Also by Michael Gannon

BLACK MAY

OPERATION DRUMBEAT

★ ★ ★

PEARL HARBOR BETRAYED

PEARL HARBOR BETRAYED

THE TRUE STORY OF A MAN AND A NATION UNDER ATTACK

MICHAEL GANNON

A JOHN MACRAE BOOK

HENRY HOLT AND COMPANY ★ NEW YORK

Henry Holt and Company, LLC
Publishers since 1866
115 West 18th Street
New York, New York 10011

Henry Holt® is a registered trademark of
Henry Holt and Company, LLC.

Library of Congress Cataloging-in-Publication Data
Gannon, Michael, 1927–
    Pearl Harbor betrayed : the true story of a man and a nation
under attack / Michael Gannon. — 1st ed.
        p.   cm.
    "A John Macrae book."
    Includes index.
    ISBN 0-8050-6698-5 (hb)
        1. Pearl Harbor (Hawaii), Attack on, 1941. 2. Kimmel,
    Husband Edward, 1882–1968. 3. Short, Walter Campbell,
    1880–1949. I. Title.

D767.92 .G36 2001
940.54'26—dc21

                                        2001024809

Henry Holt books are available for special promotions
and premiums. For details contact: Director, Special Markets.

First Edition 2001

Designed by Victoria Hartman

Printed in the United States of America

1   3   5   7   9   10   8   6   4   2

To the memory

of Esteban,

who served in the Pacific

★

Betray *v.* To be disloyal to another. To prove false to another. To disappoint the expectations of another. To violate a trust.

Oxford English Dictionary

CONTENTS

DISASTER

Friends back home used to ask about the Japs. "Hell, we could blow them out of the water in three weeks!" But here we are with our pants down and the striking force of our Pacific Fleet is settling on the bottom of East Loch, Pearl Harbor. Who wouldn't be ashamed?

Diary of 1st Lieutenant Cornelius C. Smith,
U.S. Marine Corps Reserve
Entry of 7 December 1941

$\mathbf{A}$ visitor to the navy yard at Pearl Harbor on Oahu Island, Territory of Hawaii, at sunrise, on Sunday, 7 December 1941 would have experienced one of the most dramatic daybreak scenes in the Pacific Ocean. On the south the yard bordered one of several channels of a large, cloverleaf-shaped body of water that, as morning twilight gave way at 0626 (6:26 A.M.) to light orange sunlight, presented still-dark shades of blue and gray. A slight breeze rippled its surface. On Makalapa Heights to the immediate east across East Loch and on Aiea Heights in the distant northeast, the new light picked out lush green growth on purple slopes. Overhead, cottonball clouds from the trade winds floated beneath the brightening sky.

So far this was a scene that might be repeated at any Pacific island port. But if the visitor walked out onto the yard's Ten-Ten Dock, so-called because of its 1,010-yard length, his or her eyes would behold a parade of images unlike any to be seen elsewhere for 3,000 miles around. Visible at the base of Ten-Ten, in Dry Dock No. 1, were the upper hull and superstructure of an impressively huge, gray, spectral United States Navy battleship, USS *Pennsylvania* (BB-39), flagship of the Pacific Fleet. While walking out toward the pier's end, past, to port, the moored light cruiser USS *Helena* (CL-50) and the minelayer USS *Oglala* (CM-4) secured alongside her, the visitor would begin to discern ahead the outlines of seven other majestic, gray-bathed battleships. They were moored to individual concrete quays set in a line some two hundred yards off the southeast shore of a small inland island named Ford that rose in the center of the harbor.

Two of the battleships would be difficult to see at first because they were berthed inboard of other battleships at the same quay. Toward 0700, when waxing light made it possible, the visitor could make out the precise silhouettes of all those ships' stately hulls, their jutting guns, and fighting tops. It was the rare visitor who did not find the bloodstream quickening at such a sight. The pride of the Pacific Battle Force, the battleships were, in order of station, USS *California* (BB-44) nearest to the drydocked *Pennsylvania;* *Oklahoma* (BB-37) outboard and *Maryland* (BB-46) inboard; *West Virginia* (BB-48) outboard and *Tennessee* (BB-43) inboard; *Arizona* (BB-39); and *Nevada* (BB-36).

It was America's famed Battleship Row.

At an hour past dawn the battleships were beehives of activity, white-uniformed officers and sailors seen everywhere about their decks and tops. Well over half the officers and an average of 90 percent of the ships' enlisted complements were on board. Only a few men were ashore on other duty or liberty. The morning watches were completing their watch-keeping, cleaning, and polishing duties. They and the crewmen who manned the anti-aircraft (AA) guns—two machine guns were continuously manned around the clock with two cases of .50-caliber ammunition at hand, and other crews stood by two 5-inch AA guns with fifteen rounds of ammunition for each—prepared to be relieved by the forenoon watches at 0745. At exactly that minute the forenoon crews, having breakfasted, took their assigned stations, while the morning watches went below to chow down.

Bands and guards prepared for morning colors at 0800. Catholic and Protestant chaplains laid out their sacred vessels or their hymnals for services to be held on deck following colors. One could hear, faintly, the bells of the Cathedral of Our Lady of Peace in nearby Honolulu calling worshipers to eight o'clock mass.

The Navy bands and Marine color guards paraded to their places on the main decks aft. At the stern flagstaffs seamen fastened American flags to the halyards, furled and ready to break. At the same time, other details prepared to hoist the Union Jacks—forty-eight stars on a blue field—on the bow staffs. Officers on the signal bridges looked keenly to *Pennsylvania*. When the flagship hoisted the Blue Peter, or "Prep" flag, at 0755, boatswains on that and all other ships of whatever type in the harbor piped the preparatory signal for the hoisting of colors and the playing of the national anthem. But during the interval of the following five minutes something went terribly wrong.

★

At the naval air station on Ford Island, Lieutenant Commander Logan C. Ramsey, operations officer of naval aviation Patrol Wing 2, watched with the staff duty officer in the command center as an aircraft made a shallow dive over the seaplane ramp and Hangar 6 at the south end of the island. The pilot should not have been interfering with the ceremonial silence of morning colors in the first place. In the second, he was "flathatting"— showing off at low altitude—in violation of flight rules. While Logan and the duty officer discussed the difficulty of getting the aircraft's fuselage number, a delayed-fuse bomb that the plane had dropped at 0757, which the two naval airmen had not seen fall, *exploded*. In Ramsey's words: "I told the staff duty officer, 'Never mind, it's a Jap.' I dashed across the hall into the radio room [and] ordered a broadcast in plain English on all frequencies, 'AIR RAID, PEARL HARBOR. THIS IS NO DRILL.' "[1] The transmission time was 0758.

Quickly afterward, eight other green-painted dive-bombers could be seen gliding rather than diving from the northeast toward parked aircraft in the vicinity of Hangar 6. As they pulled out, as low as four hundred feet off the deck, naval personnel on the ground could plainly see red roundels on the undersides of their wings. They were Japanese all right! They had to have come from carriers. As their bombs exploded, thirty-three out of a total of seventy U.S. naval aircraft of all types were destroyed or damaged.

The signal tower in the yard repeated Logan's alert to ships in harbor at 0800. But by that time, in mid-colors, when the hoarse klaxons sounded general quarters on all vessels, two ships in the harbor had already been struck by very-low-flying torpedo bombers, barely detectable against the horizon, sixteen in number, which swooped in from the Pearl City peninsula to the northwest over that part of the water called West Channel. Their targets were warships other than battleships that were moored to quays along Ford's opposite, or northwest, side. The first six attackers to drop aerial torpedoes took aim at an antiquated target and training ship, USS *Utah* (AG-16), and at the light cruiser USS *Raleigh* (CL-7). Three of the missiles missed and ran aground in the mud off Ford. But two hit *Utah* on her port side and one struck the portside of *Raleigh*, moored in line ahead. *Raleigh* would survive, but *Utah* was mortally wounded. The torpedo hitting *Raleigh* blew a hole in her hull thirteen feet below the waterline in the area of frames 50–60. Inrushing water flooded two forward boiler rooms and the forward engine room. As she listed to port, a fleet tug, USS *Sunnadin* (ATO-28), came alongside to steady her. That and the energetic work of her crew in counterflooding below kept *Raleigh* from capsizing. She would be holed again by a dud bomb an hour and ten minutes later.

For *Utah* the end came quickly. Two torpedoes in quick succession punctured her hull at frames 55–61 and 69–72.[2] Within a matter of a few minutes, *Utah* listed 80 degrees to port, then capsized, the two layers of 6-by-12 timbers that protected her deck from dummy practice bombs rolling overside. Ordered to abandon ship, crewmen hustled out of portholes and ran up the starboard side to her keel as, at 0810, the old vessel went belly-up. Some men were trapped inside the overturned hull, which they banged on with hammers. Despite immediate efforts to rescue them, using cutting tools borrowed from the damaged *Raleigh*, only one trapped crewman, a fireman second class, was saved. The total number of deaths on *Utah* was fifty-eight. The wreck itself sank to the bottom, where it still rests.

Directly after those hits, five torpedo bombers from the same flight, crossing over Ford Island to the East Channel, made drops at 0801 against the light cruiser *Helena*, moored inboard of the minelayer *Oglala* at Ten-Ten Dock. *Helena* was probably selected for attack by error; she was temporarily occupying the berth previously held by the now drydocked flagship *Pennsylvania*. Again, Japanese marksmanship was less than perfect as only one torpedo hit home. That successful missile, running at a depth of twenty feet, passed under the minelayer and exploded below the armor belt on *Helena*'s starboard side in the area of frames 69.5–80.5.

Twenty men were killed instantly by the blast; thirteen more died in the fires and smoke resulting. But the remaining crew saved the ship. The same cannot be said for *Oglala,* whose thin portside plates were stove in by the same blast effect. Too flooded to remain afloat, she capsized, but not before two civilian contract tugs towed her clear of *Helena.*

The remaining five torpedo bombers of the northwest flight similarly crossed over Ford but, after passing the yard, swung around to join a larger fleet of twenty-four torpedo bombers that was coming in from the southeast. The target now was Battleship Row. In three groups of twelve, twelve, and five, the attackers approached over Merry Point and the submarine base pier, making 160 knots at an altitude over water of sixty-six feet. At the optimal distance from targets, the aircraft successfully dropped three torpedoes on *California,* twelve on *Oklahoma,* nine on *West Virginia,* and one on *Nevada.* None was dropped on *Maryland* or *Tennessee* because they were berthed inboard of *Oklahoma* and *Virginia,* respectively. None was dropped on *Arizona,* which was moored at quay F-7 with a repair ship, USS *Vestal* (AR-4), outboard, covering most of her 608-foot length. It is thought that a torpedo could have passed under *Vestal* as one had passed under *Oglala,* but the official Japanese history of the attack states that no such attempt was made, and, after the attack, U.S. Navy divers did not find evidence of torpedo damage.[3] In no more than ten to twelve minutes the only torpedo attacks of the day were over. But that was more than enough time for the Japanese pilots to leave behind heavy losses of flesh and steel.

Nine of the twelve torpedoes launched against *Oklahoma* at berth F-5 hit their mark, the initial strikes opening holes portside about twenty feet below the water's surface at frames 64 and 47.5. The ship immediately took on water and began to list to port. Succeeding strikes were made at other frames from 42 to 70. As the ship's list increased, four of the last five torpedoes exploded high on the hull's armor belt, and the last, the most damaging of all, hit at the level of the main deck. *Oklahoma* was now listing 35 to 40 degrees.[4] Damage to the forward generator compartment cut off power and light throughout the ship. Tumbling officers and men made their way about with hand lanterns and flashlights. As many as possible of the crew of 1,200 slid down the ship's side into the water. When, finally, the ship turned turtle, having rolled through an angle of about 135 degrees to port, many crewmen, trapped in interior compartments, suffocated or drowned.

Thirty-two others were reached by civilian workers from the Yard who made an opening in the bottom of the hull with cutting torches and released those fortunate survivors around noon on the following day. Altogether, 415 men died on *Oklahoma.*

At the time of the attack the ship above the third deck was in Condition Xray of material readiness. That is, she was in cruising condition, the lowest level of watertight integrity. All double bottoms and lower compartments were closed, but living compartments were open and intercommunicating passageways were open to permit free passage. On the third deck and below she had made additional closings as mandated by an intermediate level of readiness called Yoke. In the highest level of material readiness on board a ship, Condition Zed, all compartments, passageways, and access openings were closed except those necessary to fight the ship. We know that at the outset of the attack Boatswain Adolph Marcus Bothne passed the word on loudspeaker for general quarters and set Condition Zed.[5] That condition apparently was set in some spaces—the ship's log was lost in the sinking—but the rapid flooding and capsizing of the ship prevented her personnel from making proper closures throughout.

Nine torpedoes also struck *West Virginia* at berth F-6, outboard of *Tennessee,* port side to stream. The "Weavy," as she was affectionately known in the fleet, was luckier than *Oklahoma* in that all but one of the torpedoes dropped on her ran at a more shallow depth and thus expended their explosive strength on the armor belt. The one deep-running missile (twenty feet) struck the rudder at frame 145.[6] At the date of this writing, Howard Huseman still remembers vividly those moments. An aviation radioman in shipborne Vought-Sikorsky OS2U Kingfisher observation planes, Huseman was getting ready to go into Honolulu on liberty, when the fire alarm and horn went off. He went up to the quarterdeck to find that one of the ship's two OS2Us had been blasted off its catapult and was barely hanging over the side; the other was on fire. General quarters sounded. His auxiliary station in drills was in the damage control center in the post office compartment on the port side, but he found no one there. He then went looking for a place where he could be of help. While he was searching, seven torpedoes in quick succession blasted against the port side. He decided to go back to the post office compartment. It was gone!

Simultaneously, *West Virginia* was hit from above by dive-bombers. One bomb passed through the firetop and the boat deck before exploding near the port side on the main, or second deck. This bomb may have accounted for the disappearance of the post office compartment. The explosion led to a fierce powder and oil fire that extended to the foremast structure up to and including the bridge. A second bomb passed through the six-inch top of turret 3 but did not explode.

Huseman caught only a brief glimpse of the attacking aircraft. His chief concern was that the ship was sinking. But thanks to expert counterflooding by crewmen below, she sank on an even keel. As *West Virginia* reached bottom, her top deck still above water, Huseman took refuge on a gun turret until picked up by a motor launch and taken ashore. He recalls that the battleship's antiaircraft guns were in action only a few minutes after the first torpedo hit, and that, apparently, they gave a good account of themselves.[7] One hundred and six men died on *West Virginia*.

Astern, though not directly because she was inboard of the repair ship *Vestal*, stood the proud 33,100-ton *Arizona*, constructed in 1915 as the second and last of the *Pennsylvania* class. Moored to quay F-7, headed down channel, *Arizona*'s bow was very close to *Tennessee*'s stern and her stern to *Nevada*'s bow, the distance in each case being two hundred feet. Not targeted by the torpedo bombers, she was still vulnerable to dive-bombers and to high-level (or horizontal) bombers that crisscrossed the sky above with 1,760-pound armor-piercing bombs. One-fourth of her AA battery was manned with ammunition available in ready boxes at the start of the attack.[8] Eyewitnesses later reported that all Xray doors and fittings were closed with very few exceptions. Many Yoke doors and fittings were also closed from the previous night. And many engineering spaces, including the shaft alleys, engine rooms, and firerooms, were in Condition Zed and locked. A gravity bomb attack on the ship was so sudden, however, that little time was allowed for setting Zed throughout the rest of the ship. Probably most of the third deck armored hatches were still open.

No fewer than eight bombs descended on *Arizona* during the middle of the torpedo launches against other vessels. (Bombs were also dropped on *West Virginia*, *Maryland*, and *Tennessee*, as well as on the repair ship *Vestal*, at the same time.) All fell between 0815 and 0820, causing damage of varying severity.[9] In one major action a bomb hit and detonated close to the port leg of the tripod of the foremast structure, causing its collapse. But by far the most severe damage—cataclysmic by comparison with anything else that winged death brought that day—was caused by a bomb dropped on the forecastle deck in the vicinity of either turret 1 or 2 that caused an intense fire that quickly engulfed the entire ship forward of the mainmast. Approximately *seven seconds* after the start of the fire—the time interval was determined by Navy analysts in 1944 on the basis of a motion picture film of the bomb hit and fire that ran at a rate of twenty-four frames per second—the ship forward of the mainmast erupted in a massive orange-black fireball that destroyed the ship forward of frame 70 and cast debris as far as *West Virginia, Tennessee, Nevada* astern, and Ford Island. Observers reported that the ship shuddered and jumped up in the water.

Arizona had on board her full allowance of smokeless powder arranged forward in six magazines to supply gun turrets 1 and 2. These surrounded 1,075 pounds of black powder in magazines on the centerline between frames 37 and 39. It was clear to the Navy analysts who in 1944 investigated the cause of *Arizona's* horrific explosion that both the smokeless and black powder detonated. But it was difficult to detonate smokeless powder with fire—and time-consuming, taking certainly more than seven seconds—whereas the ignition of black powder almost always resulted in an instantaneous explosion. That fact led investigators to theorize that a modified 16-inch (1,760-pound) armor-piercing projectile used as a bomb by the Japanese high-level bombing aircraft penetrated the armored deck and ignited the black powder, which in turn detonated the smokeless powder. But the theory proved "improbable."* "More probable" was that the fire passed down through the five armored hatches left open on the third deck, one of which was almost directly over the black powder magazine.

The analysts dismissed a popular myth that the ship blew up because a bomb passed down its stack. The myth originated with the observation by some, and with frames 46 through 208 of the film, that a jet of black smoke rose from the stack. But the navy yard at Pearl could find no damage to the insides of the stack. "The smoke issuing from the stack," the analysts concluded, "was quite obviously the result of incomplete combustion

---

*(1) Because that type of bomb contained a small charge, less than seventy pounds of TNT; and (2) because the initial fire was not one that shot skyward from a hole but, as the film showed, a spreading fire that moved laterally above the waterline.

rather than an explosion of fire."[10] As an officer on *Nevada* wrote thirty-one years later, *Arizona* would have been lucky if the bomb in question *had* gone down the stack. Wrote then Captain Joseph K. Taussig, Jr., USN (Ret.): "The stack of the *Arizona* was shaped like an inverted Y, with the upstakes angled radically from the top of the stack to the boiler rooms. A bomb dropping down the stack would have exploded in the 'uptakes' and in the spaces below."[11]

Still flying her big Sunday ensign from the stern, the twenty-six-year-old battleship slowly settled into the muck.

Four of her officers were awarded the Congressional Medal of Honor.

Altogether, 1,177 Navy and Marine personnel died on *Arizona*—nearly half the total number of fatal casualties suffered at Pearl Harbor that day. The number included her captain, Franklin Van Valkenburgh, and Rear Admiral Isaac C. Kidd, commander of Battleship Division 1, who was on the signal bridge. It was the largest fatal casualty list from any warship in the history of the U.S. Navy. Most of the dead are still entombed in the wrecked vessel, whose top deck is clearly seen from the arched white USS *Arizona* Memorial. Droplets of fuel oil still seep to the surface from her bunkers.

Two of the three torpedoes launched against *California* detonated twenty feet below the waterline where the ship's 13.5-inch armor plating gave way to thin shell plating. The explosions tore holes thirty by eighteen feet at frames 53 and 97.5. Flooding of the hull was compounded by human error. Neither Yoke nor Zed had been set. Ten inner and outboard voids had been left open below the third deck for maintenance. Her water-tight integrity compromised, *California* began listing to port. Timely counterflooding directed by a young ensign prevented her from capsizing, but salt water got into the fuel system and light and power flickered off. Then, at 0825, a bomb hit the AA ammunition magazine, taking the lives of about fifty men. It was followed shortly afterward by a second bomb that damaged the bow plates. The captain and crew made valiant efforts to douse fires, control flooding, and get up steam. *California* responded briefly. But her holes were too large. The water finally claimed her, though it was not until late Wednesday that her keel finally embedded itself in mud. Ninety-eight of her men were dead.[12]

In 1945 the Navy Department stated: "According to the best available analysis in the Navy Department, the USS *California* is the only ship that might have been saved from sinking by the closing of manhole covers that had been left open for maintenance."[13]

Oklahoma's sister ship *Nevada* was moored singly to quay F-8, at the end of Battleship Row. Though plainly exposed, she was targeted by just one of the torpedo bombers. The explosion ripped open a hole forty-eight by thirty-three feet twenty feet below the waterline well forward at frame 41. A severe dive-bombing attack beginning about 0825 made up for any additional torpedoes that might have been launched at her. One bomb hit near the foremast, wrecking the vertical area extending from the second deck to the bridge. Several bombs damaged the forecastle from side to side forward of turret 1 and down to the second deck. A bomb amidships sent fragments against the mainmast and stack, and caused many casualties to the 5-inch AA gun crews, who had been answering the Japanese since within four minutes of the torpedo explosion. Two near misses ruptured the hull on the port and starboard bows. While many of *Nevada's* compartments were flooded, her power plant was not harmed, and Lieutenant Commander Francis J. Thomas, USNR, the senior officer on board at the time, decided to stand out. Chief Boatswain Edwin J. Hill, who would receive the Medal of Honor posthumously for his action, leaped onto the mooring quay, cast off the lines while strafing fire from fighters encircled him, and swam back to the ship as she got under way. He would be killed by a bomb blast later as his ship made for the sea. The story of *Nevada's* gallant dash is told later, in chapter 9. Sixty of her men were killed that morning, and 109 were wounded, including Ensign Joe Taussig.[14]

Before the Japanese withdrew, four battleships, *Oklahoma, West Virginia, Arizona, California,* a target ship, *Utah,* a minecraft, *Oglala,* and an auxiliary, *Sotoyomo* (YT-9), would be in a capsized or sinking condition. Battleships *Pennsylvania,* which was in drydock, *Nevada, Maryland,* and *Tennessee* were damaged. Light cruisers *Raleigh, Helena,* and *Honolulu* (CL-48) were damaged. Destroyers *Cassin, Downes,* and *Shaw* were damaged. Repair ship *Vestal* and numerous small craft were damaged. Eighty naval aircraft were destroyed, 167 damaged. Naval airfields and installations at Ford Island, Kaneohe Bay, and Ewa were damaged. And those were just naval material losses. The United States Army aircraft, airfields, forts, and barracks on Oahu would also be heavily hit, as will be described in chapter 9. And the greatest losses would be human: 2,403 dead, 1,178 wounded.

Though totally surprised, the AA gunners on all ships except *Oklahoma,* whose men never had a chance, gave back what fire their weapons allowed. The overall Japanese commander of the attacking force, Vice Admiral Nagumo Chuichi, wrote later that "the enemy's antiaircraft fire reaction had been so prompt as virtually to nullify the advantage of surprise." *West Virginia* returned fire "immediately" with ready machine guns, and in fewer than five minutes with all guns. No log remains to say what gun action took place on *Arizona,* but her two ready 5-inch 25 AA guns could have commenced firing within one minute, and the remaining guns of her AA battery within about five minutes. *California's* ready machine guns at the conning tower, manned and armed, could have commenced firing upon first identification of the enemy; her machine guns in the foretop and maintop in three to four minutes; and her 5-inch 25 AA guns in about two minutes. *Nevada* estimated that both .50-caliber machine guns and 5-inch 25 AA guns opened fire within four minutes. Other estimates provided by commanding officers after the battle were: *Pennsylvania,* five to eight minutes, all batteries; *Tennessee,* three to five minutes from the sounding of the general alarm; and *Maryland,* from ten to fifteen minutes, all batteries.[15] In the attack twenty-nine of the Japanese air fleet of 354 planes were shot down, most of them by Navy gunners.

The defeat fell hardest on the shoulders of Admiral Husband Edward Kimmel, commander in chief, United States Pacific Fleet (CINCPAC) and commander in chief, United States Fleet (CINCUS). Between receiving messages and giving orders, the fifty-eight-year-old Kentuckian watched the awful drama unfold from his second deck corner office at the submarine base. For over ten months since assuming command, he had trained this powerful fleet to maximum readiness and proficiency with what ships, aircraft, and weapons he was supplied. His officers and men were at concert pitch. They were ready to sail.

And now—how could *this* happen?

While he observed the losing battle, "his jaw set in stony anguish," a witness wrote, communications officer Commander Maurice "Germany" Curts at his side, a spent .50-caliber machine gun bullet shot through the window glass and cut his white jacket. A welt on his chest was all that Kimmel suffered, but he said to Curts:

"It would have been merciful had it killed me."[16]

TOO THIN A SHIELD

Or what king, going to encounter another king in war, will not sit down first and take counsel whether he is able with ten thousand to meet him who comes against him with twenty thousand?

Gospel of Luke 14:31

Oahu is the third largest of the eight major islands and 124 islets that compose the archipelago of Hawaii. Ranging 1,500 miles in a crescent from Kure Atoll in the west to the largest island, Hawaii, in the east, the volcanic mountaintops form what Mark Twain called "the loveliest fleet of islands that lies anchored in any ocean." The U.S. Navy's anchorage at Pearl Harbor is an indentation on the southern, or lee, side of Oahu, six statute miles west of the capital city, Honolulu. From the pearl oysters that once grew there the harbor took its original Hawaiian name, *Wai Momi*—"pearl waters." The United States secured the site by treaty as a coaling and repair station in 1887. In 1908 it became a full-fledged naval station.

Providing ten square miles of navigable water thirty to forty-five feet deep, landlocked Pearl Harbor is entered from the south through a narrow coral-barred channel, which in 1911 was dredged to a depth of thirty-five feet. To the immediate south of the channel the winds are moderate, the seas are relatively smooth, and visibility is excellent. By contrast, the winds and seas to the north of Oahu are stronger and generally there is a weather belt characterized by low ceilings, squalls, rain, and low visibility.

The harbor's position in the North Pacific Ocean is 2,091 nautical miles (a nautical mile being approximately 1⅙ land miles) west to southwest of San Francisco, 4,685 nautical miles northwest of Panama, 4,767 nautical miles east of Manila in the Philippines, and 3,430 nautical miles southeast of Tokyo, Japan.

In 1941, the principal warships of the U.S. Pacific Fleet, battleships, carriers, and cruisers, were berthed to the northwest and southeast of Ford Island, which rises in the center of the harbor waters. Smaller warships and auxiliary vessels were anchored in adjacent districts. Carrier-based aircraft and patrol bomber seaplanes occupied parking aprons and hangars on Ford Island itself, site of the fleet air base. To the southeast side of the harbor stood the naval station's administrative offices, submarine base, torpedo boat piers, signal tower, magazine wharf, dry docks, repair basin, tank farms for storage of fuel oil, hospital, and other facilities—the "Navy behind the Navy." Immediately south of the naval station was a large U.S. Army Air Corps base named Hickam Field. Two other Air Corps bases, Bellows and Wheeler, were within twenty miles, to the east and northwest, respectively. A Marine Corps air station was at Ewa, a short distance west of the harbor. And the Navy operated a new air station for patrol aircraft (flying boats) at Kaneohe Bay on the eastern shore of Oahu. U.S. Army ground forces, some 58,000 strong, were stationed at Fort Shafter, Schofield Barracks, and scattered forts and camps throughout the island. "The Hawaiian Department is the best equipped of all our overseas departments," declared Secretary of War Henry L. Stimson on 7 February 1941.[1] Some journalists spoke of Oahu as the "Gibraltar of the Pacific." And, on 14 June of the same year, *Collier's* magazine, writing about "Oahu, the fortress of the Hawaiian Archipelago," stated in a subhead that, "The Navy Isn't Worrying," and titled its piece "Impregnable Pearl Harbor."[2]

But the Navy *was* worrying. And Pearl Harbor was *not* impregnable. Reason: the Army, which was officially charged with the defense of the fleet and naval station at Pearl, was, in the Navy's view, woefully unequipped to perform that task. Rear Admiral Claude C. Bloch, the Commandant of the 14th Naval District, acting as Naval Base Defense Officer, was charged with the employment of such naval units as Commander in Chief Kimmel could make available for the purpose of *assisting* the Army in its defense of the fleet. But by joint agreement between the War and Navy Departments, and by provision of the Navy's war plan (WPL-46), protection of the fleet was the core reason for the Army's considerable presence on Oahu.[3] Army Chief of Staff George C. Marshall made the point forcefully when he wrote to the newly installed commanding general of the Hawaiian Department, Lieutenant General Walter C. Short, on 7 February 1941: "The fullest protection for the Fleet is *the* rather than *a* [Marshall's emphases] major consideration for us."[4]

Six days before assuming command of the Pacific Fleet on 1 February 1941, Kimmel joined his name to that of outgoing commander in chief Admiral James O. Richardson in pointing out to Admiral Harold A. Stark, Chief of Naval Operations in Washington, that "the existing deficiencies in the defenses of Oahu and in the Local Defense Forces of the Fourteenth Naval District impose a heavy burden on the Fleet for purely defensive purposes." The most glaring of those deficiencies were: (1) the small number and obsolescent condition of land-based aircraft, requiring constant use of fleet planes for local patrol; and (2) the "critical inadequacy of A.A. guns available for the defense of Pearl Harbor, necessitating constant manning of ships' A.A. guns while in port."[5] On his own, Kimmel tackled the same subject two days later, noting that, after a hurried survey of the situation, he had become all the more concerned about the absence of means for "defending this base."[6] Kimmel could call attention to Navy General Order 142, Paragraph 42: "The Fleet must have no anxiety in regard to the security of its base."[7]

In Admiral Stark, Kimmel had a ready and willing ear. On the previous 22 November Stark had written to Richardson: "Since the Taranto incident [a British carrier-borne air attack on warships in the Italian anchorage at Toronto on 12 November] my concern for the safety of the Fleet in Pearl Harbor, already great, has become even greater."[8] The CNO showed Kimmel's communication to Marshall, who, on 7 February, confided the Navy's concerns to General Short at Fort Shafter: "Of course the facts are as he [Kimmel] represents them. . . . What Kimmel does not realize is that we are tragically lacking in this matériel throughout the Army, and that Hawaii is on a far better basis than any other command in the Army. . . . You should make clear to Admiral Kimmel that we are doing everything that is humanly possible to build up the Army defenses of the Naval overseas installations, but we cannot perform a miracle."[9] Stark probably heard the same from Marshall. We do know that he heard the same from Secretary Stimson, who stated that the Hawaiian Department "continues to hold a high priority for the completion of its projected defenses because of the importance of giving full protection to the Fleet."[10] On 10 February Stark urged Kimmel, "in view of the inadequacy of the Army defenses," to continue his faithful acceptance of "the responsibility which must rest upon the fleet for its own protection while in Pearl Harbor," despite the fact that ships' guns were not equal to an attacker's threat, and without respect to the fact that such constant vigilance took away from fleet training and readiness.[11] By 18 February Kimmel had the very feelings of anxiety that General Order 142 had been crafted to prevent: "I feel that a surprise attack (submarine, air or combined) on Pearl Harbor is a possibility. We are taking immediate practical steps to minimize the damage inflicted and to ensure that the attacking force will pay."[12] He made no claim to future ability to *repel* an attacker with the forces at his disposal. In August 1944, he would elaborate on his "feelings":

> I felt that the most probable form of attack in the Hawaiian area was submarine attack. I felt that the bombing attack by airplanes was probably second in order of probability. I felt also that the danger of torpedo plane attack in Pearl Harbor was nil because I believed that torpedoes would not run in the shallow water in that harbor. The maximum depth at any point was on the order of 45 feet with the prevailing depth in the deepest part, 40 feet. I felt that the probability of surface gunnery attack or bombardment was of a very low order of priority, but the probability of mining was considered of a high order of priority.[13]

On 5 February, Major General Walter Campbell Short arrived at Honolulu Harbor aboard the liner *Matsonia*. Twenty-four bombers from the Eighteenth Bombardment Wing at Hickam Field roared overhead in welcome to the officer who would relieve Lieutenant General Charles D. Herron as commanding general of the Hawaiian Department. After greetings at the dock from Herron, the lean, five-foot-ten-inch, somber-faced Short took up temporary residence at Admiral Richardson's house in Honolulu. There he was promptly visited by Admiral Kimmel, in civilian clothes, who welcomed him to the islands and offered him the Navy's full cooperation in every detail of his assignment. "He responded wholeheartedly," Kimmel would say later, "and I had a real regard for him before I had known him for a very long time." On 7 February, in ceremonies conducted on the parade ground of Fort Shafter, fifteen minutes by car to the east of Pearl Harbor, Herron formally passed command to Short, who, later the same day, received a third star representing temporary advancement to lieutenant general.

Two years older than Kimmel, Short was born, the son of a physician, in Fillmore, Illinois, on 30 March 1880. He was graduated Phi Beta Kappa and Distinguished Military Graduate from the University of Illinois in 1902. In February of the same year he received a Regular Army commission as a second lieutenant of infantry. During the next eleven years he served successively at posts in Texas, the Philippines, Nebraska, Alaska, and San Francisco, where in 1913 he entered the School of Musketry. An expert pistol shot, he won the U.S. National Match in 1909 and placed second in 1913. When in 1915 the School of Musketry was moved to Fort Sill, Oklahoma, he went with it, and in that state he met and married Florence Isabel Dean, of Oklahoma City.

In June 1917, Short sailed for France with the American Expeditionary Force of World War I and was sent at once to the British and French fronts. His duties were primarily in training commands, including machine gun instruction. Rising to temporary rank of colonel, he remained in Europe following the Armistice until July 1919. Reverting to major on his return, he attended the School of the Line (later Command and General Staff School) at Fort Leavenworth, Kansas. He also attended the Army War College, graduating in 1925. In 1936 he succeeded Brigadier General George C. Marshall as assistant commandant of the Infantry School at Fort Benning, Georgia. Promoted to brigadier general in 1937, he was given command of the 2nd Brigade of the 1st Division, and, in the following year, promoted to major general, he was assigned the division command. In 1940, General Marshall, then chief of staff, sent him to Fort Jackson, South Carolina, to organize the I Corps. And from there, in December of that year, Marshall selected Short to head the Hawaiian Department.

Though Short had never shirked an Army assignment, this one he was reluctant to accept, since his father-in-law was seriously ill, and he thought he should stay nearby. "But [Marshall] considered it important and ordered me [to Oahu]," Short said. In the first week of January 1941, Short conferred at the War Department with Marshall, Brigadier General Leonard T. Gerow, chief of the War Plans Division, and Colonel Carl A. Spaatz, of the Air Corps. He learned that, in addition to his primary responsibility to defend the fleet and the naval base, he was to hold Oahu against any attempt to invade, prevent sabotage, protect the other U.S. islands as far west as Wake, and aggressively train ground troops and air crews for the Pacific war that seemed increasingly predictable. Short's assessment of the situation was that the Hawaiian Department was amply prepared against submarine attack and against civilian sabotage, but that it was dangerously vulnerable to air attack by gravity bombers and torpedo bombers.[14]

Over the next two months, Short and Kimmel worked hand in glove to develop a joint defensive strategy with the means at hand. Each found the other in "complete agreement" on the broad steps that should be taken, while Rear Admiral Bloch worked with Short on the fine details—Bloch, because he, not Kimmel, was Short's opposite number. "I saw General Short frequently," Kimmel said,

> because I made it a point to see him. I think he also made it a point to see me. We conferred officially on many occasions, and at practically every official conference, Admiral Bloch was present, because Admiral Bloch was the officer in Hawaii who was charged with dealing with the Army, and at no time did I wish to by-pass him. I think I kept Admiral Bloch thoroughly informed of every dealing I had with General Short. I played golf with General Short at a little 9-hole golf course which he had established near his headquarters at Fort Shafter.[15]

Because it was later charged in a government investigation (Roberts Commission, 1942), and by certain members of Congress, that Kimmel and Short were estranged from each other in their official and social relations during the eleven months they held their commands—Harry S. Truman, for example, U.S. senator from Missouri and Democratic vice presidential nominee, asserted in *Collier's* magazine (26 August 1944) that the "root cause" of the American defeat at Pearl Harbor was the lack of cooperation between Kimmel and Short, who, Truman insinuated, were not "on speaking terms"—it is instructive also to have Short's appreciation of their association, given in 1944:

> I would say that [our relations] were extremely friendly, cordial, and cooperative. We were on a very friendly basis personally, as well as officially. We played golf together about every other Sunday, and the Sundays we didn't play golf, very frequently Admiral Kimmel dropped in to see me in the morning; because his family was away he came to my quarters more than I went to his. . . . [16]

By 28 March, Short and Bloch completed a final draft of what was called the "Joint Coastal Frontier Defense Plan, Hawaiian Department and Fourteenth Naval District." The Coastal Frontier was defined as including Oahu and the other major islands of the Hawaiian chain; also, Midway, Johnston, Palmyra, Canton, and Wake Islands. Because the agreements contained in the plan were to take effect "at once"—Short and Bloch signed the plan on 2 April—and because this was the plan that was in force on 7 December following, its principal paragraphs bear examination. First considered was the appearance in Coastal Frontier waters of hostile surface vessels. Joint air attacks made upon such warships were to be executed under the tactical command of the Navy. The Army would give the Navy use of its bomber aircraft, Boeing B-17D Flying Fortresses and obsolete Douglas B-18 Bolo medium bombers—the model was six years old and the planes themselves were five years old. The number was to be the maximum practicable. After one or repeated attacks, as required, the bombardment aircraft would revert to Army control.

In the event of an enemy air attack over and in the immediate vicinity of Oahu, defensive air operations, antiaircraft, and gas defenses were to be executed under the tactical command of the Army. The Naval Base Defense Officer (Bloch) would release to Army control as much Navy fighter strength as was practicable. After "repeated patrols or combat or for maintenance of the required alert status," Navy fighters would revert to Navy control. In another key provision, the plan placed responsibility with the Navy for long-range aerial reconnaissance of the ocean approaches to Oahu. Utilizing the Navy's twin-engine Consolidated PBY-3 and PBY-5 Catalina patrol bombers (flying boats), Bloch would be the responsible officer for instituting distant air searches. If called upon, the Army would place such bomber strength as was available under Bloch's command to supplement the Navy's distant patrol assets.

To ensure prompt exchange of information about both hostile and friendly aircraft, Army and Navy communications personnel were to install and operate common communications equipment, such as page printer teletype machines connected to the same landline circuit; and to utilize joint radio circuits on 219 and 2,550 kilocycles for voice communication. The plan anticipated that, at some future date in the year, Aircraft Warning Service radar would be supplied to the Hawaiian Department. Until such time, the Army would operate what, admittedly, was a primitive Antiaircraft Intelligence Service (AAIS), employing visual recognition of incoming enemy aircraft and radio broadcast warnings on 900 kilocycles. Four further major points were addressed in the plan: (1) the Marine Corps antiaircraft units on Oahu would be under the tactical control of the Army; (2) the possible use of balloon barrages over Pearl Harbor would be investigated; (3) smoke screens would *not* be employed over Pearl Harbor and Hickam Field, since they would hinder one's own surface and air operations; and (4) a joint harbor control post would be established for the defense of Pearl and Honolulu Harbors.[17] A slightly more detailed plan for the Hawaiian Islands proper was signed and issued on 11 April.[18]

In an important addendum, dated 31 March, the air defense officers of the two services, Major General Frederick L. Martin, for the Army Air Corps, and Rear Admiral Patrick N. L. Bellinger, for the Navy, signed off on a report that cannily predicted that a surprise attack on Oahu would likely be launched at dawn, prior to a declaration of war, and from a distance inside three hundred nautical miles. Martin was Commanding Officer, Hawaiian Air Force; Bellinger, among various other offices, was Commander, Naval Base Air Force and Commander, Patrol Wing Two. Their prescient monition could well be stapled to a dispatch dated the next day, 1 April, from Naval Operations (OpNav) in Washington to all naval districts, including the Fourteenth, advising that "Axis Powers often begin activities in a particular field on Saturdays and Sundays or on national holidays of the country concerned. . . ."[19]

The Martin-Bellinger estimate considered that in the past Orange (the code name for Japan in all the war plans of the period) had never made a declaration of war before launching hostile actions; that Orange might send into the Hawaiian area one or more submarine squadrons and/or a fast carrier raiding force to make a sudden attack with no prior warning to Pearl Harbor from U.S. intelligence; and that the damage to ships and naval installations resulting from such an attack might prevent effective offensive action by the U.S. Navy in the western Pacific for a long period of time. The best information available was that Orange possessed eight carriers (she had ten) that embarked from 20 to 60 aircraft (in fact, 27 to 104). The 1939 edition of *Jane's Fighting Ships*, the latest then available at Pearl, listed forty Orange submarines that were capable of projection into Hawaiian waters. (Nothing was known about the existence of Orange's midget submarines, which would number twenty by the following December.)

The best first means of defense against a carrier striking force was its detection by long-range reconnaissance aircraft, such as the PBY-3 and PBY-5 Catalinas, which had a theoretical range of seven hundred and eight hundred nautical miles, respectively. But, stated the estimate,

> The aircraft at present available in Hawaii are inadequate to maintain, for any extended period, from bases on Oahu, a patrol extensive enough to insure that an air attack from an Orange carrier cannot arrive over Oahu as a complete surprise. . . . In a dawn air attack there is a high probability that it could be delivered as a complete surprise in spite of any patrols we might be using and that it might find us in a condition of readiness under which pursuit would be slow to start, also it might be successful as a diversion to draw attention away from a second attacking force.[20]

Only within "narrow time limits"—a matter of four or five days, Bellinger would later define it—could the available patrol aircraft fly seaward through 360 degrees to a distance of the seven to eight hundred nautical miles required to prevent a carrier from launching an attack without prior detection.[21] Rear Admiral Richmond Kelly Turner, Director of War Plans at the Navy Department (Main Navy), concurred in that assessment—it being understood in Washington as well as in Hawaii that only a search of *all* sectors of approach to an island base deserved the name. In support of that principle, Admiral Chester W. Nimitz, who would succeed Kimmel as CINCPAC, observed on 7 January 1942 that "It cannot be assumed that any direction of approach may safely be left unguarded. . . . Neglect of any sector is apt soon to be known."[22] But a full-compass sweep of 360 degrees to the maximum range of scout planes could not then be mounted with the aircraft available; neither would it be possible for a period beyond several days, as will be seen, in the following November-December. And the Army Air Corps' assets were of minimal assistance in that regard. The comparatively short-legged B-18 medium bombers could not make the 700 to 800 mile distance (and return), and the B-17 Flying Fortresses, which could, were always so meager in number that they could cover only a few degrees of arc.

Furthermore, both services were heavily pressed by expansion training: the Army's bomber aircraft were consumed by crew training for the Philippine Air Force, and the Navy's PBYs were also totally engaged in crew training. Part of that PBY training was for crews manning new aircraft on the mainland. And part was for manning patrol wings of the fleet, with which they would be employed in offensive combat assignments stipulated in war plan WPPac-46 (effective 7 September), which included within thirteen days after the opening of hostilities a raid by Navy surface and air striking forces against Japanese bases in the Marshall Islands. Kimmel would be promised an additional one hundred PBYs, but they never arrived—they were allocated to Great Britain instead—with the result that long-range aerial reconnaissance, absent a full-fledged alert from Washington, could not be ordered as a routine procedure.

In the event of an air attack against the fleet and/or ground installations, the Martin-Bellinger estimate advised the immediate dispatch of all aircraft suitable for aerial combat both to intercept the attackers and to follow them back to their carriers. But under the present conditions, without the advance warning that long-range scout aircraft and radar could provide, the estimate acknowledged that no pursuit (fighter) planes could be dispatched "until an attack is known to be imminent or has occurred." It therefore recommended that interservice air task forces should be organized right away, that missions be assigned, and that conditions of readiness be defined so that immediate action could be taken when one of the visualized emergencies arose. Among the contingencies was a submarine attack, conducted either singly or in concert with an air attack, off the harbor channel entrance or in the fleet operating area to southward. In that event, shore-based antisubmarine aircraft would conduct patrols and take offensive action against surfaced or diving submarines in close communication with Navy destroyers.

Once his Hawaiian Department staff was assembled, General Short set about strengthening Army defensive forces. It would be a ten-month effort, and one that seems to have encountered more than its regulation share of impediments, since, repeatedly, the War Department refused to supply Short's expressed needs, either for alleged budgetary reasons or because the War Plans Division differed with Short's understanding of Oahu's vulnerability to air attack. The blame for the latter failure cannot be traced to any misconceptions by General Marshall himself: the Chief of Staff worried aloud frequently about the possibility of "a surprise or trick attack" against Oahu;[23] and in his letters to Short he expressed his pleasure at reading of the latter's progress "with regard to defense from air attack," which he called "a matter of first priority."[24] But below the Chief's level, deputies and assistants were not as understanding or supportive. A representative example of that disparity is provided by Short's identification of his number two priority ("Cooperation with the Navy" being number one): "Dispersion and Protection of Aircraft," which he proposed to the War Department on 19 February, and again on 15 March. Calling attention to the vulnerability to attack of aircraft at the Army's Hickam and Wheeler Fields, as well as at the Ford Island navy field—"On all fields the planes have been kept lined up on the field where they would suffer terrific loss [in the light of future events an ironic prediction]"—he sought money and engineer troops to build dispersal landing strips away from the main bases and to erect protective bunkers, or revetments, for those aircraft that could not be dispersed.[25] For his part, Marshall judged Short's plan to be "sound," and he answered that, as soon as Short submitted sufficient details to support the expenditures, "funds for these purposes will be included in estimates."[26] But once the proposal fell into the maw of deputies and assistants below Marshall's pay grade it met opposition and delay; one staffer, Brigadier General Harry J. Malony, Acting Assistant Chief of Staff, wrote, "War Plans Division believes: That the danger of sustained air attack against air fields in Hawaii from carrier based aviation is not serious."[27] Eventually, on 12 September, the War Department promised $1,358,000 for the work, but with the proviso that the funds would not become available until 1 January 1942.[28]

Other examples abound. In February 1941, with Marshall's concurrence on 13 March, the Army assumed responsibility for defending the new naval air station and its three squadrons of PBY patrol aircraft at Kaneohe Bay. On 14 April Short asked for procurement of a 12-inch gun battery and a war strength garrison of 2,300 men to make that defense possible. His request did not receive a favorable response. Not only air defense but urgent aviation training required the construction of ten additional airfields. No funds were forthcoming. Aircraft Warning Service (AWS) radar was, Short said, "the most important single project in the department." At present, aircraft could be visually and sound-detected at a maximum distance of four to five miles; with radar that would increase to 120 miles. Short was authorized to receive three fixed and six mobile stations. He asked the War Department that Oahu be given top priority (A1-f) in receiving the permanently placed stations. But no such installation was in place by 7 December.[29] Short had wanted to install one of the fixed AWS stations at the 10,000-foot summit of Haleakala crater on the island of Maui, seventy-six nautical miles east-southeast of Oahu, which commanded the eastern and southern approaches to Oahu. But the crater formed part of a national park, and the National Park Service, of the Department of the Interior, insisted on employing its usual long process of vetting the architecture and building plans for appropriateness, as it also insisted that the AWS station when erected not "materially alter the natural appearance of the reservation." A fuming Short thought that "the seriousness of this situation has not yet been appreciated in the War Department," and that, in view of the Pacific theater emergency, "all quibbling over details should be stopped at once." But Major General William Bryden, Deputy Chief of Staff, told Short: "It is not believed that it would be advisable to attempt to alter the informal decisions of the Department of the Interior by carrying this matter to higher authority, or to prolong the discussion through official channels."[30]

Recognizing that the aircraft repair facilities of the air depot at Hickam Field would be among the first installations targeted in a surprise attack (as it was), Short sought funds to bombproof it by moving it underground. He was denied. He recommended that funds be allocated to construct splinterproof protective shelters for antiaircraft and mobile seacoast (artillery) batteries and was denied. He requested funds to camouflage batteries at four forts and was denied. He asked for an increase in enlisted men of an antiaircraft regiment (251st Coast Artillery) and was denied. He asked that his overall garrison strength be increased from 58,000 to 71,500 and was denied.[31]

On the credit side, Short did receive the antiaircraft armament promised by Secretary Stimson, which brought his AA strength up to 98 3-inch guns, 120 37-mm guns, and 308 .50-caliber machine guns. Grateful as he was for the increase, Short knew that these weapons were relatively useless against fast modern aircraft, particularly bombers and strafers flying at 200 feet or lower. And he did receive thirty-one obsolete Curtiss P-36A pursuit planes promised him by Stimson on 7 February, as well as fifty new Curtiss P-40B Warhawk pursuits with liquid-cooled Allison engines, leakproof tanks, and pilot-protecting armor. The P-40B gave him a sporting chance against the much-touted Japanese Zero, or Zeke. Little would he think before it happened that, on 27 November, just eleven days before the Japanese attack, the War and Navy Departments would suggest sending 50 percent of his P-40 strength to Wake and Midway Islands—which would indicate to both Short and Kimmel that the intelligence services of the two departments did not consider a strike against Oahu to be imminent or likely. (Meanwhile, two hundred P-40s were being shipped to Russia.)[32]

Throughout, Short seems to have kept his composure. Though he called the Adjutant General's attention to his rebuffs from Washington,[33] on 14 April he wrote to Marshall: "Everything is going along extremely well, although there is a great deal to be done as rapidly as possible. The Navy has felt very much encouraged by the increase in our Air and Antiaircraft defense."[34] All during the spring, summer, and fall that followed he drove his men hard with infantry and artillery field exercises. With Bloch he conducted combined Army-Navy air exercises and air raid drills. With Kimmel he directed air and naval maneuvers hundreds of miles out to sea, in which Army bombers located and "bombed" the Navy's carriers. Nor was he unmindful that the Japanese might attempt landings on Oahu. With Kimmel's ships to simulate enemy warships and transports, Short had his 27th Infantry Division, representing the enemy landing force, come ashore simultaneously at widely dispersed beaches on the island, while his artillery and remaining infantry practiced repelling the invaders.[35] Hard, provident, conscientious work seems to have characterized Short's months of Hawaiian Army command. At no point in the record does the picture emerge of a derelict officer. He approached 7 December steadfast in his labors and faithful in his charge.

*

The purposes of a harbor and a fleet base were to provide upkeep, repair, refueling, and replenishing of ships as well as rest and recreation for crews after strenuous operations at sea. Just as ships could not be kept in continuous operation, so crews could not be kept at peak efficiency in peacetime without regularly scheduled days in port. And since harbors were normally viewed as havens from peril on the sea, it probably was thought by most American citizens who knew anything about Pearl Harbor from *Collier's* or other such sources that the Pacific Fleet when at Pearl was safe as bears snuggled in their den. But this harbor presented some peculiar and alarming exposures to danger. While its lochs provided ten square miles of anchorage, the 140-odd warships and other vessels that ordinarily occupied that space were moored in such congestion that, for an attacking air fleet, it would be somewhat like shooting fish in a barrel.[36] The single, narrow entrance channel, through which all ships must pass, exposed individual ships in slow line ahead to torpedo attack by submarines. Too, a ship or other obstruction sunk in the channel would block all other ships from entry or sortie. Again, because of the single channel, should a warning come of approaching enemy warships, two to three hours would be required for the fleet to sortie. Magnetic and other mines might be laid in the sea approaches to the channel. And, finally, among the major dangers in Kimmel's estimation, the topography of the land surrounding the harbor, e.g., the generally accessible Aiea Heights, made it readily possible for enemy agents from the large Japanese population of the island to keep watch on the berthing and movement of ships. But as long as the President insisted on maintaining the fleet in Hawaii, Pearl Harbor had to be its home. The only suitable alternative, deep-water Lahaina Roads, off Maui, was ruled out by Richardson and Kimmel because of its "extreme vulnerability" to submarine attack.[37]

Since the Army alone, even when reinforced by the matériel promised it by Secretary Stimson, and even, for that matter, when shored up by the Local Defense Forces of the Fourteenth Naval District, could not offer a convincing defense of the fleet and harbor against air attack, it fell to Admiral Kimmel's fleet, with its AA guns and carrier aircraft, to make up the difference, if it could. Kimmel did not think it could, fully, and he regretted that he had to try, because constant attention to defense watches in port drew energy and time from the fleet's primary responsibility under war plan WPL-46, which was to train officers and men for far-flung offensive actions in the Central and South Pacific. A *maximum* security effort in port would have made training impossible altogether; it would paralyze the fleet in place; in fact, it would call into question the reasons for having a fleet at all. With adequate personnel and matériel it would be possible to maintain a state of alert for some period of time, but Kimmel did not have (and never would have) sufficient numbers of either. And, even with them, he would have had to consider the deleterious psychological effects on personnel of long periods of peacetime watch standing. His only option was to *balance* security needs, training requirements, and crew rest. In port that delicate balance lay between rest, in order to bring fresh crews into battle, and reasonable provisions for security against surprise attack. That equilibrium had to be carefully maintained, lest the fleet be worn out on the one hand or caught unawares on the other.

It would have been helpful if Kimmel could have delegated the Navy's defense mission entirely to Bloch, but Bloch's resources were grossly inadequate, and the fleet itself had to become directly engaged, with the result that, unlike Short, Kimmel had to prepare simultaneously for both offensive *and* defensive operations. To his credit, without complaint to Washington, he threw all his energies into both tasks. And from Washington he received appropriate encouragement. Very early on, CNO Stark wrote him, praising the wisdom of the President's appointment, which "has the overwhelming approval of the Service," and adding: "I am thankful that I have your calm judgment, your imagination, your courage, your guts and your good head at the seagoing end. Also your *can do*—rather than *can't*."[38]

On 19 February, Kimmel issued Pacific Fleet Confidential Letter No. 2 CL-41 titled "Security of Fleet at Base and in Operating Areas." With only one set of minor revisions published on 14 October, this defense plan for security and condition of readiness was operating doctrine through 7 December; and, indeed, after Kimmel was relieved as CINCPAC in that same month by Admiral Nimitz, the latter continued in force the 2CL-41 directive.[39] Prescribed in 2CL-41 were three conditions of readiness for ships moored in Pearl Harbor:

> *Condition I*—General Quarters [action stations] in all ships. Condition of aircraft as prescribed by Naval Base Defense Officer [Bloch].
> *Condition II*—One-half of antiaircraft battery of all ships in each sector manned and ready. Condition of aircraft as prescribed by Naval Base Defense Officer.
> *Condition III*—Antiaircraft battery (guns which bear in assigned sector) of at least one ship in each sector manned and ready. Minimum of four guns required for each sector. Condition of aircraft as prescribed by Naval Base Defense Officer.

It was the responsibility of the Naval Base Defense Officer (Bloch) to advise the Senior Officer Embarked, normally the Commander Battleships, Battle Force, which condition the fleet should maintain. But the Senior Officer Embarked would give the order. Kimmel ordered that in port there must be *at all times* on board each ship at least 50 percent of the enlisted men and 25 percent of the officers. Furthermore, all ships must have a sufficient number of officers and men trained for the job in each watch to man all AA batteries. Ships were to be moored by sectors in such a way as to provide each a clear arc of fire. There also must be at all times a sufficient number of men on board to get the ship under way, to go to sea, and to fight the ship. After 29 April, each battleship at anchor had two machine guns continuously manned, with two cases of .50-caliber ammunition, and crews standing by two 5-inch AA guns with fifteen rounds of ammunition for each. This was a higher standard of security than prescribed in condition III. No guns in either cruisers or destroyers were manned, but, by Kimmel's order, ammunition was in the ready boxes at the guns and the gun crews normally lived near the guns at all times. It was more difficult to mount continuous peacetime watches in cruisers and destroyers because of their smaller crews, whereas with the larger number of men in battleships watches could be maintained continuously without hardship.

On Sunday morning, 7 December, it may be noted, among the battleships *Arizona* (BB-39) had 37 officers on board and all of her enlisted men with the exception of about 40; *West Virginia* (BB-48) had 80 percent of her officers and 95 percent of her crew; *Tennessee* (BB-43) had her duty watch and 38 other officers, together with all but 111 of her complement of 1,700 enlisted men; *California* (BB-44) had 49 officers and all but 6 of her enlisted complement. *Maryland* (BB-46) had all officers but one of her AA battery and all her enlisted men except a few on patrol, leave, and special liberty; *Nevada* (BB-36) had 6 of her 9 AA officers and 95 percent of her enlisted personnel; and *Pennsylvania* (BB-38), in dry dock, had 40 officers and all enlisted men except 32 petty officers on liberty. There are no figures for *Oklahoma*, whose logs and other documents were lost in the sinking. Other classes of ships showed the same high rates of personnel on board. The light cruisers *Honolulu* (CL-48) and *Helena* (CL-50), for example, had 50 percent of officers and 98 percent of crew on the former and 78 percent of officers and 98 percent of crew on the latter. Although 50 percent of crews on all ships were permitted to go ashore, few did so. And there was no noticeable evidence of alcohol abuse among either officers or crews on shore during Saturday night through Sunday morning.

On all types of vessels daily and nightly AA exercises were carried out when in port, utilizing every type of armament, 5-inch, 3-inch, 1.1-inch quadruple mounts, and .50-caliber machine guns. Unluckily for the fleet, these were wretchedly inadequate weapons for defending against low-flying aircraft moving at speeds in excess of 250 miles per hour. The .50-caliber machine guns lacked heft; the 3-inch gun was not rapid fire; and the 1.1-inch was subject to overheating and jamming after a few rounds. The Department of the Navy was slow in adopting and deploying two rapid-fire antiaircraft weapons that provided other Western navies the capacity to destroy fast modern aircraft. The first was a 20-mm gun manufactured by the Swiss Oerlikon-Bührle Company. Firing an explosive shell with a cyclic rate of fire of 600 rounds per minute, it proved particularly useful for repelling low-flying aircraft. The British Admiralty, which purchased 1,500 before the outbreak of war, and manufactured many more under license, produced a documentary film on the Oerlikon, which it showed in the United States in 1942 as part of an effort to persuade the U.S. Navy to adopt the gun, which it eventually did, but too late for Pearl Harbor. The second weapon, a Swedish-designed 40-mm antiaircraft gun, was even more effective. Called the Bofors, from AB Bofors, the company that developed it in 1929, the gun gave warships the ability to put up heavy saturating fire

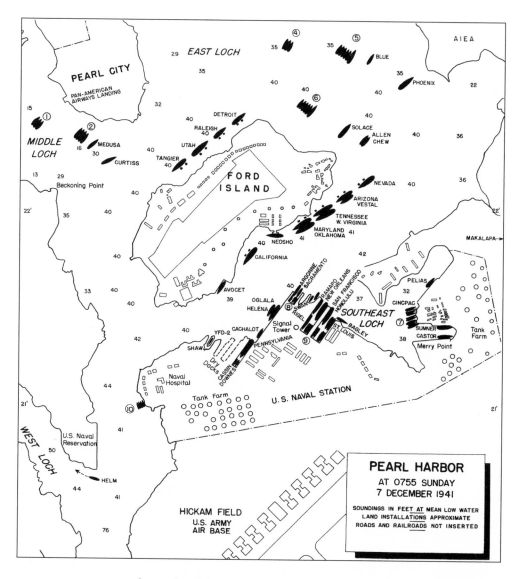

drawn by Robert M. Berish for The Rising Sun in the Pacific, *courtesy National Historical Center*

at a rate of 140 rounds per minute. Its projectiles were high explosive. Maximum practical range was 12,500 feet. Most European countries adopted the gun before the war. The U.S. Navy dawdled and finally came around to it late in 1941, again too late for Pearl Harbor. What it might have accomplished there on 7 December was demonstrated in its first use on board the carrier *Enterprise* (CV-6) and the battleship *South Dakota* (BB-55) during the Battle of the Santa Cruz Islands, on 26 October 1942, when the quadruple-mounted Bofors cleared the skies. With a more provident ordnance program at Main Navy its first successful use might have taken place eleven months sooner.

At the naval air station on Ford Island, which was surrounded by fleet moorings, there was a trained seamen guard of two hundred men and a Marine Corps detachment of approximately one hundred men and two officers. These gunners were equipped with rifles, pistols, and aircraft machine guns, both .30 and .50 caliber, but no heavier weapons. An Army company held tactical exercises on the island using four 37-mm guns, for which there were permanent emplacements.[40] Ammunition for the Army's mobile AA guns and batteries was stored underground in the Aliamanu Crater between Fort Shafter and Pearl Harbor, where Short also had an emergency command post. The practice provided security, but the time required for AA batteries to access their ammo was to prove costly on 7 December.

★

A besetting problem with which Kimmel had constantly to deal was maintaining adequate numbers of trained personnel. Officers and enlisted men were being drained away from the fleet to man new ship construction, to provide expertise in ordnance manufacturing, or to staff aircraft training centers. "During the past year," he wrote to Nimitz, who as chief of the Bureau of Navigation had responsibility for officer assignments, "the detachment of so many competent officers has reduced the number of experienced officers remaining in ships of the Fleet to such a point that I consider it *dangerous* [Kimmel's emphasis] to make further considerable reductions in our best officer personnel at this time. . . . This Fleet must be kept ready to fight, and that is impossible unless we stabilize the personnel to a much greater degree than has been done in the past." He was particularly vexed at the loss of many ordnance postgraduates who occupied key positions in the fleet, "and I can see no source from which qualified reliefs will be furnished."[41] Too, under the fleet's Aviation Expansion Program trained aviation personnel on Oahu were being sent to the mainland to train others. Each month Kimmel was required to send to the West Coast twelve trained patrol plane (PBY) crews. All across the enlisted level he was losing good men. Sailors were not reenlisting because of the high wages being paid in war industries on the mainland, and even in the repair facilities at Pearl. What enlisted personnel remained were mostly untrained new recruits. At times the number of men on board individual ships who had not heard a gun fired reached 70 percent. As late as December, Kimmel's staff estimated that the fleet needed 19,000 additional men to man ships and fill to capacity its training centers.

A blow worse than lost personnel came in April and May of 1941 when one aircraft carrier (USS *Yorktown* [CV-5]), three battleships (USS *Idaho* [BB-42], *Mississippi* [BB-41], and *New Mexico* [BB-40]), constituting Battleship Division Three, the strongest division of the fleet, and the only division with upgraded AA armament, four light cruisers, and eighteen destroyers were detached "in utmost secrecy" from the Pacific Fleet and transferred to the Atlantic, where they would be employed in meeting the German U-boat threat to Allied shipping. When Stark conveyed the news—the transfer having been decided by the President—he cautioned Kimmel: "I am telling you, not arguing with you."[42]

In a flash Kimmel lost approximately one-fourth of his fleet's strength. The Japanese Navy now held a *two-to-one advantage* over his forces. He was certain that details of the transfer would become well known in Japan, through agents in Honolulu and the Panama Canal Zone, with a further reduction in whatever deterrent Washington thought the fleet represented. Stark concurred, writing to Secretary of the Navy Frank Knox, "The truth is probably now apparent to Japan that the United States Pacific Fleet is no longer strong enough for sustaining an effective offensive against the centers of Japanese military power." And he warned Knox that "any further weakening of the Pacific Fleet at this time is almost certain to precipitate action by Japan against the British Fleet and the Netherlands East Indies."[43] None of the transferred warships would be returned to Pearl prior to 7 December, but many would be returned thereafter. When one examines the transfers of ships from the Pacific to the Atlantic, and vice versa, it is apparent how one-way that traffic was. Between 1 February and 7 December 1941 twenty-five warships were sent from the Pacific to the Atlantic, and *one,* the *Tambor*-class (1940) submarine USS *Triton,* was transferred from the Atlantic to the Pacific. Taken to the Atlantic at the same time were practically all of the fleet's trained Marine landing force at San Diego, together with their transports, leaving on the Pacific side only the Marines on the outlying islands Wake and Midway and the garrison at Pearl Harbor. While visiting Main Navy in June, Kimmel learned of plans to transfer an additional detachment consisting of one carrier, three battleships, four cruisers, and two squadrons of destroyers. In the face of his strenuous objections, the plans were dropped.

Another shortage with which Kimmel had to contend was fuel. All the reserve oil stocks were held in two tank farms, east and west of the naval station. The shortage lay not only in the amount of storage but also in the inadequate means available for moving fuel from storage into combatant ships. Early in 1941, Kimmel had reorganized the vessels of the fleet into three task forces, a fast carrier force, an amphibious force, and a battleship force. He found that it required from twenty-four to thirty hours to refuel a task force in harbor. Fuel deliveries at sea were even slower, owing to a shortage of tankers. Eleven were available, but only four had the speed and capacity for fueling combatant ships at sea. Destroyers required refueling every third day, heavier ships every fifth day. But fuel delivery never kept pace with consumption. For the entire fleet on distant operations not eleven but about seventy-five tankers would be required. The fleet's radius of action thus was severely limited by this shortage. And until more tankers, for which Kimmel constantly pleaded, arrived, even nearby exercises in operating areas would have to be curtailed. "It was this fact, and this alone," Kimmel said, "which made it necessary to have two task forces simultaneously in Pearl Harbor at certain periods."[44]

Aircraft of all types were in short supply for a fleet preparing for war. Mention has been made earlier of the small numbers of PBY patrol planes on Oahu. Kimmel's aviation staff cited other needs and problems: Carrier torpedo planes were obsolescent and spare aircraft of that category were too few. There was a serious shortage of aircraft machine-gun ammunition. No armor-piercing bombs or depth bombs for use against submarines were yet available. The level of experience of both pilots and aviation ratings was low, and there were not enough of either. Aircraft overhaul at Pearl was limited to PBYs, and transfer back and forth to the West Coast for overhaul of other types would be impractical, if not impossible, in an emergency.[45] An insistent Kimmel sometimes irritated Main Navy with his complaints about these deficiencies, and a somewhat nettled Rear Admiral John H. Towers, chief of the Bureau of Aeronautics, wrote in a memorandum to Stark:

> The impression of the Commander-in-Chief that the Bureau of Aeronautics is relegating fleet aircraft needs to a position of lower priority than the general expansion program is in error. This bureau has exerted and continues to exert every possible effort to provide the fleet with new replacement airplanes for the older models at a rate only limited by the productive output. . . . It is believed appropriate to invite the attention of the Commander-in-Chief to the fact that the Navy Department, in the face of long and determined opposition [from the Army Air Corps] has been successful in establishing the highest priority . . . for the *fleet* [Towers's emphasis]. This priority (A-1-b) is higher than that accorded any Army aircraft.[46]

Before relinquishing his command to Kimmel, Admiral Richardson advised his successor to move his Commander in Chief, Pacific (CINCPAC) headquarters and staff from the USS *Pennsylvania* to a shore installation. Accordingly, Kimmel wrote Stark suggesting this, explaining, "Facilities on the Fleet flagship are not sufficient to provide living and working accommodations for the personnel required on the staff." Stark approved and in February Kimmel transferred his flag ashore, to the submarine base. Communications to the fleet were improved by direct use of the high-power radio transmitters of station NPM on shore. Kimmel would still work aboard the *Pennsylvania* during tactical exercises, and his staff battle organization would require training on the flagship. But for most of the time, his staff lived and worked "on the beach," the staff quartered at the sub base, while Kimmel found after-work quarters for himself alone at a house in a new development on Makalapa Heights, behind the base, with a view of Battleship Row.

The new CINCPAC assembled a staff that was so bright and able that Kimmel's successor, Admiral Nimitz, would keep it on in its entirety, and every captain and commander, with one exception, would rise to flag rank during the war. Captain William "Poco" Smith was chief of staff. Tall, athletic, possessed of a quick wit and a retentive memory, Smith had served for a year and a half in Hawaii as commanding officer of the new (1937) light cruiser USS *Brooklyn* (CL-40). In the slot of assistant chief of staff and operations officer was the familiar, hardworking Captain Walter S. DeLany, who had been Kimmel's chief of staff when the latter was commanding officer cruisers, Battle Force. For War Plans Kimmel chose Captain Charles Horatio "Soc" McMorris, nicknamed after Socrates for his philosophical bent, and known affectionately as "the ugliest man in the Navy." Prior to joining the staff on 1 February, he had served in Hawaii for over a year as operations officer for Vice Admiral Adolphus "Dolly" Andrews, commander of the Scouting Force. McMorris was destined to give the most fatally wrong answer ever given to a Kimmel question. (To serve as McMorris's assistant Kimmel retained a Richardson staffer, Commander Vincent Murphy, whom the former CINCPAC regarded as "the finest officer in the United States Navy.")[47] He also kept on board Richardson's intelligence officer, Lieutenant Commander Edwin T. Layton. Fluent in Japanese, Layton had gained detailed knowledge of Japan's Imperial Navy while serving as assistant naval attaché in Tokyo from April 1937 to March 1939. In Hawaii, together with cryptographer Commander Joseph J. Rochefort, he had developed radio intelligence into a fine science. (Officially, Rochefort was combat intelligence officer under Bloch.) Commander Arthur C. Davis, a pilot, was fleet aviation officer, in charge of technical training and aviation logistics. Another Richardson holdover, he was not consulted by Kimmel on the probabilities of Japanese attack. A staffer who worked closely with Kimmel in AA defenses and firing exercises at sea was Captain Willard A. Kitts III, the fleet gunnery officer. Kitts had served with Kimmel intermittently since 1918. He described his association with Kimmel as "quite close and intimate." Communications officer Commander Maurice "Germany" Curts, who had served a year with Richardson, rounded out the staff. Outside the staff proper Kimmel had access to other strategically oriented minds, including that of Captain Charles M. "Savvy" Cooke, Jr., new skipper of the *Pennsylvania,* who had been Turner's predecessor at Main Navy as chief of War Plans. "I am sending you Savvy Cooke," Stark wrote Kimmel on 13 January, "and I feel like I am losing my arms. That boy has one of the best brains I have ever run into. . . . I am sending him to sea to protect his promotion chances."[48] Cooke did eventually advance to flag rank.

In his subordinate admirals Kimmel had the cream of the naval service afloat (excepting Ernest J. King, CINC of the Atlantic Fleet). Task Force 1 was commanded by Vice Admiral William Satterlee Pye, commander Battleships Battle Force, and as senior officer present afloat, second in rank to Kimmel. Like "Savvy" Cooke a veteran of War Plans, where he directed the preparation of WPL-46, Pye drew the praises of Stark, who wrote Kimmel: "I have always thought Pye one of the soundest strategists we have [and] I thought his handling of tactical situations outstanding. Particularly were his orders a model of clearness, brevity and effectiveness."[49] Task Force 2 was commanded by the formidable William Frederick "Bull" Halsey, Jr., commander aircraft, Battle Forces, an audacious, locker-room-talking, scotch-and-water-drinking former classmate of Kimmel's at Annapolis, who at age fifty-two, in 1935, learned to fly, and now was poised to become the wartime commander of the Third (Fifth) Fleet, with which he would win fame (and controversy) in the Pacific Ocean. Commanding Task Force 3 was the low-profile Vice Admiral Wilson Brown, newly sent from Washington to be commander, Scouting Force. Among the duty stations listed in Brown's service jacket were: commanding officer of the New London, Connecticut, submarine base, skipper of the battleship *California*, and superintendent of the Naval Academy at Annapolis. Below the level of force commanders were type commanders, of rear admiral rank, in charge of battleships, cruisers, and destroyers, and a Base Force commander of the same rank.

With his outstanding trio of force commanders, Kimmel conducted regularly scheduled air raid drills both in port and at sea, and firing exercises in the operating area south of Oahu. Monthly air raid drills would last for as long as five days, for example, 14–18 July, when simulated glide and dive-bombing attacks were made against ships of the fleet, four days in Pearl, one day at sea. The schedules, deliberately planned to be "strenuous" and "with the maximum realism obtainable," were designed to ensure that "sky lookouts" and AA batteries did not exhibit "slackness or perfunctory performances." All condition-of-readiness watches were given the opportunity for drill under various forms of attack, at night as well as in daylight.[50]

The fleet also carried out quarterly exercises during which "enemy" aircraft over Pearl Harbor dropped dummy bombs on the fleet and base installations.[51] AA firing practice was conducted against towed sleeves or flares.

In the open-sea operating area Kimmel drilled his fire control and turret crews in practice firing at fast-moving targets (sleds, not rafts). Specialized training was given in range finding, tracking, radar detection, zigzagging, towing, fueling, and damage control. Each exercise was judged and graded. A perfectionist, Kimmel never displayed or expressed satisfaction with any performance. Knowing that the fleet was on the cusp of actual warfare, when its offensive tasks in the Pacific war plan were to move against the Japanese mandated islands in the mid-Pacific and to divert Orange strength away from the Malay Barrier (the string of islands from the Kra Isthmus in the west to Timor at the eastern end of the Indonesia archipelago) through denial and capture of positions in the Marshall Islands, Kimmel drove his officers and men hard, drilled them to peak efficiency, instilled in them a fighting spirit, and taught them to be Lees and not McClellans. There were not only gun crews to be trained but also officers and men detailed to ship control, to the engine room, to the electrical installations, to the radios, to the signals, to the lookouts, to the sick bay, to the commissary, and to the numerous other billets on a fighting ship. In combat a breakdown in proficiency in any one of those responsibilities could be costly, if not fatal.

As Lieutenant Commander Layton, who came to know Kimmel the taskmaster, wrote:

> Admiral Kimmel was a very forthright officer. He could sometimes be a little starchy, but he was more starchy with senior officers who were lax than with junior officers. He was demanding in devotion to duty, setting in his own performance an outstanding example. He had little tolerance for laziness or indecision. He had an infectious, warm smile when pleased by something and a frosty demeanor if displeased.[52]

More than a few officers thought that Kimmel was overly immersed in minutiae, and that he was a bit of a school principal where appearances were concerned: he forbade officers to wear the khaki working uniform on the grounds that "it lessens the dignity and military point of view of the wearer and has a tendency to let down the efficiency of personnel"; when off duty and dressed in civilian clothes, officers were required to wear neckties and fedora-style hats that quickly became known as "Kimmels"; while cleaning the exterior of the sides of their ships, a dirty job at any time, sailors were required to wear their white uniforms (which were personal property, not government issue) instead of dungarees; and, said one chief petty officer, "We spent more for bright-work polish than the Japanese spent on fuel oil." But even those few subordinates who later criticized Kimmel for being "arrogant," "conceited," and "not well informed," or "narrow gauge" or "a martinet and detail man" who "did not delegate authority" never had the temerity to suggest that he was derelict in his duty—if anything, said his fleet operations officer, Captain DeLany, he was almost *too* devoted to his duty as CINCPAC, working longer hours at his desk than probably were necessary. The words *Kimmel* and *dereliction* were antithetical.

All criticisms aside, the distillate was that, as Captain Kitts averred, "The efficiency and training of the Fleet was at its highest level in history."[53] Other staff members and subordinate commanders agreed that in ships, gunnery, and aircraft the fleet exhibited a higher state of material readiness and personnel proficiency under Kimmel than it had ever achieved before in peacetime. Such statements were given by Pye's chief of staff, Rear Admiral Harold C. Train; Rear Admiral William L. Calhoun, commander, Base Force; and Aviation Officer Davis. Vice Admiral Halsey, who stated in 1947 that, "I don't believe there was a flag officer in the Pacific Fleet who did not feel that Kimmel was an ideal man for the job," added this encomium:

> I have never known a Commander in Chief of any United States Fleet who worked harder, and under more adverse circumstances, to increase its efficiency, and to prepare it for war; further, I know of no officer who might have done more than Kimmel did. . . . When the Roberts Comission asked me how I happened to be ready for the Japanese attack, I told them, "Because of one man: Admiral Kimmel."[54]

Was there no substantive shortcoming in this commander in chief's performance? No one critical action that he could have taken but did not? One omission that he allowed himself, which, if not allowed, might have altered history?

THREE

OPPOSITE NUMBERS:
YAMAMOTO AND KIMMEL

Most people think Americans love luxury and that their culture is
shallow and meaningless. I can tell you Americans are full of the spirit
of justice, fight, and adventure. Also their thinking is very advanced
and scientific.

Admiral Yamamoto Isoroku

On 7 January 1941, a small man of towering reputation in the Japanese
Navy took brush in hand to compose a letter to his nation's Navy Minister,
Admiral Oikawa Koshiro. The writer was Admiral Yamamoto Isoroku,
commanding the Japanese Combined Fleet. During the previous November when his flagship, the battleship *Nagato,* was anchored at Yokosuka
Naval Station, Yamamoto had confided to Oikawa an outline of the views
he was now committing to paper. He divided the scheme of his text into
five sections, entitled: "Preparations for War," "Training," "Operational
Policy," "A Plan of Operations to Be Followed at the Outset of Hostilities,"
and "Personnel." On the margin of the first page, in red ink, he brushed:
"For the eyes of the Minister alone: to be burned without showing to anyone else."[1]

Yamamoto revealed his belief that war with the United States and Great
Britain was now inevitable. In the fourth section of his text he proposed
that the necessary means of victory in that conflict was the sudden, unexpected destruction of the U.S. Pacific Fleet at Pearl Harbor in the first
hours of hostilities.

Prior to this pivotal moment in Yamamoto's professional career, Japanese naval doctrine had held that, in the case of war with the United States, the best strategy for fighting the American Navy was "attrition and ambush." A predicate of this strategy was that in any Japanese-American clash, Great Britain would remain inactive, in order not to jeopardize her Asian colonies and interests. Since the United States had given clear signs, including a fleet problem, or exercise, off Hawaii in 1925, that she was prepared to send the Pacific Fleet to protect the Philippines, the first act of Japan in the event of war should be to seize that U.S. territory—and the U.S. island of Guam as well—and thus lure the American fleet into the distant waters of the western Pacific.

When the U.S. armada left its West Coast bases—Pearl Harbor after May 1940—it would be shadowed by Japanese long-range I-class submarines that, with a cruising range of 10,000 nautical miles and a top speed of 23.5 knots, would stay abreast and ahead of the slower moving (17 knots) American formations. The submarines were equipped with Type 93 24-inch torpedoes fueled by compressed oxygen and kerosene, capable of 39-knot speed and a maximum range of 24 miles, or of 49 knots at a range of 12 miles (compared to the 2½-mile range of U.S. torpedoes). The submarines would launch their full arsenal of these high-explosive weapons at both the main body and trailing edges of the U.S. fleet, hoping to achieve substantial material and psychological damage. Then, when the fleet drew near the Japanese mandated islands, the Marshalls, Marianas, and Carolines, land-based bombers such as the Mitsubishi Type 96 would attack with the smaller Type 91 torpedo, still capable of sinking a capital ship (as this type did on 10 December 1941 when the British *Prince of Wales* and *Repulse* went down off the Malayan coast).

According to Japan's strategic theory, the U.S. fleet would have been ground down to Japan's lesser number, but higher quality, of ships by the time it reached a midway point between the Marshalls and the Philippines. There, in the final attrition phase, a Japanese advance party of fast battleships, cruisers, and destroyers would throw down a Jutland-like gauntlet and invite the U.S. fleet to pursue it. When the U.S. warships went after the bait, and darkness came, the faster Japanese vessels would turn and launch two hundred or more long-range Type 93 torpedoes at the lumbering Americans. It was expected by the strategists that 25 percent of those warheads would hit home, and that two more such nighttime launches might be made.

When daylight came, the remaining elements of Japan's fleet, including carriers, would be brought to bear in an ambush, and under the most propitious conditions, near the home islands, where lines of communication and supply favored the defender. An attempt would be made to sink the American carriers; failing that, Japanese bombers would hole the flight decks, making launch and recovery of aircraft impossible. There then would follow the decisive fleet action, as the Japanese overwhelmed the enemy with both land and carrier-based aircraft, ships' guns, and torpedoes launched by cruisers and midget submarines. At the conclusion of battle, the strategists estimated, about one-half of the American fleet would have been sunk or damaged. Forced to retire, the U.S. Navy would require at least two years to rebuild, repair, retrain, and prepare for another attack.[2]

The Operations Section of the Naval General Staff had long made this basically defensive plan the foundation of all training, war games, and maneuvers. Yamamoto, though, had begun to think as early as March or April 1940 that such an ambush strategy had three defects: (1) it conceded the initiative to the Americans; (2) it failed to take into account the fact that a southern operation, then being planned, against Malaya and the Dutch East Indies would divert major components of the fleet away from a western Pacific battle; and (3) the strategy, assuming as it did that Japan would continue to have a Navy in quality superior to or at parity with the Americans' Pacific Fleet, ignored the fact that the United States was then engaged in a massive and rapid expansion of naval forces, and that, if Japan remained too long in a defensive posture, new construction would give the U.S. Navy a decisive edge in any collision of forces, when it came.

Yamamoto had gotten to know the United States, her resources and her people, during two tours of duty, first as a student of the English language at Harvard University in 1919–21, and then as naval attaché at the Japanese embassy in Washington during 1926–28. From his extensive travels through the United States, where he visited, among other sights, the oil fields of Texas and the automobile plants of Detroit, he had come to know the country's vast resources, its industrious people, and its potential manufacturing might. In January 1941, he had no doubt that the shipyards and aircraft plants of America would eventually overwhelm Japan's naval assets.

Already, in 1938, with Japan in China and Europe sliding toward war, the U.S. Congress, at President Franklin D. Roosevelt's urging, had authorized a 20 percent growth in naval strength. Then, on 19 July 1940, with France defeated, Britain reeling, and an aggressive Japan looking southward, Roosevelt had signed the Two Ocean Navy Bill, authorizing the largest-ever naval expansion.

Two new carriers, *Yorktown* (CV-5) and *Enterprise* (CV-6), joined the United States fleet in 1939. Two of a new class of battleship, *North Carolina* (BB-55) and *Washington* (BB-56), with speeds (28.5 knots) approaching that of the Japanese battleships *Kirishima* and *Hiei* (29.8 knots), were due for completion in 1941 at the New York and Philadephia navy yards, respectively. Four new battleships of the *South Dakota* class were scheduled for commissioning in 1942. Six battleships of the even larger (45,000 tons displacement) and faster (33 knots) *Iowa* class, with 40,000-yard-range 16-inch main guns, were in the contract stage. In aircraft carriers (soon to displace the battleship as the dominant ship type), construction was accelerated: the *Wasp* (CV-7) had been commissioned in April 1940; the *Hornet* (CV-8) was due out of the ways in the fall of 1941; and no fewer than seventeen carriers of the *Essex* class (short-hull and long-hull groups) were expected to be at sea in the years 1942–45. Similar expansion was under way in other categories of warships: heavy and light cruisers, destroyers, and submarines.

Since Japan could not keep up with America's industrial productivity, and since the longer Japan's naval power waited to engage the American fleet the smaller the chance of victory, there was no alternative, Yamamoto concluded, but to make a preemptive strike against the Americans as soon as practicable. "We should do our best," he wrote, ". . . to decide the fate of the war on the very first day." If the enemy's main body was in Pearl Harbor, Japanese carrier aircraft and submarines should sink the principal ships (carriers and battleships) at their moorings and blockade the harbor entrance. If the U.S. fleet was at sea, it should be located and sunk off soundings. For the United States the result would be that "the morale of the U.S. Navy and her people" would "sink to the extent that it could not be recovered."[3] The entire air strength of the First and Second Carrier Divisions must be committed to the operation, and the strike itself should be made on a moonlit night or at dawn. Should Japan hesitate to attack Pearl Harbor, worrying about possible heavy damage to her own forces, and "continue crouching in the Far East," the Americans, with an eventually dominant fleet, "would proceed to Japan to bomb and burn down the cities." The same early assault principle must be applied in the Philippines, so that U.S. air forces there would be destroyed in concert with the Hawaii operation, and thus securing the Navy's flanks for a southern operation to capture Malaya and the East Indies.[4]

In the last section of his letter to Oikawa, Yamamoto asked to be relieved of his position as commander in chief of the Combined Fleet, since he "earnestly desired" that "I should be appointed C. in C. of an air fleet, so that I would have direct control of the attacking units."[5] But that was not to be.

★

Yamamoto was born on 4 April 1884, the seventh child of a schoolmaster named Sadakichi Takano in the small Japanese village of Kushigun Sonshomura, inland from the east coast ports of Yokohama and Kobe. His father, aged fifty-six, gave the infant his age as a name—Fifty-six—Isoroku in Japanese. Yamamoto, meaning "base of the mountain," would be added thirty years later when Isoroku was adopted by a prominent family of that name. At age sixteen the youth successfully passed the examination for entrance to the naval academy at Eta Jima. Four years of spartan training followed, and Isoroku was graduated seventh in his class in 1904, the same year in which his future adversary Husband E. Kimmel was graduated from Annapolis.

Like Kimmel, Isoroku was sent directly to the fleet, in his case as an ensign on the cruiser *Nisshin*. Earlier that year, on 8 February, the warship had participated in a surprise night attack on the much larger Russian Far Eastern fleet at Port Arthur, where destroyers badly damaged three Russian battleships, sank a cruiser, and blockaded the harbor. But the larger naval battle of the Russo-Japanese War of 1904–05 loomed ahead, as Admiral Togo Heihachiro, whose flagship *Mikasa* was guarded by a screen of vessels that included *Nisshin*, awaited a twenty-seven-ship Russian fleet from the Baltic that was bent on relieving Port Arthur. On 27 May 1905, Togo, outnumbered five to two, met the Russians in the Straits of Tsushima and routed them, sinking or causing the surrender of ten of the twelve Russian capital ships. During this engagement the five-foot-three-inch and

130-pound Isoroku was wounded when one of the *Nisshin*'s own guns exploded, fragments from which severed at their roots the middle and index fingers of his left hand and caused 120 scars on the lower half of his body. "Whenever I go into a public bath," he would say afterward, "people think I am a gangster."[6]

Isoroku's career followed predictable lines for an officer who graduated seventh in his class and distinguished himself in battle. By 1914, as a lieutenant, he was chosen for a two-year course of study at the Naval War College in a suburb of Tokyo, where, among other studies, he familiarized himself with the principles of naval warfare articulated shortly before the turn of the century by the American naval theorist Captain Alfred Thayer Mahan. Using the British Empire as his template, Mahan had argued that sea power was the key to the rise of imperial nations. The nation that would rule, Mahan said, was the nation that concentrated its ships and firepower on a contender's main fleet and forced the issue of dominance in a decisive battle *à toute outrance*, as the Royal Navy had done at Quiberon Bay (1759), the Nile (1798), and Trafalgar (1805).

In 1916, now a lieutenant commander, Isoroku registered as an adopted son of Yamamoto Tatewaki, whose surname he adopted. Two years later, at thirty-four years of age, he married Reiko Mihashi, from his home province. They would produce four children, two boys and two girls. Between the two assignments in the United States already mentioned, Yamamoto was promoted to captain and, in 1924, was named second in command of the Kasumigaura Aviation Corps. Until that date, his professional interests had been mainly directed to gunnery. From this point forward he concentrated his focus on naval aviation, then in its infancy. In 1928 he was assigned briefly to gunships as captain of *Izuzu*, a light cruiser used for training. In December of the same year, he reached his dream command as skipper of the 36,000-ton, twenty-eight-knot carrier *Akagi*, which, converted from a battle cruiser, was one of the largest carriers in the world's navies. In November–December 1941 she would be the flagship of the six-carrier task force that attacked Pearl Harbor. But, here again, Yamamoto's sea command was cut short, when it was decided by the Navy Ministry, less than a year later, that he should accompany the Japanese delegation to the London Naval Disarmament Conference, scheduled to begin on 21 January 1930, where he served as an aide to Vice

Admiral Sakonji Seizo. The conference was called to review naval limitations and Pacific area security compacts agreed to by the United States, Great Britain, Japan, France, and Italy at the Washington Naval Conference in 1921–22. Intent on ending a naval arms race, the five powers had agreed then to a strict proportionality in their respective strengths in capital ships, that is, in those ships of more than 10,000 tons or in ships mounting guns exceeding eight inches in caliber (effectively battleships and aircraft carriers). The ratios of such ships were established at 5 each for the United States and Great Britain, 3 for Japan, and 1.67 each for France and Italy. Other provisions required the scrapping of some warships that were already afloat or under construction, and a ten-year moratorium on capital ship construction. In another effort to maintain peace in the Pacific, signatories who held island possessions, such as the Japanese mandates and the U.S. Philippines and Guam, accepted restrictions on their further fortification.

Prior to 1921, the Japanese Navy had hoped to build and sustain a fleet of eight battleships not older than eight years and eight cruisers. But the expenditures required, it was discovered, would consume one-third of the overall national budget—an impossible burden. The Washington Conference provided a rationale for abandoning the 8-8 dream, which, in turn, meant giving up for the time being a developed strategy. That strategy held that with an 8-8 fleet Japan would possess 70 percent of America's naval strength, thus making it possible to oppose an attacking American fleet in the western Pacific. But with only 60 percent of America's strength, which the 5-5-3 ratio imposed, Japan would have to pull back from her assumption that the United States was the hypothetical enemy, and content herself with a "nonbelligerent" navy. That view was put forward, on returning home from the conference, by Navy Minister Kato Tomosaburo:

> One cannot, very broadly speaking, make war without money. . . .
> Even supposing Japan's armaments were to rival those of America in strength, the nation could not, as it did in the Russo-Japanese War, fight on a shoestring. Where then would the money come from? The answer is that there is no country other than America that could oblige Japan with the foreign credit required—and this would obviously not be forthcoming if America were the enemy. . . . The conclusion is that a contest between Japan and America is unthinkable.[7]

Those in the Navy and the public who agreed with the minister that the Washington treaty both saved Japan economically and advanced her stature internationally came to be called the "treaty faction." Those, on the other hand, who thought that the third greatest naval power in the world had been shamed by the pusillanimity of its conference delegates became known as the "fleet faction." Leadership of the latter group was seized by Fleet Admiral Kato Kanji, who, as a naval adviser at the conference, had argued vainly for a ratio permitting Japan seven-tenths of America's strength in tonnage. Upon accession to the office of chief of the Navy General Staff, Kato further characterized the inferior ratio allotted Japan as an insult to Japan's standing as a major power, as a sign to China of Japanese weakness, and as a stain of subservience to the "Anglo-American hegemony." The indignation stirred up by Kato found its most ready audience among junior officers, but over time, Kato was able to rally a number of important flag officers to his side. It bears mention that no one, in high station or low, was so hawkish as to demand hostilities with the Americans just yet. But the fleet faction kept that prospect fresh in its mind (as did the Orange Plan theorists at the U.S. Navy War College in Newport, Rhode Island).

At the London Conference of 1930, which Yamamoto attended, the five powers reviewed what had been accomplished in disarmament during the past eight years and entertained motions for new action. Various refinements to the 1922 document were adopted, including new limitations on heavy cruisers, in which category Japan had heavily invested during the decade. The Japanese delegation demanded a 10:7 ratio in cruisers, but was permitted only 10:6. Furthermore, the conference imposed a halt on Japanese construction in that category for a five-year period so that the United States could pull even. Japan also was required to reduce its tonnage in submarines, a category in which she had also built heavily.

The reaction in the fleet faction was one of resentful anger. Navy Chief of Staff Kato resigned in protest, but his allies in the fleet faction drove all the major leaders of the treaty faction into retirement or onto the reserve list. In a stroke, the navy lost much of its moderate leadership at the upper level. One of the victims of this purge was Yamamoto's closest friend in the service, Vice Admiral Hori Teikichi, head of the Naval Affairs Bureau. Many thought that he possessed the most brilliant mind in the Navy. Another Yamamoto friend, Vice Admiral Inoue Shigeyoshi, on the Aviation Section of the Navy General Staff, who narrowly missed being purged himself, stated that the loss of a man of Hori's stature and gifts was more costly to the service than a 10 or 20 percent reduction of its fleet ratio. Yamamoto, whose sympathies were clearly with the treaty faction, also escaped the purge unharmed. He called the action taken against Hori an "outrage." By 1933, the direction of the Imperial Navy was fully in the hands of the fleet faction. In the same year, Japan withdrew from the League of Nations, another post–World War I international effort to maintain peace.[8]

★

Yamamoto, who returned from the London Conference a rear admiral, took up new duties as head of the Technical Division of the Navy's Aeronautics Department. In 1933 he was back on board the *Akagi* as commander of the First Carrier Division. Not without continuing opinions on armament controls, he considered a 10:7 and even a 10:6 treaty better than no treaty at all. With no restrictions to control her, the United States would vanquish everyone in an arms race: given her industrial capacity, she would have Japan reduced quickly to 10:5 or 10:4, or to an even lower ratio. In his mind, Japan must keep the fetters on America that the treaty system provided, while working through diplomatic channels to secure terms as favorable to Japan as possible.[9] Such a channel opened in 1934. The London Naval Treaty would expire in 1935 and the Washington treaty in 1936. In anticipation of those lapses, the five powers agreed to meet in London for preliminary talks on how to proceed past those two dates.

Yamamoto, who was then back to shore duty with the Naval General Staff and the Navy Ministry, was appointed chief naval delegate at the preliminary talks, where he would work hand-in-glove with Ambassador Matsudaira Tsuneo in representing Japan's interests. He was reluctant to go, and numerous times tried to duck the assignment. Certainly, he was an unlikely choice, given his pro-treaty views, since the Navy that assigned him that delicate and critical position was dominated by the fleet faction, headed by the Navy Minister, Admiral Suetsugu Nobumasa. On 8 June 1934, Suetsugu told his principal active and retired admirals that the best policy for Japan was to "abrogate the existing treaties and have no treaties and no restrictions." The next best policy was to insist on parity with the West. The second was a policy Yamamoto could support. In either event,

Suetsugu contended, Japan should not fear an armaments race with America. A number of reasons for such a dauntless stance have been suggested: the U.S. economy was in the grip of a long-standing depression, and funds for new naval construction were scant. Japan's economy, at the same time, was strong, and thus in the near term she could probably stay abreast of the United States in a naval construction race. Too, as Mahan and the battles of Tsushima and Jutland suggested, Japan should not quail before future dangers but, instead, if she truly wished to grow in imperial power, she must be willing to cast all her resources into the contest. In doing so, she could take confidence in the fact that not only had her naval engineers and technicians created ship and weapons designs on a parity with or better than those found in the Western navies, but the Navy's past experiences in battle had led to the development of better tactics, including surprise night attacks, faster and more limber ship maneuverability, and superior firepower.[10]

While Yamamoto did not in any way share that confidence, he was gamely committed to winning parity for Japan in all weapons categories under the rubric of a "common upper limit" on overall tonnage. When the London talks opened on 23 October, he startled the British by further arguing that all offensive weapons, such as battleships, carriers, and heavy cruisers, should be destroyed or radically reduced in number—in effect, "heaping burning coals upon their heads." In that bold move to position the other powers in a corner, Yamamoto was closely following his instructions. (His words must have seemed all the more impertinent since they came from a mere rear admiral, when the chief naval delegates of the other powers were full admirals. During the course of the talks, on 15 November, he was promoted to vice admiral.) Overcoming their shock, the British responded coolly that since they had to defend colonies in many more seas than the Pacific, Yamamoto's second proposal was unacceptable on its face. When Yamamoto presented the same propositions to the Americans on the next day, the U.S. delegates responded in similar fashion, stating that they had two coastlines to defend, and as for the parity matter, the ratios fixed at Washington twelve years before had, they said, served the cause of peace very well. On those grounds, by and large, the talks foundered, and remained deadlocked for over two months, with Britain stymied in her attempt to work out a compromise, with many bluffs and counterbluffs exchanged, and with each of the three major powers calculating how to avoid blame for the talks' collapse, which came on 30 December, when the Japanese government in Tokyo gave notice that it was abrogating the Washington treaty.

Yamamoto had been faithful to his charge, but he had little reason to share in the fleet faction's jubilation back home. He continued to believe that treatyless oceans presented a perilous state of affairs, especially for Japan. And he wanted Emperor Hirohito to know that "there was no appearance whatsoever of two powers [the United States and Great Britain] combining to oppress the third [Japan] at these talks." In the conclusion of his official report to the throne, dated 19 February 1935, he stated: "I deeply regret that it was not possible to persuade Britain and America to accept the imperial government's views, and am convinced of the necessity for still further efforts in this direction."[11]

When the Second London Naval Conference opened in December 1935, Japan's delegation was led by Admiral Nagano Osami, a protégé of Admiral Kato Kanji. There was no surprise, but certainly plenty of dismay, among the other powers when, during the opening sessions of the conference, Japan's "further efforts" consisted of a repetition of Yamamoto's earlier position, without change or compromise: Nagano demanded parity, a common upper limit, reduction in overall tonnage, and abolition of all battleships and carriers. A deep gloom settled over the conference deliberations during the weeks that followed, as the other delegations came to realize that, owing to Japan's intransigence, a dangerous naval race was in the offing. On 15 January 1936, the four Western powers formally voted down Japan's "impossible" demands. The Japanese delegation thereupon retired from the proceedings, pledging as they did so that their nation would not start a naval race. But that is exactly what, in less than a year, it would do.[12] In the viewfinder: Pearl Harbor.

*

Following his return from the talks in 1934, Yamamoto found himself at loose ends. Though assigned to both the Navy Ministry and the Naval General Staff, he had been given no special responsibilities or tasks, in keeping, it appears, with a traditional Japanese practice of shunning for a time plenipotentiaries and other delegates to international conferences, as though they were assumed to have come home stained by foreign contaminants. To his friend Hori Teikichi, he occasionally spoke of his desire to retire. Each time, Hori succeeded in dissuading him. In his case, Yamamoto should not have been particularly surprised by his dismissal. Few admirals in the leadership of the two naval factions knew what to make of his apparent independent spirit. Though nominally a moderate and a member of the treaty faction, he had gone to London, reluctantly at first, but in the end willingly, to deliver and plead a set of demands from the fleet faction that included, among other things, abolition of the aircraft carrier, by that date his own new passion. How to account for his ambivalence must have been a question that bothered both sides in the ideological debate. Perhaps the answer was that Yamamoto truly believed while in London that he could bluff and win with a losing hand—that a treaty on his impossible terms might actually be secured. But back in Tokyo, wiser by half, he no doubt realized that his personal disquietude resulted from the realization that he had been coldly used by the fleet faction admirals to wreck the scheduled conference of 1935; and that he had been naive to think he could alter their purposes. Remarkably, his friends in the treaty faction, forgiving him that transgression while acknowledging his undoubted naval patriotism, rallied around him for support.

During this period in limbo Yamamoto was not without his divertissements. A gambling addict, he played poker at night into the wee hours; in London he had relieved the First Sea Lord, Admiral A. Ernle M. Chatfield, of twenty pounds by that means. And the U.S. Chief of Naval Operations, William H. Standley, learned to respect his skills at bridge. Takagi Sokichi, a naval officer who worked under Yamamoto in a variety of posts, wrote of him:

> Few men could have been as fond of gambling and games of chance as he. . . . *Shogi, go,* mahjongg, billiards, cards, roulette—anything would do. At parties and the like, although he could not drink, he would make up for it by organizing "horse races" on paper and getting the younger officers accompanying him or the young women serving at a teahouse to bet fifty sen on the outcome.[13]

Yamamoto's professional career was resurrected in 1935, when he was appointed chief of the Aeronautics Department, in command of all navy aviation. Air warfare had become his primary professional interest, and now that international restraints had been rejected he could throw all his energies into the promotion of the carriers and air arm that he had been instructed to oppose in London. Believing that the Navy's main strength would shift from battleships, the other "offensive weapons" of London renown, to carrier-borne aircraft, he vigorously opposed the current diversion of a major share of the Navy's resources to the design and construction of two mammoth 63,700-ton "unsinkable" battleships, *Yamato* and *Musashi,* with 18.1-inch main batteries.[14] His surely was a quixotic effort in a Navy still wedded, through Mahan, to the primacy of battlewagons in any fleet that would aspire to rule the seas. The big-ship, big-gun admirals were obsessed with the realization that, at one stroke, the two battleships would advance the Navy's strength in capital ships from 60 percent of American strength to a position of dominance. That the battleship in whatever size was fast becoming an anachronism, as Yamamoto argued, was simply beyond their comprehension. (The U.S. Navy also continued to place its faith in the central role of the battleship.) Though he failed to stop the design phase and to reduce the funding of the behemoths, the farsighted Yamamoto did significantly advance the Navy's air assets by other means, and it was a newly invigorated vice admiral who received a call in 1936 to assume the office of navy vice minister, a position that gave him access to the money and power required to create a naval aviation arm second to none in the world.

Prior to the collapse of the Second London Naval Conference, the Navy Ministry and the Naval General Staff had represented two separate interests and sets of talents. To the Navy Ministry went officers who excelled in politico-administrative detail and whose interests ran to policy. The General Staff, by contrast, attracted warrior-type officers who demonstrated ability in operational command. With the ideological victory of the fleet faction, men of like mind could be found in both billets by 1936, and the differences between ministry and staff became blurred. By 1936, too, the Japanese Navy was distinctly pro-German, and becoming more so. A higher number of officers served as attachés and members of their staffs in Berlin than in Washington or London. The same people who formed the new "German faction" also exhibited a pronounced anti-Americanism, part of it aroused by a U.S. Navy fleet problem (maneuvers) conducted in the previous year near Midway, 1,300 nautical miles to the northwest of

Hawaii. (From that problem the U.S. Navy learned that its Pacific Fleet would be defeated by superior Japanese speed and weaponry should it venture into the western Pacific.) It is in 1936 that one finds the first recorded hint of a strategy to come: in November of that year the Navy War College completed a study, entitled "Strategy and Tactics in Operations Against the United States," in which it was proposed: "In case the enemy's main fleet is berthed at Pearl Harbor, the idea should be to open hostilities by surprise attacks from the air."[15] No doubt that study was read with high interest by the new air-minded vice minister, who, we do know, was much influenced in this period by his friend Vice Admiral Inoue Shigeyoshi, head of the Aviation Section of the Navy General Staff. Inoue's tenet was: "He who commands the air commands the sea."[16] Together, these two airpower advocates succeeded in making certain that Japan's accelerated naval construction program (the Third and Fourth Replenishment Plans) that began in 1937 included carriers and advanced-model aircraft in the mix.

Between 1937 and 1941, in addition to one super battleship, six cruisers, and a number of destroyers and submarines, Japan added to her strength four fleet carriers: *Akagi* (a conversion), embarking 104 aircraft; *Hiryu*, 73; *Shokaku*, 84; and *Zuikaku*, 84. In addition, she added three light fleet carriers: *Taiyo*, *Chuyo*, and *Unyo*, each embarking 27 aircraft. Altogether, during the nineteen years that passed since the Washington Treaty of 1922, the Japanese almost doubled the size of their Navy in terms of tonnage. By 1941 her naval forces slightly exceeded in number the U.S. Pacific Fleet in all categories excepting carriers, where her then existing six fleet and four light fleet carriers greatly outnumbered the U.S. Pacific Fleet's three—a testament to the enterprise of Yamamoto and Inoue.[17] Their influence can also be discerned in the design and manufacture of new models of aircraft for the carriers. The premier dive-bomber in production by 1941 was the Aichi Type 99 (D3A1 to D3A2), which the Americans and British code-named "Val." The first-line torpedo bomber was the Nakajima Type 97 (B5N1 to B5N2), known to the West as "Kate." The Type 97 was also employed as a high-altitude level (horizontal) bomber. And the primary carrier-based fighter was the Mitsubishi Type 0 (A6M2 to A6M8) "Zero" or "Zeke." (Type numbers corresponded to the last one or two digits of the first production year in the Japanese calendar, according to which the year

1940 was 2600. Hence the Nakajima Type 97 was brought into service in 1937, and the Mitsubishi Type 0 was first produced in 1940.) The Zero was unquestionably the finest carrier fighter afloat at the outbreak of the Pacific war, when its speed, rate of climb, maneuverability, range, and firepower made it superior to any American fighter, carrier or land based, Navy or Army, including the Navy's first-line Grumman F4F Wildcat. Its sole weaknesses were the absence of self-sealing fuel tanks and armor protection for the pilot. The naval air arm was divided into flotillas, two or more of which formed an air fleet. By December 1941 there were two air fleets in being. The 1st Air Fleet was carrier-borne. Its 500 pilots, the cream of naval aviation, had about 800 hours flying time each, many of those hours in combat over China. There was no mightier shipborne air force in the world. Its destiny was to attack Pearl Harbor. The 11th Air Fleet was land-based. With about the same number of pilots, the 11th would accompany the southern operation. The entire inventory of operational aircraft at the end of 1941 was estimated at 3,400.

★

A man sometimes of seeming contradictions, Yamamoto did not want to take the aerial armada he had assembled to war against the United States and Britain, each of which, he knew, would quickly rally to help the other. In the course of such a conflict, he stated freely, America would soon outbuild Japan, hence in the end defeat her. He would be just as outspoken in his opposition to talk of a Tripartite Pact that would formally link Japan to the aggressor states Germany and Italy. During the year before that axis was formed, on 27 September 1940, when extreme nationalists in Japan were pushing for the pact, Navy Minister Admiral Yonai Mitsumasa insisted that Yamamoto be accompanied everywhere by armed plainclothes police, lest he be eliminated from the scene by rightist assassins. In the end, Yonai, who agreed with Yamamoto's view, decided that the only way to save his life was to send him off to sea.[18] Thus, on 30 August 1939, Yamamoto, who had served under four successive governments as Navy vice minister, donned his formal white uniform with the Order of the Sacred Treasure, First Class, upon the left breast, and presented himself at the Imperial Palace to be invested with Japan's highest command at sea, commander in chief of the Combined Fleet. He would retain for now the rank of vice admiral.

Back at the redbrick building that housed the ministry, the new commanding officer, equivalent to the U.S. Navy's commander in chief, United States Fleet (CINCUS), held a press conference at which he stated: "For a navy man, the post of C. in C. of the Combined Fleet is the greatest honor possible. . . . I feel overwhelmed at the great task with which I have been so undeservedly entrusted, but I mean to do my humble best in the service of His Imperial Majesty."[19] In honor of the occasion the teetotaler CINC downed a beer in a single draft.

Yamamoto took formal command of the Combined Fleet on board his flagship, the battleship *Nagato,* on 1 September 1939. It was the same day on which Germany invaded Poland, launching the Second World War. Yamamoto at once tightened training exercises and placed the 40,000 officers and men in his command on notice that they must prepare for any eventuality. Training was conducted in daylight, twilight, night, and early dawn. Gunnery drills took place off Sukumo and Cape Ashizuri. Carrier aircraft launches were made off Yokosuka. Wintertime torpedo attacks were rehearsed at Hashirajima in the Inland Sea. But the training was not relentless, since Yamamoto, like all fleet commanders, knew that after four straight weeks of constant and intense work, efficiency declined and accidents increased. So rest and recuperation periods were regularly scheduled at Kure, Sasebo, and Beppu. All knowledgeable observers agreed that, after a year under Yamamoto's discipline, the Combined Fleet was in its highest-ever state of readiness.

In September 1940, the new Navy Minister, Admiral Oikawa Koshiro, summoned the Navy's highest-ranking admirals to a conference in Tokyo. Oikawa wanted everyone's consent to the signing of the Tripartite Pact. All present nodded agreement. Yamamoto was the only one to speak: "I haven't the slightest intention of raising any objections to steps on which the minister has already decided," he said, resignedly. But, in the *praeteritio* style of Cicero, he did object by warning that America and Britain, from whose territories Japan imported 80 percent of her raw materials, were likely to embargo those materials in response to the pact. Then what would Japan do? The anger he hid at the conference came out in a letter he sent afterward to Admiral Shimada Shigetaro, who commanded the China Area Fleet: "At this stage, to express shock and indignation at American economic pressure is either childishly impetuous or . . . extraordinary inattentiveness to recent events."[20] It was during this same visit to Tokyo that

Yamamoto met with Prime Minister Prince Konoye Fumimaro, himself a moderate who sought to resolve Japanese-U.S. tensions through diplomatic negotiation, and to Konoye's question, How would the navy fare in the event of a war with America, made his famous answer: "If we are ordered to do it, then I can guarantee to put up a tough fight for the first six months, but I have absolutely no confidence as to what would happen if it went on for two or three years."[21]

Yamamoto was now convinced that Japan's descent into war was ineluctable, impelled by forces, both personal and material, that would not be thwarted. He had now exhausted whatever credit and leverage he might have had in the attempt to deflect the inevitable. What else remained for him, a professional officer of the Emperor, but to prepare his forces for battle? "Now that things have come to this pass," he told his friend Baron Harada Kumao, "I'll throw everything I have into the fight. I expect to die in battle on board the *Nagato*."[22]

It was with this mind-set, then, that Yamamoto proposed to Navy Minister Oikawa that the unavoidable war with America must begin with a surprise air attack on Pearl Harbor and the airfields of Oahu. It was an operational plan that he had first discussed, so far as we know, in either March or April 1940, with his then chief of staff Vice Admiral Fukudome Shigero. "It may be said that except for the late Admiral Yamamoto," Fukudome wrote in December 1955, "I was the only person acquainted with detailed plans of the operation from the moment of its conception."[23] Next to know was Oikawa, but, without waiting for the minister's reaction, Yamamoto drafted a three-page outline of what came to be called the *Hawai sakusen* ("Hawaii Operation") and presented it to a trusted old friend, Rear Admiral Onishi Takijiro, chief of staff of the 11th Air Fleet. Although the 11th was not carrier-based, Yamamoto valued the sound judgment and practical airman's sense possessed by Onishi. If anyone could find defects in the scheme, taken simply as an aviation project, it would be he. In one sign of his good judgment, Onishi enlisted the assistance of someone less conventional and cautious than himself: Commander Genda Minoru, an air staff officer on board the carrier *Kaga*, known to his friends as "madman Genda," for his radical ideas of air warfare. The two officers—one senior, the other junior; one solid, the other mercurial— came to the conclusion that the plan was "not impossible" to achieve. But when Onishi presented their joint study to Yamamoto's chief of staff, Fuku-dome, at the end of April 1941, he fingered two seemingly insurmountable problems.

The first was the expectation that aerial torpedoes dropped into the shallow (thirty to forty-five foot) water of Pearl Harbor would strike and stick in the mucky bottom before they could run their courses. The second was that the success of an attack of that kind depended on the maintenance of absolute secrecy, which seemed highly unlikely given the large number of people who would have to be involved in its planning and execution. [24]

Onishi gave the plan only a 60 percent chance of succeeding. Fuku-dome, interestingly, gave it only a 40 percent chance: "Had I from the very beginning been entrusted with the study of the idea instead of Onishi, I would certainly have recommended to Commander in Chief Yamamoto that the Hawaii Operation be abandoned."[25]

But Yamamoto would not be deterred by percentages. He was comfortable with the hand he held.

★

Husband Edward Kimmel's ancestors on his father's side emigrated from Bavaria in 1755 and settled in Somerset County, Pennsylvania colony. His father, Marius Manning Kimmel (1832–1915), attended Princeton University until his junior year, then accepted an appointment to the United States Military Academy at West Point, from which he was commissioned a second lieutenant of cavalry in 1857. During the following four years he fought against the Comanche Indians in the Battle of Nescutunga Valley and against Mexican marauders on the Rio Grande. When the Civil War broke out, then Major Kimmel served in defense of Washington in the First Battle of Bull Run on 21 July 1861. He then obtained leave to go home to Kentucky, where he changed sides, resigning from the Union army and accepting a commission in the Confederate forces. In the latter uniform he served as chief of staff to Major General Earl Van Dorn in the defense of Vicksburg in 1862. Following the surrender at Appomattox, Kimmel rode southwest to become a civil engineer on the Vera Cruz–City of Mexico Railroad, then under construction. For six years beginning in 1866 he engaged in a number of business enterprises in Missouri, then moved to Henderson, Kentucky, where he married and, at 512 North

Green Street, began raising a family of seven boys and girls. Mrs. Kimmel was born Sibbella Lambert, the daughter of Joel Lambert and Polly Husband, of Henderson, hence the introduction of "Husband" into the family as a given name.

Young "Kim," or "Hubbie," as Husband was called within the family, was a serious boy, his brother, Singleton, older by twelve years, would remember in later years: "The Admiral used to haunt my office." (Singleton was the city and county road engineer.) "He learned everything he could about the business, served as my surveying party rodman for a while. He always wanted to know the whys and wherefores of everything. I remember that when he was still in high school he went out and surveyed the old Lambert farm, plotted it, drew a map of it, located all the buildings."

At age sixteen Kim was valedictorian of his graduating class at Barrett High School. Afterward, inspired by his father's diploma from the military academy, he applied to his congressman from the Second District of Kentucky for an appointment to West Point.[26]

While waiting for the decision he completed his freshman year at Central University in Richmond, Kentucky. Told then that the allotments for West Point were filled, he secured an appointment to the United States Naval Academy, at Annapolis. The academy that he entered on 21 May 1900 was less an institution of higher learning than it was a training establishment or novitiate.

Cadets (the title of midshipman did not come into use until 1904) learned by the book, that is, by texts in tabloid form that had to be committed to memory. Innovative thinking was expressly discouraged. Cadets developed "a slavish adulation for the book" rather than "a quickening of the intellect."[27] In 1902 only 12 percent of the faculty were civilian academicians; the balance were academy graduates who had passed through the same regimen. Indeed, at Annapolis the intellect was deliberately subordinated to the will, and the subjects of instruction were frequently employed as a means of punishment; for, if any one subject ruled the curriculum, it was discipline. Molding character was thought more important than enlargement of the mind. Controlled by an iron hand of authority in every sector of his life, the cadet was understood not to be an individual aspiring to naval service but as one *belonging* to the service; hence, to resign from the academy required permission to do so. The overall and intentional effect of discipline was mastery over self, in the sense that it was thought to produce men who displayed, as the great naval historian and strategist Alfred Thayer Mahan (class of 1859) expressed it, "uncomplaining, noble self-abnegation."[28] A Cistercian monk could not have put it better.

One by-product of self-mastery was the development in each cadet of a deep personal sense of honor. Reputation and a good name were paramount values, to be esteemed both in the academy and in later service at sea. Cadets were taught to "guard their own honor and the honor of the service." Death should be preferable to dishonor. By such exhortations cadets were persuaded that, like medieval knights, they possessed a morality superior to that of civilians. It was a morality to be expressed not in self-absorption, much less in conceit, but in refined manners, punctilious courtesy, and becoming modesty. When taking on their first fleet assignments after graduation, passed midshipmen presumably would know not to assert themselves too much among their peers and certainly never to take initiatives that would outshine a superior. They would be loyal, obedient, and efficient officers according to their ranks, and the discipline through which they had passed at Annapolis would always abide as a ready anchor to windward.

At least that was the theory, and it seems not to have had any lasting deleterious effect when one considers the accomplishments of Kimmel's contemporaries at the academy, many of whom, a half century later, went on to become the principal naval leaders of World War II: Harold R. Stark, Ernest J. King, Chester W. Nimitz, William F. Halsey, Raymond A. Spruance, Royal E. Ingersoll, Robert L. Ghormley, John H. Towers, John S. McCain, Wilson E. Brown, H. Kent Hewitt, Milo F. Draemel, Aubrey W. Fitch, Richmond Kelly Turner, William S. Pye, and Thomas C. Kinkaid. The last-named, future commander of the Seventh Fleet, became Kimmel's brother-in-law when his sister Dorothy gave her hand in marriage to Kimmel on a snowy evening in January 1912 at St. Anne's Episcopal Church, Annapolis.[29] It would be difficult to argue that the sterile intellectualism of the academy appreciably hindered those particular classes, on whom "the stars fell," either in the prosecution of their careers or in the achievement of their wartime victories.

As for Cadet Kimmel, who would also rise to high position, second only to that of Chief of Naval Operations, he successfully observed the academy discipline as a "regulation" cadet, passed his courses, became a member of the varsity gymnasium team, played on his class football team, managed the varsity crew, and reached the cadet rank of brigade adjutant. Not the least of his accomplishments had been to form numerous strong friendships with quality individuals. One such staunch relationship had bonded him with Harold Raynsford "Betty" Stark, in the class (1903) ahead of him. Stark got his nickname from upperclassmen during his plebe year at the academy. His hazers mistook a distant Stark relative's name from the Revolutionary War period to have been Betty, instead of Molly. But Betty stuck. Kimmel was able to escape the academy as Kim, except that Stark would later call him by the Turkish "Mustapha," because Kimmel sounded like "Kemal," as in Mustapha Kemal, president of the Turkish Republic (1923–1938). Their paths would intersect many times in the years ahead.

✶

After graduating thirteenth in his class of sixty-two on 1 February 1904, Passed Midshipman Kimmel was ordered to duty in the battleship USS *Kentucky*, where he served in the gunnery department. Other tours of duty followed in battleships, cruisers, and destroyers, as the novice officer rose in rank. In 1914, as a lieutenant, he became aide and fleet gunnery officer on the staff of the commander in chief of the Pacific Fleet. During the years 1913–15 he was engaged in the task of rescuing stranded Americans from the coast of Mexico, then in the throes of revolution. On 18 July 1914, while on board ship, he was wounded twice in the right arm and in each leg by shots fired from shore. When the United States entered the World War in 1917, the now lieutenant commander was detailed as a U.S. naval observer to the British Grand Fleet at Scapa Flow to demonstrate a photographic system for the analysis of gunnery scores that he had had a major hand in developing. Afterward, he served as squadron gunnery officer with the five battleships that formed the so-called American Battle Squadron attached to the British fleet. Later, in 1918, as executive officer of the *Arkansas*, he witnessed the ignominious surrender (and scuttling) of the German High Seas Fleet at Rosyth.

In the early 1920s, Commander Kimmel served three years as production officer in charge of 6,700 civilian workers in the Naval Gun Factory at

Washington Navy Yard, after which he was made captain in charge of the Cavite Navy Yard in the Philippines. He then served two years on the Asiatic Station as commander of Destroyer Division 45, a part of whose mission was to guard U.S. Army round-the-world aircraft on their leg between Hong Kong and Calcutta. That duty was followed by studies at the Naval War College in Newport, Rhode Island, where he completed the senior course, the greater part of which was taken up by analysis of the latest version of War Plan Orange, the Navy's secret projection of how it would fight and win the "inevitable" naval war with Japan. Two years of duty at the Navy Department in the Policy Section of Naval Operations preceded another two years in destroyers, this time as commander, with the rank of captain, of a squadron of Battle Force destroyers.

In every assignment, Kimmel acquired an outstanding annual performance evaluation ("Officer's Record of Fitness") from direct superiors: "an all-around officer of great promise," "energetic, forceful and of pleasing personality," "good common sense and initiative," "a splendid officer of high character," "excellent in organization, management, and in handling personnel." So impressive was Kimmel's proficiency in ship movements, the then Chief of Naval Operations, Admiral William V. Pratt, added his own encomium to the fitness report of April 1933: "Captain Kimmel is a humdinger. He is a driver and a worker most efficient and he does it all without antagonizing people; I like him because he says what he thinks, never fools you, and his judgment is excellent. He is eminently qualified for promotion and I expect to see him get to the very top someday. He will make good."[30]

It was axiomatic that for advancement to flag rank an officer must first serve as commanding officer of a battleship. Kimmel received that compliment later in 1933 when he was given command of the 27,000-ton USS *New York* (BB-34), built in 1914. It was a ship on which he had been stationed briefly, when on the staff of Admiral Hugh Rodman, with the British Grand Fleet, in 1917. (His senior air officer on board, Lieutenant Logan C. Ramsey, would later, in August 1937, write a prescient article for the United States Naval Institute *Proceedings* entitled, "Aerial Attacks on Fleets at Anchor." In 1941, while serving Kimmel again as operations officer of Patrol Wing 2 at Pearl Harbor, Ramsey would be the first to sound the attack alarm on 7 December.) After only a short stint as skipper of the *New York,* Kimmel was transferred to become chief of staff for Commander Battleships, Battle Force. Yet another Washington assignment followed in 1935, as budget officer for the entire naval establishment. On 13 October 1937, to no one's surprise, he was promoted to rear admiral.

Back at sea, the new flag officer became Commanding Officer Cruisers, Battle Force. Early in 1939, he commanded a good will tour around South America with a division of three heavy cruisers, visiting ports in Venezuela, Brazil, Argentina, and, via the Straits of Magellan, Chile and Peru. In June of that year, he was reassigned to the command of Cruisers, Battle Force (consisting of three divisions of light cruisers) in the Pacific Fleet, relieving his old friend from academy days, Rear Admiral Harold R. Stark, who had been appointed Chief of Naval Operations (CNO). Kimmel hoisted his flag in the USS *Honolulu.*

As the months of 1940 came and went, it was clear to Kimmel and his fellow flag officers at Pearl that the Orange plan, which they had first encountered in an earlier form at the Naval War College, was moving ever closer to the execution phase. Japan was threatening to unleash a sixth initiative since 1896 to dominate the nations and territories of eastern Asia. In the Sino-Japanese War of 1896 she had seized the island of Formosa (Taiwan) off the southeastern coast of China. In the Russo-Japanese War of 1904–05, she had gained predominant control over Manchuria and Korea, annexing the latter in 1910. In 1931 she had seized the three northern provinces of China and formed them into a puppet state named Manchukuo. In 1937 she had invaded the major population centers of China—Peking (Beijing), Shanghai, and Nanking—and, by the following year, she had occupied almost all the principal cities, ports, and railroads of north and central China. In 1939 she occupied Hainan Island off the coast of China, and the Spratlys, coral islands that lie between southern Vietnam and Borneo, athwart the sea-lanes between Singapore and Manila—perfect submarine bases.

Two events in September 1940 demonstrated that Japan's appetite was hardly sated. First, as a result of Germany's defeat of France, she stationed troops in northern French Indochina. The U.S. government, which earlier, in July, had responded to Japan's continuing war in China by placing an embargo on exports to Japan of aviation fuel and the highest grades of iron and steel scrap, now cut off all grades of those metal exports. And, second, on 27 September, Japan signed the Tripartite Pact with Germany and Italy, which provided that the three powers would come to one another's assistance if one of them was attacked by a nation not yet involved in the European or Sino-Japanese wars. Emboldened by her Axis partnership, and fueled by ambitions to establish a western and southwestern Pacific empire that she euphemistically styled the Greater East Asia Co-Prosperity Sphere, Japan now cast ravenous eyes in the direction of southern Indochina and other European colonies to the south of her: the Dutch East Indies, whose oil fields had become a strong attraction after the mother country's surrender to Germany; and rubber and tin-rich Malaya, only half-protected by a beleaguered Great Britain. If the Japanese fleet moved south against those colonies of nominal allies of the United States, it was possible that the United States Navy Pacific and Asiatic Fleets would become engaged; it was certain if the list of Japanese targets was enlarged to include the U.S. territory of the Philippine Islands.

✫

Rear Admiral Kimmel was still in command of Cruisers, Battle Force, when, on Sunday, 5 January 1941, after returning to the Pearl Harbor fleet landing following a round of golf with his chief of staff, Captain Walter S. DeLany, at the Army's Fort Shafter course, he was met by a staff officer who announced that the admiral was to report immediately aboard the fleet flagship, then alongside one of the docks. Upon going aboard, Kimmel was escorted to the quarters of the chief of staff, who showed him a dispatch from the Navy Department to Admiral James O. Richardson, Commander in Chief, United States Fleet (CINCUS). The dispatch read that, effective 1 February 1941, Admiral Richardson was relieved of his command, and that President Franklin D. Roosevelt had appointed in his stead as CINCUS and as Commander in Chief, United States Pacific Fleet (CINCPAC) Husband E. Kimmel, with the designated rank of admiral. DeLany was with him when he received the news. "The blow dazed him," DeLany told the Associated Press. "I've never seen a man more surprised."[31]

Kimmel went at once to Admiral Richardson's quarters in Honolulu to assure him that he had in no way sought this appointment, second only in the Navy to that of Chief of Naval Operations in Washington, and to express his conviction that, from his knowledge of Richardson's efficient command of the fleet, there was no justification for his being relieved only thirteen months into his command. Kimmel, furthermore, sent a letter, dated 12 January 1941, to CNO "Betty" Stark:

> When I got the news of my prospective assignment, I was perfectly stunned. I hadn't any intimation that Richardson's relief was even being considered; and even had I known that his relief was being considered, I did not in my wildest dreams really think that I would get the job. Nevertheless, I am prepared to do everything I can when I take over on about the first of February.[32]

Some months later, Kimmel would learn why Richardson was relieved. He had angered President Roosevelt during a White House luncheon meeting on the previous 8 October by opposing, in what Roosevelt considered disrespectful language, the permanent stationing of the fleet at Pearl Harbor. Prior to May 1940 Pearl had been home base for only a Hawaiian detachment, consisting of a carrier, heavy cruisers, and destroyers. Roosevelt thought that the presence of the fleet in mid-Pacific waters would deter Japan from seizing European colonies in the Far East. Richardson had disagreed and had argued, furthermore (and too boldly for Roosevelt's taste), that only the bases on the U.S. West Coast could provide the dockyard and supply services, the manpower, and the auxiliary vessels that the fleet would need for war. Kimmel would also learn that he had not been the President's first choice to replace him. That had been Rear Admiral Chester W. Nimitz, chief of the Navy's Bureau of Navigation, which had charge of all naval training and all officer appointments. Widely admired in the Navy, Nimitz was also a Roosevelt confidant, and thus he probably was not overly surprised by the President's offer. But knowing that he was being jumped over fifty more senior officers, thus risking their ill will (though it had not bothered Stark to be promoted over fifty seniors when he was made CNO in 1939), he respectfully declined. In his stead he recommended for CINCUS and CINCPAC his old cadet-mate Kimmel, who would jump only thirty-one numbers. "He had an excellent service reputation," Nimitz would write in 1962, "so good—in fact—that he was promoted from grade to grade after having been selected by Selection Boards. His reputation was good enough to persuade me, as Chief, Bureau of Naval Personnel, Navy Dept., to nominate him as the relief of Admiral J. O. Richardson, C-in-C Pacific Fleet."[33] Pointing out that he and Kimmel had known each other since their academy days, former CNO "Betty" Stark said of Kimmel in a 1966 interview: "We became warm friends in those early days and our contacts were many through the years. In 1941 when a vacancy occurred in the command of the Pacific Fleet I strongly urged [upon the Secretary of the Navy, Frank Knox] the appointment of Admiral Kimmel for that most important Command, and he was so appointed. I could have paid him no higher compliment."[34]

When Knox and Stark then presented Kimmel's name to the President, Roosevelt responded, "Of course! Why didn't I think of him?"[35]

After the appointment was publicly announced, it was greeted with approval throughout the service; it is not recorded how many, if any, of the senior flag officers over whom Kimmel was jumped manifested a grievance. As for the U.S. Army, it took cautious measure of the man. Under the date 7 February 1941, U.S. Army Chief of Staff General George C. Marshall wrote to the newly installed Lieutenant General Walter C. Short, commandant of the Army's Hawaiian Department:

> My dear Short: I believe you take over command today; however, the reason for this letter is a conversation I had yesterday with Admiral Stark.
>
> He spoke of Admiral Kimmel, the new Fleet Commander, regarding his personal characteristics. He said Kimmel was very direct, even brusque and undiplomatic in his approach to problems; that he was at heart a very kindly man, though he appeared rather rough in his methods of doing business. I gather that he is entirely responsive to plain speaking on the part of the other fellow if there is frankness and logic in the presentation. Stark went so far as to say that he had in the past personally objected to Kimmel's manners in dealing with officers, but that Kimmel was outstanding in his qualifications for command, and that this was the opinion of the entire Navy.
>
> I give you this as it might be helpful in your personal dealings with Admiral Kimmel, not that I anticipate that you would be supersensitive, but rather that you would have a full understanding of the man with whom you are to deal.[36]

When shown this communication by the writer in May 2000, Admiral Kimmel's sole surviving son, Edward R. Kimmel, commented, "Sounds like my dad. He kept us three boys in line."[37] (Husband and Dorothy Kimmel had three sons: Manning Marius, born 22 April 1913, was graduated from the Naval Academy and entered the submarine service. During the Second World War Commander Kimmel became skipper of the submarine USS *Robalo*, which was sunk by a mine in the Balbac Strait north of Borneo, on 2 July 1944, with the loss of all hands. Thomas Kinkaid was born on 29 September 1914. Also an academy graduate, he commanded surface ships during the war. He died, a retired captain, at Annapolis on 24 January 1997. Edward Ralph was prevented from entering the academy by poor eyesight. He served as a reserve naval officer during the war, rising to the rank of lieutenant commander.

In 1966, middle son Tom recalled:

> The most outstanding impression I have of my father [who was still alive] from the very first day I can remember is his complete honesty, forthrightness, and sense of fairness. He simply would not be a party to anything that was not completely honest and above board. He was a very poor bargainer, because he much preferred to pay a fair price and not enter into any "deals" with anyone. He had a quick temper and would not tolerate disobedience or willful neglect or carelessness. Such infractions he dealt with immediately in no uncertain terms. However, when the incident was over, it was completely finished and he held no grudges. My two brothers and I have always had the greatest respect and admiration for our father. In times of crisis, when something "big" came along, he was always ready to deal with the problem quickly, intelligently, and thoroughly. He seemed to save his temper for the small, relatively unimportant matters.[38]

If, indeed, there was a sometimes harsh surface to Kimmel, as Stark informed Marshall, and as son Tom appeared to acknowledge, one understands better the gossip, widespread in the Navy, that Roosevelt wanted the "two toughest sons-of-bitches" in the Navy to run the Pacific Fleet and the Atlantic Fleet (before 1 February 1941 called the Atlantic Squadron).[39] For commander in chief of the latter theater (CINCLANT) he had chosen, effective 1 February 1941, Admiral Ernest J. King, about whom Roosevelt stated gleefully, "He shaves with a blowtorch." One of King's six daughters had her own assessment: "My father is the most even-tempered man in the Navy; he is always in a rage."[40]

On Saturday morning, 1 February 1941, Husband E. Kimmel stood under the guns of turret No. 4 on the quarterdeck of the fleet flagship *Pennsylvania* for the change of command ceremonies. After a reading of orders with Admiral Richardson, the new CINCUS and CINCPAC watched as his four-starred flag was broken from the maintruck. Every high-ranking officer at Pearl watched with him, but not his wife and sons.

Dorothy had remained on the mainland when Kimmel began his latest tour in the islands; Manning and Tom were serving together on board the submarine S-38 based in the Philippines; and Ned was a junior at Princeton. The father of the family cut a fine, athletic figure in his starched white uniform. Five feet ten inches tall, with his ramrod straight posture he seemed taller. A ruddy youthful complexion formed the background to a prominent nose and clear blue eyes. His dark blond hair was turning prematurely gray. When he spoke the voice was soft Kentuckian.

Kimmel knew that, from this day, he would wear the coveted four stars of fleet command on his shoulder boards. But for how long? His new rank of admiral was a designated rank that went with the office, not with the officer. If relieved, he would revert to his permanent lower grade. This first-ever change of fleet command ceremony to take place at Pearl Harbor was not an occasion for vainglory. Realism, even humility, were the uniform of the day. What had happened to Richardson, for whatever reason, could also happen to him.[41]

After a formal luncheon attended by the two principals, and members of their staffs, incoming and outgoing, Kimmel repaired to his flag cabin in the *Pennsylvania,* where his communications officer handed him a dispatch from CNO Admiral Stark. It informed him of the contents of a telegram sent on 27 January by U.S. Ambassador Joseph C. Grew in Tokyo to the State Department. A member of Grew's embassy staff, first secretary Edward S. Crocker, had been advised by the Peruvian minister, Ricardo Rivera-Schreiber, of a rumor circulating in Tokyo to the effect that, in the event of broken relations between Japan and the United States, the Japanese fleet intended to make a full-scale surprise attack on Pearl Harbor. The dispatch concluded:

> The Division of Naval Intelligence places no credence in these rumors. Furthermore, based on known data regarding the present disposition and employment of Japanese naval and army forces, no move against Pearl Harbor appears imminent or planned for in the foreseeable [*sic*] future.[42]

On 5 February Kimmel received from the Navy Department a copy of a letter drafted by Rear Admiral Richmond Kelly Turner, the fifty-five-year-old, six-foot, lantern-jawed director of war plans (OP-12). Called "Terrible Turner" by coworkers for his alleged overbearing ego and stormy temper, the newly minted flag officer had sometimes insightful (and more often very wrong) estimates of Japanese intentions and capabilities. His letter draft was for the use of Secretary Knox and was addressed to Secretary of War Stimson. Stark approved the draft, and Knox signed and mailed it on 24 January.

Turner and his War Plans staff clearly had been impressed by what a single British carrier, HMS *Illustrious,* had accomplished in a nighttime raid against the Italian naval base at Taranto on the night of the previous 12 November. Flying twenty-one antiquated, fabric-covered, open-cockpit, biplane Swordfish bombers—ten to drop flares and bomb dockyards, and ten to release torpedoes against warships at anchor—the Fleet Air Arm pilots disabled three battleships, the new *Littorio* and two of the older *Giulio Cesare* class. Knox's letter read in part:

> The security of the U.S. Pacific Fleet while in Pearl Harbor, and of the Pearl Harbor Naval Base itself, has been under renewed study by the Navy Department and forces afloat for the past several weeks. This reexamination has been, in part, prompted by the increased gravity of the situation with respect to Japan, and by reports from abroad of successful bombing and torpedo plane attacks on ships while in bases. If war eventuates with Japan, it is believed easily possible that hostilities would be initiated by a surprise attack upon the Fleet or the Naval Base at Pearl Harbor.

In my opinion, the inherent possibilities of a major disaster to the fleet or naval base warrant taking every step, as rapidly as can be done, that will increase the joint readiness of the Army and Navy to withstand a raid of the character mentioned above.[43]

It may be assumed that this text caught Admiral Kimmel's full attention.

FOUR

THE BREWING STORM

All the seas, everywhere,
are brothers one to another.
Why then do the winds and waves of strife
rage so violently through the world?

Japanese Emperor Mutsuhito,
Meiji the Great (1867–1912)

China was always the sticking point. During the fateful years 1937–1941, all diplomatic efforts by the United States and Japan to resolve mounting dangers of war between the two powers turned on Japan's continued aggressive presence in China—the "China Incident," as the war was called in Japan. Throughout the four years since 7 July 1937, when Japanese Army troops marched across the Marco Polo Bridge west of Peking, every major diplomatic note exchanged between Washington and Tokyo had the assault on China as its text or subtext. In unmistakable language, the U.S. State Department condemned the Japanese incursion and called the world's attention to its violation of the first paragraph of Article I of the Nine-Power Treaty of Washington, signed by Japan on 6 February 1922, which read: "The Contracting Powers, other than China, agree: (I) to respect the sovereignty, the independence, and the territorial and administrative integrity of China."[1] But beyond announcing, on 16 July 1937, a list of nonaggression principles that it hoped all nations in the Far East would observe, the United States did nothing substantive to stop the aggression—

even to mediate, as China asked Washington to do. U.S. Secretary of State Cordell Hull drew back from direct engagement on the advice of his chief of the Division of Far Eastern Affairs (FE) (becoming later in the same year Advisor on Political Relations [FE]), Dr. Stanley K. Hornbeck, who believed that "any step that might be taken by this Government toward action 'in a mediatory capacity' would (at this moment) be premature and ill-advised; would be likely to aggravate rather than to ameliorate the situation."[2] The noninterventionism proposed by Hornbeck would form the basis of Hull's policy throughout the remainder of the decade.

Other nations, too, claiming that they lacked appropriate authority and means, drew back from engagement: Great Britain, France, the Netherlands, Norway, Sweden, and Denmark. And so the march of Japanese soldiers proceeded unchecked through the central Chinese provinces amid mounting stories, both verified and unverified, of Japanese atrocities committed against helpless civilians, including the stunning act of genocide inflicted on the residents of Nanking in December 1937.[3] In the same month, Japanese bomber aircraft and naval units on the Yangtze River attacked and sank the U.S. Navy gunboat *Panay,* causing two deaths and leaving fifty sailors and passengers wounded. There was a brief excitement in the American press, and some pugnacious posturing in the Department of the Navy, but the crisis passed thanks to adroit action by U.S. Ambassador to Japan Joseph C. Grew and an apology sent to Washington from the Japanese Foreign Ministry.

By 1939, with Hull still pursuing a cautionary course, the American public was becoming increasingly offended by Japanese behavior in China. One reason was expanded coverage of the war in the press by correspondents sympathetic to China, who represented the Associated Press, United Press, International News Service, *The New York Times,* the *New York Herald Tribune,* the *Chicago Tribune,* and *The Christian Science Monitor.* Another and equally effective force in turning American opinion against Japanese militarism was the informal collection of "China hands"—Foreign Service veterans and Christian missionaries both active and retired who had worked in China and now expressed their heartsickness at what was happening to the Chinese people. The missionaries were particularly effective in rallying support for China, since as a body they were greatly respected by the American people for being well-educated, devout, self-sacrificing men and women who had no obvious ideological bias. Their letters, articles, and lectures spread word of Japanese atrocities committed against the most innocent of people, including children. They reported that, because it was known that Japanese soldiers had the locations marked on their maps, the Japanese were deliberately bombing American churches, hospitals, colleges, and schools, most of which had the American flag painted on their roofs. The most dangerous place to be in an air raid, they said, was an American mission. Furthermore, they warned that Japan seemed bent on destroying Chinese culture and on brutally reducing the country to a vassal state.

Notable among the lecturers was the congregational medical missionary, and later congressman, Dr. Walter Henry Judd, who during the period 1939–1941 delivered some fourteen hundred lectures across the United States about China's travail. An article by him in the February 1941 *Reader's Digest,* "Let's Stop Arming Japan," cited a recent Gallup Poll which found that 82 percent of the American people favored ending all exports of war materials to Japan.[4] No doubt the missionaries' efforts contributed to that arousal of the American conscience. Sympathy increased for the Chinese Nationalist leader Generalissimo Chiang Kai-shek, who was battling both the Japanese and the Communists of Mao Tse-tung. Meanwhile, hundreds of thousands of U.S. citizens gave scant Depression-era dollars to China Relief. And children found gory pictures of Japanese war-making on cards accompanying their bubble gum.

Against that background spines stiffened all over Washington. Already, in July 1939, the U.S. government had renounced the 1911 Treaty of Commerce with Japan, thus opening up the possibility of applying economic pressure on Tokyo. Henry Morgenthau, Jr., secretary of the Treasury, who had long wanted to give aid to China but had been obstructed from doing so by Hornbeck, on the grounds that it would provoke Japan "prematurely," recounted how, when visiting State in December 1939 to solicit Hull's support for an embargo on sales of molybdenum (a metallic element used to toughen alloy steels) to Japan, Hull, who was still committed to "the precept of inaction," summoned an adviser from the Far Eastern Division for an opinion. That adviser favored the embargo. "He then sent for Dr. Hornbeck," Morgenthau recorded later, "and again I almost fell out of my chair when Hornbeck agreed that this ought to be done. He said, 'As a matter of fact, we are working on several other ways to put the screws on the Japanese and this is just what we ought to do.'"[5]

Not everyone was on the same page, however, in that December. Ambassador Grew in Tokyo was convinced that Japan would never yield to economic pressure. On the first day of the month, he cabled State that no sanctions contemplated in Washington would cause Japan to give up her conquests in China. She would rather fight, and she had the warrior instinct to fight to the death. "On one issue [Japanese] opinion can be definitely said to be unanimous: the so-called New Order in East Asia has come to stay. . . . The minimum interpretation envisages permanent Japanese control of Manchuria, Inner Mongolia, and North China."[6] But Grew's apparent resignation to events was operating outside the American groundswell. Indeed, as one of his Foreign Service officers, John K. Emmerson, wrote later, "Sad as it is to contemplate over the perspective of the intervening years, the Embassy did not play a crucial role in the unfolding Japanese-American drama."[7] The major players on the U.S. side were Hull and Hornbeck at State; Morgenthau at Treasury; a Cabinet hawk, Harold Ickes, secretary of the Interior, who controlled petroleum reserves; and, to a lesser degree, because his gaze was always fixed across the Atlantic, President Roosevelt.

The Morgenthau-Hornbeck rapprochement led to Roosevelt signing, on 25 July 1940, a proclamation ending the sale to Japan of all petroleum, petroleum products, and scrap metals; but, two days later, owing to fervent objections from Under Secretary of State Sumner Welles, a Europeanist who opposed even the risk of a distracting war with Japan, the embargo, as the press called it, was watered down to a ban on aviation gas and No. 1 heavy melting iron and steel scrap.[8] However weakened, the first sanctions were in place.

In Japan the reaction was swift and predictable. The government directed its ambassador in Washington, Kensuke Horinouchi, to make urgent inquiries about the cutoff. This Kensuke did, meeting with Welles at State. The under secretary explained, first, that the controls were being applied only because of his country's own fuel requirements. (There was some justification for this statement, since, at the time, Japan was making huge purchases of U.S. aviation grade gasoline, and the commanding general of the IX Corps, based at San Francisco, reported that, within six to nine months, Army Air Corps and U.S. Navy aircraft would be short of fuel if the purchases continued.) But Welles surely dissembled when he went on to say that the cutoff was not directed at Japan or at any other specific foreign country.[9] During the month that followed, Tokyo transmitted three formal notes of protest. All were rejected. The State Department took the occasion to point out Japanese actions that were damaging to American rights and interests in China. No one stepped back from what historian Herbert Feis called "our first firm counteraction." The U.S. position was hardening. And Roosevelt himself was emboldened to consider how he might further ratchet up the penalties.

On 24 September, elements of the Japanese Army marched into northern French Indo-China, having compelled the defeatist Vichy government to render no resistance. This first overt, in-your-face act of aggression since China in 1937 was a sign to Washington that Japan was determined, despite Washington's first sanctions, to continue her expansionist policies. Roosevelt required no time at all—two days—now that he had the confidence that came from knowing that the British Royal Air Force had earlier that month defeated the German Luftwaffe in the skies over England, to employ the ratchet effect. In reproof of the Japanese seizure, this time *all* grades of iron and steel scrap were embargoed. At the same time, Roosevelt arranged for a highly publicized loan to the Kuomintang government of Generalissimo Chiang Kai-shek at Chunking. In Tokyo the penalty was expected, and without question it hurt, but Japan had decided that with her access to iron ore from conquered territories, as well as from Malaya, she could ride it out.

Hard on the heels of the Indo-China incursion, on 27 September Japan signed the Tripartite Pact with Germany and Italy, in the first article of which Japan "recognizes and respects the leadership of Germany and Italy in the establishment of a new order in Europe." The second article states that "Germany and Italy recognize and respect the leadership of Japan in the establishment of a new order in Greater East Asia." In the third article the Axis nations, as they came to be called, pledged to come to the aid of one another "when one of the three Contracting Parties is attacked by a power at present not involved in the European War or in the Sino-Japanese Conflict." That unnamed but unmistakably inferred power was the United States. Less unmistakable were several phrases in the document, which were noted and commented on when a copy reached Washington. What, for example, was intended by "new order"? What geography precisely made up "Greater East Asia"? And if Germany attacked the United States, instead of the obverse, was Japan then obligated by this language to join Germany in war? Even the Japanese government, it turned out later, was not clear about the precise meanings of the articles it signed, and had had the principal role in drafting.

The German alliance had long been sought by extremist elements of the Japanese Army, since any German conquests in western Europe would free up the colonies of those subjugated nations in Southeast Asia for Japanese absorption. It should be noted, moreover, that the Army dominated all decision making at the higher reaches of Japanese polity, and had for some time. In the preceding July, Army firebrands brought down the government of Prime Minister Yonai Mitsumasa, a moderate who had tried to conciliate the American government, without success. All such peaceful efforts were doomed to failure, as German diplomats acknowledged in 1945, "because Japan, far from restoring the sovereignty and integrity of China, only asked for recognition of the situation she had established in China, in open violation of existing treaties."[10] On those terms, realistically, the Yonai Cabinet should never have expected to exact a consenting treaty from the United States. And so it seemed to the General Staff of the Army, which had a history of intervening in matters of state. On 16 July it compelled its cabinet representative, Minister of War General Hata Shuroku, to resign. Under the peculiar procedures of the cabinet, that action precipitated the resignation of the entire cabinet.

The General Staffs of the Army and Navy held unusually strong and independent positions under the Prussian-style Meiji Constitution adopted in the late nineteenth century. The central institutions of government were an Imperial House, the Diet (legislative assembly), and the cabinet headed by a prime minister. The Emperor, since 1926 Hirohito, was head of state and supreme commander of the Army and Navy. He was assisted by a lord privy seal as political secretary and adviser. But operational control of the services fell to the chiefs of the General Staffs, who made up the Supreme Command. Subject theoretically to the Emperor, the Supreme Command acted outside the administrative authority of the cabinet, including that of its Army and Navy minister members. Military strategies, plans, and operations were the sole prerogative of the chiefs of staff, and they need not to be disclosed to anyone save the Emperor, to whom they had direct access.

The Army and Navy ministers served on the cabinet at the pleasure of the Chiefs. At any time, a chief of staff could withdraw a minister, and, by not appointing a replacement, bring down the government. It was a power frequently employed. In November 1937, following the start of the China Incident, the Emperor and chiefs of staff created what was called Imperial General Headquarters for coordinating military affairs. And, later, the headquarters and the cabinet developed a liaison conference system to keep both entities informed. That liaison, under various names, would last throughout World War Two. On occasion of grave national decisions, the liaison personnel, sitting as an Imperial conference, would confirm policies already decided on in the presence of the Emperor and lord privy seal, in order solely to invest them with unimpeachable prestige and authority. As a rule, the Emperor would not speak during those proceedings. The distillate of this system of governing was that Japan had, first, a cabinet entrusted with powers to administer domestic and foreign policy but lacking control of, and sometimes even knowledge of, military operations; second, a military that was so independent of governmental, or civilian, control it was a law unto itself; and third, a head of state who sanctioned the decisions made.[11]

On 22 July, a new cabinet was formed under another moderate prime minister, Prince Konoye Fumimaro, who had served in the position before (1937–39), when the Army launched its operations in China, and who this time, concerned about Army domination of the cabinet, was reluctant to reassume the premiership—but he did, finally, out of sense of duty to prevent, if he could, war with the United States and Britain. Choice of the General Staff for war minister in the cabinet was General Tojo Hideki, a narrow-minded leader (called "Razor Brain") of the Army firebrands, and reason enough for Konoye to reconsider his agreement to serve a second term. Konoye, who proved to be a weak person in a strong position, made an injudicious choice for foreign minister when he selected Matsuoka Yosuke, a graduate of the University of Oregon, who, widely known for his egocentrism and ranting, mercurial behavior, was hardly the definition of a diplomat, one who "sits in silence, watching the world with his ears."[12] Stimson, who was Secretary of State at the time, would remember Matsuoka from the latter's abrupt behavior in dismissing American and British objections to Japan's invasion of Manchuria in 1931, and from his insolent conduct while leading the Japanese delegation out of the League of Nations in 1933.

About the only cabinet member whom Konoye might approach for help in averting war was a holdover from the Yonai cabinet, Navy Minister Admiral Yoshida Zengo, who represented the Navy's reluctance to go to war anytime soon, especially against the United States. But two months after being reseated, Yoshida, repelled by the move toward a German alliance, resigned during the Axis pact debates. Konoye, and, from outside the cabinet, Admiral Yamamoto Isoruku, who by then commanded the Combined Fleet, similarly opposed the pact, Yamamoto telling the prime minister at the debate's conclusion: "It's too late to do anything about the Tripartite Pact now, but I hope at least that you'll make every effort to avoid war with America."[13] The reason he gave was not opposition to that war as such but that the Japanese fleet, while very much improved in readiness, was not yet primed for combat. Despite his declared hopes for peace in the interim, Yamamoto, like a number of others in the Navy, was gradually coming around to the view that war with the United States was inevitable. And, if indeed it was, as he had written six months before, Japan's only chance to dominate in the Pacific was to strike offensively, and as soon as it was primed, before the American naval construction program marginalized Japanese naval power and made Japan's imperial ambitions moot. Under Yamamoto's influence, a growing number of high-ranking officers in the Navy began closing ranks with the Army.

★

On the American side, where there was also a growing sense of inevitability, most voices urged delay. Ambassador Grew cabled State that "we must strive by every means to preserve the status quo in the Pacific at least until the European war has been won or lost." But the normally cautious Grew startled Hull and Hornbeck with a call for a "show of force" in the region, "together with a determination to employ it if need be."[14] Such an action posed risks that went well beyond what the American people were prepared to accept. The presidential election platforms of both the Democratic and Republican parties that fall flatly rejected the acceptability of American participation in any foreign war. Roosevelt, the Democratic candidate, made the same rejection, "except in case of attack."[15] Wendell Willkie, his opponent, concurred, endorsing aid to Britain and China, but "short of war."

Both candidates were fully aware of the isolationist temper in much of the country, though it had subsided since 1935 when the majority of U.S. citizens had expressed opposition to further foreign entanglements. A Gallup poll taken that year revealed that 70 percent of respondents thought that American entry into the "Great War" of 1914–18 had been a mistake. There was widespread revulsion at the carnage, at the fortunes made by armaments manufacturers, at the false propaganda, and at the failed peace. Some of the resentment originated from German-Americans and Irish-Americans, for ethnic reasons, but the antiwar sentiment was sufficiently wide-based that Congress passed, on 20 August 1935, a Neutrality Act that forebade the export of arms, munitions, and implements of war to *all* combatants in future wars, without distinction as to aggressor or victim. The arms ban sections of four Neutrality Acts passed between 1935 and 1939 were repealed on 3 November 1939. That made possible financial loans to China, and arms sales to Britain, which went to war against Germany in the preceding September, on a "cash and carry" basis. And when Britain ran out of cash, it enabled Roosevelt to sell Congress on passage of the Lend-Lease bill (HR-1776), on 11 March 1941, that continued such aid.[16] By that date sympathy for Britain's cause had grown strong in the country; Gallup polls found that the public supported the Lend-Lease program by a margin of more than two to one.[17]

Interestingly, the Gallup poll for 10 January 1941 asked the benchmark question, Was it a mistake for the United States to have entered the first World War?, and received the response: 39 percent yes, 42 percent no, with 19 percent having no opinion. The same question asked again on 6 April elicited almost exactly the same numbers.[18] If the Gallup poll was an accurate measure, the isolationist mood was softening. But there remained a strong inclination to keep American troops out of the European war. On 3 February and 10 March, the poll asked separately if the United States should enter the war against Germany and Italy. The first poll received answers of 15 percent yes and 85 percent no; the second 17 percent yes, 81 percent no.[19] The public was realistic, however, as shown in the poll published on 27 April, which asked, Do you believe that the United States will go into the war in Europe sometime before it's over, or do you think we will stay out?, the answers were: Will go in, 82 percent; Will stay out, 18 percent.[20] Similarly, when asked on 28 April, If it appeared that there was no other way to defeat Germany and Italy except for the United States to go to war against them, would you be in favor of the United States going to war?, 68 percent answered yes, 24 percent no, with 8 percent having no opinion.[21]

The Gallup poll asked comparatively few questions about Japan. During the whole of 1940 there were only two, and it was the same question asked twice: Do you think our Government should forbid the sale of arms, airplanes, gasoline, and other war materials to Japan? On 14 February 75 percent answered yes, 25 percent no; on 20 October 90 percent answered yes, 10 percent no.[22] On 24 February 1941 the poll asked, Do you think the United States should try to keep Japan from seizing the Dutch East Indies and Singapore? The yes response were 56 percent, the no response 24 percent, and those with no opinion numbered 20 percent. It would seem that, in the minds of respondents, the question addressed only such restraints as diplomacy and embargoes on war materials, rather than armed intervention, since when the same question was asked on 14 March, and the kicker, "should risk war if necessary" was added, the affirmative replies dropped to 40 percent and the negative rose to 39 percent.[23] Two more questions about Japan were asked during the remainder of 1941. The first, on 7 September, disclosed how far the public had advanced by that date in its willingness to risk war. To the question, Should the United States take steps now to keep Japan from becoming more powerful, even if it means risking a war with Japan?, the responses were 70 percent yes, 19 percent no, with 12 percent having no opinion.[24] The final question about Japan before 7 December, asked in the interview period from 27 November to 1 December, read: Do you think the United States will go to war against Japan sometime in the near future? The respondents, nearly two to one, thought so: 52 percent yes, 27 percent no, with 21 percent having no opinion.[25] That, approximately, is what the American citizenry was thinking, as reported by the only semidependable instrument history can rely on for the period.

What was the President of the country thinking about where Japan and Germany were concerned during 1941? The answer: Franklin Roosevelt was thinking about the same thing that Ambassador Grew had proposed to

Secretary Hull: a show of force. Taking Japan first, Roosevelt thought that the militarists in Tokyo were best handled, not by cowering in harbors, but by overt demonstrations of will and power. While probably not directly influenced by Hull's backroom adviser Hornbeck at State, who consistently underestimated Japan's naval strength and willingness to fight, the President certainly thought in parallel with him. In order to warn Japan about her continued occupation of China territory, and to deter her, as well, from any intended operations in southern Indo-China, Malaya, and the Dutch East Indies, Roosevelt thought it apropos to resurrect in miniature the Great White Fleet of his uncle Theodore. In early February he conceived the notion of sending a detachment of the Pacific Fleet—carriers, approximately four cruisers, and a squadron of destroyers—on a temporary visit to the Philippines and Far East waters, going down through the Phoenix and Gilbert or the Fiji Islands, then reaching over to Mindanao and Manila. The notion was strongly supported by Hull, but just as vigorously opposed by Stark, who thought that what Roosevelt called a "bluff" might turn out to be a *casus belli*. He sternly lectured the President, and, because of their long friendship, he knew he could do so without offending him:

> We want to give Japan no excuse for coming in in case we are forced into hostilities with Germany who we all consider our major problem.
>
> The Pacific Fleet is now weaker in total tonnage and aircraft than the Japanese Navy. [This was before the detachment of one-fourth of the fleet's strength to the Atlantic in May and June.] It is, however, a very strong force and as long as it is in its present position it remains a constant serious and real threat to Japan's flank. If any considerable division is sent to Manila it might prove an invitation to Japan to attack us in detail and thus greatly lessen or remove our serious naval threat to her for a considerable period to come. I believe that it would be a grave strategic error at this time to divide our Pacific Fleet.

Stark laid out more of his reasoning:

> Right now, Japan does not know what we intend. If we send part of the Fleet to the Asiatic now, we may show our hand and lost [*sic*] the value of any strategic surprise. We might encourage Japan to move,

rather than deter her, and also we might very well compromise our own future operations.

Toward the end of his presentation to Roosevelt, Stark referred to a cable received from the American embassy at Tokyo, dated 7 February, in which the mercurial Ambassador Grew, now back to pulling his talons after a brief fling as a hawk, said, "Risk of war would be certain to follow increased concentration of American vessels in the Far East. . . . The risk should not be taken unless our country is ready to force hostilities."[26]

To Kimmel at Pearl, Stark wrote about his "two hour struggle (please keep this absolutely secret) in the White House," and said that, while Hull opposed him, "You may be amused to know that the Secretary of War, Colonel Stimson, has been of very great assistance to me in this connection in recent conference."[27] He told Kimmel that the President had backed off for the time being. "I have fought this over many times and won, but this time the decision may go against me."[28] Kimmel replied on 18 February: "While my political horizon is limited, I believe we should be prepared for war when we make this move."[29] Between 10 and 25 February the question of sending a fleet detachment to the Far East came up twice again at the White House. The President was finding it hard to make a decision. He knew he should be doing something, but what? In this and other matters affecting relations with Japan the White House was drifting. The initiatives all belonged to Japan. Policy makers from the President down seemed to be particularly troubled by the question of what the United States should do if Japan were to attack Malaya and the Netherlands East Indies. Stark, who was not bound by partisan politics or factions, is a good source for the indecision and confusion that abounded from February to July. To Kimmel he wrote, on 25 February:

> The difficulty is that the entire country is in a dozen minds about the war—to stay out altogether, to go in against Germany in the Atlantic, to concentrate against Japan in the Pacific and the Far East—I simply cannot predict the outcome. Gallup polls, editorials, talk on the Hill (and I might add, all of which is irresponsible) constitute a rising tide for action in the Far East if the Japanese go into Singapore or the Netherlands East Indies. This can not be ignored and we must have in the back of our heads the possibility of having to swing to that

tide. . . . This would mean that any reinforcement to the Atlantic might become impossible, and, in any case, would be reduced by just so much as we would send to the Asiatic [Fleet]. And that might be a very serious matter for Britain.[30]

In April, Roosevelt finally got his way with a warship foray into the western Pacific, but, at Stark's urging, the form of the voyage was a nonthreatening southern route "practice cruise" to Australia and New Zealand. The ships taking part were the heavy cruisers *Chicago* and *Portland*, the light cruisers *Brooklyn* and *Savannah*, and Destroyer Squadron (Desron) 3. Their crews received a hearty welcome in the Commonwealth nations, and some solid training was obtained along the way. No harm was done and possibly some good was achieved. But Stark was truly alarmed by Roosevelt's newest "harebrained scheme." He quoted the President in a personal letter to Kimmel, dated 19 April:

> The President said (and incidentally when I open up to you this way I don't expect you to quote the President and I know that there is nobody who can keep things secret better than you can): "Betty just as soon as those ships come back from Australia and New Zealand, or perhaps a little before, I want to send some more out. I just want to keep them popping up here and there, and keep the Japs guessing." This, of course, is right down the State Department's alley. To my mind a lot of State Department's suggestions and recommendations are nothing less than childish (don't quote me) and I have practically said so in so many words in the presence of all concerned.[31]

Popping up all over the Pacific to say "Boo!" to the Japanese was to play a dangerous game, in Stark's view. Following an alternative tactic, he decided this time to see Roosevelt's chips and raise him. He proposed a plan to send a carrier force out northwest of Hawaii to a point within striking distance of Japan, which would really give the Japanese a thrill, given "their unholy fear of bombing." (In his letter of 25 February, Stark had advised Kimmel that, in planning offensive raids after the opening of hostilities, he should consider carrier bombing attacks on the "inflammable Japanese cities—ostensibly on military objectives.") The tactic worked. "I thought for once, if I could, I would give the State Department a shock," Stark wrote to Kimmel. "I had a broad inward smile when the State

Department in effect said: 'Please Mr. President, don't let him do it'; or words to that effect. It was a little too much for them."[32]

Whenever he turned his gaze to the Pacific Roosevelt was edgy and erratic. Or so Stark thought. To his confidant and former director of war plans "Savvy" Cooke, skipper now of the flagship *Pennsylvania*, Stark complained, "To some of my very pointed questions, which all of us would like to have answered, I get a smile or a 'Betty, please don't ask me that.'" He confided to Cooke that he had more than once offered to resign. "Policy seems to be something never fixed, always fluid and changing." He said of his letter, "I think you should burn it after showing it to Kimmel."[33] (Fortunately for history Yamamoto's and Stark's addressees did not always observe that admonition.) If it is true, as is often alleged, that Roosevelt all along wanted to go to war, it is far from certain that war with Japan was the war he wanted—at least not now.

✷

By contrast, where Germany was concerned, Roosevelt was totally focused, resolute, confident, and daring, to the extent of giving Admiral Ernest J. King, commander in chief of the Atlantic Fleet, license to make war at the time of his choosing in the North Atlantic Ocean. There the enemy was the one arm of the German Navy (Kreigsmarine) that by summer 1941 was still playing a significant offensive role in the war against England. Hitler's heavy units were then frozen in port, the Führer not willing to see happen to them what happened to the battleship *Bismarck,* which was famously sunk by a combined air-sea force of the Royal Navy on 27 May 1941. The still active arm was the submarine fleet (*Unterseebootwaffe*), commanded by Admiral Karl Dönitz. From the first week of September 1939, Dönitz's U-boats had waged a tonnage war (*Tonnagekrieg*) against Britain's merchant fleet of freighters and tankers in a campaign to sink more British tonnage than could be replaced with new construction. Britain depended on her ocean trade for all her fuel oil and refined gasoline, most of her raw materials, and half of her food. Dönitz's staff had calculated in 1940 that the U-boats would have to inflict a monthly loss rate of 700,000 gross register tons (GRT) in order to strangle Britain's armed forces and industries and to starve into submission Britain's people. (The British had estimated that 600,000 would do them in.) By July 1941, however, they had never reached that goal, nor would they in the entire course of the war, excepting

November 1942, when they sank 118 ships for a record 743,321 GRT. Because of the unexpectedly productive American shipyards, in that same November merchant ship construction passed and continued to pass thereafter, with ever increasing plurality, the figures for merchant ship losses to U-boats. It was clear by that date that Dönitz's tonnage battle was not winnable.

But it was not so clear earlier, in 1940 and 1941, when Roosevelt worried that what German chancellor Adolf Hitler had failed to do with his Luftwaffe he might well accomplish with his Unterseebootwaffe: take Britain out of the war. That would be a disaster for the British people, but it would be an equal disaster for American arms should they be called upon to rescue the European continent from Naziism, since the British Isles were the indispensable jumping-off point, and an unsinkable aircraft carrier, for mounting that endeavor. Too, a technologically advanced German armed force, with perhaps the entire British Home Fleet under its swastika, would pose a grave threat to America's own security. Therefore, in September 1940, with solid Gallup poll backing (62 percent), Roosevelt transferred fifty obsolete World War I–era four-stack destroyers to Britain in exchange for bases under ninety-nine-year leases in the Bahamas, Jamaica, Antigua, St. Lucia, Trinidad, and British Guiana. Ten of the destroyers barely made it across the Atlantic, but even in lame condition the old tin cans could be put to work in the Royal Navy's antisubmarine effort. By strict interpretation the warship transfers violated the neutrality provisions set down in the Hague Conference of 1907, and a grateful Winston Churchill wrote nine years later that the exchange "was a decidedly unneutral act by the United States" that would have "justified" Hitler in declaring war.[34] Berlin was appropriately indignant, but the declaration would not come until fourteen months later, after Pearl Harbor.

Acting boldly during February and March, Roosevelt froze German and Italian assets in the United States; seized German and Italian ships in U.S. harbors "to prevent their sabotage"; and created a Support Force of twenty-seven destroyers to escort merchant ship convoys from North American ports as far as Iceland. In March he devised the Lend-Lease program so that the U.S. industrial base could become the "arsenal of democracy." On 9 April he authorized the establishment of U.S. military bases and meteorological stations in Greenland. And, nine days later, he extended the "Western Hemisphere," which, he said, the United States had a duty to defend, to about 26 degrees west longitude, or 2,300 nautical miles east of New York. The new jurisdiction, covering some four-fifths of the Atlantic, including Greenland and the European Azores, Roosevelt brazenly called the Pan-American Security Zone. In July, he extended his conception of the Western Hemisphere even farther, to 22 degrees west to include Iceland; and at the (forced) invitation of the Icelandic government, he dispatched an occupation force of 4,095 Marines to Reykjavík. The United States was edging into the Battle of the Atlantic. And with the occupation of Iceland, it was compromising its condemnation of the Japanese occupation of northern Indo-China, as Tokyo was quick to point out.

★

During spring, summer, and fall of 1941 there were incidents at sea. On 10 April, while rescuing survivors from a torpedoed Dutch freighter off the coast of Iceland, the destroyer USS *Niblack* made sonar contact with what she thought was a submerged U-boat, range closing. *Niblack* dropped three depth charges—the first American shots fired in World War II. No visible damage resulted, and German naval archives make no mention of the event, leading to the conclusion that the sonar contact was a false one. On 21 May, a 5,000-ton American freighter, SS *Robin Moor,* sailing under the stars and bars in the South Atlantic, was torpedoed and sunk by *U-69* (Kapitänleutnant [hereafter Kptlt.] Jost Metzler). The crew and passengers were found and rescued. Calling the sinking "ruthless," Roosevelt declared an "unlimited national emergency" on 27 May. Berlin turned a deaf ear to Washington's demand for restitution. On 20 June, *U-203* (Kptlt. Rolf Mützelburg) attempted to attack the U.S. battleship *Texas* in the western approaches to Britain, but during a sixteen-hour pursuit was not able to overtake the faster battlewagon. Her commander, Mützelburg, explained to Dönitz that he thought the warship was British because it was east of the Pan-American Security Zone and inside the declared German blockade area surrounding the British Isles. On the U.S. side, the event would not become known until after the war.

Officially, Hitler did not want such incidents to occur, since he was not yet ready to make war against the United States. Dönitz dutifully issued warnings to his commanders to scrupulously avoid all U.S. naval and merchant vessels. And there were no further incidents until 4 September, when inadvertent action by a Royal Air Force Coastal Command bomber caused *U-652* (Kptlt. Georg-Werner Fraatz) to launch two torpedoes, ten minutes apart, at a World War I–era, 200-ton flush-deck "four-piper" destroyer, USS *Greer,* which was steaming toward Iceland with mail, freight, and military passengers. It was the first German attack on a U.S. Navy warship in the war. The bomber involved, an American-made Hudson, had warned *Greer* by blinker light that a U-boat lay submerged athwart her track about ten miles ahead; then, when seeing the destroyer come upon the position and begin a sonar tracking pattern, the bomber dropped four depth charges randomly and headed back to base. Coming to periscope depth, *U-652's* commander saw that the destroyer was of the same class that had been traded to Britain, and, thinking that the depth charges had come from *Greer,* considered himself justified in attacking her. Both torpedoes missed. *Greer* thereupon dropped nineteen depth charges, without effect, and broke off the engagement ten hours after first contact. In Washington, Roosevelt seized on this first "exchange-of-fire" event to demand that the U-boat responsible for the "unprovoked" attack (which he would later learn was not an exact description) be "eliminated" (which was not exactly possible). In a "fireside chat" to the nation on 11 September he denounced the U-boats as "rattlesnakes of the Atlantic" and declared that henceforth U.S. warships would "shoot on sight" (as the press put it) all German and Italian vessels discovered in Security Zone waters. Sixteen days later, addressing a Navy Day audience, Roosevelt himself used the "shoot on sight" phrase in presenting his newly assertive position, which drew a 62 percent approval rating in a Gallup poll published on 2 October.[35]

Most histories about this period assign the origin of Roosevelt's "shoot on sight" order to the *Greer* event. But documents found in the Modern Military Branch collection of the National Archives and in the Operational Archives and Library of the Naval Historical Center at the Washington Navy Yard disclose that the "shoot on sight" order was originally given two months before, in July.[36] After *Greer* Roosevelt was merely articulating in public operational war orders that Admiral King had issued to his escort ship captains on 1 and 18 July: "Destroy hostile forces which threaten shipping of U.S. and Iceland flag"; "My interpretation of threat to U.S. or Iceland flag shipping, whether escorted or not, is that threat exists when potentially hostile vessels are actually within *sight or sound contact* of such shipping or its escorts [emphasis added]."[37] And on 19 July King added a spatial dimension to his order: Operation Order No. 6-41 directed U.S. naval forces to attack any U-boats or other German or Italian (and, one supposes, Japanese, if he thought that there were any around) warships found within one hundred miles of an American-escorted convoy to or from Iceland.[38] Thus, King went to war four and a half months before 7 December—notice of which action was never transmitted by Main Navy to Admiral Kimmel at Pearl Harbor.

No Axis ships were detected or attacked in the undeclared war that King waged beginning in July. Had there been, according to the third article of the Tripartite Pact, Japan (theoretically) would have been obligated to come to the aid of her German ally. Of course, the loss of just one U-boat or one surface vessel might not have been enough to trigger the pact's provisions. But if that surface vessel was a *capital* ship the outrage might have risen to a different order of magnitude. That King was plainly prepared to go that far may be gathered from an extraordinary step he took on 5 November, when he dispatched Task Force 1, consisting of battleships *Idaho* and *Mississippi* (transfers from Kimmel's Pacific Fleet), cruisers *Tuscaloosa* and *Wichita,* with three destroyers, to sink the German pocket battleship *Admiral Scheer* (or possibly the superbattleship *Tirpitz,* sister ship of *Bismarck*), which British naval intelligence predicted would sortie from her base in Norway and enter the transatlantic convoy lanes. Under King's direct command, Task Force 1 took up attack positions athwart the Denmark Strait (between Iceland and Greenland), through which *Scheer/Tirpitz* was expected to pass. As events unfolded, it was *Scheer* who was the intended intruder, and she was kept in port by machinery damage. Had the German raider attempted to force the strait, as planned, it is very likely that she would have been sunk by the combined firepower of King's task force, and Hitler would have had no option but to declare war on the United States. The noted German historian Dr. Jürgen Rohwer told this writer that, while the loss of fifty men in a U-boat could be kept quiet, the loss of a capital ship with one thousand hands could not. Pride, face, and anger would have caused the Führer to move his declaration of war forward from December to November. Japan, we may assume, would have followed suit. Pearl Harbor would have gone on maximum alert, and, both because the Japanese Combined Fleet was not ready to sail that early in November, and because the element of surprise would have been lost altogether, the events of 7 December *might not have happened at all, or as they did*.[39]

★

The Roosevelt administration's identification with Britain's war against Germany was further tightened during 1941 through the adoption of two formal war plans. The first, called the ABC-1 [American–British Commonwealth] Staff Agreement, represented the fundamental strategy that would be followed by the two powers in the Atlantic-European and Pacific theaters. It resulted from Anglo-American military staff conversations begun at London in September 1940 and concluded at Washington in January–March 1941. A key passage read:

> Since Germany is the predominant member of the Axis Powers, the Atlantic and European area is considered to be the decisive theatre. The principal United States military effort will be exerted in that theatre, and operations of United States forces in other theatres will be conducted in such a manner as to facilitate that effort. . . .
>
> Even if Japan were not initially to enter the war on the side of the Axis Powers, it would still be necessary for the Associated Powers [the United States and the British Commonwealth] to deploy their forces in a manner to guard against Japanese intervention. If Japan does enter the war, the military strategy in the Far East will be defensive. The United States does not intend to add to its present military strength in the Far East but will employ the United States Pacific Fleet offensively in the manner best calculated to weaken Japanese economic power, and to support the defense of the Malay barrier by diverting Japanese strength away from Malaysia.[40]

First proposed in U.S. military circles in a famous "Plan Dog" memorandum authored by Admiral Stark in November 1940, the "Germany first" strategy would be followed even if (as would happen) Japan attacked the United States before the Germans made an attack or declaration of war. The strategy rested on the assumption that the defeat of Germany ensured the defeat of Japan, but not the obverse. Meanwhile, as plainly stated here, the operations of the Pacific Fleet would be *offensive* as well as defensive. It would not be correct to assert, as some have during the years since, that the Pacific strategy was to be a "holding operation."[41] Only one serious disagreement divided the U.S. and British delegations. The British thought that their base at Singapore was essential for the defense of the Malay Barrier, and they urged that a detachment of the U.S. Pacific Fleet be sent to defend that base. The American naval delegation, arguing that Singapore could not be held, even with the detachment, if Japan seized airfields in southern Indo-China, from which she could bomb Singapore at will, insisted that the Pacific Fleet not be divided. The stalemate was acknowledged in the ABC-1 Staff Agreement. Though an effort was made to devise an ABCD (American–British Commonwealth–Dutch) Agreement similar to ABC, the effort failed after one week of discussion. One of the rocks on which it foundered was the uncertainty on all three sides on where Japan might strike next and on what self-interested measures would then be taken by such disparate partners as the distant United States, the British in Malaysia, the orphaned Dutch East Indies, and the locally concerned Australia and New Zealand. President Roosevelt, for his part, was puzzled about what course he could take, given Congress's reluctance to consider a declaration of war against anybody; though he personally believed that the United States should oppose with force a Japanese entry into Malaysia, because it would give Japan a near monopoly on rubber and tin.[42]

In the footsteps of ABC-1 came a comprehensive war plan produced in May by the Joint Board, soon to be renamed the Joint Chiefs of Staff. Called the United States Joint Army and Navy Basic War Plan, or, more commonly, Rainbow 5, the plan incorporated leading features of ABC-1. From it was derived the basic Navy plan WPL-46, and from it again Admiral Kimmel developed the operating plan that governed specifically the Pacific Fleet, WPPac-46, which was promulgated by him on 21 July. The first offensive action of the Pacific Fleet was to "make reconnaissance and raid in force on the Marshall Islands."[43] WPPac-46 was approved by Stark on 9 September. But with war plans at the tactical level there was no certainty that what read well on paper would play out the same in execution. In the oft-cited expression of Count Helmuth von Moltke (1800–1891), "No battle plan survives contact with the enemy." In this instance, the events of 7 December would put the offensive features of WPPac-46 on temporary hold.

*

At Tokyo the Konoye cabinet was reeling from new restrictions imposed in February by Secretary Hull, after consultation with the President, on the export to Japan of copper, brass and bronze, zinc, nickel, and potash. And during the weeks and months of 1941 that followed, one after another of materials and products that could serve the Japanese war effort were placed under control, e.g., lead, jute, burlap, borax, phosphate, carbon black, cork, and animal and vegetable fats.[44] Exports of crude oil and regular gasoline were still off the table, but Hull found indirect means in that field, too, for punishing the Japanese warlords for what they *had* done in China and for what they *might* do next: in February and March he directed U.S. flag tankers to avoid Japanese ports, and he closed off further exports of oil drilling and refining machinery, storage tanks, containers, and even drums. Faced with these shortages in the energy field, the Japanese cabinet, with Foreign Minister Matsuoka in the lead, applied stiff pressure on the Netherlands East Indies (NEI) to provide unhindered access to her oil fields, technology, and equipment, as well as to her other raw materials. What Japan was demanding amounted to colonial domination of the NEI replacing that previously exercised by the defeated Dutch government in Europe. Because they feared that a U.S. cutoff of all oil exports would precipitate an armed takeover of the colony, NEI government officials sought a delicate balance, giving Japan just so much petroleum and raw materials as would keep her industries and military forces pacified, and, on the other hand, asking the United States to keep her own oil flowing westward lest there be unfortunate consequences for the NEI, including armed invasion. Hull and Hornbeck agreed to observe this policy, for the time being.

In February, the Konoye cabinet dispatched a new ambassador to the United States in an announced effort to improve political and economic relations. He was Admiral Nomura Kichisaburo, a former foreign minister, known for his dignity, character, and friendly inclinations toward the United States and Britain. Premier Konoye viewed the appointment of a moderate legate as a means both of buying time and of securing, if possible, reversal of export controls. Nomura himself seems not to have been optimistic of selling the New Order of Greater East Asia, given the anger in America over Japanese aggression in China, but, encouraged by former naval colleagues who wanted to avoid war, he agreed to try. At the date of his confirmation by the Emperor, he may not have been aware, given the bifurcation of Japanese officialdom, that his nation's independently operating warlords were then engaged in an intensive program of constructing airfields, seaplane bases, and fortifications throughout the mandated Marshall and Caroline Islands west-southwest of Hawaii. When on 14 February he presented his papers to Roosevelt, whom he had met before, he exhibited, as expected, a respectful, affable, and accommodating demeanor, to which Roosevelt responded in kind. To the President Nomura made clear that he was on a mission of peace. And in his discussions he never wavered from that course.

Altogether, from February through 7 December, the stately antifascist would meet with Roosevelt eight times, with Hull forty-five times, and with Welles six times. Interspersed were meetings with old naval acquaintances Stark and Turner. Hull said of him, "He spoke a certain—sometimes an uncertain—amount of English. His outstanding characteristic was solemnity, but he was much given to a mirthless chuckle and to bowing. I credit Nomura with having been honestly sincere in trying to avoid war between his country and mine."[45] Hull's conversations with the emissary were conducted after work in the secretary's private apartment at the Wardman Park Hotel. A small group of State Department staffers attended and recorded the discussions. Hornbeck, who dismissed the proceedings as a sham and abhorred the thought of compromise where China was concerned, was the least frequent in his attendance. It was Hull who had the hardest task in maintaining a diplomat's poker face and a semblance of interest in what Nomura had to say, because he knew every day beforehand what words the emissary would speak.

In August 1940 War Department cryptanalysts had created an electromechanical decryption device that penetrated the high-grade Japanese diplomatic cipher code-named "Purple." With this equipment the Army and Navy alternated daily in "breaking" intercepted Japanese diplomatic (DIP) radio traffic. Thus Hull, who was one of the few Washington officials to see the machine's product, called "Magic," was privy to all of Nomura's instructions from Tokyo, as well as to his reports home.

On 16 April Hull nudged the discussions along a more "get to the point" track by presenting four principles on paper that concisely represented the American position. In offering them to Nomura he invited the Japanese government's comment on them. They read:

1. Respect for the territorial integrity and the sovereignty of each and all nations.
2. Noninterference in the internal affairs of other countries.
3. National equality, including equality of commercial opportunity.
4. Maintenance of the status quo in the Pacific except where it might be altered by peaceful means.[46]

Tokyo would not comment on the principles until 11 May, possibly because it was hard-pressed to think of a reasonable reply that was not a capitulation, or, because the Konoye cabinet was preoccupied with another diplomatic development: on 13 April Foreign Minister Matsuoka concluded with Soviet Foreign Minister V. M. Molotov a Russo-Japanese Neutrality Pact. By its terms Russia and Japan would maintain peaceful relations with each other, and should either power be attacked by one or several third powers, the other would remain neutral throughout the duration of the conflict. The pact had advantages for each of the signers, if two duplicitous nations could trust each other's signatures. For Russia it meant that if she were invaded by Germany (as she would be, on 22 June) she need not worry about being stabbed in the back by a Japanese assault on her maritime provinces. For Japan it meant that she need not keep forces on the Manchurian border that abutted her traditional enemy, and could now execute her long-planned *hokushu nanshin* strategy: "Hold north, go south."

When the Japanese reply to Hull's four principles came on 11 May, it took the rhetorical form of *ignoratio elenchi*, i.e., it totally ignored Hull's principles and instead made demands of its own, namely, that the United States should ask Chiang Kai-shek to negotiate peace with Japan, and, if he refused, should halt all further assistance to his government; that the United States should restore normal trade relations with Japan; that the United States should help Japan access natural resources, such as oil, rubber, tin, and nickel, in the southwest Pacific; and that the United States should recognize the Tripartite Pact as a purely defensive instrument. Since no regard whatever was paid in this reply to such benchmark international concepts as sovereignty, noninterference, equality, and peaceful means, it was clear to Hull and his associates that there existed little basis for meaningful negotiation. Still, after an interval, he gamely carried on his diplomatic discussion, hoping against hope that the principled Nomura might be able to convert his handlers. That there was little chance of that happening was confirmed at an Imperial conference on 2 July when the Japanese government declared its firm intention to advance the Greater East Asia Co-Prosperity Sphere to the south irrespective of events elsewhere, and took the first public steps, including the mobilization of over a million conscripts, recall of Japanese merchant ships in the Atlantic, and censorship of mail, to place the nation on a war footing. Secretly, it authorized the Navy's carrier aircraft to begin practice bombing and torpedo attacks at Kagoshima Bay, where the surrounding hills and shallow water resembled the topography of Pearl Harbor.[47]

Then, on 12 July, U.S. Army and Navy cryptographers, who alternated in the decryption of Japanese diplomatic traffic, received a communication from Tokyo to the Vichy government in France announcing that if Vichy did not give Japan permission to occupy the southern half of French Indo-China by the twentieth of that month, Japan would forcibly do so unilaterally. On the basis of this Magic intelligence, Washington and London conferred on how best to impose appropriate economic penalties. When Vichy succumbed, granting Japan a joint protectorate of Indo-China, Japanese transports started carrying troops south toward the harbor of Camranh Bay and the airport at Saigon, the occupation of which would complete a virtual encirclement of the American Philippines. In response, on 26 July, after consulting by telephone with Hull, President Roosevelt issued an executive order freezing Japanese assets in the United States and choking off most of what remained of Japanese-American trade, which meant that now virtually *all* oil exports were embargoed. This drastic step was taken with the full realization by Roosevelt and Hull, who was recuperating from an illness in White Sulphur Springs, West Virginia, that it could lead to war with Japan, but with the conviction that anything less would be tantamount to countenancing and encouraging the Japanese conquests. Roosevelt's belief at the time (shared by Churchill) was that Japan would not engage the United States in hostilities unless and until Great Britain was defeated by Germany.

Secretaries Hull, Stimson, and Knox approved of the President's action.

General Marshall was nervous about the military's state of unpreparedness, and hoped for a delay in the outbreak of hostilities.[48] Admiral Stark forthrightly opposed the freeze order because war with Japan was not yet the war he wanted. Duking it out with Germany was the course to follow, the bellicose CNO wrote privately to "Savvy" Cooke (and Kimmel) on 31 July: "Protecting the Western Atlantic on a large scale . . . would almost certainly involve us in the war and [I told the President] that I considered every day of delay in our getting into the war as dangerous, and that much more delay might be fatal to Britain's survival. I reminded him that I had been asking this for months in the State Department and elsewhere, etc. etc. etc."[49]

For the full impact of the President's order to be appreciated, it should be noted that Japan's own oil wells and synthetic plants produced less than 12 percent of her annual civilian and peacetime military consumption. About 88 percent of her petroleum needs was imported, and 80 percent of that came from the United States.[50] The Navy held about two years' worth of operating oil in reserve, but for all of Japan's ambitious undertakings she would need oil resources in far greater measure than that, which could only be found now in the NEI. The Indies capital city of Batavia understandably shuddered with apprehension but bravely joined the American action by sharply reducing her own oil exports to Japan.

The reader may wish to pause at this oak-cleaving moment to reflect on what has happened. An aggressor state, Japan, has presented the Western powers with a third (after China and northern Indo-China) flaunting of international law. What is more, it has placed itself in a position to threaten the American Philippines. The United States has responded by placing the tightest possible tourniquet on those unjust purposes. But a Rubicon has been crossed, since after 26 July there were *no more peaceful sanctions* at American disposal. Meanwhile, neither side could, or had shown a willingness to, back down from their standoff. Absent a truly creative diplomatic intervention, the Japanese-American collision, if history will permit the interpretation, was now on automatic.[51]

Over the next four months there would be at least two clear opportunities to sever auto from matic, but they would not be taken, by either side.

AN AIR OF INEVITABILITY

Dear Kimmel: I have [had] a talk with Mr. Hull who has asked me to hold it very secret. I may sum it up by saying that conversations with the Japs have practically reached an impasse. As I see it we can get nowhere toward a settlement and peace in the Far East until and unless there is some agreement between Japan and China—and just now that seems remote.

Betty
23 September 1941

The Japanese cabinet had a slightly different appearance as it entered the final months of peace. The independently acting, inconsistent, and vainglorious Foreign Minister Matsuoka was gone. His last offense had been to consult repeatedly with the Emperor without Premier Konoye's prior knowledge or consent—most recently, following Germany's invasion of Russia on 22 June, for the purpose of pressing Hirohito to authorize an attack on the country with which Matsuoka had, just ten weeks before, concluded a nonaggression pact. To remedy that behavior, the entire cabinet resigned, on 16 July, and re-formed two days later with Konoye nominally still at the helm and Matsuoka replaced as foreign minister by the stable and politically more moderate Admiral Toyoda Teijiro.

Konoye now attempted a creative act of diplomacy. He would personally meet with Roosevelt on U.S. soil, at, for example, Hawaii. In proposing the meeting to his cabinet he stated his intention to hold firmly to the Greater

East Asia Co-Prosperity Sphere, which included a continued military presence in China, while seeking an American recognition of Japan's peaceful intentions. It was hard for the Navy to say no to that. And even the Army, in the person of General Tojo, minister of war, grudgingly agreed that probably no harm would come from such an initiative—provided the prime minister understood that, if his talks failed, he would be expected to lead his country into war against America. Even thus constrained, Konoye may have expected, naively, that somehow in the warm course of personal conversation the ice would melt and he would return home with a formula that both appeased the militarists and saved the peace. He even told Ambassador Grew, at a private dinner on 6 September, that he could agree in theory with Hull's "Four Principles" of the previous 16 April, though they would require "adjustments" and their implementation would take time.[1]

From 10 to 15 August President Roosevelt met with British Prime Minister Winston Churchill aboard the battleship HMS *Prince of Wales* (soon to be sunk off Malaya) anchored at Argentia Harbor, Newfoundland. The publicly announced result of their conversations was a somewhat euphonious Atlantic Charter that testified to the unity of Anglo-American purpose and to the commitment of both their nations to peace. Secretly, however, the two heads of state drafted strong statements rejecting Japanese attempts to dominate East Asia, which each pledged to deliver. Roosevelt, for his part, asked Hull to arrange for Ambassador Nomura to be present at the White House on Sunday, 17 August, when he returned from Argentia. That afternoon, with a now healthy Hull in attendance, he heard out Nomura's transmittal of Konoye's offer to meet in Hawaii. Without acknowledging the invitation, Roosevelt read aloud a stiff rebuke of Japanese pretensions to military domination of East Asia; followed by a craftily phrased (by Sumner Welles) second statement of the United States' desire to remain friends with Japan.

It was eleven days later, when Ambassador Nomura handed him a second message from Premier Konoye suggesting that they meet, and very soon, since Japanese-American relations were mutating rapidly, that Roosevelt responded, and affirmatively, suggesting that the two meet for as much as three or four days, and perhaps at Juneau, Alaska, which was not quite as far for him. That evening, at Hull's apartment, the secretary told Nomura that certain matters had to be settled before such a meeting could take place, for instance, Japan's withdrawal from China, so that it was known by both parties in advance that an agreement would in fact be signed. Nomura balked, suggesting that matters *other than* China be settled beforehand, in order to get both countries over a presently difficult patch. Hull demurred. He would not have the Chinese believe that the United States had sold them out. The sticking point, again.[2]

On 6, 23, and 27 September, Nomura presented Hull proposals from Tokyo that, he thought, Roosevelt and Konoye could agree upon before a personal meeting took place between the two. He also suggested 10–15 October as a suitable conference date, and said that Konoye, together with a full admiral, a full general, and a staff of twenty, were standing by, waiting to depart. But, as happened so often before in these negotiations, none of the Japanese proposals approached the irreducible standards of the "Four Principles." Hull had learned through the medium of Magic that Konoye's professed acceptance of the principles was a sham. Intercepts of diplomatic traffic revealed that the Japanese government was proceeding apace with plans for conquest while talking peace in the White House and in Hull's apartment. Furthermore, the proposals received through Nomura permitted Japan to:

(1) refuse to renounce aggression and territorial aggrandizement;
(2) refuse to withdraw troops from northern China and Inner Mongolia; and
(3) refuse to state that she would not make war against the United States if war broke out between the America and Germany.

Finally, while in her proposals Japan suggested that she might undertake certain behavioral changes *over time*, what she asked from the United States was that it *immediately:*

(1) lift all economic sanctions against Japan;
(2) discontinue the shipping of American troops, planes, and other war material to the Philippines; and
(3) halt all military aid to China, British Malaya, and the NEI.

An agreement based on that imbalance, Roosevelt and Hull knew, would never be acceptable to the American people, who had their own pride. If instead Japan had offered, as she never did in these penultimate papers, to permit the United States a gradual adjustment of policies and operations to match the gradualism she demanded for herself, there *might* have been the possibility of a truce of sorts, of a softening of wills, of deep breaths taken by both sides. And if, on the other hand, the United States had not played so much the role of stern, moralistic headmaster, and had, as historian Herbert Feis expressed it, been willing "to ease Japanese failure" by granting limited concessions, there *might* have evolved a Camp David–type understanding that allowed both parties to step back from the brink. But all that is speculation in hindsight, and not very well grounded, since on 16 October the Konoye cabinet fell, and on the next day, the premiership was conveyed to the pro-Axis General Tojo, for whom the search for peace was a matter of no concern.[3]

CNO Admiral Stark in Washington sent a warning to Admiral Kimmel in Hawaii, Hart in the Philippines, and King in the Atlantic:

> The resignation of the Japanese Cabinet has created a grave situation. . . . Hostilities between Japan and Russia are a strong possibility. Since the U.S. and Britain are held responsible by Japan for her present desperate situation there is the possibility that Japan may attack these two Powers. In view of these possibilities you will take due precautions including such preparatory deployments as will not disclose strategic intentions nor constitute provocative actions against Japan.[4]

Kimmel responded to the warning with an eleven-point report on the special dispositions he made at base and at sea. Among these dispositions, he had put the Battle Force on twelve-hour sailing notice; delayed the sailing of *West Virginia* to Puget Sound for overhaul; dispatched two submarines to Wake Island; dispatched additional Marines to Wake, Johnston, and Palmyra Islands; dispatched twelve patrol planes to Midway; and placed six submarines on short notice for departure to Japanese home waters. These orders and deployments would remain in force through the next such warning, which would come on 24 November. Biweekly air raid drills and twenty-four-hour-manned machine guns on battleships continued as before. From Stark he received an "OK on the dispositions which you made in connection with the recent change in the Japanese cabinet."[5]

The language of the 16 October message, particularly its inclusion of a possible Japanese attack on Russia, shows the hand of Kelly Turner, director of war plans (OP-12), who had arrogated to himself the functions of naval intelligence (Office of Naval Intelligence), about which he seemed to know little. It was Turner who had predicted on 19 July that a total trade embargo, such as was imposed on Japan seven days later, "would probably result in a fairly early attack by Japan on Malaya and the Netherlands East Indies, and possibly would involve the United States in early war in the Pacific," none of which happened.[6] In the same month, Stark wrote to Savvy Cooke: "We have felt that the Maritime Provinces [of Russia] are now definitely Japanese objectives. Turner thinks Japan will go up there in August. He may be right. He usually is."[7] He usually was wrong.

In a more fundamental error, with calculable consequences for Kimmel, Turner assured Stark that Hawaii was equipped with Magic, and that Kimmel, his fleet intelligence officer, Commander Edwin T. Layton, and Commander Joseph J. Rochefort's Combat Intelligence Unit were "receiving the same decrypted information" that was available in Washington. Though Magic decryption equipment had been sent to Admiral Hart in the Philippines, and even to cryptographers at Bletchley Park in England, none had been sent to the Army and Navy commanders in Hawaii! "I inquired on two or three occasions as to whether or not Kimmel could read certain dispatches when they came up," Stark later testified, "and which we were interpreting and sending our own messages and I was told that he could."[8] During the postwar Joint Congressional Committee Hearings on the Pearl Harbor Attack (hereafter JCC), Stark was asked, "Who was it that told you that they had a system out in Honolulu or Pearl Harbor of decoding and decrypting Jap messages?" He answered: "Admiral Turner." Asked the same again, Stark replied, "Well, Admiral Turner told me he [Kimmel] could do it. I did not consider it necessary to go further."[9] For both Stark and Turner this was a telling admission. For Kimmel it may explain why certain information vital to his sea and air defenses was never sent to him by the Navy Department. CINCPAC had been told by Stark that the Army and Navy had broken certain Japanese codes and ciphers, and various paraphrases of Magic-originated information had been sent to him prior to the July embargo, but none afterward, until the first week of December. When Turner was asked in the same proceedings, "Did you ever tell Admiral Stark that Admiral Kimmel was getting that [Magic] information?" Turner answered, "Yes, sir, on three occasions. . . . I asked Admiral Noyes [Rear

Admiral Leigh Noyes, director of naval communications] about it and so reported to Admiral Stark."[10] Then, the question was posed to Noyes: "Did you ever inform the Chief of War Plans Division, Captain Turner, that the Commander of the Pacific Fleet was decrypting intelligence information of a character similar to that which you were receiving in the Navy Department?" To which Noyes answered, "No." He added: "I would never have made the statement that all ciphers could be translated in Pearl Harbor." A month before 7 December, Secretary Knox's aide Captain Frank E. Beatty asked Turner, in Knox's name, "Is Admiral Kimmel getting these 'magic' messages?" Turner replied, "Beatty, of course he is. He has the same 'magic' setup we have."[11]

In 1961, after two decades of reflection on the Japanese attack of 7 December, Rear Admiral (Ret.) Samuel Eliot Morison, official U.S. Navy historian of naval operations during World War II, considered the various officers who had been blamed on the U.S. side, and concluded, in a letter to Vice Admiral John F. Shafroth (Ret.), that "If I were pushed to name one person as being more careless or stupid than all the rest it would be Kelly Turner." He went on to say: "I have come out of this study with a more charitable feeling toward Gen. Short and Adm. Kimmel than I felt before. . . . If you and your friends are getting up any sort of petition to have Admiral Kimmel's status restored or record changed, you can count on me to sign it."[12] At this date, the obvious question that remains is, Why instead of taking Turner at his word did Stark not ask *Kimmel* if he was receiving Magic? (Not until 1944 would Kimmel learn the nature of the intercepted material affecting his command that Magic contained.) At the least he could have asked Noyes directly or asked Rear Admiral Theodore S. Wilkinson, director of the Office of Naval Intelligence (ONI), or asked Wilkinson's predecessor, Captain Alan C. Kirk. But, content apparently with secondhand information on such a centrally important matter, and perhaps being under the spell of his vicar, Turner, he put the question to none of those men.

★

From August to November the United States Army and Navy accelerated their preparedness for war. General Marshall stated that his forces in the Philippines would not be ready for combat until 5–10 December. Stark stated that his fleets would not be ready for offensive action until January or February 1942.[13] Both service chiefs urged the President to buy time by "stringing out the negotiations," though not at the cost of American principles and obligations. Repeatedly, they urged "That no ultimatum be delivered to Japan."[14] Marshall explained in 1944: "Our state of mind at that period—I am referring now to both Stark and myself—was to do all in our power here at home, with the State Department or otherwise, to try to delay this break to the last moment, because of our state of unpreparedness and because of our involvements in other parts of the world."[15]

From August through November the Army exhibited a sharp change of mind with respect to the Philippines. On 14 August the chief of Army strategic plans, Brigadier General Leonard T. Gerow, advised Marshall that "the ability of the Philippine Islands to withstand a determined attack with present means is doubtful."[16] Marshall had to make a decision. He knew that if Japan made a military strike south against Malaya and/or the NEI, she could not allow U.S. air bases in the Philippines, which lay along the China Sea sealanes between Japan and those British and Dutch possessions, to interdict Japanese naval and commercial shipping. If Japan moved south, she would have to seize and hold those islands. But were the islands defensible? Should the Army yield them as sacrificial pawns and save the American troops, munitions, and aircraft there for other battles to come? Or should the Army make a good faith effort to strengthen the defenses so that the Philippines had a realistic chance to defend themselves against assault? Marshall chose the latter course. He was encouraged to do so by two developments. The first was the contagious optimism of General Douglas MacArthur, recalled to active duty on 26 July as commanding general, United States Army Forces in the Far East (USAFFE). One of the Army's celebrated veterans of World War I and a former chief of staff, he had served six years as military adviser to the Philippines Commonwealth Army. In July 1941, when that army was federalized, MacArthur expected that he could increase its numbers to 120,000 regulars and reserves by mid-December. He also assumed command of some 22,000 U.S. Army regulars and Philippine Scouts, who had been well trained by outgoing Philippine Department commander Major General George Grunert. With those forces and a little help from the Army Air Corps, MacArthur thought that he could ride out a Japanese assault, and so persuaded Marshall. More than just a "citadel" at Manila Bay, he would defend the entire archipelago, a claim, as Marshall would learn later, that was oversanguine to a fault.[17]

The second factor was an equally optimistic chief of the Army Air Corps, Lieutenant General Henry H. "Hap" Arnold, who was touting the virtues of the Boeing Company's new B-17D model of the Flying Fortress four-engine heavy bomber. Accompanied by Secretary Stimson and Arnold, Marshall flew out to the Boeing plant at Seattle to see for himself. There the Boeing people put the B-17D through a number of impressive bombing runs and antifighter machine-gun displays that proved convincing in theory. (In actual combat, including the Battle of Midway [4–6 June 1942], the aircraft's bombing accuracy against ships at sea proved notoriously lacking.) Marshall and Stimson bought the theory and decided that the presence of such technologically advanced weapons, as they assumed the Fortresses to be, on Philippine bases would not only materially assist MacArthur in defending the islands but likely would deter a Japanese invasion fleet from proceeding south through the China Sea along MacArthur's flank. To that end, on 26 August, Marshall ordered a first squadron of nine B-17s from Hickam Field on Oahu to be ferried to the main island of Luzon. Taking off on 5 September, the squadron was staged through Midway, Wake, then southwest at night over the Japanese mandates to Port Moresby, New Guinea, and Darwin, Australia; arriving at Clark Field north of Manila on 12 September. The historic first flight of land-based bombers from Hawaii to Clark, which was serviced by primitive maintenance, refueling, and navigational and weather information stations, proved that the Philippines could be reinforced by air.[18] Thereafter on 30 September, Marshall staged two more squadrons (twenty-six Fortresses) from San Francisco through Hawaii to Clark, gave orders to send thirty-five Fortresses to Clark in December (these landed at Hickam for refueling in the middle of the Japanese raid), and discussed sending out six to nine of the new four-engine Consolidated B-24 heavy bombers, soon to be named the Liberator but known to Marshall as the "super Flying Fortress." Thinking offensively, Marshall advised Stark that the operating radius of the B-24 allowed it to bomb the Japanese cities of Osaka and Tokyo with full and partial bomb loads, respectively.[19] He did not say from what base.

What had happened was that the War Department, relying on what turned out to be inflated estimates of both what MacArthur could accomplish with the ground forces at hand and what heavy bomber aircraft could achieve in repelling invasion forces sent either south to British and Dutch possessions or to the Philippines themselves, shifted the American defensive effort 4,700 nautical miles west of Hawaii. Not only were no additional B-17s to be sent to reinforce Hawaii, but Hickam Field would be all but denuded of its own B-17s in order to supply the Philippines. By 7 December, when the Philippines boasted thirty-five of those craft, the largest concentration of B-17s in existence anywhere, Hickham, which in June had twenty-one, could count only six in operating condition, and they were not being used for practice search or attack missions over Hawaiian waters but to train crews for the Philippine Air Force. General Marshall testified about the projection of bomber strength westward before the JCC on 7 December 1945:

> We turned from the meeting of the demands in Hawaii and not fulfilling the Martin-Bellinger request for 180 B-17s of which in all we possessed all over the world 148 at that particular time. . . . We did our utmost one way or another to provide the things that the Navy thought were needed and the Army commander in Hawaii thought were needed. . . . From the latter part of August, having given Hawaii all we could afford to give them up to that time . . . we turned and tried to do something for General MacArthur, and most of that went through the Hawaiian Islands, incidentally, by Navy or by air.[20]

The projection westward was an understandable strategic decision, one with which Admiral Stark fully agreed, as he wrote to Savvy Cooke: "We are delighted with the Army move putting the Filipinos in harness; we recommended this. Also it is being supplemented by a considerable number of planes, fighters and bombers."[21] It was also a decision with which Admiral Kimmel agreed, having written Stark on the preceding 26 May: "It is easily conceivable that 50,000 troops and 400 airplanes on Luzon might prove a sufficient deterrent to Japan to prevent direct action."[22] But one might pardon Admiral Kimmel and General Short a certain amount of envy as they watched those majestic flocks of bombers passing through Hawaii on their migration to distant danger sites. Kimmel could have used the B-17s both for distant aerial reconnaissance and for attacking a

Japanese surface fleet if one appeared in Hawaiian waters. That he himself had urged the transfer of long-range bombers to Luzon might have weakened his case later when he argued that he did not have sufficient aircraft to mount a 360-degree distant search of the ocean approaches to Oahu; but his critics never mentioned the fact.

★

Four times Kimmel had asked Stark to be kept informed of all secret information about Asian and European developments that might affect his fleet's security and mission. In February he had written Stark about his concern that "information of a secret nature" was not arriving in any significant amount. His concern was well placed, because, though he did not know it, Admiral Hart and later General MacArthur received Magic-generated intelligence from Washington even though they were equipped with Purple decryption machinery themselves. Kimmel wondered if the paucity of intelligence sent his way was owed to a "misunderstanding" between Naval Operations and the Office of Naval Intelligence as to which office was responsible for keeping him informed. On 22 March Stark answered that "ONI is fully aware of its responsibility in keeping you adequately informed." Yet by the end of May, when Kimmel made a personal visit to Washington, he was persuaded (correctly) that much was being held back, and he handed Stark a written restatement of what he regarded to be a "cardinal principle":

> The Commander-in-Chief, Pacific Fleet is in a very difficult position. He is far removed from the seat of government, in a complex and rapidly changing situation. He is, as a rule, not informed as to the policy, or change of policy, reflected in current events and naval movements and, as a result, is unable to evaluate the possible effect upon his own situation. He is not even sure of what force will be available to him and has little voice in matters radically affecting his ability to carry out his assigned tasks. This lack of information is disturbing and tends to create uncertainty, a condition that directly contravenes that singleness of purpose and confidence in one's own course of action so necessary to the conduct of military operations.

It would seem that this was the propitious moment for Stark, among other replies he might make, to ask Kimmel if he was receiving Magic. But he did not. Kimmel went on to discuss a conflict that would bear heavily on him and his staff after 27 November, as will be shown:

> This is particularly applicable to the current Pacific situation, where the necessities for intensive training of a partially trained fleet must be carefully balanced against the desirability of interruption of this training by strategic dispositions, or otherwise, to meet impending eventualities. . . . It is suggested that it be made a cardinal principle that the Commander-in-Chief, Pacific Fleet be immediately informed of all important developments as they occur and by the quickest secure means available.

Much of the news conveyed by Stark was not by "quickest secure means," i.e., naval radio communications, but by personal letters that, having traveled overland to California, thence by China Clipper flying boat, took up to a week in arriving. So Kimmel made the same appeal for a third time, on 26 July, to which Stark made the perfunctory reply: "If you do not get as much information as you think you should get, the answer probably is that the particular situation which is uppermost in your mind has just not jelled sufficiently for us to give you anything authoritative." Armed with copies of Admiral King's "shoot on sight" operation orders given after the 4 September *Greer* event, Kimmel approached Stark again, on 12 September, with a fourth appeal for information—"But what about the Pacific?" Stark's reply, dated 23 September, was made a subject of his interrogation during the Naval Court of Inquiry (NCI), in 1944:

> Q. You [Stark] intended . . . to indicate to Admiral Kimmel that you would keep him fully and promptly informed as to all diplomatic developments which you learned, at least from the Secretary of State?
> A. That's right.[23]

Thus, Stark told Kimmel both that ONI would keep him informed and that he personally would keep him informed. But in the event neither kept him informed, particularly after July.

During October a minimum of "secret" information (and no raw Magic) was arriving at Pearl Harbor, and it was not much more specific in content, distinguishable in tone, timely in arrival, or enlightening in foresight than what appeared in the Associated Press dispatches in the daily Honolulu *Advertiser*. What had to be particularly maddening to Kimmel was Stark's penchant for nixing or fudging what little intelligence the department did send. On the day after the 16 October warning, Stark wrote in a personal letter: "Personally I do not believe the Japs are going to sail into us and the message I sent you merely stated the 'possibility,' in fact I tempered the message handed to me [by War Plans?] considerably." Again, in the same letter, like a Broadway Hamlet, Stark stated, "You will also recall in an earlier letter when War Plans [Turner] was forecasting a Japanese attack on Siberia in August, I said my own judgment was that they would make no move in that direction until the Russian situation showed a definite trend."[24] Stark's confused signals may have reminded Kimmel of Lord Raglan's order, later called "fatally lacking in precision," to Lord Lucan at Balaclava, which led to the ruin of the Light Brigade.[25]

★

Meanwhile, during the same four-month period (August–November), things heated up in the North Atlantic, where the first American blood was shed on the night of 16–17 October. An eastbound British slow convoy, SC 48, composed of forty-nine loaded merchant ships in eleven columns, protected by only one destroyer and four corvettes, had been attacked the night before by a patrol line of U-boats, resulting in the loss of four freighters. Five U.S. Navy destroyers, including the now-famous *Greer*, proceeded to the assistance of SC 48. A second night attack by the U-boats found the barely year-old USS *Kearny* (DD-432) silhouetted against a burning freighter in the bridge optics of the surfaced *U-568* (Kptlt. Joachim Preuss). Thinking the destroyer to be British, as he subsequently signaled Admiral Dönitz, Preuss launched a torpedo into *Kearny*'s starboard side. The damaged but tough *Gleaves*-class destroyer survived the attack, and, escorted by *Greer*, managed to make the Atlantic Fleet anchorage of Hvalfjordhur at Iceland; but there she delivered eleven American seamen dead and twenty-four wounded.

Four more "incidents" quickly followed. On 5 September, a U.S. freighter, *Steel Seafarer*, was sunk by a German bomber 220 miles south of Suez, with no loss of life. On 19 October another U.S. freighter, *Lehigh*, steaming in ballast off West Africa, was sunk in daylight by *U-126* (Kptlt. Ernst Bauer). The vessel had large American flags painted on each side of the hull. Her crew was rescued. American protests to Berlin were ignored. On 30 October, while accompanying westbound convoy ON 28, the armed 8,000-ton U.S. Navy fleet oiler USS *Salinas* (AO-19) absorbed two torpedoes from the surfaced *U-106* (Kptlt. Hermann Rasch). Navy gunners raked the water where the U-boat submerged, but with no effect. Rasch signaled Admiral Dönitz that he had sunk the tanker, but *Salinas* reached port safely in St. Johns, Newfoundland.

The primary incident in that undeclared war between the United States and Germany in the North Atlantic occurred the next day when the old (1920) "four-piper" destroyer USS *Reuben James* (DD-245) was attacked while escorting fast convoy HX 156 about six hundred miles west of Ireland. The warhead of a torpedo launched by *U-552* (Kptlt. Erich Topp) exploded on the port side near the No. 1 stack, and, seconds afterward, another, more destructive explosion, probably from ignition of the forward magazine, blew off the entire bow section, flooding the ship. Then, as the stern sank beneath the surface, several depth charges mounted there detonated when they reached their prescribed depths, causing death to a number of bluejackets in the water. Of the 160-man crew nearby destroyers picked up only forty-five survivors, and no officers. *Reuben James* was the first U.S. Navy ship to be sunk in World War II. Her loss caused hardly a ripple of attention on the surface of the American public, who considered that those sailors knew the risks they were taking when they enlisted; the public's interest was more fixed, anyway, on the upcoming Army-Navy football game.[26] CNO Stark was one of the few to express alarm: he wrote Kimmel, "Believe it or not, the REUBEN JAMES set recruiting back about 15%."[27]

On the good news front, Stark was pleased to inform Kimmel that the government was apportioning men to the Navy Department from Selective Service, as the draft was known. That meant a bonanza of 533,000 men for the Navy and 105,000 for the Marines. Kimmel welcomed the promise of draftees. "We should lose no time in getting our ships filled up," he responded on 12 August. "This Fleet can use 20,000 additional men today." His four-page letter was unique in that it revealed Kimmel at his most optimistic. Never before or since was he so sanguine about the condition of his fleet as he was in the narrow window of mid-August. "I feel that gunnery in the Fleet is better than we have any right to expect," he wrote, "considering the enormous changes in personnel and the lack of permanency of the officers. . . . The morale of the officers and men of the Fleet is very satisfactory, and everyone is working to the limit of his capacity. . . . Bloch is doing a great job. . . . The Honolulu people have been very fine in their continued efforts to entertain the officers and men of the Fleet in their homes and on their plantations." Kimmel described the good effect that had been achieved by "Health Cruises" to the West Coast that enabled one-fourth of the fleet personnel at a time to enjoy leave with their wives and/or families. (Stark had readily approved the West Coast visits earlier in the summer.) And Kimmel bragged of his new recreational facilities at Pearl, which included baseball, softball, and football fields that were in daily use; a swimming pool that was filled to capacity at all times; a stadium seating 6,000 men that was suitable for boxing and wrestling matches, ships' entertainments, and movies; and a Fleet Recreation Center that featured ten bowling alleys, eleven pool tables, and a reading and writing room, as well as a large soft drink and sandwich stand, and "an enormous bar where beer is served." Clearly, the CINCPAC was on an unaccustomed trajectory. God's in his Heaven, and all's well with the fleet. He concluded jauntily, "Keep cheerful. We are ready to do our damnest."[28]

Then, just as dramatically, ten days later, Kimmel was back to his usual role of carper. He had on hand, he complained to Stark, only thirty-five in-commission F4F-3 and F4F-3A modern carrier fighters and seventeen obsolescent carrier aircraft, when his operating allowance for three carriers and two Marine fighter squadrons was ninety. "I think you should take some drastic action to remedy this deplorable condition," he scolded Stark; whose reply in its entirety read: "Dear Mustapha [Stark's private nickname for Kimmel]: See our serial 0136723 of 12 Sept. Best we can do. Keep cheerful. Betty."[29] But Kimmel had other categories of shortage: modern carrier torpedo planes to replace obsolescent types; modern cruiser (catapult) planes to replace obsolescent types; patrol planes, including the new Martin PBM-1 Mariner, of which there were none in the Hawaii area; spare parts for the PBY; special radio equipment for patrol planes; aircraft torpedoes; armor-piercing bombs; aircraft machine-gun ammunition; and, finally, pilots and aviation ratings. It was in trained manpower where the fleet was particularly hurting, and increases from the draft would be of little help in the near term. Regular and experienced officers had been detached at an alarming rate. Some 3,000 sailors, more than half of them rated, had been taken from the fleet to man new construction. Of those remaining, 68 percent did not intend to reenlist; wages offered in the Pearl Harbor area, not to mention the West Coast, were too attractive to skilled men. Greater permanence of personnel was required to achieve that ship, unit, and fleet efficiency essential to maintain readiness to fight. The Pacific Fleet, Kimmel argued to Stark on 15 November, "must not be considered a training fleet for support of the Atlantic Fleet and the shore establishment."[30]

Kimmel's attention to his carrier needs highlights a quality of his naval leadership that has been overlooked in the historical literature. At a time when most naval authorities in the United States and Japan, indeed worldwide, counted the battleship as a navy's indispensable weapon, when strategists eagerly envisioned decisive main-battery salvos in blue-water engagements like the Battle of Jutland, and, accordingly, when most fleet commanders planned operations around the use of the great-hulled, strutting brutes that were the battle line of the fleets, Kimmel, like his Japanese opposite number, Yamamoto Isoruku, believed that the opening stages of the Pacific war would be, and should be, a *carrier* war and not a clash of battleships or heavy cruisers. On 22 October he wrote Stark: *"The type of operations we have planned in the early stages of the war puts a premium on aircraft operations from carriers* [emphasis added]."[31]

Elsewhere, Kimmel had developed his strategy, which emphasized *light* forces, particularly air power:

> In the Pacific our potential enemy is far away and hard to get at. He has no exposed *vital* interests within reach of Pearl Harbor, and has a system of defense in the Mandates, Marianas and Bonins that requires landing operations, supported by sea forces, against organized land positions supported by land-based air. This is the hardest kind of opposition to overcome and requires detailed preparation and rehearsal. It also requires a preponderance of light forces and carrier strength, in which we are woefully deficient in the Pacific. Our present strength is in battleships—which come into play only after we have reduced the intervening organized positions. They [battleships] will have to be used to "cover" the intervening operations

and prevent interference therewith, but their real value can not be realized until the intervening opposition has been overcome and a position obtained from which solid strength can be brought to bear. The Japanese are not going to expose their main fleet until they are . . . forced to do so by our obtaining a position close enough to threaten their vital interests.[32]

What was gall and wormwood to Kimmel's warrior soul was that his fleet was so reduced in light force and carrier strength that its offensive capabilities were severely crippled. Moreover, the Pacific Fleet was lacking in auxiliary vessels—tankers, cargo ships, transports—to the degree that he could not mount an overseas expedition, "even on a small scale," for many months. A reconnaissance and raid in force on the Marshalls, mandated in WPL-46, he could carry out on schedule, as he could also *prepare* to capture and establish control over the Caroline and Marshall Island area [emphasis added]," but actual occupation of the Marshalls and the Carolines and an advance westward across the Pacific could not be attempted before he was given thirty or forty troop transports—he currently had *one* in commission—an equal number of supply ships, seventy-five tankers, *and* a 30 to 50 percent increase in the fighting strength of the fleet.[33] The earliest date of a small-scale voyage westward Kimmel put at February 1942.[34] (This was, in fact, the month when Kimmel's relief, Admiral Chester W. Nimitz, employed the fleet in their first offensive operations in the Marshall and Gilbert Islands.) And the earliest date when the fleet could operate in Philippine or Japanese home waters was midsummer 1942. Stark sought to cool Kimmel's offensive ardor, writing him on 25 November that, as for cruising in Japanese home waters, "neither ABC-1 or [sic] Rainbow 5 contemplate [sic] this as a general policy. . . . Opportunity for raids in Japanese waters may present themselves, but this will be the exception rather than the rule."[35] (This was the same CNO, of course, who earlier, on 25 February, had urged Kimmel, in his planning for offensive raids to take place after hostilities began, to consider carrier bombing attacks on the "inflammable Japanese cities.")

The import of all this—the deficiency in auxiliaries, the reduced fighting strength of the fleet, the midsummer 1942 date when Kimmel could first operate in the western Pacific—will not be lost on the reader who remembers that one of Japanese Admiral Yamamoto's expressed reasons for destroying or crippling the Pacific Fleet at its anchorage was to prevent that fleet from menacing the left flank of Japan's southward movement of conquest through the China Sea. As Navy Minister Admiral Shimada Shigetaro expressed it to Rear Admiral Fukudome, Yamamoto's chief of staff, "There would be little chance to exploit a conquest of Southeast Asia if our long Southern Operation line, stretching far below the equator, was flanked by a dominant U.S. fleet, prepared to strike at the best time and in a manner of its own choosing."[36] With the Southern Operation long completed by the time Kimmel's fleet could appear on the horizon, Yamamoto and his navy had nothing to fear from the U.S. warships berthed at Pearl Harbor. It were better that Japanese spies in the hills overlooking Pearl counted auxiliaries instead of warships; or, if they did, that Navy strategists in Tokyo did not discount them. It were better, too, that certain critics of Kimmel had paid more attention to auxiliaries than they did, so as not to exaggerate, as some have, what Kimmel intended to achieve with his battle line. Ironically, the evidence was clear to any knowledgeable eye that an attack on Pearl Harbor was not even necessary for Japan's immediate purposes of conquest.[37]

It is true that Kimmel and his chief planner, "Soc" McMorris, had developed an offensive plan of action for execution by the fleet at some date after the opening of hostilities. Drafted in March and finalized in July, Plan Optional Dash One, or Plan 0–1 (or WPUSF-44), was a contingency plan for thrusting the Pacific Fleet into blue-water battle with the Japanese Fleet in the Central Pacific, probably along the 1,028-nautical-mile Wake-Midway line.[38] Typical of thirty-four years of Orange Plan scenarios, it presupposed the availability of material resources, including auxiliaries, that were in fact lacking. The plan plainly represented the aggressive instincts of "the two foremost thrusters of the fleet," Kimmel and McMorris, but by November–December it hardly represented any current reality, much less intent. Failure to consider a fleet's auxiliary train, because of an obsession with that fleet's eight battleships, can lead to a skewed assessment of what a fleet is capable of achieving. And, it must be said, an obsession with Kimmel's background as a battleship gunner—"Although a battleship orientation was not uncommon in the navy of 1941," one recent author writes, "Kimmel's case was extreme"—can lead to a skewed depiction of Kimmel as some kind of naval Luddite in the matter of carriers and light forces, as in this portrayal from the same author:

Kimmel's appreciation of air power, except for reconnaissance, was rather primitive. He thought of carriers as auxiliaries: They could sally forth on raids, but their place in a fleet engagement was with the battle line. The CINCPAC didn't understand, and sometimes irritated, his aviators. "Fly-boys," he called them.[39]

That same canard was being advanced as late as 2001, when an Army colonel, writing in *MHQ: The Quarterly Journal of Military History*, argued that "Admiral Kimmel, for example, having spent his career in a navy built around the battleship . . . simply could not conceive of carriers operating apart from battleships." By telling coincidence, the editor of *MHQ*, in a prefatory "Note to Our Readers" in the same issue, wrote: "A history is only as good as its sources."[40]

In both instances the view taken of Kimmel is not supported by the pertinent original documents, as cited here. Furthermore, such a gratuitous position would have a hard time reconciling itself to Kimmel's operational doctrine as applied by his subordinate commander Vice Admiral Halsey, on 28 November, when Halsey's Task Force 8 sortied "under war conditions" to ferry Marine F4F fighters aboard the USS *Enterprise* (CV-6) to Wake Island. It did so accompanied by his trudging battleships, as though heading for a typical exercise in the operating area; but, once at sea, Halsey sloughed off his three battleships, which busied themselves for a time in exercises, and then returned to Pearl. Similarly, when Admiral Newton's Task Force 12, built around USS *Lexington* (CV-2), left Pearl for Midway on 5 December to fly off air reinforcements to that island, it consisted, besides the carrier, of three heavy cruisers and five destroyers—*no* battleships. (A third task force, TF-3, under Vice Admiral Wilson Brown, consisting of the heavy cruiser USS *Indianapolis* (CA-35) and five destroyers, departed Pearl on the same 5 December to conduct landing exercises on Johnston Island.) Like Yamamoto Isoruku, Husband E. Kimmel was a farsighted pioneer in his keen understanding of the carrier war to come. Both men understood that the battleship was too slow, and its reach too short, to keep pace with that war.

In the Pearl Harbor literature much has been made of the fact that Halsey announced to *Enterprise*'s crew that they were operating under war conditions, that radio silence would be observed, that all torpedoes and bombs were to be armed, that any submarine sighted or detected was to be sunk, and that any aircraft not identified as American was to be shot down. His aggressive spirit and tactical preparedness have sometimes been interpreted to show that Kimmel, by contrast, lacked those qualities. Apart from the fact that it was Kimmel who authorized Halsey to go on a war footing, it was also Kimmel who, in direct violation of Stark's restraining order, went to war conditions himself on the same date, 28 November, when he ordered all sea and air forces to depth-charge any submerged submarine detected by sonar in the harbor approaches and in the fleet operating area. Neither Newton nor Brown was put on a war footing; nor, unlike Halsey, was either told of the 27 November war warning.

★

By 18 October the shakeups in the Japanese cabinet were complete. The militarists were in control. Tojo Hideki, now a full general, was prime minister. He also held the cabinet offices of war minister and home minister, the latter office in charge of national police. Admiral Toyoda Teijiro was replaced as foreign minister by Togo Shigenori, a senior diplomat and moderate, who hoped that war with the United States could be put off until that power's entry into the war against Germany, and who, under the Emperor's mantle, wrung from Tojo a reluctant pledge to make yet one more effort to secure an accommodation with Hull and Roosevelt. In that endeavor Togo could take no comfort from the desire of Ambassador Nomura to quit his post and return home. Arguing that those Americans who trusted him were "poor deluded souls" for thinking that he had any influence with the new military cabinet, Nomura wrote, on 23 October: "I don't want to be the bones of a dead horse. I don't want to continue this hypocritical existence, deceiving other people.... Please send me your permission to return to Japan." To which Togo replied, under the same date: "I appreciate the efforts you are making.... We express our hope that you will see fit to sacrifice all of your own personal wishes, and remain at your post."[41]

Meanwhile, in the Japanese Imperial General Headquarters at Tokyo, as well as in naval, air, and army bases both in the home islands and in occupied territories of China and Indo-China, preparations for war moved ahead at an anxious pace. Weather conditions dictated the schedule to be followed. The Southern Operation to make Japan self-sufficient in oil, rubber, tin, bauxite, and other raw materials through the capture of Malaya and the NEI had to be mounted no later than December, before the north-east monsoon roiled the South China Sea. Effective occupation of the British and Dutch possessions had to be completed during the Manchurian winter, when traditional enemy Russia would find it difficult, though not impossible, to menace Japan's exposed northern flank. And Yamamoto's transpacific raid on Pearl Harbor would have to be launched no later than December, before the onset of winter gales and worsened visibility in the northern route, or Vacant Sea, which was chosen in preference to the calmer southern or central routes because it was distant from normal shipping tracks. In Japanese home waters the carriers and other warships assigned to the Hawaiian operation diligently practiced refueling at sea, which was not as commonplace then as it would become later in the war, and in various home bays air crews rehearsed the complicated approach patterns that would have to be flown in the Oahu airspace. At the same time, aircraft flew bombing-run drills to prepare for strikes they would be ordered to make on the same 7 December (8 December in the Phillipines) against Clark Field on Luzon Island, where General MacArthur's air staff husbanded their growing fleet of B-17 Flying Fortresses.

The Japanese Army had not at first agreed with its Navy counterparts that the Philippines should be attacked at all. Its forces were not as strong as originally hoped: since, by mid-August Russia had not dispatched her Siberian troops to the German front, it appeared that only eleven out of Japan's fifty-one divisions and 700 out of 1,500 in-commission Army aircraft (remembering that much of Japan's manpower and equipment was tied up in the occupations of China and Indo-China) could be committed to the Southern Operation. But, the Navy argued successfully, Japan could not permit an unsinkable aircraft carrier, which was the Philippines, to stand, unmolested, astride her southward advance, trade routes, and communications. In mid-August Army strategists agreed with that imperative, and undertook the development of detailed operational plans based on the joint decision to attack and occupy the Philippines. Since an attack on the Philippines would bring the United States into the war anyway, Yamamoto's plan for a simultaneous carrier-borne attack to disable the American fleet at Pearl Harbor made all the more sense to the Army.

On 20 October the two services agreed on a final plan for making war at one and the same time against the British Commonwealth, the NEI, and the United States. Hostilities were to open with six different but nearly simultaneous operations. These were: (1) a surprise air attack on Pearl Harbor and Oahu airfields for the purpose of destroying or neutralizing the U.S. Pacific Fleet; (2) occupation of Siam with the object of obtaining a base for operations against Malaya; (3) landings in northern Malaya and on the Isthmus of Kra as first stages in the capture of Singapore; (4) bombing raids on the U.S. B-17 Flying Fortresses based at Clark Field on Luzon Island in the Philippines; (5) seizure of the U.S. Pacific islands of Guam and Wake in order to isolate the Philippines; and (6) invasion of the British Crown Colony of Hong Kong. The air attacks on Clark Field were to be followed by landings of ground forces on Luzon and Mindanao Islands; landings in northern Malaya were to be followed by landings in British Borneo; and capture of Jolo Island in the Sulu Sea would help make possible capture of the NEI. Second and third phases of the Southern Operation would establish a defensive cordon, or perimeter, that would run from the Kuriles through Wake Island, the Marshall and Gilbert Islands, the Bismarck Archipelago, New Guinea, Timor, Java, Sumatra, and Malaya to Burma, and west to India.[42]

✳

On 5 November an Imperial conference placed its imprimatur on the general war plan. At the same time, its participants agreed to have Nomura make one last effort to secure an agreement with Washington. Two proposals in sequential order, lettered A and B, were to be placed before Hull and Roosevelt. Proposal A was a reformulation of previously stated Japanese positions, including Japan's right to maintain armed forces in northern China, Mongolia, and Hainan for "a necessary period" (which Nomura was to interpret as "about twenty-five years"). All other troops presently in China would be withdrawn when that country agreed to make peace with Japan. Similarly, upon the signing of such a treaty, Japan would withdraw her troops from Indo-China. The Tripartite Pact with Germany and Italy would remain in force. Unwritten but understood in these terms was the requirement on Washington's part to force Chiang Kai-shek's government into a peace treaty under threat of denying it all further economic and military aid. Should Washington refuse to comply, Nomura was to produce Proposal B (largely the work of Foreign Minister Togo), which posited a modus vivendi—a temporary war-preventing truce—based on the following terms:

1. Both the Governments of Japan and the United States undertake not to make any armed advancement into any of the regions in Southeastern Asia and the Southern Pacific area excepting the part of French Indo-China where the Japanese troops are stationed at present.
2. The Japanese Government undertakes to withdraw its troops now stationed in French Indo-China upon either the restoration of peace between Japan and China or the establishment of an equitable peace in the Pacific area. In the meantime the Government of Japan declares that it is prepared to remove its troops now stationed in the southern part of French Indo-China to the northern part of the said territory upon the conclusion of the present arrangement which shall later be embodied in the final agreement.
3. The Governments of Japan and the United States shall cooperate with a view to securing the acquisition of those goods and commodities which the two countries need in Netherlands East Indies.
4. The Governments of Japan and the United States mutually undertake to restore their commercial relations to those prevailing prior to the freezing of the assets. The government of the United States shall supply Japan a required quantity of oil.
5. The Government of the United States undertakes to refrain from such measures and actions as will be prejudicial to the endeavors for the restoration of general peace between Japan and China.[43]

On 5 November Togo cabled Nomura that an agreement with Washington must be secured no later than the twenty-fifth of that month. Since Nomura was in the dark about war-making schedules that were driving events at home, he must have been alarmed by the imposition of a deadline, as he read Togo's grim message:

> Because of various circumstances, it is absolutely necessary that all arrangements for the signing of this agreement be completed by the 25th of this month. I realize that this is a difficult order, but under the circumstances it is an unavoidable one. Please understand this thoroughly and tackle the problem of saving the Japanese-U.S. relations

from falling into a chaotic condition. Do so with great determination and with unstinted effort, I beg of you.[44]

Neither Kimmel nor Short was advised of this deadline.

To brace up Nomura's drooping spine, and to assist him in arguing the reasonableness of Proposal A, Togo sent a second, seasoned, diplomat to Washington, Kurusu Saburo, who, as ambassador in Berlin, had been a signatory of the Tripartite Pact. When Togo transmitted the text of Proposal A to Nomura, he told the ambassador that he was to exert every effort to keep Hull's Four Principles off the table.

Coincidentaly, on that same 5 November, General Marshall and Admiral Stark met in Washington to make military recommendations to the President. On their table was a request from Chiang Kai-shek for U.S. military intervention should the Japanese attack Kunming and sever the Burma Road, over which U.S. and British Commonwealth aid reached the Nationalist government. In their estimate the service chiefs strongly advised against such intervention, even by airpower alone. Such action, they stated, would engage the United States in a Far Eastern war, when the ABC-1 agreement and Rainbow 5 plan clearly stipulated that "the primary objective" of U.S. policy was the defeat of Germany, which was considered "the most dangerous enemy." From other sources it is known how impatient Stark was with the way in which the China incident kept pulling the United States into deeper and darker thickets, far distant from where he wanted the action to be. On 17 October he had written Kimmel:

> The stumbling block of course, is the Chinese incident and personally without going in to all its ramifications and face-saving and Japanese army attitude, civil attitude and Navy attitude, I hardly see any way around it. I think we could settle with Nomura in five minutes but the Japanese Army is the stumbling block.[45]

The service chiefs' recommendations on 5 November were that material aid to China and the contributions of the American Volunteer Group (Flying Tigers) be accelerated, but "that no ultimatum be delivered to Japan." Their estimate includes three other points that merit more than passing attention. The first is the clear recognition on Stark's part that Kimmel lacked the warships and auxiliaries to operate in the western Pacific, for which Stark states, he "would have to be strengthened by withdrawing practically all naval vessels from the Atlantic" and he "would require tremendous merchant tonnage." The second point is a contribution from Marshall on the reinforcement of the Philippines, with special reference to the B-17 fleet and "the potency of this threat" in deterring Japanese operations south and west of the islands. "The present combined naval, air, and ground forces," the Army chief said, "will make attack on the islands a hazardous undertaking." But where the capability of the B-17 was concerned, War Department planners had made a gross miscalculation, as Marshall acknowledged after the war.[46] To have effective and credible deterrent power of the kind Marshall (and Stimson) envisioned, the Philippines needed *thousands* of the heavy bombers, not the two hundred scheduled to be on location by April 1942. (And, of course, one could not allow half of the existing force to be destroyed on the ground, as MacArthur would allow, with seven to ten hours' prior notice of what had happened at Pearl Harbor on 7 December.)

The third point is the statement, probably authored by both chiefs, that "the only current plans for war against Japan in the Far East are to conduct defensive war, in cooperation with the British and Dutch, for the defense of the Philippines *and the British and Dutch East Indies* [emphasis added]"; and the chiefs did recommend to the President that the United States go to war if Japan attacked British or Dutch territory or mandated territory.[47] The question may be asked, Was the United States *committed* to go to war if Japan attacked only Malaya and/or the NEI but not the Philippines or any other U.S. territory?

The answers to that question are circumstantial, since no document from the President or from the departments of State, War, or Navy has surfaced to prove a formal commitment to that effect. The evidence that does exist is mostly of British origin. In his statement before the Joint Congressional Committee, Secretary Stimson, drawing on his diary, recalled the President's unminuted cabinet meeting of Friday, 7 November. The President opened with what he said was his first-ever general poll of the cabinet:

> As to whether it was thought the American people would back us up
> if it became necessary to strike at Japan, in case she should attack
> England in Malaya or the Dutch in the East Indies. The Cabinet was

unanimous in the feeling that the country would support such a
move. The Cabinet voted this way even though only Mr. Hull and the
President [beside himself and Knox] knew of the efforts which we
had been making to reinforce the Philippines with the big bombers
and which we in the Army felt could be effective support in case any
attack should be made on the British or Dutch in southeastern Asia.[48]

It has long been suggested that a secret oral commitment to give armed
support to Britain was made by Roosevelt to Churchill during their
Atlantic Conference at Argentia, Newfoundland, on 9–13 August 1941,
though Churchill had to be aware that the U.S. Constitution required public congressional approval of such action, and minutes of their meeting of
11 August kept by Sumner Welles state that ". . . the President had desired
to make it clear that no future commitments had been entered into,"
except as authorized under the terms of the Lend-Lease Act.[49] In his
famous two-hour Vote of Confidence address to the House of Commons
on 27 January 1942 Churchill revealed that at the Atlantic Conference the
"probability" was established "that the United States, even if not herself
attacked, would come into a war in the Far East. As time went on one had
greater assurance that if Japan ran amok in the Pacific, we should not fight
alone."[50] Recently, British historian John Costello compiled War Cabinet
minutes and Foreign Office messages from December 1941, archived at
the Public Record Office in Kew, that tend to confirm such a commitment
on Roosevelt's part, made not to Churchill but to Britain's ambassador in
Washington, Lord Halifax, on 4 and 7 (London time) December. On the
latter date, Churchill cabled Halifax: "From your recent telegrams we
understand we can rely on armed support of the United States if we
become involved in hostilities with Japan."[51] Admiral Kimmel was not
informed of this "commitment," nor, more remarkably, was Admiral Hart,
whose Asiatic Fleet was most proximate to the scene of a Japanese-British
clash. But Hart learned of it from the U.S. naval attaché in Singapore, who
cabled him at 1526 on 6 December (Singapore time):

[British Commander in Chief, Far East, Air Chief Marshal
Sir Robert] BROOKE POPHAM RECEIVED SATURDAY FROM WAR
DEPT LONDON QUOTE WE HAVE NOW RECEIVED ASSURRANCE [sic]

OF AMERICAN ARMED SUPPORT IN CASES AS FOLLOWS: AFIRM [*sic*]
[A] WE ARE OBLIGED EXECUTE OUR PLANS TO FORESTALL JAPS
LANDING ISTHMUS OF KRA OR TAKE ACTION IN REPLY TO NIPS
INVASION ANY OTHER PART OF SIAM XX BAKER [B] IF DUTCH
INDIES ARE ATTACHED [*sic*] AND WE GO TO THEIR DEFENSE XX
CAST [C] IF JAPS ATTACK US THE BRITISH XX[52]

A startled Hart radioed Stark: "Learn from Singapore we have assured
Britain of armed support under three or four eventualities. Have received
no corresponding instructions from you."[53] In 1944 Stark testified that he
had no knowledge in December 1941 of such assurances.[54] Hart also sent
the information to Kimmel, but it arrived after the attack on Pearl.[55] With
our only witnesses to that agreement Churchill, Halifax, and Brooke-
Popham, the reader may wonder, Did Roosevelt in fact make the commitment described, or did the British ambassador hear only the words he
decided to hear and none others? In other words, was the wish father to
the "commitment"? We shall perhaps never know. If, in fact, Roosevelt *did*
make such a commitment, was there any chance that he could get consent
to it through the Congress? Of that, it is certain we shall never know.

★

On 7 November Ambassador Nomura presented Proposal A to Secretary
Hull, who feigned close attention to its terms, since he had already read it
through the lens of Magic. Though Nomura asked for a quick reply, Hull
knew, again through Magic, that a fallback Proposal B was in the offing.
While Nomura was nervously working against a 25 November deadline (as
Hull also knew), it suited the State Department to play for time, mindful of
the Stark-Marshall memorandum of two days before. Proposal A neither
contained anything fundamentally new nor offered any real recessions
from previously stated Japanese positions, and Hull said as much to
Nomura on 15 November, when, finally, he formally made reply. He particularly pointed out that the proposal did not include withdrawal of troops
from China and rejection of the Tripartite Pact. On that same date, special
legate Kurusu reached Washington; two days later, accompanied by the
ambassador, he called on both the secretary and the President. Hull found
him a disagreeable sort: "Kurusu seemed to me the antithesis of Nomura.

Neither his appearance nor his attitude commanded confidence or respect. I felt from the start that he was deceitful."[56]

Then, on the eighteenth, there occurred a remarkable mutation in the Japanese position. Kurusu, for all his off-putting first impression, showed himself capable of accommodation. With no instructions from or the pre-knowledge of Tokyo, he suggested to Hull that instead of each government rigidly continuing to pursue earlier argued positions, which were found to be so much at odds, they might want to strike out on an entirely fresh and different course, deciding, for example, to restore temporarily the status quo ante of early July—prior to the Japanese occupation of southern Indo-China and the U.S. imposition of the freeze order. (That this initiative ran counter to the Japanese military timetables would indicate that Kurusu arrived unaware of his nation's plans for Pearl Harbor.) Hull immediately resonated to the creative impulse of this move. Knowing from Magic that a Proposal B setting forth a modus vivendi was about to be presented, Hull saw in this moment an opportunity for the U.S. government to produce a conciliatory document of its own. Just the day before, the hardlining Trea-sury Secretary Morgenthau had suggested the carrot of gradually restoring oil supplies to Japan if that nation phased out her occupation of Indo-China. And Roosevelt himself, just before or after his first meeting with Kurusu on the seventeenth, suggested in a memorandum to Hull that for a six-month duration the two powers agree:

1. U.S. to resume economic relations—some oil and rice now—more later.
2. Japan to send no more troops to Indo-China or Manchurian border or any place South (Dutch, Brit. or Siam).
3. Japan to agree not to invoke the Tri-partite pact even if U.S. gets into European war.
4. U.S. to introduce Japs to Chinese to talk things over but U.S. to take no part in their conversations.

Later on Pacific agreements.[57]

What Hull had in mind was a *three*-month truce that would give time for Stark and Marshall to prepare their forces. In his conception, during that period Japan would evacuate southern Indo-China and limit her force in northern Indo-China to 25,000 in exchange for a recision of the freeze order of 26 July. He placed responsibility for drafting the American modus vivendi document in the hands of State's Far Eastern Division, which also had in hand suggested hard-nosed terms for a temporary settlement in a memorandum drafted by Harry Dexter White, an assistant secretary of the Treasury, and transmitted to State by Morgenthau.[58] Before the American document took final form, however, Hull had to deal with the Japanese Proposal B, which Nomura and Kurusu formally presented him on 20 November.

By that date the two Japanese negotiators were in a bind. The day before, Kurusu had been sharply rebuked by Togo for proposing his own temporary limited arrangement, and both emissaries were admonished that there would be no withdrawal from southern Indo-China "merely on assurances that conditions prior to this freezing act will be restored."[59] Thus, the one bargaining chip the emissaries held was taken from them. They were stuck with Proposal B, which they were instructed to present forthwith. When they did so, Hull, who had already read the Magic copy, had to restrain his outrage, as he wrote in his *Memoirs,* lest he give the Japanese "any pretext to walk out of the conversations." He found the proposal "preposterous" and called it in his testimony before the JCC and in his *Memoirs* an "ultimatum."[60] Certain nonpartisan historians since have characterized Hull's reaction as somewhat overdrawn.[61] The Japanese document was not intended to represent a final settlement. It was a stopgap arrangement on the basis of which further negotiations might proceed toward a comprehensive understanding. As such it was little different in nature from the modus vivendi document that Hull's own people were preparing.

One factor that drove Hull's intemperate reaction was a Magic decryption of 20 November from Togo to his emissaries instructing them to interpret Article I of Proposal B as requiring the suspension of all U.S. aid to Chiang Kai-shek.[62] China remained the sticking point, and Hull maintained that that particular condition was "unacceptable." He had no difficulty in persuading Roosevelt to the same view. Historian Roberta Wohlstetter has commented, pointedly, that "from the extremity of his [Hull's] denunciation of Plan B, one would never have guessed that such a proposal [suspending aid to China] was currently being debated in his own Department."[63]

With Japan's Proposal B dead on delivery, all that remained as a possible bridge over troubled waters was State's own modus vivendi, which was passing through three successive drafts. As well as helping to inspire those drafts, the White-Morgenthau memorandum also became the basis of a so-called Ten-Point Program outlining U.S. terms for a future, final, and general settlement of disputed issues. Hull regarded the Ten Points as essentially a restatement of principles that long guided U.S. foreign policy. But points three and four required the Japanese to get out of China and Indo-China and to stop subverting the Chiang Kai-shek regime. In its bare-knuckle form, the Ten-Point document would not normally be the paper that a seasoned diplomat would want to put in front of potential enemies in the barometric chamber of endgame negotiations—unless one wanted war. Other, less intransigent options would be exhausted first. But Hull, as we shall see, would follow his own drummer. Nomura and Kurusu could not follow theirs, as Togo, in Tokyo, prescribed the beat for them. There were "reasons beyond your ability to guess why we wanted to settle Japanese-American relations by the 25th," Togo cabled them on the twenty-second, but "if the signing can be completed by the 29th" and "if everything can be finished" by that date, "we have decided to wait until that date. This time we mean it, that the deadline absolutely cannot be changed. After that, things are automatically going to happen."[64]

Neither Kimmel nor Short was advised of this extended deadline.

In the days 21–26 November Hull submitted copies of the penultimate drafts of State's modus vivendi proposal and Ten-Point Program to service chiefs, and to the emissaries of Great Britain, Australia, the Netherlands, and China. Admiral Stark and Acting Assistant Chief of Staff Major General Leonard T. Gerow, acting for Marshall, approved of the modus vivendi, Gerow noting, "The adoption of its provisions would attain one of our present major objectives—the avoidance of war with Japan."[65] The reactions that came in from the embassies and their home governments were mixed. The Dutch were generally in support of the truce document, though they worried about the amount of oil they would have to deliver. Australia came on board, somewhat reluctantly. Churchill, answering for the British, was tepid: "What about Chiang Kai Shek? Is he not having a very thin diet? Our anxiety is about China."[66] And the Chinese were plainly livid: Chinese Ambassador Hu Shih and Chiang's brother-in-law T. V. Soong made anxious complaints to Roosevelt, Hull, Stimson, and Knox that not only China's military morale but her very survival was in danger of being sacrificed by this act of "appeasement."[67]

In the midst of Hull's consultations, Stimson had, on the twenty-fifth, what he called in his diary a "very full day indeed." At 9:30 A.M. he and Knox met in Hull's office to discuss the three months' truce that Hull planned to lay before the Japanese that day or the next. He joined Hull in thinking that there was not much chance of the Japanese accepting it. At noon he met for an hour and a half at the White House with Roosevelt, Hull, Knox, Marshall, and Stark. The President opened the meeting by stating that "we were likely to be attacked perhaps as soon as next Monday [1 December], for the Japanese are notorious for making an attack without warning, and the question was what we should do. The question was how we should maneuver them into the position of firing the first shot without allowing too much danger to ourselves. It was a difficult proposition."[68] Much has been made of this Roosevelt statement by some revisionist historians, who see in it evidence that the President was deliberately provoking Japan into war. This theory is hard to reconcile, however, with the fact that all the principals at the meeting had earlier agreed that Hull should make one more effort to delay or avert war by presenting the Japanese emissaries with State's modus vivendi document. Stark and Marshall had the greatest stake in that agreement and wanted no war with Japan *at all*. More likely, Roosevelt was simply venting his doubt that the Togo government would accept the document—and what then? He would not be an aggressor himself.

The "difficult proposition," of course, placed at a distinct military disadvantage the commanders in Hawaii and the Philippines who now would be expected to absorb the first blows—perhaps disabling blows—without, under this policy, being given the chance to make preemptive, protective strikes of their own. It is not thought (by this writer) that the President had Hawaii in mind when he made his statement, since those islands were so distant from the longitudes where Japanese actions were expected. Roosevelt, obviously, was looking for political cover with Congress and the public. Let the enemy fire the first shot; let an outraged citizenry shoot back. He did not reckon, however, with Admiral Kimmel's war plan WPPac-46, which stipulated that the Pacific Fleet would shoot and ask questions later if the Japanese so much as stuck their noses into the

Hawaiian tent, say, within five hundred nautical miles out. And, as events unfolded, it was Kimmel who *did* fire the first shot in the Pacific war, Roosevelt's policy notwithstanding.

Following the White House meeting, Stimson returned to his office in the Munitions Building, sometime before 4:30 P.M., where G-2 (Army Intelligence) handed him a sighting report that five Japanese divisions had come down from Shantung and Shansi in China to the port of Shanghai, where they had embarked on ships (thirty, forty, fifty?), the first formations of which were seen steaming south of Formosa along the China coast. At 4:30, Stimson called Hull to inform him, and sent a copy of the report to Roosevelt. When Stimson resumed his diary the next day, the twenty-sixth, he related a 9:20 A.M. telephone conversation with Hull, who "had about made up his mind not to give (make) the propositions [State's modus vivendi] that Knox and I passed on the other day to the Japanese but to kick the whole thing over—to tell them that he has no other proposition at all." After digesting that stunning volte-face from Hull, Stimson called the President to ask his reaction to the Japanese troop movements southward toward Indo-China. When the secretary learned that Roosevelt had not received the message, he relayed it to him over the phone. "He [Roosevelt] fairly blew up," Stimson recorded, "—jumped up into the air, so to speak, and said . . . that that changed the whole situation because it was an evidence of bad faith on the part of the Japanese."[69]

On the same day, Hull sent a memorandum for the President recommending that "at this time I call in the Japanese Ambassadors and hand to them a copy of the comprehensive basic proposal for a general peaceful settlement [Ten-Point Program] and at the same time withhold the modus vivendi proposal." What reasons did Hull give for this astonishing overnight reversal in American policy, so detrimental on its face to the interests of Stark and Marshall? He gave three in the memorandum: (1) the opposition to the modus vivendi by the Chinese government; (2) the "half-hearted support" given to it by the British, Dutch, and Australians; and (3) the American public's expected opposition to it. He now recommended against the truce proposal, he wrote, "without in any way departing from my views about the wisdom and the benefit of this step [modus vivendi] to all of the countries opposed to the aggressor nations." On its face, this last clause reads like the statement of a man who either has used the abandonment of the modus vivendi as an occasion for expressing his pride in having attempted such a creative alternative or has lost the courage of his convictions or has had his mind changed by someone superior to him, who could only have been the President. Unfortunately for the third notion, the only firsthand, direct, and contemporary evidence we have is the memorandum in which *Hull recommends* the change *to* Roosevelt. For conspiracy theorists, a possible riposte would be to allege that Roosevelt made the decision to abandon the modus vivendi and ordered Hull to counterfeit a memorandum that would give the White House cover. It is unlikely that the strict moralist Hull would ever have participated in such a fabrication. But there are second- and thirdhand sources that revisionists have seized on for alleging that it was Roosevelt, not Hull (who consistently took personal responsibility for the decision), who held back the modus vivendi.[70] While their use may not convince orthodox historians who rely on original documents of proven provenance for understanding and explaining core historical moments, once- and twice-removed sources have the virtue at least of reminding one that history is not always tidy. The single thing that one can say with certainty in the present case is that Hull's language in the memorandum was ambivalent.

In his statement to the JCC in November 1945, Hull emphasized that he had abandoned the modus vivendi because: (1) the chance of the Japanese accepting the proposal was remote; (2) American opinion would have opposed the supplying of even limited quantities of oil to Japan; and (3) there was serious risk that Chinese morale and resistance would collapse if the truce document was presented. It is interesting that neither in his memorandum nor in his statement did Hull mention the report of Japanese troop movements southward as a factor in his decision. Nor did he consult with Stark or Marshall about his decision, before presenting the Japanese emissaries with the red meat of the Ten-Point Program. Ironically, on the same 26 November the two service chiefs signed another memorandum to the President stating that "the most essential thing now . . . is to gain time."[71]

Were there other factors perhaps at play in Hull's decision? Two possibilities come to mind. The first was the error-filled influence of his principal adviser on Far Eastern Affairs, Stanley Hornbeck, who had consistently mistaken Japanese intentions and had grossly underestimated Japanese military capabilities. As a purveyor of faulty information, the uncommonly purblind doctor was to Hull what Kelly Turner was to Stark. On 31 October he had advised Hull: "Japan is today a weakened and comparatively weak power, and . . . would not for long be a formidable menace to the United States or Great Britain, *or,* if engaged in war with the United States, would not be a formidable opponent."[72] Hornbeck urged the secretary to take a firm stand against the Japanese, arguing that Japan earnestly wanted to avoid a fight with the United States, and that, if pushed into one, would be defeated quickly and easily. An example of Hornbeck's perspicacity is provided by a memorandum he addressed to Hull on 27 November, eleven days before the Japanese attack:

> Were it a matter of placing bets, the undersigned would give odds of five to one that the United States and Japan will not be at "war" on or before December 15 . . . ; would wager three to one that the United States and Japan will not be at "war" on or before the 15th of January . . . ; would wager even money that the United States and Japan will not be at "war" on or before March 1.[73]

It is unknown how much of a factor the fatuous Dr. Hornbeck was in the November decisions taken by Hull, but it may have been considerable. Too, we find reports of Hull's general "weariness" and "grimness" during the same period.[74] Along with burnout went a good deal of exasperation. Assistant Secretary of State Adolf A. Berle, Jr., recorded in his diary for 1 December: "Promptly this morning I went in to see the Secretary. He was alone and unhappy. He said that everybody was trying to run foreign policy: Stimson, who felt bitterly about the Far East; Knox; and pretty much everyone else. 'They all came at me with knives and hatchets,' he said."[75] Hull's biographer Julius W. Pratt attributed the secretary's decision to forgo a truce and to lay out instead the strongest possible terms for a settlement to a righteous belief in the positions he had taken for four years, and now was determined to see stated for the record, in Japan as well as in his own country. Pratt concluded that his decision taken on the overnight of 25–26 November "was a petulant one by a tired and angry old man."[76]

Roosevelt approved Hull's decision, for what precise reasons it is not clear, other than that he had trusted Hull all along to manage the Japanese crisis while his and the American public's attention was fixed on Europe and the Atlantic. And, as historian Herbert Feis observed, Roosevelt probably recognized that, for what the American modus vivendi offered, the Japanese "would not have recalled the expeditions then heading south and west."[77] Accordingly, at 5:00 P.M. on the twenty-sixth, after Hull called Nomura and Kurusu to his apartment at the Wardman Park, the secretary handed them his Ten-Point "comprehensive basic proposal." This constituted the formal American reply to their modus vivendi document of six days before. No doubt both men blanched to read, among other terms, the raw, uncompromising language of points three and four:

3. The Government of Japan will withdraw all military, naval, air and police forces from China and from Indo-China.
4. The Government of the United States and the Government of Japan will not support—militarily, politically, economically—any government or regime in China other than the National Government of the Republic of China with capital temporarily at Chungking.[78]

When transmission of this document reached Tokyo, Foreign Minister Togo testified after the war, "The reaction of all of us [in the cabinet] was, I think, the same. Ignoring all past progress and areas of agreement in the negotiations, the United States had served upon us what we viewed as an ultimatum containing demands far in excess of the strongest positions theretofore taken."[79]

Thus, a second chance for a delay of hostilities was lost. Each power's final note had been interpreted by the other as an ultimatum. There would not be a third chance.

On the next morning, the twenty-seventh, Secretary Hull said to War Secretary Stimson, "I have washed my hands of it [the standoff] and it is now in the hands of you and Knox—the Army and the Navy."[80]

Neither Kimmel nor Short was advised.

By that same morning, the Japanese Navy's Pearl Harbor Striking Force, *Kido Butai*, was under steam, two days at sea, on an eastward course of 095 degrees. Destination: Hawaii.

SIX

WAR WARNINGS

And we are here as on a darkling plain
Swept with confused alarms . . .

Matthew Arnold,
"Dover Beach"

Upon receipt of the news that Secretary Hull had spurned the Japanese truce overture, Secretaries Stimson and Knox directed their respective chiefs of war plans to prepare warnings of imminent hostilities for transmission to all American commands. The sending of such messages was precipitated by Stimson, who invited Knox and Stark to join him and General Gerow, chief of the Army War Plans Division (Marshall being away observing maneuvers in North Carolina), in his office at the Munitions Building. Since this was the same day, 27 November, when the latest memorandum from Marshall and Stark asking for *more* time reached the White House, it is not surprising to read in Stimson's diary entry for that day that Gerow and Stark pressed the same issue in the meeting. "I said," Stimson recorded, "that I was glad to have time but I didn't want it at any cost of humility on the part of the United States or of reopening the thing which would show a weakness on our part."[1]

Stimson then reported to the group that, earlier that morning, he had discussed the Pacific situation with the President by telephone, and that he had recommended to the President that General MacArthur, "who was in the forefront of the threatened area," should be alerted to the diplomatic standoff. MacArthur had already received war warnings of various sorts, but now was the time, Stimson urged the President, to send him "a more definite warning," which he also called "a final alert"—one that "it would not be necessary to repeat . . . over and over again during the ensuing days."[2] There is no firm evidence for concluding that it was the finality of the Ten-Point note that prompted Stimson to make this recommendation; it seems more likely that it was the known (through Magic) extended dead-line of the twenty-ninth, two days hence, when Japan would go on auto-matic, that drove the secretary's initiative. The President approved his recommendation and directed that such a message putting the Philippines "on the qui vive for any attack" be sent.

Accordingly, Gerow produced warning language that he and Marshall had drafted the previous day, before Marshall's departure. On its basis, with Stark's help, Gerow fashioned a final version. Stimson called Hull for an exact statement about the status of negotiations, and Hull's reply was incorporated in the first sentence of the message. Although the drafting of operational messages was a function of uniformed staff, Stimson thought himself justified—since he had been the one instructed to send the message—in making his own contribution, which was the insertion in the second sentence of the words: BUT HOSTILE ACTION POSSIBLE AT ANY MOMENT. It was decided by the drafting group that the same message sent to MacArthur should be wired to three other Army commanding officers of theaters or outposts, *viz:* the Hawaiian Department; the Western Defense Command, at the Presidio in San Francisco; and the Caribbean Defense Command, at Quarry Heights, Canal Zone, Panama, except that those three radiograms should include an extra sentence, reading: BUT THESE MEASURES SHOULD BE CARRIED OUT SO AS NOT COMMA REPEAT NOT COMMA TO ALARM CIVILIAN POPULATION OR DISCLOSE INTENT. As Stimson explained before the JCC in March 1946, "In Hawaii, because of the large numbers of Japanese inhabitants, it was felt desirable to issue a special warning so that nothing would be done, unless necessary to the defense, to alarm the civil population and thus possibly to precipitate an incident and give the Japanese an excuse to go to war and the chance to say that we had commit-ted the first overt act."[3] Unfortunately for General Short in Hawaii, this addition was a sentence too far. And the words *alert* or *final alert* were not used. The ultimate form of the radiogram sent to Short read:

SECRET

PRIORITY NOVEMBER NOVEMBER 27, 1941

NO. 472

COMMANDING GENERAL, HAWAIIAN DEPARTMENT, FORT SHAFTER, T.H. NEGOTIATIONS WITH JAPAN APPEAR TO BE TERMINATED TO ALL PRACTICAL PURPOSES WITH ONLY THE BAREST POSSIBILITIES THAT THE JAPANESE GOVERNMENT MIGHT COME BACK AND OFFER TO CONTINUE PERIOD JAPANESE FUTURE ACTION UNPREDICTABLE BUT HOSTILE ACTION POSSIBLE AT ANY MOMENT PERIOD IF HOSTILITIES CANNOT COMMA REPEAT CANNOT COMMA BE AVOIDED THE UNITED DESIRES THAT JAPAN COMMIT THE FIRST OVERT ACT PERIOD THIS POLICY SHOULD NOT COMMA REPEAT NOT COMMA BE CONSTRUED AS RESTRICTING YOU TO A COURSE OF ACTION THAT MIGHT JEOPARDIZE YOUR DEFENSE PERIOD PRIOR TO HOSTILE JAPANESE ACTION YOU ARE DIRECTED TO UNDERTAKE SUCH RECONNAISSANCE AND OTHER MEASURES AS YOU DEEM NECESSARY BUT THESE MEASURES SHOULD BE CARRIED OUT SO AS NOT COMMA REPEAT NOT COMMA TO ALARM CIVIL POPULATION OR DISCLOSE INTENT PERIOD REPORT MEASURES TAKEN PERIOD SHOULD HOSTILITIES OCCUR YOU WILL CARRY OUT THE TASKS ASSIGNED IN RAINBOW FIVE SO FAR AS THEY PERTAIN TO JAPAN PERIOD LIMIT DISSEMINATION OF THIS HIGHLY SECRET INFORMATION TO MINIMUM ESSENTIAL OFFICERS.

MARSHALL[4]

The message's path on the twenty-seventh can be tracked as follows: it was received in the War Department [WD] code room for encryption at 6:00 P.M. Washington time (12:30 P.M. Hawaii time); filed in the WD signal center at 6:11 P.M. Washington time (12:41 P.M. Hawaii time); received in the Hawaiian Department signal center at 6:46 P.M. Washington time (1:16 P.M. Hawaii time); decrypted in Hawaii at 7:52 P.M. Washington time (2:22 P.M. Hawaii time); and was placed in the hands of Chief of Staff Colonel Walter C. Phillips, who presented it to General Short about 2:30 P.M. Hawaii time. Short talked it over with Phillips and, after "a very few minutes," decided to place the Hawaiian Department on No. 1 Alert. The alert was in effect thirty minutes later. He imposed a heavy guard around all military installations as well as vital civilian structures such as power stations, highway bridges, and telephone exchanges. At 5:40 P.M. Hawaii time, Short had an acknowledgement encrypted for transmission to Washington. The wire was received in the WD code room at 5:57 A.M. on the twenty-eighth, Washington time. Its passage thereafter through the War Department will be considered below. Short's reply in its entirety, addressed to "Chief of Staff," read as follows:

NO. 959

REPORT DEPARTMENT ALERTED TO PREVENT SABOTAGE PERIOD

LIAISON WITH NAVY REURAD [with reference to your radiogram]

FOUR SEVEN TWO TWENTY SEVENTH

SHORT[5]

On the same day, Short's chief intelligence (G-2) officer, Lt. Colonel Kendall J. Fielder, was sent a sabotage/espionage message, No. 473, by Brigadier General Sherman Miles, assistant chief of staff, G-2, in the War Department. It read:

JAPANESE NEGOTIATIONS HAVE COME TO PRACTICAL STALEMATE

STOP HOSTILITIES MAY ENSUE STOP SUBVERSIVE ACTIVITIES MAY

BE EXPECTED STOP INFORM COMMANDING GENERAL AND CHIEF

OF STAFF ONLY

MILES[6]

Fielder showed the message to Short and Phillips about the same time that the No. 1 Alert was ordered. Then, on the following day, the twenty-eighth, Short personally received two more sabotage alerts from Washington. The first (No. 482), from the adjutant general, Major General Emory S. Adams, urged "that you initiate forthwith all additional measures necessary to provide for protection of your establishments comma property comma and equipment against sabotage comma protection of your personnel against subversive propaganda and protection of all activities against espionage stop." But Adams added the caution that Short should not take actions that were illegal or that violated civil rights.[7] The second message (No. 484), from Major General Henry H. Arnold, commander in chief of the Army Air Forces, and marked for the attention of Major General Frederick L. Martin, commander of the Hawaiian Air Force, repeated the substance of Adams's message.[8]

Since the Marshall warning message (No. 472) made no mention of a possible Japanese military strike at Hawaii, Short considered the message's phrase "hostile Japanese action" to mean, in his case, sabotage and uprisings. With three warnings of such activities, Short concluded both that the greatest danger facing his command was internal and not external, and that the three latest messages, all sent *after* the receipt of his No. 959 acknowledgment of No. 472, confirmed the appropriateness of the alert he had ordered.[9] Alert No. 1 was defined as "a defense against acts of sabotage and uprisings within the islands, with no threat from without."[10] It was the lowest of three levels of alert in the Hawaiian Department. Short sent a copy of the 27 November warning from Marshall to his Navy opposite number, Admiral Bloch, and advised him that the Army had gone on Alert No. 1. This caused some misinterpretation in Bloch's headquarters, as well as in Kimmel's, where, because the maximum Navy state of alert was Condition I, just the reverse of Short's No. 1, everyone seemed to understand that Short had declared an all-out alert. Short's all-out, or No. 3, required "the occupation of all field positions by all units, prepared for maximum defense of Oahu and the Army installations on outlying islands."[11] Not surprisingly, when Kimmel's intelligence officer Lieutenant Commander Edwin T. Layton looked out his window on the evening of the twenty-seventh and saw Army trucks moving, troops marching, and, he thought, weapons being deployed, "I presumed that they were going into full condition of readiness, including the emplacement of anti-aircraft and other mobile weapons around Pearl Harbor and other important points on Oahu."[12] But those movements were to protect installations and equipment against ground sabotage. When, in the JCC proceedings of 23 January 1946, Short was asked why Kimmel and Bloch were under the misapprehension that the Alert No. 1 meant all-out alert instead of alert against sabotage only, he snapped: "The only way I can account for that would be poor staff work on the part of the staff of the Fourteenth Naval District. . . . We had furnished them with ten copies of our staff operating procedure, which somebody in that naval staff must have dug into and known what it meant." Apparently, it did not occur to anyone on either Bloch's or Kimmel's staffs to ask a Hawaiian

Department staff member what the Army was *doing* during its alert. And Kimmel admitted in 1944 that "I did not inquire into the particular details."[13]

Short had, he thought, good reason for expecting local attempts to inflict damage on Army and Navy assets. Thirty-seven percent (about 161,000 persons) of the population of Oahu was of Japanese descent. Of those about 40,000 were aliens. Many were suspected (unfairly as it turned out) of disloyalty. Furthermore, Short had to worry about 239 registered Japanese consular agents, as well as 70 or 80 more Japanese who were thought to be informants to the Japanese consulate. With a sizable number of Japanese living in close proximity to airfields, Short regarded his aircraft as particularly vulnerable. Dispersed in scattered bunkers, their fuel tanks, gas-filled engines, and ammunition could easily be torched by fifth column saboteurs sneaking across the unfenced airport perimeters. (Funds for fencing airfields had finally been allocated by the War Department, but not in time to have the barriers erected by November–December.) Short was mindful that an Army inspector's report, dated 9 July, had pointed up the vulnerability of Hickam Field, adjacent to Pearl Harbor, to "a few bold, ruthless and intelligent saboteurs."[14]

Rear Admiral Bloch, who had responsibility for defense of Navy assets in the yard proper, already had armed naval personnel patrolling the two tank farms, upper and lower. The upper farm, adjacent to a public highway, had an "unclimable" fence; it was also protected by three elevated sentry stations equipped with searchlights. Marines alternated with the Army in maintaining constant guard over the water supply and electric power lines. It was thought impossible, by Bloch, to achieve absolute security of the Pearl yard without disruption of its work. Though an elaborate system of photograph passes and random surprise searches was in effect, there was no guarantee that a saboteur might not successfully penetrate the yard among the 5,000 employees of civil contractors, the 5,000 civil service employees, and the several thousand naval personnel who entered the yard each day.

✶

Short stated after the war that he did not believe the 27 November war warning message (No. 472) had been authored by Marshall, though his name was affixed to it. He was correct in that, since, as shown above, Marshall was in North Carolina observing maneuvers when the message was drafted by Gerow, Stimson, and Stark. Marshall had worked with Gerow the day before on language for a warning to MacArthur in the Philippines, but it was not he who inserted the caution "not to alarm civilian population." That, it appears, was Stimson's doing. On his own, Gerow might have included the words "needed measures for protection against subversive activities should be taken immediately," but he was persuaded by the deputy chief of staff (Major General William Bryden), Miles, and Colonel Charles W. Bundy, chief of the War Plans Group, to send that particular warning as a separate G-2 dispatch: that would be Miles's No. 473 on the twenty-seventh.[15]

What tipped Short off to the absence of Marshall's hand was the directive to undertake reconnaissance. Marshall would have known that, by agreement with the Navy on 31 March, aerial reconnaissance of the approaches to Oahu was the responsibility of the Navy. Army aircraft flew regular inshore patrols, but distant (six hundred miles out) air patrols were a Navy function, by signed agreement well known to, and signed off on, by Marshall. Short stated in his testimony before the JCC that, "This message was written basically for General MacArthur in the Philippines and then adopted to the rest of us, and in the Philippines they had no such agreement. The Army was responsible for reconnaissance and they got together with the Navy and agreed upon what sectors that each would cover."[16] (It is not recorded that Short knew this in November 1941.) In response to that part of the directive, Short did order Aircraft Warning Service radar reconnaissance daily from 0400 to 0700—the most dangerous three hours (the two and a half hours preceding dawn and one half hour after) for a dawn air attack, as specified in the Martin-Bellinger estimate. He placed the Army's Interceptor Command and Information Center on the same schedule. In addition, radar would operate daily, *except Sundays,* from 0700 to 1100 and from 1200 to 1600, except Saturdays and Sundays, for training and maintenance work. (The Japanese aircraft would make their approach *after* the predicted 0400–0700 window, and on a Sunday.) At this time, and through December, Short had only six mobile radar stations; three planned fixed stations were not yet operative, their booms and antennas still on a pier in Oakland, California.

That Short did not think himself obligated to go beyond the No. 1 Alert was owed, he said later, to two known facts about Marshall: first, at the time Short was appointed to the command in Hawaii, Marshall "had definitely indicated his intention to direct personally any genuine prewar alert."[17] Second, the one previous Marshall-authored alert to Hawaii had been so overt in language and intent that no one could mistake its meaning. On 17 June 1940, when there was information in Washington suggesting that Japan might make a military move against the United States, but hardly the amount of intelligence and threat that existed in November 1941, Marshall wired an alert to the then commander of the Hawaiian Department, Major General Charles D. Herron. The wire may stand as a model of what a war alert should look like:

JUNE 17, 1940.

NO. 428

IMMEDIATELY ALERT COMPLETE DEFENSIVE ORGANIZATION TO
DEAL WITH POSSIBLE TRANS-PACIFIC RAID, TO GREATEST EXTENT
POSSIBLE WITHOUT CREATING PUBLIC HYSTERIA OR PROVOKING
UNDUE CURIOSITY OF NEWSPAPERS OR ALIEN AGENTS. SUGGEST
MANEUVER BASIS. MAINTAIN ALERT UNTIL FURTHER ORDERS.
INSTRUCTIONS FOR SECRET COMMUNICATION DIRECT WITH CHIEF
OF STAFF WILL BE FURNISHED YOU SHORTLY. ACKNOWLEDGE.[18]

Herron at once placed the department on the only alert he had in his procedures—total. Within the hour he conferred with his opposite number, Bloch and with Vice Admiral Adolphus Andrews, commander of the Hawaiian Detachment. There was no corresponding Navy Department warning. The same day, Herron wired the War Department an acknowledgment as unambiguous as Marshall's warning:

ALL ANTI-AIRCRAFT OBSERVATION [posts manned] AND
DETACHMENTS IN POSITION WITH LIVE AMMUNITION AND ORDERS
TO FIRE ON FOREIGN PLANES OVER RESTRICTED AREAS AND IN
DEFENSE OF ANY ESSENTIAL INSTALLATIONS. SOME LOCAL
INTEREST IN AMMUNITION ISSUES BUT NO EXCITEMENT. NAVY
INSHORE AND OFFSHORE AIR PATROLS IN OPERATION.[19]

The all-out Marshall-Herron alert remained in force until 20 June, when Marshall ordered it tapered down; it ended for all practical purposes on 16 July. Herron assured Marshall that the alert did not "dull the keen edge, or exhaust morale."[20] When Herron was relieved by Short in February 1941, Herron briefed his successor on the 1940 alert, and, according to Short, "acquainted me with the relation which had existed between himself and General Marshall during the all-out alert which began June 17, 1940. In that alert, General Marshall had directed the alert and had closely supervised its continuance."[21] Short argued before the JCC, in January 1945, that he had taken the Marshall-Herron alert as a "precedent" of what he might expect to receive if Marshall ever wanted him to go on all-out alert. He expected that the Chief of Staff, who had personally supervised the thirty-day-long 1940 alert, "would certainly have the time and interest not only to read and understand my succinct report . . . but to send further word in the event that he disagreed in any way with the measure I had taken in obedience to his November 27 directive."[22] But no further communication was received from Marshall, corrective or otherwise.

Like the November 27 directive, the Marshall-Herron alert was a "do-don't" message: *do* take the following measures; *don't* excite the local population. But the *do* parts of the 1940 warning were explicit and unambiguous, starting with the verb *alert*. By comparison with the plain Army language of Marshall in June 1940, the November 1941 message, No. 472, was awkward in expression, abstract in tone, and unsure in intent. It did not seem to come from the same hand (which it did not). And it contained no warning whatever of a possible sea-air attack—"trans-Pacific raid"—on Hawaii. In fact, Short observed, among the military intelligence estimates prepared by G-2 at the War Department and sent to his department, "in no estimate did G-2 ever indicate the probability of an attack on Hawaii."[23] And no Magic intercepts had been sent to him. There were other problems, Short contended: if the War Department had wanted him to upgrade his alert to No. 2, which read, "defense against sabotage and uprisings and, in addition, defense against an air attack or against an attack by surface and subsurface vessels,"[24] it would not be possible to obey the injunction to "limit dissemination [of the warning] to minimum essential officers." If No. 2 were declared, he would have to inform officers all up and down the line—air, antiaircraft, coast artillery, and infantry. As it was, under Alert No. 1 Short informed only his staff, General Martin of the Army Air Forces, Major General Henry T. Burgin, commander of the coast artillery, and the two infantry division commanders. Furthermore, if Alert No. 2 or No. 3 had been ordered, there would have been no way to keep the warning secret, not to mention refrain from alarming the locals:

> All of the coast artillery, all of the anti-aircraft artillery, and all of the air would have immediately taken up their duties as described in that alert. Part of the coast artillery was right in the middle of the town. Fort de Russy was within two or three blocks of the Royal Hawaiian Hotel. The public couldn't help seeing that they were manning their seacoast guns. Placing live ammunition. Some of the guns were practically in the middle of the park.[25]

Use of Alerts No. 2 or No. 3 would also have interfered with his training mission, Short argued. In large part, his command was made up of newly commissioned officers and recent enlistees and inductees. They required constant training in order to achieve battle readiness. If they were taken out of training to man alert posts, they would not be properly prepared to carry out their specialized tasks. "The War Department message had not indicated in any way," Short testified to the JCC, "that our training mission was modified, suspended, or abolished, or that all troops were to go immediately into tactical status."[26] The same problem would face the Army Air Forces, which had the mission of training bomber combat crews and of ferrying B-17s to the Philippines. General Martin was then making maximum use of his few bombers and more numerous pursuit (fighter) planes for combat training. "If war were momentarily expected in the Hawaiian coastal frontier," Short said, "these considerations would give way. But every indication was that the War Department expected the war to break out, if at all, only in the far Pacific and not at Hawaii."[27] No warning of a possible Japanese attack on Hawaii had been received at Fort Shafter since the Marshall-Herron alert of June 1940. In the Army Pearl Harbor Board investigation, Marshall confirmed Short's reading of those facts:

> We anticipated, beyond a doubt, a Japanese movement in Indochina and the Gulf of Siam, and against the Malay Peninsula. We anticipated also an assault on the Philippines. We did not, so far as I can recall, anticipate an attack on Hawaii; the reason being that we thought, with the addition of more modern planes, that the defense

there would be sufficient to make it extremely hazardous for the Japanese to attempt such an attack.[28]

Yet, as Short was to learn shortly after exactly that attack on Hawaii materialized on 7 December, Generals Marshall and Gerow, as well as Colonel Bundy, were all the while confident that Short had *at the least* ordered Alert No. 2 against air raids. Marshall particularly was amazed and acrid that Short had failed to go on all-out alert, when the commanders in the Philippines, the Canal Zone, and at San Francisco, who had received basically the same message, *did* go on full alert. Short's basic defense was, Why, when I sent my acknowledgment stating the alert I had ordered, was I not told that it was insufficient? As he stated in the JCC, "The War Department had nine days in which to tell me that my action was not what they wanted. I accepted their silence as a full agreement with the action taken."[29] (On the twenty-ninth Short sent the War Department a detailed report on the precautions he had taken against subversion and sabotage. That report, specifically acknowledging the sabotage warning, No. 473, was not answered either.)

We can track the course of Short's first acknowledgment (No. 959) through the corridors of the Munitions Building, from the time, 5:57 A.M. on the twenty-eighth, when it arrived in the WD code room. Specifically marked as a reply to WD's No. 472, the dispatch was clipped together with a dispatch from General MacArthur (who was responding to the parallel warning sent him the day before), which had arrived in the code room about an hour before. MacArthur had declared an all-out alert that included extensive air reconnaissance. In the way the two dispatches were clipped, the MacArthur message was on top. Their first distribution was in Marshall's office, where the chief wrote on the top document (MacArthur's), "To Secretary of War GCM." He did not initial either the top or the under document at the space marked "Chief of Staff." The routing slip shows that the two messages left Marshall's office at noon on the twenty-eighth and made their way to Stimson's office, where the secretary initialed each of them, "Noted—H.L.S." The messages were then walked to the War Plans Division, where General Gerow initialed both, "L.T.G." While there, both messages were read by Colonel Bundy, head of the Plans Group, and by Colonel Charles K. Gailey, executive officer of the division. Gailey initialed the routing slip that had been attached in Marshall's office, and the messages passed thenceforth into the War Department files. Not one of the officers (or the secretary) through whose hands Short's reply passed found any reason to correct it by transmission of a more explicit warning. In the JCC hearings, Marshall was asked,

> Would this be true from an Army viewpoint, that when an overseas commander is ordered to take measures as he deems necessary and to report measures taken to you, is he correct in assuming that if his report is not the kind of action that you had in mind that you would thereafter inform him specifically of the difference?
>
> General Marshall: I would assume so.[30]

In the Army Board investigation of 1944, General Gerow accepted the blame for not having recognized the insufficiency of the reply from Fort Shafter. He agreed that, as War Department rules read, "The merit of a report is not measured by its length. A concise presentation of important points usually is all that is required." And to the question asked him, "Would General Short's reply comply with that regulation?" he answered, "Yes, sir," although he suggested that, if the message had read, "alerted against sabotage only," he might have caught its import more clearly.[31] Marshall refused to let Gerow accept the blame for not picking up on the inadequacy of Short's report. "He [Gerow] had a direct responsibility and I had the full responsibility."[32] Marshall went on to express the breakdown in this language: "It did not register on Colonel Bundy, it did not register on General Gerow, it did not register on me and it carries Mr. Stimson's initials also."[33] Marshall's biographer Forrest C. Pogue has commented that Marshall was attempting to do so many things—"hold too many threads of operations in his hand"—that he simply missed noticing the kind of signal Short was sending and missed as well his own opportunity to intervene. Inability to take each order in turn and to give it exactly the attention it deserved was to Pogue "a reasonable defense from an overworked Chief of Staff, but it did not exonerate him."[34] Marshall testified that the officer expressly charged with checking on compliance with orders sent was Bundy. About an hour and a half after the Pearl Harbor attack, Marshall had a conversation with Bundy. The officer stated to the chief that he had gotten the impression from the words "liaison with Navy" that Short and Bloch had activated the Joint (Coastal Frontier) Defense Plan.[35] Which they had not.

> Confusion now hath made his masterpiece!
>
> *Macbeth,* Act II, Sc. 3

Bundy was killed in an airplane crash while en route to Hawaii shortly after 7 December.

★

On the morning of the twenty-seventh, just prior to receiving his war warning from Washington, Short met for three hours with Kimmel at the latter's headquarters. With Kimmel were Admirals Bloch, Halsey, Brown, and Bellinger, and certain staff members, including "Soc" McMorris. Short had brought along Major General Martin and his chief of staff, Lieutenant Colonel James. A. Mollison. At conferences such as this one Short had learned that, according to the best naval intelligence, the Japanese carriers were either in home ports or were proceeding south. That knowledge would give him some confidence later in the day in declaring the alert against sabotage only. He had to have been reassured, too, when, in the course of this particular conference, Colonel Mollison having observed that the Japanese had the *capability* of making an air attack on Oahu, Kimmel turned to his fleet war plans officer and, according to Short, asked, "What do you think about the prospects of a Japanese air attack?" and McMorris answered, "None."[36] (Ten days later, Short, Kimmel, and, of course, McMorris would rue that fateful response.) Even the principal item on that morning's agenda lent itself to easing disquiet: the War and Navy Departments had authorized the reduction of Short's P-40 fighter strength on Oahu by about half, the balance to be sent to Wake and Midway Islands. The fact that Marshall and Stark felt comfortable in making that recommendation persuaded those around the conference table that Washington "did not consider hostile action on Pearl Harbor imminent or probable."[37]

★

On Oahu Short ordered all aircraft, following each day's training exercises, to be cleared of all ammunition and to be clustered together on the "warming up aprons," wingtip to wingtip, nose to tail, so that they might be more efficiently guarded against ground sabotage. At Hickam that meant ten feet between wingtips and 135 feet between noses and tails. Of course, when Japanese bombers and strafers came streaking in over the hills of Oahu after dawn on 7 December, they found their Army aircraft targets unbelievably bunched together for best effect. Short *could* have chosen a different expedient that would have allowed his aircraft to remain dispersed, fueled, and armed, requiring only warm-up time to get airborne: to quadruple or quintruple the guard on aircraft from his garrison of 21,273 men at Schofield Barracks.

The sabotage never happened.

When confronted later with that irony, Short stated that, if he had been sent certain Magic intercepts that he did not learn about until 1944, he would have ordered things otherwise.[38]

His fellow service commander, Admiral Kimmel, would say the same.

✴

About the same time, on the afternoon of the twenty-seventh, that Kimmel was handed a copy of Short's war warning, the Pacific Fleet commander received his own Navy war warning dispatch from Washington. It began, somewhat dramatically, "This dispatch is to be considered a war warning." Kelly Turner claimed pride of authorship of that opening sentence. He and Royal Ingersoll, with an assist from Stark, were the principal architects of the text that followed. The language was vetted by Roosevelt. Sent by Naval Operations (OpNav) at 2337 on the twenty-seventh, the message, addressed to both Kimmel (CINCPAC) and Hart (CINCAF), read in its entirety:

SECRET

FROM CHIEF OF NAVAL OPERATIONS FOR ACTION

CINCAF–CINCPAC

NOVEMBER 27, 1941

272337   (CRØ921)

THIS DISPATCH IS TO BE CONSIDERED A WAR WARNING X

NEGOTIATIONS WITH JAPAN LOOKING TOWARD STABILIZATION OF

CONDITIONS IN THE PACIFIC HAVE CEASED AND AN AGGRESSIVE
MOVE BY JAPAN IS EXPECTED WITHIN THE NEXT FEW DAYS X THE
NUMBER AND EQUIPMENT OF JAPANESE TROOPS AND THE
ORGANIZATION OF NAVAL TASK FORCES INDICATES AN AMPHIBIOUS
EXPEDITION AGAINST EITHER THE PHILIPPINES THAI OR KRA
PENINSULA OR POSSIBLY BORNEO X EXECUTE AN APPROPRIATE
DEFENSIVE DEPLOYMENT PREPARATORY TO CARRYING OUT THE
TASKS ASSIGNED IN WPL46 X INFORM DISTRICT AND ARMY
AUTHORITIES X A SIMILAR WARNING IS BEING SENT BY WAR
DEPARTMENT X SPENAVO INFORM BRITISH X CONTINENTAL
DISTRICTS GUAM SAMOA DIRECTED TAKE APPROPRIATE MEASURES
AGAINST SABOTAGE[39]

Before exegeting this message in its parts it would be advisable to examine it as a whole. Turner insisted in December 1945 that "there was only one war warning and that was on the 27th of November."[40] But that could be so only if one considered messages containing the words "war warning" and none others. Just three days before, on the twenty-fourth, OpNav sent Kimmel and Hart a signal that was no less a war warning. It read:

SECRET

FROM CHIEF OF NAVAL OPERATIONS FOR ACTION

CINCAF CINCPAC COM 11 COM 12 COM 13

COM 15

242005   CRØ443

CHANCES OF FAVORABLE OUTCOME OF NEGOTIATIONS WITH JAPAN
VERY DOUBTFUL X THIS SITUATION COUPLED WITH STATEMENTS
OF JAPANESE GOVERNMENT AND MOVEMENTS THEIR NAVAL AND
MILITARY FORCES INDICATE IN OUR OPINION THAT A SURPRISE
AGGRESSIVE MOVEMENT IN ANY DIRECTION INCLUDING ATTACK ON
PHILIPPINES OR GUAM IS A POSSIBILITY X CHIEF OF STAFF HAS
SEEN THIS DISPATCH CONCURS AND REQUESTS ACTION ADEES
[ADDRESSEES] TO INFORM SENIOR ARMY OFFICERS THEIR AREAS X
UTMOST SECRECY NECESSARY IN ORDER NOT TO COMPLICATE AN
ALREADY TENSE SITUATION OR PRECIPITATE JAPANESE ACTION X
GUAM WILL BE INFORMED SEPARATELY

COPY TO WPD, WAR DEPT, AND TO OP-12 <u>BUT NO OTHER</u>
<u>DISTRIBUTION.</u>[41]

In fact, Turner is recorded as having been disappointed that the November 24 phrase "in any direction" was not included in the warning of the twenty-seventh.[42] What Turner could have acknowledged further, if he had sifted through the contents of CINCPAC's in basket, was that, prior to the twenty-fourth Kimmel had received *five* other official messages from Stark that could broadly be characterized as "war warnings": on 21 January, 3 February, 13 July, 21 August, and 16 October.[43] Kimmel also received during those eleven months a stream of personal letters from Stark, many of which reflected the darkening skies and rising waters, though some, as shown earlier, nixed or fudged on warning information given in the official communications. Typical, and particularly interesting because it fell between the twenty-fourth and twenty-seventh, was a letter from the CNO, dated the twenty-fifth, written after that day's notable noon meeting at the White House. Leading with a comment about Roosevelt and Hull, Stark wrote:

> Neither would be surprised over a Japanese surprise attack. From many angles an attack on the Philippines would be the most embarrassing thing that could happen to us. There are some here who think it likely to occur. I do not give it the weight others do, but I included it [in the warning of the twenty-fourth] because of the strong feeling among some people. You know I have generally held that it was not time for the Japanese to proceed against Russia. I still do. Also I still rather look for an advance into Thailand, Indo China, Burma Road area as the most likely.
>
> I won't go into the pros and cons of what the United States may do. I will be damned if I know. I wish I did.[44]

The letter arrived at Pearl on 3 December.

After that nearly yearlong litany of portents and lamentations—Kimmel called it the "plethora of premonitions, generalized warnings and forebodings"—sent via official ciphered radiograms or by personal mail on board the weekly China Clipper, Kimmel was not likely to be startled by 27 November's opening sentence, or by the text that followed. It fell right in with the rest of Washington's literature. It had, as Admiral King (later COMINCH and CNO) complained in November 1944, a "sameness of tenor" that failed to set it apart from previous messages.[45] But King was not exactly an objective critic. He had been in Stark's office when the final language of the warning was drafted, and had said nothing.[46] What was more important, it can be argued, was what Kimmel (and Short) had *not* been sent: raw Magic intercepts, of which more later. They had not even been sent news of the Japanese deadline dates of 25 and 29 November.

★

In examining the language of the Navy warning of the twenty-seventh, one finds that it is just as vague and open to conflicting interpretations as the Army warning of the same date. Even Turner's "war warning" sentence could be understood as a catch basin for any and all events to come, as assembled by hindsight. But there are certain specific differences between the two messages, starting with their reports on the status of American-Japanese negotiations. In the Army message it was stated that negotiations "appear to be terminated for all practical purposes with only the barest possibilities" of continuance. In the Navy message the negotiations had "ceased"—a statement that was to puzzle Kimmel over the next nine days as he read about continuing negotiations in the Honolulu newspapers. Not learning of Japan's 29 November deadline when "things [were] automatically going to happen" until 1944, Kimmel commented before the JCC, in January 1946: "So far as Japan was concerned, the talking which went on after November 26 was play-acting. It was a Japanese stratagem to conceal a blow which Japan was preparing to deliver. . . . The Navy Department knew the scheme [and did not tell me]."[47] Where the Army warning stated that future Japanese moves were "unpredictable," the Navy warning made site-specific predictions ("indications") of attacks against "either the Philippines, Thai, or Kra Peninsula or possibly Borneo." That the "United States desires that Japan commit the first overt act" was a vital condition that found no mention in the Navy message; nor did the Navy message enjoin Kimmel (as the Army message did Short) to undertake "reconnaissance." The "Do-Don't" Army message commanded:

Do be on guard.
Don't alarm civilians.
Do take measures deemed necessary.

Don't disclose intent.

Do carry out tasks assigned in Rainbow Five.

Don't commit the first overt act.

The Navy message contained no Don'ts and two Do's: (1) "Execute an appropriate defensive deployment preparatory to carrying out the tasks assigned in WPL-46," and (2) "Inform district [Bloch] and Army [Short] authorities." While U.S. mainland naval districts as well as Guam and Samoa were directed to take measures against sabotage, no such directive was addressed to Oahu in the Navy message. "Spenavo" in the second to last sentence was special Naval Observer in London, Admiral Robert Ghormley. The Navy message asked for no acknowledgment. What is most striking about both warning messages is that neither mentioned Hawaii as a probable or even possible target, though in the later Pearl Harbor investigations both Marshall and Stark averred that their respective messages were intended to prompt all-out alerts in Hawaii against such an attack. Marshall stated in December 1945 that, "I feel that General Short was given a command instruction to put his command on the alert against a possible hostile attack by the Japanese. The command was not so alerted."[48] When asked in the JCC hearings what additional dispositions he had expected Kimmel to make beyond those he had already taken after the 16 October warning, Stark answered: "Full security measures [presumably Condition I], not only for ships in port but for ships at sea; measures regarding the safety of Pearl Harbor; distant reconnaissance"—that last despite the fact that, in compliance with WPPac-46, as Stark well knew, long-range aerial reconnaissance was not to be mounted until W-Day, the day that war began with Japan.[49]

Much popular (and some published) criticism of Short and Kimmel since 7 December seems to have assumed that explicit and unmistakable warnings were sent them of probable Japanese attacks on their positions. If anything, the NCI concluded in 1944, the Navy's 27 November warning "directed attention away from Pearl Harbor rather than toward it."[50] The meanings that afterward were read into these messages by the War and Navy Departments were in them only indirectly or obscurely. Turner testified in the NCI that the Navy message meant what it said.[51] But did it say what it meant? Stark's defense of the Navy message in the JCC hearings consisted of saying that "there was grave danger of Japan striking any-where. . . . The words 'war warning' had never before been used in any of my dispatches to the commander in chief, Pacific Fleet. . . . That certain signs indicated an amphibious expedition against either the Philippines, Thai, or the Kra Peninsula, or possibly Borneo . . . did not, in our opinion, rule out or preclude an attack elsewhere. Our dispatch of the 24th . . . warned against a surprise aggressive movement in any direction."[52]

Kimmel's and Short's most severe critic in the JCC was staff member Edward P. Morgan, an attorney and investigator from the Federal Bureau of Investigation, appointed by committee chairman Senator Alben W. Barkley, Democrat of Kentucky, upon the recommendation of FBI direc-tor J. Edgar Hoover. Morgan produced a 266-page (printed) report that was generally hostile to the two commanders. In the matter of the war warnings, Morgan advised the committee (his italics): *The more the evi-dence is considered, the more apparent becomes the realization that the only thing to have altered the defensive picture would have been to tell both the responsible commanders that a surprise air attack was to be visited on Pearl Harbor by Japan.*[53] His sarcasm aside, Morgan was more right than he knew. Remembering the Marshall-Herron alert of 1940, it is not diffi-cult to construct the language of what would have been an adequately explicit and unmistakable joint warning to Short and Kimmel:

IMMEDIATELY GO ON HIGHEST LEVEL ALERT AGAINST POSSIBLE
TRANS-PACIFIC RAID X EXECUTE JOINT COASTAL FRONTIER
DEFENSE PLAN INCLUDING DISTANT RECONNAISSANCE ALL
SECTORS AND AIRCRAFT WARNING SERVICE MAXIMUM HOURS X
ISSUE ALL AMMO X UNITED STATES DESIRES JAPAN COMMIT FIRST
OVERT ACT X AVOID BOTH PUBLIC HYSTERIA AND INCIDENT
OCCURRING IN LOCAL POPULATION THAT JAPAN MIGHT TAKE AS
PRETEXT X GUARD AGAINST SABOTAGE AND SUBVERSION X
MAINTAIN ALERT UNTIL FURTHER ORDERS X REPORT IN DETAIL
                                          MARSHALL STARK

It is not too much to suggest that the Army-Navy cooperation that Pearl Harbor critics wanted to see practiced in Hawaii might also in this instance be desirable in Washington. Marshall and Stark enjoyed a close professional and personal association. They served together on the Joint Board. Stark assisted in the drafting of the Army warning. Gerow knew Marshall's thinking. If the War Plans and Operations people could have set aside their prerogatives and traditions of sending separate and different messages to their respective commanders, and if the drafters could have asked the help of a service publication editor (from, say, the U.S. Naval Institute *Proceedings* or the *Field Artillery Journal*) to assist them in *writing exactly what they meant to say,* perhaps the warnings of 27 November would not have gained status as tragically obscure military communications.

At 0110 on 29 November (but under the date 28 November) OpNav sent Kimmel a copy of the Army message No. 472 for "information." Kimmel already had a copy of No. 472 via courier from Short. (And Kimmel had shared his "war warning" in paraphrase with Short.) But OpNav added to the Army message an order it had omitted from its own warning of the twenty-seventh: "Undertake no offensive action until Japan has committed an overt act."[54] This was stronger than the "United States desires" language in the Army message, and the offensive nature of Kimmel bristled at having to conform to its "paralyzing" stricture.[55]

★

Kimmel might have been sent a different, if not more specific, kind of warning if Commander Arthur H. McCollum had had his way. McCollum was head of the Far Eastern Section in the Foreign Intelligence Division of the Office of Naval Intelligence (ONI) in the sixth wing on the second deck of the Navy Department at Constitution Avenue and 17th Street in Washington. On 4 or 5 December, as he recollected, when convinced that "everything pointed to an immediate outbreak of hostilities between Japan and the United States," he drafted a warning message for transmission to the fleet. After showing it to his immediate chief, Captain William A. Heard, he took it to Wilkinson, the director of ONI, who told him it had to be approved by Kelly Turner, who by that date was reserving all evaluation of intelligence to himself.[56] Turner showed McCollum the warning messages of 24 and 27 November and asked McCollum if he didn't think those were enough. McCollum gushed, "Well, good gosh, you put in the words 'war warning.' I do not know what could be plainer than that, but, nevertheless, I would like to see mine go too." Turner then struck through several passages of McCollum's text and said that if it went out it would have to go as edited. McCollum testified that he left the altered draft with Wilkinson and did not know what happened to it thereafter. No copy survives.[57] A different version of its fate was given by Turner, who claimed that, upon seeing the 24 and 27 November warnings, McCollum tore up his proposed dispatch.[58]

Neither of the two principals here, Turner or McCollum, should be released without further examination. After the war, "Terrible" Turner claimed that, in the first week of December 1941, his belief was that Hawaii was directly at risk:

> I was satisfied in July that we would be at war with Japan certainly within the next few months. I believed during the first part of December that the probability of a raid on Hawaii was 50-50. . . . I felt that there were two methods, two strategic methods that the Japanese Fleet would pursue. One was to go down and base their fleet in the Mandates with the hope that our fleet would go after them, and they would be in a good position. The other was to make a raid on Hawaii. There were two major methods and without evaluating it too much, too greatly, I thought it was about a 50-50 chance of the raid on Hawaii.[59]

But, as Turner's biographer points out, "no specific mention of this belief appeared in the final version of any dispatch which he drafted for the CNO to send to CINCPAC"; although, in a different context, Turner suggested that Pearl Harbor was mentioned in one of the preliminary drafts of the 27 November warning.[60]

On 7 October 1940, then Lieutenant Commander McCollum sent a memorandum to the director of ONI, Captain Walter Stratton Anderson. Four pages in length, on legal-size paper, the memorandum proper was followed by an additional page of summary. From the main text and seven-point summary we may draw a condensation of McCollum's thinking: The United States faces hostile powers in both the Atlantic and the Pacific; British naval power currently insulates the United States from assault by Germany; Japan may threaten British lines of communication in the Indian Ocean and Mediterranean; and the U.S. Pacific Fleet is capable of harassing and nullifying Japanese assistance to Germany and Italy in their war against the British. McCollum then suggests the following course of action for the United States:

A. Make an arrangement with Britain for the use of British bases in the Pacific, particularly Singapore.

B. Make an arrangement with Holland for the use of base facilities and acquisition of supplies in the Dutch East Indies.

C. Give all possible aid to the Chinese Government of Chiang Kai-Shek.

D. Send a division of long-range heavy cruisers to the Orient, Philippines, or Singapore.

E. Send two divisions of submarines to the Orient.

F. Keep the main strength of the U.S. Fleet now in the Pacific in the vicinity of the Hawaiian Islands.

G. Insist that the Dutch refuse to grant Japanese demands for undue economic concessions, particularly oil.

H. Completely embargo all U.S. trade with Japan, in collaboration with a similar embargo imposed by the British Empire.

McCollum concluded: "If by these means Japan could be led to commit an overt act of war, so much the better." Or, as he expressed it in his summary, "It is to the interest of the United States to eliminate Japan's threat in the Pacific at the earliest opportunity by taking prompt and aggressive action against Japan."[61]

In a new book, whose jacket claims that the Japanese attack on Pearl Harbor "was *deliberately provoked* through an eight-step program [shown above] devised by the navy [emphasis in the original]," Robert B. Stinnett contends that McCollum's memorandum became the blueprint for actions subsequently taken by President Roosevelt to ensure an uncontested Japanese act of war against the fleet at Pearl Harbor. His is not, to be sure, the first revisionist attempt to posit a vast conspiracy by Roosevelt and his minions, including, according to Stinnett, the midlevel Far Eastern specialist McCollum, to force the United States into war by a secret and deliberate contrivance that placed the fleet in harm's way. In McCollum's case, Stinnett is able to assemble circumstantial evidence in the officer's eight-step plan for holding that McCollum's blue-sky scenario became the template for what happened in fact. Stinnett could argue, for example, that, as proposed under McCollum's item F, Roosevelt did keep the fleet in

Admiral Yamamoto Isoroku, commander in chief, Japanese Combined Fleet. *National Archives* (80-JO-63430)

Admiral Husband E. Kimmel, commander in chief, United States Fleet, and commander in chief, Pacific Fleet, center, flanked by his operations officer, Captain Walter S. DeLany, left, and his chief of staff Captain William W. "Poco" Smith. *National Archives (80-G-456842)*

Admiral Nagano Osami, chief,
Japanese Naval General Staff.
National Archives (80-JO-63422)

Japanese photograph taken during the attack depicts a geyser of water rising
from a torpedo hit on the port side of USS *Oklahoma*. The "Kate" aircraft that

Vice Admiral Nagumo Chuichi, commander in chief, Japanese First Air Fleet. *National Archives (80-JO-63423)*

dropped the torpedo is seen, upper center, banking away. Another Kate can be seen at the upper right. *National Archives (80-G-30554)*

Half of the U.S. Pacific Fleet was in the Harbor. *National Archives (80-G-32414)*

Commander Fuchida Mitsuo, leader of the air attack on Pearl Harbor. *U.S. Naval Institute*

The twisted, sinking wreckage of USS *Arizona* burns after the explosion of her forward powder magazines. *National Archives (80-G-32916)*

Naval Air Station personnel at Kaneohe Bay pass by one destroyed and one damaged Catalina patrol bomber. *National Archives (80-G-32833)*

Aircraft and hangar wreckage at the Army's Hickam Field. *National Archives (80-G-32896)*

Damaged aircraft at the Naval Air Station on Ford Island. In the foreground
is a dismantled wing of a PBY Catalina patrol bomber. In the left background
is what appears to be a still-intact Catalina. Vice Admiral Halsey later said

Kimmel's forces were at the highest level of efficiency; they were surprised because they lacked the scout planes to perform a compass sweep of 360°. *National Archives (80-G-19948)*

After three bomb hits, the forward ammunition magazine of destroyer USS *Shaw* explodes. *National Archives (90-G-16871A)*

Battleships USS *West Virginia*, left, and USS *Arizona*, right, are shown sinking in the harbor. USS *Tennessee*, center, was damaged by two armor-piercing bombs. *National Archives (80-G-33058)*

Workmen from the Navy Yard cut through the capsized hull of USS *Oklahoma* to rescue crewmen trapped below. At right is USS *Maryland*. *National Archives (80-G-32741)*

October 1941. The single entrance to the harbor is at top, and the Navy Yard with its two fuel farms is to the left. Ford Island is at the center with battleship row off its left (southeast) shore. The attackers missed several million barrels of

fuel, which, if destroyed, would have put the fleet out of commission for six months. *National Archives (80-G-182874)*

Lieutenant General Walter
C. Short, commanding
general of the Hawaiian
Department. The Japanese
tactical victory also aborted
Short's career. *U.S. Naval
Institute*

Rear Admiral Claude C.
Bloch, commander,
Fourteenth Naval District.
National Archives (302296)

Rear Admiral Richmond Kelly Turner, chief, War Plans Division, Navy Department. *National Archives (302369)*

Admiral Harold R. Stark, chief of Naval Operations. *U.S. Naval Institute*

Frank Knox, secretary of the Navy. *National Archives (40229)*

The miscalculations of these three men paved the way for Japan's successful surprise attack. After the attack they found a scapegoat in the Pacific Fleet commander, Admiral H. E. Kimmel.

General George C. Marshall, chief of staff, United States Army, left, and Henry L. Stimson, secretary of war. Washington knew a Pacific attack was coming but refused to jeopardize the security of their code-breaking success by contacting Kimmel directly. The "war warning" arrived at Pearl after the last attacking plane had departed. Even with advance warning the U.S. forces in Hawaii could have neither repelled nor neutralized the attack. Washington misjudged Japan's superior weaponry and the size and skill of her attacking forces. *National Archives*

Hawaii; that, under item C, all possible aid was given to Chiang Kai-shek; and that, under item H, the United States instituted a total trade embargo on Japan. (These were all Stanley Hornbeck proposals.) Items A, B, and G happened for well-known reasons, associated with mutual defense pacts. Under item E McCollum cannot take any credit for the first submarine reinforcements sent to the Asiatic Fleet by Stark in October 1939, a year before his memorandum. The submarine reinforcements sent to CINCAF in October 1940 and again in October 1941 were in response to a worried Admiral Hart's pleadings, having no connections to McCollum or to his "conspiracy" memo. And it is more than a stretch to say, as Stinnett does under item D, that the Pacific "pop-up" cruises that Roosevelt proposed to Stark in 1941, and which were never carried out, constituted a "division of heavy cruisers" sent to "the Orient, Philippines, or Singapore."[62] Stinnett seems to say, if McCollum proposed it, Roosevelt must have done it— *post hoc, propter hoc*. Alas for his conspiracy theory, Stinnett cannot place McCollum's memorandum in the President's hands at any time, as he himself concedes.[63] Many a book since Harry Elmer Barnes's *Perpetual War for Perpetual Peace* in 1953 has tried and failed to establish Roosevelt's complicity in the Japanese attack, while withholding his supposed foreknowledge of the event from Kimmel and Short. The smoking gun so devoutly sought by those who have wanted to blame Roosevelt for the sacrifice of capital ships, aircraft, and 2,403 lives on Oahu in an alleged effort to find a back door into the European war *has never been produced*.[64]

What may have been the most revealing, ironic, and dissembling moment in the brief history of McCollum's memorandum occurred during his testimony in the JCC hearings, on 30 January 1946:

SENATOR SCOTT W. LUCAS (*D-Il*): Captain [McCollum], with all the knowledge that you had as an Intelligence officer, and in view of the top position that you held in Intelligence at that time, do you know of anyone in your branch of the service or any other department of the Navy who attempted to trick or maneuver the Japs into attacking the United States on December 7, 1941?

CAPTAIN MCCOLLUM: No, sir.

SENATOR LUCAS: That is all.[65]

★

The sole operational order contained in the 27 November Navy warning read: "Execute an appropriate defensive deployment preparatory to carrying out the tasks assigned in WPL 46." The murky nature of the warning message is perhaps best demonstrated by this sentence, which has been parsed repeatedly in the historical literature. The warning's authors, it will be remembered, were Admirals Turner and Ingersoll, with the approval of Stark and the imprimatur of Roosevelt. If we turn to the authors' later explanations of the "defensive deployment" order, which may or may not have been enhanced by hindsight, we find a certain disharmony of interpretation. Ingersoll stated that the deployment order had reference mainly to the Asiatic Fleet, whose CINC, Hart, was a coaddressee along with Kimmel, and that the subtext for Hawaii was a directive to establish submarine patrols:

> I think the preparatory deployments that would not constitute provocative action and disclose strategic intention against Japan referred more to the withdrawal of certain units of the Asiatic Fleet from the China Sea area toward the southern Philippines, rather than to any particular deployment of the Pacific Fleet, with the possible exception of sending out submarines for observation.[66]

In one place, Turner defined defensive deployment as "a spreading out of forces. A naval deployment means to spread out and make ready for hostilities. To get into the best positions from which to execute the operating plans against the enemy." He continued:

> Since . . . the danger position of Hawaii was to the north, because there were no little outlying islands there from which observation would have been made . . . an appropriate deployment would have sent some fast ships, possibly with small seaplanes, up to the north to assist and possibly to cover certain sectors against approach. . . . Of course, these ships would naturally have been in considerable danger, but that was what they were there for, because fighting ships are no use unless they are in a dangerous position so that they can engage the enemy.[67]

In another place, Turner focused his explanation on what else the fleet was expected to do in its own defense:

It will be noted that the dispatch orders a defensive deployment. We expected all war scouting measures to be undertaken, submarines to be sent out to protect our Fleet and territory against enemy naval forces; we expected the carriers with their protective vessels to put to sea and stand in readiness for war; we expected, in the Asiatic, the movement of ships to be made to the South in accordance with the plan agreed on. We expected a high degree of readiness on board ships against attack of any form.[68]

Stark's explanation made no mention of the Asiatic Fleet as having been the prime addressee, or of "spreading out forces." His concern, he said, in endorsing the language used, was that Hawaii "take action against surprises." Where Kimmel was concerned, defensive deployment meant "taking a position as best he could with what he had for the defense of his fleet, whatever he had either at sea or in port, to the best of his ability and to guard against being caught unawares." "This appropriate defensive deployment was a new term to me," Kimmel stated. "I decided that what was meant was something similar to the disposition I had made on October 16, which had been approved by the originator of both these dispatches."[69] Elsewhere, Stark said that he had anticipated that Kimmel would invoke in Hawaii full readiness (which would be the fleet's Condition I) and that he would institute distant aerial reconnaissance.[70]

There are three problems with these after-the-fact explanations. The first is that we have no way of knowing, apart from the trust we place in the oaths they took before testifying, how far these officers may have read into the key phrase "defensive deployment" what, later, they thought they had meant, or even wished they had meant. These are honorable men, but Monday-morning quarterbacking tempts even the best of men. Second, their expression here of specific expectations raises once again the question, If this is what they meant, why did they not say so at the time, when it counted? Third, it should be remembered that, following the words "defensive deployment" there came the important qualifier, *"preparatory to carrying out the tasks assigned in WPL 46* [emphasis added]." Turner and Stark both stated that, under that rubric, Kimmel was expected to establish "all war scouting" (Turner), or "distant aerial reconnaissance" (Stark). But that is not what WPL-46 directed, particularly in its more detailed form, WPPac-46 (the U.S. Pacific Fleet Operating Plan, Rainbow

No. 5 [Navy Plan 0–1, Rainbow No. 5]), which was approved by Stark on 9 September 1941, and which should have been well known to all principals throughout OpNav.[71]

It would appear that, if the drafters of the 27 November Navy warning had wished Kimmel to divert from WPPac-46, they would have told him so, and in language that was not what the Italians call *sfumato*—blurry, ambiguous, and up to the imagination. But they did not. One may reasonably assume, therefore, that Kimmel was justified in holding to his original orders in the absence of any countermand. And those orders were predicated on the following time schedule:

> At the date of issue of this plan [WPPac-46], the U.S. Pacific Fleet has virtually mobilized, and is operating, with intensive security measures, from the Pearl Harbor base. It is expected, therefore, that the major portion of the Fleet can be ready for active service within four days of an order for general mobilization. To provide for the contingency of M-day [mobilization] being set prior to the date on which hostilities are to open, the day of execution of this Plan is designated throughout the Plan as W-day [Japan in the war]. The day that hostilities open with Japan will be designated J-day [Japan]. This may or may not coincide with W-day.[72]

Upon commencement of W-day (also called Phase IA) and not before, the Patrol Plane Force, designated Task Force 9, will:

(1) Having due regard for time required to overhaul and upkeep planes and for conservation of personnel, maintain maximum patrol plane search against enemy forces in the approaches to the Hawaiian area.

(2) Initially base and operate one patrol-plane squadron from Midway. At discretion increase the number of planes operating to westward of Pearl Harbor to two squadrons, utilizing Johnston and Wake as the facilities thereat and the situation at the time makes practicable. . . .

(8) Modify patrols as necessary in order to carry out tasks assigned in Marshall Raiding and Reconnaissance Plan (Annex II to Navy Plan 0–1).[73]

In the Marshall Islands plan task forces would (a) reconnoiter the Marshalls, particularly Eniwetok atoll, preparatory to a raid in force and to eventual capture; and (b) raid the Marshalls with ships and aircraft and small landing groups in order to destroy enemy mobile forces, fixed defenses, and facilities. The U.S. seaborne force would depart Pearl Harbor beginning on J-Day plus one and continuing through J-Day plus five. All elements would proceed to rendezvous at Point Tare (latitude 16 degrees north; longitude 127 degrees east), arriving on J-Day plus eleven. Beginning about J-Day plus thirteen the force would carry out the raiding plan, based on information acquired by patrol plane reconnaissance. The Patrol Plane Force (Task Force 9), leaving two squadrons (twenty-four aircraft of which twelve could be utility aircraft) at Oahu, would have advanced in "maximum practicable strength" prior to J-Day plus five to Wake, Midway, and Johnston Islands. The Wake-based aircraft would make preliminary air reconnaissance of Taongi and Bikar Atolls on J-Day plus five, and thereafter conduct search to prevent surprise attack from the westward. The Midway-based aircraft would search sectors to the southwestward of Midway to prevent surprise attack across that sector. And the Johnston-based aircraft would search along the fleet's route of advance to longitude 178 degrees west. All aircraft would be expected to make such additional air reconnaissance immediately prior to the attack as best met the existing situation. Upon completion of the raid, the patrol aircraft would be withdrawn from the advance bases, if necessary, to avoid disproportionate losses. Kimmel asserted before the JCC that "without [this air reconnaissance] the task forces might be exposed to surprise attack if they entered the dangerous Marshall area."[74]

✶

All the same, Kimmel did give consideration to mounting distant aerial reconnaissance around Oahu on 27 November. He had before him the Martin-Bellinger report of 31 March, and, no doubt, he referred again to its bleak estimate: "The aircraft at present available in Hawaii are inadequate to maintain, for any extended period"—beyond "perhaps four or five days," Bellinger would testify in May 1945[75]—"from bases on Oahu, a patrol extensive enough to ensure that an air attack from an Orange [Japanese] carrier cannot arrive over Oahu as a complete surprise." Only within those "narrow time limits" could the available PBY-3 and PBY-5 Catalinas fly outbound legs of the seven hundred nautical miles thought to be the distance required to detect a carrier before it launched its aircraft. And, even then, through unlucky timing or poor visibility, "in a dawn air attack there is a high probability," Martin and Bellinger had written, chillingly, "that [an attack] could be delivered as a complete surprise in spite of any patrols we might be using."[76]

For a complete sweep on a 360-degree arc to the maximum range of the patrollers, eighty-four aircraft would each be required to make a single flight of sixteen to eighteen hours. Since the same planes and crews could not make such a flight every day, the Navy required a fleet of 250 operational aircraft if it hoped to conduct effective reconnaissance over a protracted period. Admiral Bloch, Bellinger's immediate superior in the airman's capacity as Commander, Naval Base Defense Air Force and Commander, Patrol Wing 2, and whose responsibility it was to implement distant reconnaissance, had only *forty-nine* ready status patrol aircraft at his disposal for that purpose in the first week of December, most of which were being used for training in anticipation of the offensive combat assignments in the Marshalls raid. Kimmel stated before the JCC that, "I had been ordered, not once but twice, to be prepared to carry out the raids on the Marshalls under WPL-46, which meant the extended use of the fleet patrol planes from advanced bases in war operations."[77] For those planes spare parts were extremely scarce—many of the Catalinas on hand were grounded by cracked engine nose sections—experienced aviation machinist mates were also in short supply, and there were no spare crews. The newer PBY-5 types, ferried to Hawaii in October and November, were experiencing shakedown problems and required extensive modifications to qualify them for continuous operation, not to mention combat. Twelve older PBY-3s (of squadron VP-22) at Pearl returned from Midway on 5 December in parlous material condition; and ten of the twelve were due for overhaul. In sum, extended reconnaissance would have incapacitated many of the PBYs after just four or five days of distant scouting. Addressing the issue twelve days after the Japanese attack, Bellinger wrote in a memorandum to Kimmel that "the material situation of the patrol squadrons made the maintenance of continuous extensive daily searches impracticable. . . . Under the circumstances, it seemed advisable to continue intensive expansion training. . . . Operations by the PBY-5s was certain to result in rapid automatic attrition of the already limited number of patrol planes."[78]

In the JCC hearings, war plans chief Soc McMorris testified that, after receipt of the 27 November warning, Kimmel and his staff carefully considered the availability of flyable patrol planes, the status of training, the patrol wings' responsibility for supplying trained personnel for new squadrons, the tasks assigned the wings in WPPac-46, and the fact that, given aircraft shortages and maintenance limitations, seaward patrols would be "largely token searches." The question was one on which Kimmel and his staff had gone up and down the scale many times. The conclusion, McMorris stated, was that "training would suffer heavily and that if we were called upon to conduct a war, that we would find a large proportion of our planes needing engine overhaul at the time we most required their services." Exhaustion of crews was another consideration. Kimmel therefore decided to concentrate on expansion training until more aircraft, or more information, became available.[79]

No witness in later investigations or hearings cited a specific order given after the reconnaissance matter was deliberated upon and decided, although Bloch stated that Kimmel made his decision on 27 November.[80] For his part, Kimmel said, simply, "However, I want it clearly understood, it was my responsibility and I would give the orders to the planes."[81] The Navy court in 1944 judged that the "the mission of this reconnaissance was not due to oversight or neglect. It was the result of a military decision, reached after much deliberation and after weighing the information at hand and all the factors involved."[82] Halsey, the senior Navy air commander in the Hawaiian area, said after the war, "Any Admiral worth his stars would have made the same choice."[83]

Kimmel's critics have drawn attention to the fact that he did not share knowledge of, or consult about, the 27 November warning with Rear Admiral Bellinger, his commander of Patrol Wings 1 and 2, as though that was a serious negligence. Several observations might be made in that connection. Bellinger already had his marching orders within the narrow confines of his fourfold mission: daily reconnaissance over the operating area; training; distant reconnaissance beginning on W-Day; and departure of the wings for the Marshalls raid prior to J-Day plus five. He had rarely been engaged in broad-based executive decisions at the staff level and probably did not come to Kimmel's mind as a necessary consultant now. His remarks to Kimmel made in the memorandum of 19 December reveal that his mind was at one with Kimmel's on the inadvisability of attempting a 360-degree search over an extended period, a fact that was already well known to Kimmel, thus obviating any need for further consultation. In any event, Bloch, Bellinger's immediate superior, was in regular consultative contact with Kimmel. Finally, Bellinger was not alone among officers to whom neither the existence nor the content of the war warning was communicated by Kimmel. As the latter stated before the JCC: "[Bellinger] was not the only air man we had there. He was rear admiral in charge of this patrol wing. . . . I did not tell a great many other admirals about the war warning. I did not tell a great many other people in Hawaii about the war warning. But Admiral Bellinger was there directly under my orders, and I felt capable of giving him any orders that he required."[84]

✭

Kimmel's critics have furthermore argued that while Oahu may not have had sufficient patrol aircraft for a 360-degree search, it did have enough for an arc of lesser scope. Following the Marshall-Herron alert of June 1940, Kimmel's predecessor, Admiral Richardson, for a brief time had increased the regular training searches out of Oahu from a distance of 180 nautical miles to 300. Since only six aircraft were employed, it was only a very partial search, and, in Kimmel's view, "At no time did [Richardson] have, in my opinion, any real reconnaissance flying from Pearl Harbor that would have been successful, except by chance, in discovering an attack in time to be of any real use."[85] In his fourth endorsement to the findings of the NCI, dated 13 August 1945, Secretary James V. Forrestal expressed his opinion that "there were sufficient fleet patrol planes and crews, in fact, available in Oahu during the week preceding the attack to have flown, for at least several weeks, a daily reconnaissance covering 128 degrees to a distance of about 700 miles."[86] His opinion raises a number of questions. A 128-degree sector is just over one-third of the compass rose, but which one-third would be covered? Richardson did not cover 128 degrees but his small patrol concentrated on a sector from west to northwest. Those happened to be the sectors from which Pearl Harbor had been successfully "attacked" by air at dawn on 30 March 1938 during the U.S. Navy's Fleet Problem XIX. Two carriers, USS *Saratoga* (CV-3) and USS *Ranger* (CV-4), launched the attacking SBU-1 biplane aircraft. (USS *Lexington* [CV-2] was scheduled also to participate, but was forced to make for Honolulu when an epidemic throat infection afflicted 500 of her company.) Under the overall command of Vice Admiral Ernest J. King, commander, aircraft, Battle Force, who had broken his three-star flag in *Saratoga,* and had chosen Bellinger for his chief of staff, *Ranger* advanced on Oahu from French Frigate Shoals to west-northwestward, while *Saratoga* steamed from the northwestward behind an eastward-moving front of bad weather. *Ranger,* we know, launched at 0500. The aircraft from both carriers caught patrolling Army Air Corps aircraft at low altitudes and achieved what was declared to be a successful attack. The Navy's postproblem report concluded that "with the forces then based on Hawaii it would be impossible to defend the area."[87]

But if Kimmel had relied on that example and deployed a partial search from the west to northwest, his scout planes would have missed the Mitsubishis, Nakajimas, and Aichis that descended from due north on 7 December.[88] Prior to the Japanese attack, Kimmel, his senior air commander Halsey, and his intelligence chief Layton all expected that any air attack attempted against Oahu would be made from the Marshalls, to the southwest. If a partial search sector were designed to include the southwest, as seems likely, the patrols would have been even farther removed from due north. Of course, the sector searched daily could have been rotated around the compass rose, in a kind of Russian roulette, but such a plan as that would not have avoided the second major question: how would a maximum effort around 128 degrees have averted the physical attrition of planes and crews that undermined the full compass search? As Kimmel told the JCC: "I decided that I could not fritter away my patrol-plane resources by pushing them to the limit in daily distant searches of one sector around Oahu—which within the predictable future would have to be discontinued when the patrol planes and crews gave out.... Had I directed their use for intensive distance searches from Oahu, I faced the peril of having these planes grounded when the fleet needed them and when the war plan was executed."[89]

Some Kimmel critics have asked why he did not mount at least a narrowly conducted search employing just a few aircraft over some arguably "more dangerous sector" as a way of covering his behind in the event a Japanese attack did materialize. Kimmel anticipated that meretricious argument during the JCC hearings: "Now I might have made a token search and I might have been able to come here and say I made a token search. It was not worth anything but I made it, and therefore I am all right. I did not do that. I have never done that kind of thing, and I will not do it."[90]

Had a daily patrol been run due north to a range of seven hundred miles, what might the pilots and crews, who had no radar, been able to see with their Mark I eyeballs, even when enhanced by 7×50 binoculars? Not very much or very clearly, particularly if they did not know what to look for. Going north from Oahu there is an extensive weather belt characterized generally by low ceilings, squalls, rain, and low visibility. A Pacific region meteorologist in Honolulu told the writer that intense low pressure systems cross the area north of Oahu west to east, one after another, during December. And a meteorologist-forecaster at the National Weather Service Forecast Office at the University of Hawaii said that typical of weather systems to 600 miles north of Oahu in December are stratocumulus cloud bases of 2,000 feet, and tops of 6,000 to 7,000 feet.[91] Aircraft having to fly below 2,000-foot cloud bases would have a drastically reduced radius of visibility. Japanese pilots who participated in the attack reported later that on 6 and 7 December the skies north of Oahu were overcast. Vice Admiral David C. Richardson, USN (Ret.), longtime Navy pilot and, in his last assignment, deputy commander in chief, Pacific Fleet, has written about those latitudes in a letter:

> The areas to the north are in the tradewinds. 15 to 25 kt. wind strength is usual. Seas are normally choppy. Cumulus clouds scud. These weather factors strongly affect visibility required to see even large ships like carriers at sea. Wakes rapidly disappear. I can't begin to count the times I have searched for my carrier on return leg and suddenly spotted it looming large and near. (Nor my feeling of relief.) Widespread rain squall conditions were more to be feared than Japanese fighter pilots.[92]

We know something about the conduct of a daily intensive air search out of Oahu in this period of history, because, in the wake of the events of

7 December, distant reconnaissance was immediately undertaken there utilizing surviving patrol aircraft strength and PBY-5 as well as B-17 reinforcements that were rushed to the island from the mainland. Kimmel's replacement as CINCPAC, Admiral Nimitz, was convinced that "the attack of 7 December will be followed by others."[93] He was proved wrong in that, but the distant reconnaissance flights he commanded brought together some reliable data pertinent to what might have been attempted prior to 7 December, if Kimmel had thought the flights advisable. On 7 January 1942, Nimitz had a total force of 67 PBYs and 42 B-17s, but each day, because of maintenance and crew rest requirements, he could only send out 25 of the former and 12 of the latter. The result was that, while he had hoped to cover 360 degrees, his long-range aircraft were covering only 290 degrees to a range of 700 nautical miles. Neither the PBY-5s nor the B-17s, it turned out, could achieve a radius beyond 700 miles, with reasonable margin for safe return, while carrying bombs, as they were mandated to do under a war alert—depth charges against submarines in the case of the PBYs. The remaining 70 degrees of the compass rose was covered, inadequately, by B-18s, Vought OS2U-3 Kingfishers and VJs to distances of 200–300 miles.

Aircraft departed on search daily at 0600. The ground speed of a two-engined PBY during search averaged 100 knots, taking into account that one of the aircraft's legs, outbound or inbound, had to contend with head-winds, particularly in the northern quadrants. Average ground speed of the four-engined B-17 at low altitudes was 150 knots. Flight time per search for a PBY was 16.5 hours; that for a B-17 11.7 hours. Average radius of visibility for the PBY was 15 miles; for the B-17 25 miles. The pilot's rule of thumb was that the separation between his outbound and inbound tracks at the extremity of his range was double the distance of his visibility. If visibility was 15 miles, he would travel a 30-mile leg along the outer rim of the search perimeter before turning home to base. The divide narrowed as he approached base. In the month of January the PBY flew its last 550 miles in darkness.[94]

Applying these data to what is known of the Japanese strike force's approach to Oahu yields interesting material for speculation. It is a given that visual detection of that force on the night of 6–7 December was not possible because of darkness. But, it may be asked, could the Japanese carriers have been sighted during the *daylight* hours of the *day before,* by a patrol aircraft flying the 0-degrees (north) sector to the maximum scouting range of a PBY or B-17? The answer is dependent, of course, on the known position times of the Japanese carriers. The "Japanese Attack Plan" reconstructed from postwar U.S. military interrogations of Japanese naval officers specified that the striking force was scheduled to rendezvous for refueling and supply on 3 December at point C, latitude 42 degrees north, longitude 170 degrees west, well northwest of Oahu. The force was then to proceed from the rendezvous point southeast to point D, latitude 31 degrees north, longitude 157 degrees west, arriving at that position, about 575 nautical miles north of Oahu, at 1130 on the sixth. From that point, following a topping off of fuel tanks, the carriers would begin a sprint south down the 158 degree meridian at twenty-four knots toward a launch position at point E, latitude 25 degrees north, longitude 158 degrees west, or 230 nautical miles due north of Oahu.[95] Twilight on the sixth began at 0508, sunrise was at 0626, sunset was at 1719, twilight ended at 1838. Moonrise was at 2005.

From the tracking chart we can calculate that a PBY-5 taking off on the sixth at 0600, an average time to be "on the step" in Kaneohe Bay, and flying north along the 158 meridian at 100 knots would reach 31 degrees north, 158 degrees west at approximately 1145 on the clock while the carriers were refueling to the east outside the PBY's visibility range; though a flight along the 157-degree meridian would intercept the refueling carriers at approximately 1204. Similarly, we can calculate that a B-17 lifting off from Hickam Field at 0600 and proceeding north along the 158-degree meridian would pass west of point D at approximately 0952 when the carriers were still to the northwest outside the aircraft's twenty-five-nautical-mile visibility range; however, a flight north along the 157-degree meridian would place the B-17 within its visibility range of the still southeast-bound carriers for a window of approximately seventeen minutes, from 1010 to 1027. These positions and times are highly speculative. Assuming that the Japanese carriers lay within the PBY's average fifteen-mile radius of visibility, or the B-17's average twenty-five-mile radius, what was the likelihood of their being sighted? Weather conditions would go far in determining the answer. From Japanese aviators—the official records, including deck logs and war diaries, were largely destroyed shortly before the Japanese surrender[96]—we have partial meteorological information.

Captain Fuchida Mitsuo, who led the air attack, wrote in 1952, "We had maintained our eastward course in complete secrecy, thanks to thick, low-hanging clouds. Moreover, on 30 November, 6 and 7 December, the sea, which we feared might be rough, was calm enough for easy fueling." After a presunrise takeoff of the attacking air fleet on the seventh, Fuchida set a flight course due south at 0615. "We flew through and over the thick clouds which were at 2,000 meters [6,562 feet]. . . . But flying over the clouds we could not see the surface of the water, and, consequently, had no check on our drift."[97] From other sources we learn something about conditions before the sixth. Captain Genda Minoru, who planned the attack, and was aboard the flagship *Akagi,* told interrogators that during the passage to Hawaii the fleet "didn't expect to meet any shipping, and fog and stormy weather would impair visibility conditions, anyway."[98] A prisoner of war told U.S. interrogators that the weather was closed in until the afternoon of the fifth.[99] From interrogation of a carrier pilot U.S. intelligence learned that during the fleet's passage, at least up to 2 December, "the weather was foggy part of the time."[100] Sadao Chigusa, chief ordnance officer of the destroyer *Akigumo,* recorded in his diary that "stormy weather" had attended the fleet's passage as far as 5 December (Hawaii time).[101]

There is no report of weather conditions on the sixth as such that the writer has been able to uncover, but it is not unreasonable to assume that they generally conformed, if not to the stormy, to the cloudy conditions before the fifth and on the seventh. Any PBY patrolling the northern sector would have had to fly beneath the cloud bases, and it is problematic how much haze hampered visibility below those bases. If, instead of the PBY, a B-17 had been assigned to the northern sector on 6 December, its wider radius of visibility might have given it an edge in detecting ships below, but the B-17 would have had to fly, ponderously in its case, beneath the cloud bases. With the little observational weather evidence we have available from the period, though, on the other hand, with our general understanding today that meteorological conditions north of Oahu are usually marginal, particularly in winter, perhaps the most that one can say is that, if Kimmel had in fact ordered distant air reconnaissance over the sector north of Oahu, the flight crews may likely not have sighted the Japanese carriers; and that one may reasonably agree with what Martin and Bellinger concluded in their estimate of 31 August: namely, that in a dawn attack (certainly where the northern sector was concerned) there was "a high probability that [it] could be delivered as a complete surprise in spite of any patrols we might be using."[102]

★

If, as Kimmel argued, and, as he said, Washington plainly knew, he could not both conduct a distant air search *and* have his patrol planes ready in "maximum practicable number" to undertake their first wartime missions in the Marshalls raid, was there *no other means* he might have seized upon to post sentinels around his perimeter? There was, in fact, such a means, and it dated from the age of sail, when it acquired the name *picket ship*. Technologically inferior to aircraft, of course, in speed and coverage, and likely to be destroyed by the enemy it detected, the picket ship did have a justifiable use in modern times, which can be expressed in the maxim: *in extremis extrema tenenda sunt*.[103] While Kimmel may not have thought he could spare his task force vessels for sentry duty, he and Bloch had other vessels at their disposal that could have been deployed for that duty, including submarines. Those other vessels sat low on the water, thus would have limited radius of vision, but they still had the practical potential of sighting by chance a carrier's tall island on the horizon. Fleet-type submarines could cover 7,000 to 10,000 nautical square miles per day: with brackets on the periscope shears (supports) they could place eyes thirty-five feet above water. Even so, the small number of vessels and the marginal vision they provided meant that only a comparatively few sectors could be covered, such as the north and the south.

Kimmel had been urged to deploy small surface vessels to the northward and southward by Stark as early as 10 February. Warning him that "in view of the inadequacy of the Army defenses, the responsibility . . . must rest upon the fleet for its own protection while in Pearl Harbor," Stark went on in the same communication to propose the following expedient:

> It is noted that no provision is made in the Local Defense Force plans of the Fourteenth Naval District for the employment of vessels as a part of an aircraft warning net in the waters to the northward and southward of Oahu. It is suggested that in coordinating the plans of the Commander-in-Chief, U.S. Pacific Fleet, and the Commandant, Fourteenth Naval District, this matter be given consideration. It is

possible that large sampans equipped with radio might prove useful for this purpose during the war.[104]

The Hawaiian "sampan" was a flat-bottomed skiff, built along oriental lines, propelled by a diesel engine, and, because of its sea-keeping capability, widely used on prolonged cruising in the Hawaiian fishery. Crewed by Hawaiian Japanese, the sampan fleet was based at Kewalo Basin, about twelve miles from Pearl Harbor. The vessel's use proposed here as a naval picket boat was not as far-fetched as might be thought by modern readers. One has only to remember the Japanese use of small fishing vessels in a picket boat line positioned 600–700 nautical miles east of their home islands on 18 April 1942, the date of Lieutenant Colonel James H. Doolittle's B-25 bombing raid on Tokyo and other Japanese cities. The U.S. Navy task force, including the carrier USS *Hornet,* from which the bombers were to be launched, was sighted by a picket boat while still 650 nautical miles from Japan. The task force twice changed course, but another outlier was encountered after each alteration. The pickets got off their sighting reports. It then became necessary to launch immediately, though the plan had been to launch at 500 miles distance. This meant both that the attack, scheduled to take place at night, had to be made during daylight and that the air crews, forced to fly 150 additional miles, risked not having enough fuel to make landing fields in China.[105]

On 21 December 1945, before the JCC, Admiral Turner testified as follows:

> We informed—the Chief of Naval Operations informed—the Commander-in-Chief of the Pacific Fleet in at least three official communications during 1941 that it would be desirable to use ships to the northward and on one occasion to the southward of Hawaii for detecting approaching raiders, in addition to the use of airplanes, and we had endeavored to get small craft to send out and be on look-outs. One of these letters suggests the use of five sampans that had just been condemned [legally appropriated for public use under the right of eminent domain] by a court out there and the use of yachts which we were trying to get to them.[106]

Kimmel had still other craft that might have proved useful as pickets, and, together with the sampans, should have been numerous enough to guard sectors to the northward and southward, as recommended by Stark.

These were five submarines, four old destroyers, four small minesweepers, three Coast Guard cutters, the gunboat USS *Sacramento* (PG-19), one net vessel, one gate vessel, two self-propelled oil lighters, and twelve tugs.[107] Of the last-named Ingersoll wrote on 13 August to Kimmel that "should the fleet leave, [they] might be used for patrol purposes."[108] One is reminded of what Samuel Eliot Morison said about the Navy's (Admiral King's) costly delay in deploying a coastal picket patrol composed of small craft to detect German U-boats off the U.S. East Coast in 1942: "More of the Dunkirk spirit, 'throw in everything you have,' would not have been amiss."[109] When in the JCC hearings, on 21 December 1945, Kimmel's picket boat assets were discussed by Senator Homer Ferguson (R., Mich.) and Admiral Turner, the following exchange took place:

> Senator Ferguson: Why didn't we use those then?
> Admiral Turner: I do not know, sir.[110]

Kimmel's comment on surface distant reconnaissance, made before the Army Board in 1944, was laconic: "The use of surface craft for distant reconnaissance against an air attack would have required so many ships that their use was considered entirely impracticable for this purpose."[111] The NCI in the same year concluded, somewhat moralistically:

> Neither surface ships nor submarines properly may be employed to perform this duty, even if the necessary number is available. . . . A defensive deployment of surface ships and submarines over an extensive sea area as a means of continuously guarding against a possible attack from an unknown quarter and at an unknown time, is not sound military procedure either in peace or in war.[112]

But in extremis?
It worked for the Japanese.

★

What Kimmel *did* do after receipt of the 27 November warning dispatch was the following: He maintained in force the tightened readiness measures he had taken after the 16 October warning. He issued new orders for "full security measures" to be taken by ships in operating areas and at sea.[113] In Pearl

Harbor proper he and Bloch warned all antisubmarine patrol forces to take additional security measures against submarines.[114] He issued orders to the fleet to "exercise extreme vigilance" against submarines in operating areas and to depth-charge all contacts expected to be hostile in the fleet operating areas.[115] He gave the depth-charge order despite Stark's previous resistance, dating from 23 September, to such an order. Stark had told Kimmel that "if conclusive, and I repeat conclusive, evidence is obtained that Japanese submarines are actually in or near United States territory," a "strong warning" should be sent to Japan. But Kimmel decided on his own to give the "bomb on contact" order, and so informed Stark, who made no reply.[116] (There would be no *conclusive* evidence until 7 December.) "The Pearl Harbor operating area was some 2,000 miles from the nearest Japanese possession," Kimmel reasoned. "I knew that if we sent any submarines into a Japanese operating area they wouldn't hesitate a moment to bomb them."[117] Kimmel's estimate of Japanese intentions after receipt of the 27 November dispatch was that if an attack was made against the Philippines, then

> there was a very good chance that a mass submarine attack would occur in the Hawaiian area. I thought an air attack was still a remote possibility, and I did not expect an air attack to be made on Pearl Harbor at this time due to the tenor of the dispatches, the other information available to me, the difficulties of making such an attack, and the latest information I had from the Navy Department and other sources was that the greater portion of the carrier forces were located in home waters.[118]

He issued orders for Task Forces 8 (departing 28 November) and 12 (departing 5 December) taking Marine F4F fighters 2,004 nautical miles to Wake and 1,300 miles to Midway, respectively, to conduct en route morning and afternoon air searches out to 300 miles from their positions for any sign of hostile shipping. Thus, Kimmel *did* have distant air reconnaissance in the western and northwestern sectors, and to a greater distance than could have been achieved by patrol planes based on Oahu. Furthermore, he ordered a patrol plane squadron to proceed from Midway to Wake and to search the ocean en route; and while at Wake, to search varying sectors on 2 and 3 December to a distance of 525 miles. He ordered another squadron from Oahu to replace the squadron that went from Midway to Wake. It proceeded by way of Johnston Island, 700 miles to the southwest, making a reconnaissance sweep along both legs. After reaching Midway, that squadron flew distant searches of varying sectors of not less than 500 miles on 3, 4, 5, and 6 December. On the seventh, five of that squadron's PBYs were searching the sector from 120 to 170 degrees from Midway to a distance of 450 miles. Another two PBYs of that squadron flew a sweep on the seventh while rendezvousing with the *Lexington* 400 miles from Midway. Four others remained at Midway, each loaded with depth charges, on ten-minute notice.[119] As Kimmel testified before the JCC:

> In the week before December 7, these reconnaissance sweeps of the patrol plane squadrons moving from Midway to Wake; from Pearl Harbor to Johnston and from Johnston to Midway; from Wake to Midway and Midway to Pearl Harbor, covered a total distance of nearly 5,000 miles. As they proceeded, each squadron would cover a 400-mile strand of ocean along its path. They brought under the coverage of air search about 2,000,000 square miles of ocean area.[120]

At the same time, on and after 27 November, Kimmel maintained surface patrols of varying ocean sectors by two submarines out of Wake and two out of Midway.[121]

Nor were the PBYs on Oahu standing idle. In addition to daily employment in expansion training, PBYs flew scout training missions on 1, 2, 3, and 4 December northward and northwestward of Oahu to a distance of about 400 miles. While these flights did not constitute distant reconnaissance as such, it is worth remarking that they exceeded in distance the flights conducted by Admiral Richardson after the Marshall-Herron alert of 1940. On the fifth, the PBYs held ground arming drills with live bombs. On the sixth and seventh the PBYs that flew the scout training missions were down for maintenance and upkeep, "in order not to depreciate the material readiness of the planes," said Lt. Comdr. (in 1941) Logan Ramsey, who drew up the wing tactical exercises for Patrol Wing 2.[122] Moreover, since 15 November and continuing each day of the week preceding the Japanese attack, including the seventh, three PBYs flew a dawn patrol over the operating area south of Oahu.[123] Lifting off the water at Kaneohe Bay at just after 0600, the Catalinas each flew, with tanks topped off with 1,000 gallons of gasoline, with two depth charges on wing racks, and with all machine guns armed, pie-shaped sectors over the fleet operating area south of Oahu to a distance of 300 miles.[124] It was on the dawn patrol flown on the seventh, as will be shown, that Catalina 14P1 sighted and attacked a Japanese submarine. In addition, on the morning of the seventh, four other Catalinas were near Lahaina Roads off Maui Island to the east conducting exercises with U.S. submarines in inter-type tactics for communication and recognition.

Finally, Kimmel activated certain features of the Joint Coastal Frontier Defense Plan, including an inshore and offshore patrol of the immediate Oahu perimeter by ship; activation of the harbor control post; deployment of sonobuoys to detect enemy submarines; operation of torpedo nets at the entrance to Pearl Harbor and Honolulu; and daily sweeping of channels. Furthermore, beginning 30 November, he kept and updated a daily memorandum entitled "Steps to be taken in case of American-Japanese war within the next 24 hours." (The last issue of the preparedness memorandum, dated 6 December, was presented to the JCC on 15 January 1946.) And he directed his war plans officer Soc McMorris, to draw up a memorandum of "Recommended steps to be taken in case of American-Japanese War within the next forty-eight hours" (completed on 5 December).[125]

✳

Meanwhile, a confident United States citizenry, including the millions who did not know the location or even the name of Pearl Harbor, basked in the knowledge of America's oceanic remoteness from the fields and seas of battles then raging. Where Japan was concerned, many in the Midwest read approvingly an editorial in the *Chicago Tribune*, which held:

> What vital interests of the United States can Japan threaten? She cannot attack us. That is a military impossibility. Even our base at Hawaii is beyond the effective striking force of her Fleet.[126]

CLIMB NIITAKAYAMA

Our objective lies more than three thousand miles away. In attacking this large fleet concentration it is to be expected that countless difficulties will be encountered in preserving the absolute security of the plans. If these plans should fail at any stage, our Navy will suffer the wretched fate of never being able to rise again. The success of our surprise attack on Pearl Harbor will prove to be the Waterloo of the war to follow.

Rear Admiral Ugaki Matome
Chief of Staff, Combined Fleet

When in April 1941 Onishi Takijiro and Genda Minoru presented their analysis of the Pearl Harbor attack proposal to its author, Admiral Yamamoto Isoruku, it was considered by the C-in-C, Combined Fleet alongside analyses undertaken independently by his own staff. Taking the two analyses together, we find in them two propositions that would be deleted before adoption of a final plan: (1) that not one but repeated raids should be mounted against Pearl Harbor in order to secure a thorough crippling effect; and (2) that landings should be made on Oahu for the purpose of capturing all or as many as possible of the U.S. naval officers at Pearl. Yamamoto made a few amendments in the Onishi-Genda analysis and, sometime in April, ordered it to be sent to the Naval General Staff for their reaction.

While awaiting staff response, Yamamoto proceeded to move from analysis to a formal plan of operations. To draw up that plan he appointed four study groups headed by a brilliant and eccentric senior staff officer, Captain Kuroshima Kameto. Working naked at his desk (the flagship *Nagato* lacked air conditioning), chain-smoking and burning incense through an intense period of intellectual labor, Kuroshima produced a document that Yamamoto could take to the Naval General Staff at the end of April. There it met with serious resistance and lay fallow for several months. On 7 August Yamamoto sent Kuroshima himself to argue the plan's virtues before the General Staff, but staff members were unmoved. First, the staff wanted the Combined Fleet to be kept under *its* control, not the obverse; and second, staff members thought that Yamamoto's operation was far too much of a gamble. Even if a striking force were to approach Oahu successfully and without detection, what guarantee was there that the American fleet would be in the harbor on the day chosen? Kuroshima did win one concession: that the Navy's annual map maneuvers at the War College be moved from November (sometimes December) to September, and that a special section be devoted to the Pearl Harbor problem. That would enable the operation, if approved, to proceed before adverse weather conditions occurred in the North Pacific, if that was selected as the preferred route, which would make the passage impossible.

Also in August, an unusual order arrived at the desk of Lt. Comdr. Fuchida Mitsuo, a newly promoted staff member in the Third Carrier Division. It directed him to return to the carrier *Akagi,* from which he had just been transferred, and to reassume the lower-ranking duties of a flight commander. His puzzlement was relieved when, on board his old carrier, he was let in on the still very secret plan to bomb Pearl Harbor, and told that he would lead the attacking air fleet. Placed in charge of training the air crews of all participating carriers, Fuchida created a series of "near-combat" exercises in Kagoshima Bay, where the topography happened to resemble that at Pearl Harbor, but in which no secrets would be revealed, since, so far as his aviators were aware, Kagoshima could represent a foreign harbor anywhere in the Far East, such as Singapore. There, for many weeks, the carrier pilots unknowingly simulated the attacks they would make at Pearl Harbor only months later in December.[1]

In suburban Tokyo, on Meguro Street, a few minutes walk from the Meguro railway station, stood the four-story black building of the Naval

War College. There, in a sealed room on the east wing, thirty carefully selected Combined Fleet commanders and staff members gathered on 2 September to begin tabletop map maneuvers, or "war games," to test the feasibility of the Hawaiian Operation. The officers were organized into three teams, designated "N" (Nippon), "A" (America), and "E" (England). When the exercises were completed, on 13 September, it was judged that four U.S. Navy capital ships had been sunk and one seriously damaged, two carriers were sunk and one damaged, six cruisers were sunk or damaged, and 180 aircraft were shot down. But Japanese losses had also been heavy, including one *Akagi*-class carrier and one *Soryu*-class carrier sunk, and two slightly damaged, as well as 127 aircraft shot down. The amphibious landing and capture proposition was rejected because of insuperable logistical problems. The other results and the collected written materials were delivered to Yamamoto's flagship, *Nagato*, then anchored at Hashirajima, the anchorage of Kure.[2]

Opposition to the plan mounted among both task force command staffs and members of the Naval General Staff. The commanders of the First and Second Air Fleets, Vice Admiral Nagumo Chuichi and Vice Admiral Kondo Nobutake, respectively, sent written messages to Yamamoto urging him to abandon the plan. It was Nagumo who eventually would command the Pearl Harbor Striking Force. Two other officers carried their objections personally to Yamamoto—Rear Admiral Kusaka Ryunosuke, chief of staff to Nagumo, Commander of the First Air Fleet; and Rear Admiral Onishi Takijiro, who occupied the same position with the Eleventh Air Fleet. Onishi, the reader will remember, was the first line officer to whom Yamamoto had confided his plan, in the previous January; on that review he had given the plan a 60 percent chance of success. After the two officers expressed their views, Yamamoto is purported to have replied:

> But what would you do if, while we were engaged in the South Pacific, the U.S. Fleet launched air raids on Japan from the east? Are you suggesting that it's all right for Tokyo and Osaka to be burned to the ground so long as we get hold of oil? Still, the fact is I'm determined that so long as I'm C. in C. we shall go ahead with the Hawaiian raid. I'm sure there'll be many things that are difficult for you, or go against the grain, but I'm asking you to proceed with preparations on the positive assumption that the raid is on.[3]

With this and other arguments plus a full display of his not inconsiderable charm and powers of persuasion, the C-in-C overcame his visitors' objections and, as they departed the gangway, won their pledges of support. During 9–14 October, Yamamoto conducted tactical war games on board *Nagato,* and upon their completion, with all the ships assigned to the Striking Force assembled in the western sector of the Inland Sea (an inlet of the Pacific in southeastern Japan, extending 240 miles between Honshu on the north and Shikoku and Kyushu on the south), he had all the commanding officers of ships and aircraft brought together to receive a detailed briefing on the raid. Many of the officers present were hearing of it for the first time. To command the Striking Force Yamamoto had named Nagumo, who had opposed the operation. He was an unlikely choice for another reason: though commander of the First Air Fleet, he had only marginal experience in aviation. He won the command through seniority, Yamamoto's request to have the command himself having been rejected by the Naval General Staff.

Now all that remained was to receive the approval of that staff. Yamamoto dispatched Kuroshima again to staff headquarters in Tokyo armed with the latest operational draft and a personal written message from the C-in-C stating, in essence, that he was no less determined at that date to make the surprise attack on Hawaii, and that he would stake his rank and position on bringing it off. Impressed by Yamamoto's confidence, Chief of Staff Admiral Nagano Osami decided to give the operation a green light. Rear Admiral Fukudome Shigero, who had been Yamamoto's chief of staff until the preceding April and, in that capacity, had given the plan only a 40 percent chance of success, and was now on the naval staff as chief of the First Division, was present when Nagano said, "If he has that much confidence, it's better to let Yamamoto go ahead." The only condition the chief imposed was a requirement that the Striking Force turn back at once if it suffered a setback en route, such as premature discovery by the enemy, an on-board explosion, or an inability to refuel from tankers owing to high seas.

When the new Navy minister, Admiral Shimada Shigetaro, who had sought every means of avoiding war with the United States and who would have preferred that the United States struck the first blow so that Japan could declare war with honor, also, and reluctantly, came on board, the

Naval General Staff sought the additional support of the chief of the Army General Staff. The Army's endorsement was necessary for the plan to be advanced to the level of the Imperial General Headquarters, which alone could approach Hirohito for the Emperor's sanction. The Army came approved, and the imperial sanction was received on 5 November.[4]

Contrary to the conventional historical view of Hirohito as an enigmatic, passive, and generally benign monarch who was duped by his ultranationalist military chiefs, the "divine" descendant of Emperor Mutsuhito (1867–1912), known after death as "Meiji the Great," was in fact an active driving agent in Japanese war-making from Manchuria in 1931 through Pearl Harbor to final ignominious defeat in 1945.[5] In the latter part of 1941 the Emperor took a direct role in promoting the military's preparations for war and in establishing a deadline for negotiations with Washington. Of the Hawaii Operation he said, approvingly, "This surprise attack operation, comparable to the Battle of Okehazama [a feudal-period battle in central Honshu, Japan, in 1560], is extremely bold. Of course its success will largely depend on the luck of the battle. However, so long as the enemy fleet is anchored there on the day of the attack, it is possible to sink two or three battleships and aircraft carriers."[6] On 5 November Admiral Nagano gave the Emperor a detailed briefing on the Imperial Navy Operations Plan for War Against the United States, Britain, and the Netherlands. It was at that audience, Hirohito's most recent biographer states, that "Hirohito gave the final go-ahead to attack Pearl Harbor."[7]

On the same day, Imperial Navy General Staff Order No. 1 was issued to Yamamoto "by Imperial Order":

1. The Empire has decided to schedule various operational preparations for completion in the early part of December in view of great fears that she will be obliged to go to war with the United States, Britain, and the Netherlands for her self-existence and self-defense.
2. The Commander-in-Chief Combined Fleet will make necessary operational preparations.
3. Detailed instructions will be given by the Chief of the Naval General Staff.[8]

Under the same date, but actually not until 8 November, Yamamoto issued his own Combined Fleet Top Secret Operation Order No. 1, which showed that the fleet was *already* prepared not only for the Hawaii but also for the Southern Operation, as well as for further operations (Phase Two) to consolidate victories in those two theaters. The extraordinary order, 100 pages in length, had been drafted by the indefatigable Kuroshima, who explained its comprehensive nature by saying that he believed "an order should . . . include all potential operations."[9] The Naval General Staff printed 700 copies of the order, but, save in the original, *omitted* the Hawaii Operation.[10] Only in one known fragment of that original do we have language about Pearl Harbor:

1. The Task Force will launch a surprise attack at the outset of war upon the U.S. Pacific Fleet supposed to be in Hawaiian waters, and destroy it.
2. The Task Force will reach the designated stand-by point for the operation in advance.
3. The date of starting the operation is tentatively set forth as December 8 [Japan time; December 7 Hawaii time], 1941.[11]

✶

Being prepared for combat did not mean, however, that aerial bombing performance had been brought to concert pitch, at least in Yamamoto's estimation. One day late in October, having learned of Yamamoto's dissatisfaction from Combined Fleet air staff officer Comdr. Sasaki Akira, Fuchida went personally to see the C-in-C on board *Nagato*. There he reviewed the air training to date in Kagoshima Bay and proposed to Yamamoto that demonstration maneuvers be conducted in Saeki Bay utilizing all six carriers dedicated to the Pearl Harbor mission. Yamamoto agreed, pointing out that he wanted to see the aircraft drop their bombs or torpedoes not at safe distances from but within close proximity to their targets. Accordingly, four days of maneuvers were laid on for 4–7 November. In four groups—dive-bombers, torpedo bombers, horizontal bombers, and fighters—the aircraft displayed their newly acquired skills in mock attacks on Saeki, in northern Kyushu, which served as Pearl Harbor. Yamamoto pronounced himself satisfied.[12]

But there was one problem affecting the torpedo bombers that remained unresolved. Though they were now pressing their attacks close in to their targets, the torpedo-bomber pilots were achieving a disturbingly low percentage of hits. Part of the reason, it was decided, was the tendency of the torpedoes, when dropped, to plunge too deep in the water before ascending to their programmed attack depth, 13 to 20 feet. The water depth at Pearl Harbor was only 30 feet, except in the channels, where it was 45 feet. The successful British aerial torpedo attacks at Taranto had generally been made in depths of 84 to 90 feet, with a few runs made at 66 to 72 feet. The Japanese studied the site and took photographs, but Genda said after the war that Taranto had had no influence on the Japanese tactics for Pearl Harbor.[13] Unless some modifications were made to the Japanese torpedoes it was certain that they would dive uselessly into the muck at shallow Pearl. This had been one of the two chief concerns about the raid expressed by Onishi in April.

The principal expedient devised by Japanese engineers to prevent that happening was the attachment of extended wooden fins to four metal horizontal and vertical tail fins of the Type 91 aerial torpedo ("Thunder-fish") then in use. The four other tail fins were left as they were. When the torpedo was dropped by an aircraft, the function of the wooden fin extensions was to "catch" the surface of the water and thus retard the torpedo's plunge, before breaking away. Similar, though smaller, breakaway wooden fins were affixed to two antiroll stabilizer fins that protruded from the aft upper body of the weapon. After an initial, relatively shallow dive, the modified torpedo assumed a specifically programmed depth, usually 13 to 20 feet, the latter depth designed to place its 452-pound warhead below a warship's armor belt. Once launched, the torpedo became an independent, self-propelled submarine, with guidance system, engine, propellers, rudders, and hydroplanes, which steered itself to immolation against the pilot's target. The minimum run underwater required to arm the contact pistol (detonator) was about 650 feet, which was well suited to Pearl Harbor's narrow waters. In tests of three such Modification 2 torpedoes, one hit bottom at 12 meters (39.3 feet), but the other two made successful runs to target. On that basis Fuchida estimated that, out of the 40 drops planned for, 27 Thunderfish would hit home. (In the actual attack, there were 36 successful drops, of which 25 scored hits; 11 others missed, malfunctioned, or bore into the muck; four met unknown fates.)

Still one more refinement was required, and that was finding what should be the pilot's correct altitude, airspeed, and trim for making the drop. Sometime during the period 11–13 November the answers were found and the success rate in hits climbed to 82 percent.[14] It was a tactic worked out just in time, since to make an aerial torpedo attack at Pearl Harbor on 8 December (7 December in Hawaii), carriers would have to depart by 26 November (25 November in Hawaii). The importance of all these operational advances may be measured by the fact that by far the most significant damage received by the Pacific Fleet's capital ships on 7 December was inflicted by torpedo action.

✱

Why, then, did Admiral Kimmel not have his battleships protected against such attacks by torpedo baffles, or nets, extended out from and down ships' sides that faced the water, in order to deflect torpedoes from ships' hulls? There were reasons. The nets would interfere with ship movements inside the harbor, and their time-consuming removal would substantially delay an emergency sortie out the channel. Such nets had not been provided the fleet and Pearl Harbor had no facilities for manufacturing them. The most important reason was that Kimmel and his staff believed that any torpedoes launched in Pearl's shallow water would dive steeply and bury themselves in the muck before hitting their targets. They had been encouraged in that view by CNO Stark, writing to Kimmel on the preceding 15 February:

> Consideration has been given to the installation of A/T baffles within Pearl Harbor for protection against torpedo plane attacks. It is considered that the relatively shallow depth of water limits the need for anti-torpedo nets in Pearl Harbor. In addition the congestion and the necessity for maneuvering room limit the practicability of the present type of baffles. . . .
>
> A minimum depth of water of seventy-five feet may be assumed necessary to successfully drop torpedoes from planes. One hundred and fifty feet of water is desired. The maximum height planes at present experimentally drop torpedoes is 250 feet. Launching speeds are between 120 and 150 knots. Desirable height for dropping is sixty feet or less. About two hundred yards of torpedo run is necessary before the exploding device is armed, but this may be altered.[15]

In the JCC hearings, Kimmel was asked to read aloud an additional passage from Stark's letter:

> Kimmel (reading): As a matter of interest the successful attacks at Taranto were made at very low launching heights at reported ranges by the individual aviators of 400 to 1,300 yards from the battleships, but the depths of water in which the torpedoes were launched were between 14 and 15 fathoms.
> Chairman: That is 90 feet?
> Kimmel: Yes, sir.[16]

Stark's letter concluded with a comment on A/T nets (baffles), which he described as very expensive and extremely heavy. The anchors and moorings took up about 250 yards of space perpendicular to the line of the net and required a long time to lay. He acknowledged the need for deployment of a light and efficient net that could quickly be laid out and removed, and expressed his hope that such a net would become available "in the near future."[17] But no such net was made available before 7 December, indicating, we may assume, Stark's continuing view that torpedo bombers should be of no concern at Pearl.

Arriving by Clipper, Stark's letter was read by Kimmel on 8 March; after which, as the CINCPAC routing sheet shows, it was read by his staff, one of whom, Gunnery Officer Kitts, made this notation: "From considerations listed in letter, it appears Pearl Harbor does not need nets."[18] When a companion letter from Stark arrived for Bloch, it, too, was passed through Kimmel's staff. Aviation Officer Davis commented on the routing slip: "Remember Taranto! I don't think Pearl Harbor need worry, however— too shallow."[19] On 12 and 20 March, respectively, Kimmel and Bloch replied to Stark, concurring with his judgments, Bloch expressing a particular concern: "Most of the available berths are located close aboard the main ship channels, which are crossed by cable and pipe lines as well as ferry routes. The installation of baffles for the fleet moorings would have to be so extensive that most of the entire channel area would be restricted."[20]

On 13 June, however, a modification of his earlier judgments was sent by Stark to commandants of the various districts, including Bloch's Fourteenth, with a copy to Kimmel. In it Stark reported recent developments permitting torpedoes to be launched in water considerably less than seventy-five feet deep, and to make excellent runs. "Hence," he wrote, "it can not be assumed that any capital ship or other valuable vessel is safe when at anchor . . . if surrounded by water at a sufficient distance to permit . . . a sufficient run to arm the torpedo." Then, as was often his wont, he diluted that caution with a qualifier: "It may be assumed that depth of water will be one of the factors considered by any attacking force, and an attack launched in relatively deep water (10 fathoms [60 feet] or more) is much more likely."[21]

In his fourth endorsement (critical of Kimmel) to the findings of the NCI in 1944, Secretary of the Navy James V. Forrestal stated:

> The records of the Navy Department indicate that in April 1941 there was circulated in the Department an Intelligence Report which described the demonstration of an aerial torpedo in England. It appears from this report that the torpedo described was equipped with special wings, and that it required no greater depth of water for its successful launching than the depth at which it made its normal run. It further appears from the records of the Navy Department that the British report aircraft torpedo attacks during the year 1940 in which torpedoes were successfully launched in 42 feet of water.[22]

The last of Forrestal's three sentences makes reference to a British periodical summary entitled "Naval Aircraft," No. CB 3053 (1), which summarized operations for the period ending 20 September 1940. Included were descriptions of British aerial torpedo attacks at sea on the German battle cruiser *Scharnhorst*, the Vichy French battle cruisers *Strasbourg* and *Dunkerque*, at Oran, and the battleship *Richelieu* at Dakar. In the attack on *Richelieu* in July 1940, the report stated that, "the charted depth was only 7 fathoms [42 feet]." This report, received in the Navy Department on 21 June 1941, was not sent on to Kimmel.[23] Forrestal's first two sentences probably refer to one of three U.S. Navy intelligence reports, the first dated 15 May 1941, the second 26 June 1941, and the third 5 September 1941. All three describe the operational British 18-inch, 42-knot Mark XII aerial torpedo fitted with glider wings. In an official enumeration of intelligence reports on aerial torpedoes received at the Navy Department, none is listed as having been dated at or received in April 1941.[24]

The May document identifies the new torpedo as the Mark I TORA, and gives this general description:

> The TORA consists of a normal aircraft torpedo with air rudders removed and fitted with wings and tailplane. A gyroscopic unit applies aileron in response to deviation in roll and yaw so that after release the tora glides in an approx. straight path, at an angle of about 1 in 5 and at about a constant speed unit [until?] it strikes the water. It is thus possible to drop a torpedo from heights above those in use for release of ordinary torpedoes and at a considerable range from the target.
>
> To avoid damage to the torpedo and disturbance of its water path it is necessary to jettison the wings and tailplane just prior to entering the water. To effect this a paravane is towed below the tora and on striking the water operates a quick release mechanism.[25]

There follows a fifteen-page highly technical description of TORA components, attachments, rigging sequence, and so on. Nowhere, however, is mention made of the water depth required, the depth to which the TORA dived upon reaching water, or the length of run needed to arm the warhead. An official Navy Department document prepared in 1945 or 1946 specifies: "There is no evidence that the report or enclosure was sent to C. in C. U.S. [Kimmel]."[26]

The second intelligence report, dated 26 June, describes the same aerial torpedo but under two new names, Paratorp and Torraplane. By this date two squadrons of Beaufort bombers had been equipped with the weapon. Here it is stated that the torpedo "enters the water at 9 degrees incidence" [9 degrees to the horizontal] and will "reach the proper depth without driving too deeply or broaching to, when dropped from an airplane." Again, the report reads, the torpedo "would enter the water smoothly without ricochet or danger of striking the bottom."[27] The oblique angle of entry "is controlled by means of wooden air rudders fixed to the horizontal rudders of the torpedo, which are in turn actuated by a servo motor within the torpedo itself." The additional information contained in the foregoing sentence is drawn from the third intelligence report, originating with the U.S. naval attaché in Ottawa, Canada, which was based on conversations held with RCAF flying officers in aerial torpedo squadrons, and received in the Navy Department on 8 September. Again, no precise numbers are given for the initial depth reached after entry, but normally the depth setting, rather than placed for impact against the hull, is deeper than the draft of the target vessel both as a means of circumventing a torpedo net and for the purpose of placing the torpedo's electromagnetic Duplex pistol type of detonator below the ship's hull, where the change in magnetic field generated by the hull activates the detonator.[28]

The last two of the three intelligence reports cited above *were* sent to Admiral Kimmel, according to Navy Department records.[29] If they were read at Pearl it would seem that the fact that the British had succeeded in dampening the initial dive of an aerial torpedo would have been picked up by somebody and would have set alarm bells ringing in Kimmel's staff offices, for the Japanese arguably could do the same. But later staff testimony makes no mention of the British breakthrough. That of fleet gunnery officer Kitts on 21 August 1944 may stand for the rest:

> My views were that the particular kind of aircraft attack, namely, by torpedoes, was possible in Pearl Harbor. In that, we had considered counter-measures, such as nets and balloon barrages. The feeling in general in my own mind was that the feasibility of a successful torpedo attack in Pearl Harbor—to my mind, that was minimized by the receipt of information copies of one or two letters addressed by the Chief of Naval Operations to the District Commandant [Bloch], indicating to me that the water at Pearl Harbor was so shallow that the success of a torpedo attack on ships in Pearl Harbor was dubious. Nets were considered. The difficulty of procuring these nets, on which there was a low priority, and the need of moving the fleet on short notice from berths for a sortie, the difficulties of cluttering up the harbor with these nets—it was my understanding that all these factors placed the nets not only in a low priority, but gave us a feeling that the risk of a successful torpedo attack was slight.[30]

Kimmel and Bloch, too, make no mention at the time or later of any familiarity they had with aerial torpedo launching advances such as those recounted above. Indeed, in October 1945, while preparing his testimony to be given in the JCC hearings, Kimmel wrote to CNO King asking to see, as though for the first time, the intelligence report on British aerial torpedo developments to which Secretary Forrestal made reference in his fourth endorsement to the NCI findings.[31] Subsequently, two of the reports discussed above (15 May 1941 and 5 September 1941) were sent by messenger to Kimmel, who had a temporary office in the Navy Department.[32] The discontinuity of information here—Navy Department records that indicate certain torpedo reports were sent to Kimmel, despite the seeming ignorance of the existence of those same reports on the part of Kimmel and his staff—leaves the student of these events in an uncertain mind. The question of what Kimmel and his staff knew about aerial torpedo advances in 1941 and when they knew it must be answered at this date by acknowledging that we simply cannot say.

Of one thing we may be certain: in later years, Kimmel understood thoroughly how decisive the breakthrough in torpedo delivery during 1941 had been. In an aide-mémoire dated 15 August 1945, he wrote: "The fact that the Japanese aerial torpedoes could be launched in less than 40' of water and make successful runs was unquestionably a considerable factor in the Japanese decision to make the attack on the fleet at Pearl Harbor."[33]

✶

On 7 November Admiral Yamamoto ordered all ships assigned to the Hawaiian Operation to depart their various anchorages on or about the fifteenth and to proceed as single vessels or in small formations to rendezvous in isolated Tankan (Hitokappu Wan) Bay, Etorofu Island, in the northern Kuriles, arriving no later than the twenty-second. On the same day, Yamamoto issued Combined Fleet Top Secret Operation Order No. 2, implementing Order No. 1 and establishing 8 December (7 December Hawaii time) as "Y" Day—the approximate date for the commencement of operations. An Imperial Naval Order issued by the Imperial General Headquarters on 2 December would confirm Yamamoto's No. 2 and declare 8 December to be "X" Day—the exact date on which the raid on Hawaii would be made: "The hostile actions against the United States of America shall commence on 8 December."[34] The provisional date ("Y") and the finally determined date ("X") proved to be one and the same.

The fleet that assembled in Tankan Bay consisted of, for aerial attack: the Navy's six first-line carriers, *Akagi* (flagship) and *Kaga* (1st CV Division), *Soryu* and *Hiryu* (2nd CV Div.), and *Zuikaku* and *Shokaku* (5th CV Div.); for guard and support: battleships *Hiei* and *Kirishima* (3rd BB Div.)

and heavy cruisers *Tone* and *Chikuma* (8th CA Div.); for guard and escort: light cruiser *Abukuma* and destroyers *Tanikaze, Urakaze, Isokaze, Hamakaze, Akigumo* (17th DD Div.), *Kasumi, Arare, Kagero,* and *Shiranuhi* (18th DD Div.); for patrol: submarines *I-19, I-21,* and *I-23* (2nd SS Div.); for bombardment of Midway Island on return voyage: destroyers *Akebono* and *Ushio* (7th DD Div.); and for supply: tankers and auxiliaries *Kyokuto Maru, Kenyo Maru, Kokuyo Maru,* and *Shinkoku Maru* (1st Supply Train), *Toho Maru, Toei Maru,* and *Nihon Maru* (2nd Supply Train).

These were not the only naval vessels assigned to the Hawaii Operation, however. Already at sea was the Advance Expeditionary Force composed almost entirely of fleet submarines, twenty in number. Most were assigned to blockade of Oahu and strangulation of the entrance and sortie channel at Pearl. Two were assigned to reconnaissance of key points. And five were each to launch a deck-borne forty-five-ton midget submarine in the southern approaches to Pearl. Seventy-four feet in length, carrying two crewmen and armed with two torpedoes, the midgets' mission was to pass submerged beneath the torpedo net guarding the channel entrance and to launch torpedoes at capital ships from inside the harbor. Since the existence of the midgets that formed what was called the Special Attack Unit had successfully been kept secret, it was thought that the American defenses would miss their penetration. In one midget that was captured after beaching off Bellows Field, U.S. investigators would find silhouettes of Oahu from every angle of approach, exact silhouettes of all ships of the fleet, and charts of Pearl Harbor that were impressively accurate. Meanwhile, the larger boats outside the harbor would torpedo any American ships that tried to sortie during or after the air assault, and to the east, interdict any surface reinforcements dispatched from the West Coast.

The entire submarine force was under the command of Vice Admiral Shimizu Mitsumi, C-in-C of the Sixth Fleet, who accompanied the advance force to a point short of Oahu on board his flagship, the cruiser *Katori.* The submarines departed Kure and Yokosuka Naval Stations between 18 and 20 November for rendezvous and final refueling at Kwajalein in the Marshalls. (A few, delayed in leaving Japan, proceeded directly to Hawaii.) Yamamoto had permitted the participation of this more conventional naval force in the operation on the grounds that, according to the tactical war games projections, aircraft alone were not likely to destroy the American battle line. Fuchida, however, was said to be furious about their inclusion. First, the confident airman argued, they were not needed. Second, they presented the serious risk of compromising the air attack if one of their number was detected prematurely. He would be proven right on both counts.[35]

★

While these movements of ships and boats were under way, the Japanese Foreign Ministry and military engaged in a number of calculated deceptions. On 7 November, the date when Y-Day was set, an unnamed Japanese, reportedly acting at the request of Foreign Minister Togo, visited Ambassador Grew and urged "repeatedly" that, irrespective of the merits of the Japanese diplomatic position, it was "of the highest importance that the Washington conversations be continued and not [be] permitted to break down."[36] Equally insistent were Togo's messages later to his negotiators in Washington, Nomura and Kurusu. On 28 November, when the Striking Force was well out to sea on its passage to Hawaii, the foreign minister sent the following signal: "In two or three days the negotiations will be de facto ruptured. This is inevitable. However, I do not wish you to give the impression that the negotiations are broken off. Merely say to them [Secretary Hull and his aides] that you are awaiting instructions." Four days later, Togo told them that "the date set [29 November] has come and gone and the situation continues to be increasingly critical. However, to prevent the United States from becoming unduly suspicious we have been advising the press [that] . . . the negotiations are continuing."[37] These "deceit plan messages," as they came to be called, were decrypted and read in Washington, though knowledge of their content was not shared with Kimmel or Short.

On the military side, sailors from the Yokosuka Naval Barracks were sent on liberty to Tokyo and Yokohama on highly visible sight-seeing tours to project an image of ordinary peacetime casualness. And the Pacific liner *Tatsuta Maru*, with a full passenger list, including Americans who wished to evacuate, was permitted to depart Yokohama for Honolulu and San Francisco on 2 December; though she reversed course on the eighth (Japan time) upon receipt of orders from the Navy Ministry. In accordance with the deception plan, the Striking Force proceeded to the Kuriles under strict radio silence. The Morse code sending key that was wired to the continuous wave radio transmitter on each ship was sealed or dismantled, and in some cases fuses were removed from the circuitry, to ensure that the attack fleet was dumb but not deaf, so as to preclude the possibility that an errant transmitted signal might give away the position of the carriers to American direction-finding (DF) receivers. Oscilloscopes attached to those receivers, furthermore, could distinguish the transmission patterns of the various ships, e.g., those of the *Akagi* from those of the *Kaga*. That imposition of radio silence, say *all* the Japanese who oversaw or participated in the raid and who wrote or spoke about it in later years, remained in force until the launch of aircraft on 7 December.[38] In the meantime, communications between ships were conducted by means of signal flag by day and blinker light by night.

★

When were the Japanese carrier pilots told of the objective for which they had been training? The question admits of several answers depending on the witness speaking. One carrier pilot told postwar interrogators that all officer pilots—but no petty officer or enlisted—were briefed on the operation aboard the *Akagi* in Shibushi Bay on 5 October. The briefers were Yamamoto and the chief of staff of the carrier fleet, Rear Admiral Kusaka Ryunosuke. The pilots were told, said this unnamed source, that the attack would be made on 8 December (Japan time). A second carrier pilot, identified as Shiga Yoshio, independently confirmed the particulars of the foregoing account, including the site and the roles of Yamamoto and Kusaka, but differed on the date, which he set at 5 November. According to Shiga, the pilots' reaction to the briefing was one of general pessimism: "All felt that it was a suicide mission."[39] These two interrogation responses bear about them an air of unreality. First, it is not credible that pilots would be briefed by the C-in-C Combined Fleet. Second, Yamamoto had not even by the latter date issued his Order No. 1 establishing 8 December as Y-Day.

Far more likely is the date of 23 November given by historian Gordon W. Prange, based on extended interviews he conducted with Kusaka, Genda, and Fuchida. On that date, which was one day after the Striking Force had assembled in its jump-off point, Tanken (Hitokappu Wan) Bay, and on board the flagship, carrier *Akagi* (Red Castle), force commander Vice Admiral Nagumo Chiuchi went over their destination and targets with the captains and staffs of the carriers, battleships, cruisers, and destroyers, as well as with the three submarine skippers and the commanding officer of the tanker fleet. He explained that if during their passage to Hawaii there should be an agreement struck in the Washington negotiations the Striking Force would be ordered to return to home bases without executing. Similarly, he told his commanders and staffs, should the force be detected by the enemy prior to or on X-Day minus two, the force would reverse course. If discovered on X-Day minus one, however, he, Nagumo, would make a decision whether to continue the advance, based upon the circumstances. If an enemy force confronted them on X-Day, *Kido Butai* would fight it out with them at sea, calling up the remaining vessels in the Inland Sea for reinforcement.[40]

Nagumo seems to have been of two minds on the question of how many attacks should the Striking Force make on Pearl Harbor and the Oahu airfields. On the one hand, he told his commanders that their single two-wave morning attack, as planned, should be sufficient to cripple, if not altogether destroy, the U.S. Pacific Fleet. On the other hand, he issued under the same date Operation Order No. 3 that stipulated (as Genda and Fuchida had been pressing) that "if the land-based air power has been completely knocked out, repeated attacks will be made immediately in order to achieve maximum results."[41]

On the same day, after lunch, Nagumo told the assembled officer pilots for the first time that they were going east to attack Pearl Harbor. On hearing the news, according to Fuchida, quite aside from pessimism, "their joy was beyond description."[42] Genda and Fuchida then provided the young airmen a day-and-a-half-long (23–24 November) detailed briefing on the attack. There would be two waves of aircraft, they informed them, the first to launch when 230 nautical miles north of Oahu, timed to arrive over Pearl Harbor and surrounding airfields at about 8:00 A.M. Hawaii time; the second to launch from 200 miles out, timed to arrive over targets at about 0900. Fuchida himself would lead the first wave, consisting of fighter aircraft (Mitsubishi A6M2 Type 21 Reisen Zero), torpedo bombers (Nakajima B5N2 Type 97 Kate), high-level (horizontal) bombers (the same Type 97, each fitted with one 1,760-pound armor-piercing gravity bomb), and dive-bombers

(Aichi D3A1 Type 99 Val). Lt. Comdr. Murata Shigeharu would lead the centrally important torpedo flight.

The second wave, consisting of all types except torpedo bombers—they were expected to be too vulnerable to AA fire after their surprise use in the first wave—would be commanded by Lt. Comdr. Shigekazu Shimazaki. The two waves would be preceded by a flight of two Aichi E13A1 "Jake" reconnaissance floatplanes with three-man crews catapulted from the heavy cruisers *Tone* and *Chikuma*. Their purpose was to determine what ships of the U.S. fleet were at Pearl Harbor and which (if any) were at Lahaina Roads on the neighboring island of Maui. The scouting period over targets was set to last one hour, but when Murata and other pilots objected that the planes' necessary breaking of radio silence and their subjection to sighting might jeopardize the critical element of surprise, it was agreed by Genda, Fuchida, and, later Nagumo, to halve the time to thirty minutes.

Genda went over the sequence and spacing of takeoffs from the six carriers, the process of forming up aloft, the courses to be flown, rendezvous points, changes in altitude to be executed, and the exact approach routes to targets. He emphasized that the essential ingredients of success were teamwork, surprise, timing, and simultaneity of attacks. For example Murata's flight of forty torpedo bombers would divide into two groups and strike the battleships and cruisers moored to the southeast and northwest of Ford Island from two different directions at the same time. Fuchida explained the various signals that he would use during the first wave's approach to targets. Upon reaching the northern tip of Oahu, he would fire one flare if it appeared that the aircraft had caught the enemy with his guard down, in which case one particular sequence of attacks would take place; he would fire two flares if it appeared that the enemy had been alerted, in which case another, different, sequence would be followed. And if, when Pearl Harbor came into view, Fuchida was convinced that surprise had indeed been achieved, he would break radio silence and signal the carriers: *"Tora! Tora! Tora!"* ("Tiger! Tiger! Tiger!")

In daylong breakout sessions with twenty-six separate groups of pilots, Fuchida went over the operation in exacting detail. Using models of Pearl Harbor, and Oahu, with miniature mock-ups of ships and ground installations, as well as maps and diagrams, he pinpointed each group's targets and approach routes, and drilled the officers (and their enlisted personnel) on their responsibilities until they had them thoroughly memorized.

It was the last time that Genda and Fuchida had the air crews of all the carriers together, and they made the most of it. Neither wanted to dampen the enthusiasm of the pilots, but Fuchida had to acknowledge to them the possibility that the American fleet would not be in the harbor and could not be found. In that disappointing event, Fuchida told interrogators after the war, "we would have scouted an area of about 300 miles around Oahu and were prepared to attack. If the American fleet could not be located, we were to withdraw." (Interestingly, no mention was made of attacks instead on land installations such as repair facilities and the fuel farms.) The carriers would take up station about fifty miles south of Oahu, recover their scouting aircraft, and retire to the Marshalls to await further instructions.[43]

There were many such imponderables facing Nagumo, Genda, and Fuchida, not in any particular order: Suppose the American defenders had distant aerial reconnaissance under way in the sector north of Oahu— agents associated with the consulate in Honolulu had not reported any— where Nagumo's carriers would make much of their final dash toward launch position in full daylight, and suppose the skies overhead were clear, what then? Suppose American naval intelligence had divined the Japanese intention and, even now, was preparing to ambush the *Kido Butai* (as U.S. Navy carriers, acting on superb intelligence, would trap the Japanese in the Battle of Midway [4–6 June 1942], when Nagumo again was task force commander). Suppose fog socked in the carriers on X-Day, foreclosing the possibility of recovering aircraft, thus causing Japanese air losses to be higher than those of the Americans? Suppose the negotiators in Washington reached an accord, and the Hawaii expedition was recalled, and the Americans then reneged: could a surprise operation be remounted weeks or months later when thousands of sea and air crewmen were privy to the secret?

★

Following last-minute preparation of the ships for battle, which included the rigging of rolled mattresses (mantelets) around the exterior of bridge and island structures to protect against bomb splinters, Nagumo's formidable armada weighed anchor and sortied into the North Pacific. The time was 0600 on 26 November (Japan time). Chief Ordnance Officer Sadao

Chigusa, on board the destroyer *Akigumo,* wrote in his diary, "0600. At last we left Hitokappu Bay for Hawaii to attack Pearl Harbor, seeing M[oun]t Berumarube disappear behind us. . . . A northwest wind of 5–6 m/second (10–12 knots) blew, and it was very cold with occasional gusts of driving snow. . . . The sally of our great fleet was really a majestic sight."[44] *Kido Butai* steamed east at a steady 12 to 14 knots, the carriers in parallel columns of three, with the tankers trailing. The two battleships and two heavy cruisers flanked the carriers. The light cruiser and the destroyers formed the perimeter, or screen. The three submarines advanced at twenty-three knots to take up scouting stations 200 miles ahead.

The course chosen, 095 degrees, would take the fleet through the "Vacant Sea," which was practically devoid of commercial shipping, between the southern routes that lay between Hawaii and the ports of China and the northern great circle routes that lead near the Aleutians. Two other courses had been considered. One, a central route, would have taken the fleet directly toward the Hawaiian archipelago; the other, a southern route, would have passed the fleet through the Marshall Islands to the southwest of Hawaii. Both had the advantage of providing calm seas for refueling, as against conditions in the Vacant Sea, which normally offered twenty-four days of storm for every seven days of calm. But both posed dangers of encountering commercial vessels en route and of being sighted by U.S. Navy patrol flights out of Wake, Midway, Palmyra, and Johnston Islands. The refueling problem presented by gale winds and heavy seas on the northern route could be overcome, it was decided, by training. Too, the very improbability of a punishing North Pacific crossing assisted in the deception plan. Maintaining surprise was the overriding key to a successful operation. Hence the 095 degree heading, on which, to its own surprise, the fleet found fair seas during its first six days. The choice of Sunday, 7 December (Hawaii time) for the attack was owed primarily to the fact that, as the Honolulu consulate had reported, the U.S. Pacific Fleet followed the habit of entering harbor on Friday or Saturday after exercises and of departing on Monday or Tuesday. Also the Sunday date coordinated well with attacks scheduled in the Southern Operation.

The first refueling at sea of four of the carriers and the cruisers took place five days out. We know that the carrier *Kaga* took an oiler in tow, distance apart seventy to eighty meters, using a manila hauser about six inches in diameter; after the tow was passed, and speed of the vessels was reduced to eight knots, fuel was passed through a hose about eight inches in diameter, rubber outside, metal inside, supported by a two-inch wire jackstay. Fuel intakes were fitted on both quarters of *Kaga*. Oiling took about six hours. Carriers *Soryu* and *Hiryu,* though the fastest of the carriers, had the lowest fuel capacities (4,000 metric tons), hence they had to be replenished daily. Fuel tanks on the short-legged destroyers had to be topped off every other day. From the diary kept by her ordnance officer, we learn that the newly commissioned destroyer *Akigumo,* replenished whenever the opportunity presented itself, day or night, with the donor tanker either alongside or astern.[45] Visibility was usually so bad when the tankers approached the warships that towing spars for position-keeping were almost constantly in use.

Meanwhile, all ships posted lookouts as a guard against possible U.S. air interdiction. *Kaga,* for example, had twenty-one sure-eyed men on two-hour tricks manning seven AA machine-gun positions around the clock. But no enemy aircraft would be sighted during the voyage; nor would any warships. Encountering U.S. flag merchant shipping was no problem, since on the day after the 16 October war warning OpNav had ordered all merchant transpacific traffic diverted to a southern route that ran well clear of the Japanese mandates, south through the Solomon Islands, then west of the Santa Cruz Islands, then through the Torres Straits between Australia and New Guinea, "taking maximum advantage of Dutch and Australian patrolled areas."[46] Nagumo may have learned of this course alteration from Japanese intelligence.

In ships' radio shacks operators listened for the latest encrypted intelligence on Pearl Harbor. It came from consular agents in Honolulu, relayed to *Kido Butai* through the Imperial General Staff, with unexplained delays of three to five days. Thus, the report "Activities in Pearl Harbor as of 0800/28 November [Hawaii time]" reached the ships on 2 December [Japan time]. It read:

> Departed: 2 battleships (*Oklahoma* and *Nevada*), one carrier (*Enterprise*), 2 heavy cruisers, 12 destroyers. [This was Halsey's Task Force 8 ferrying Marine F4Fs to Wake. He in fact took nine destroyers.]

Arrived: 5 battleships, 3 heavy cruisers, 3 light cruisers, 12 destroyers, 1 tanker.

Ships making port today are those which departed 22 November.

Ships in port on afternoon of 28 November estimated as follows:

6 battleships (2 *Maryland* class, 2 *California* class, 2 *Pennsylvania* class).

1 carrier (*Lexington*).

9 heavy cruisers (5 *San Francisco* class, 3 *Chicago* class, and *Salt Lake City*).

5 light cruisers (4 *Honolulu* class and *Omaha*).[47]

Operators listened, too, for special code phrases, the meanings of which would be known to cryptographers on board the flagship *Akagi*, phrases such as "the fate of the Empire," "the cherry blossoms are all in their glory," and the one for which Nagumo anxiously awaited:

THIS DISPATCH IS TOP SECRET. THIS ORDER IS EFFECTIVE 1730 ON 2 DECEMBER COMBINED FLEET SERIAL 10. CLIMB NIITAKAYAMA 1208 REPEAT 1208[48]

Niitakayama was the highest mountain in Japanese-occupied Korea. The code phrase was the order to "Proceed with attack." The 1208 (8 December Japan time) was the date for the attack.

The signal crackled through *Akagi*'s earphones on 2 December.

There had been no diplomatic breakthough in Washington. The operation was go.

Shortly after receipt of the order, Nagumo's Striking Force crossed the 180th meridian into the Western Hemisphere.

✫

Among the critical predicates of success in the Hawaii Operation, joining the ability to refuel ships in the rough North Pacific seas and avoidance of premature discovery by the enemy, was the availability of continuous intelligence about the presence of principal U.S. fleet warships in Pearl Harbor. That information was supplied on an almost daily basis through the Japanese consulate in Honolulu by a trained naval intelligence agent named Yoshikawa Takeo. Arriving by ship at Honolulu on 27 March 1941 under the cover of a junior diplomat named "Tadashi Morimura," the twenty-nine-year-old, English-speaking Yoshikawa took up ostensible duties as chancellor of the consulate. He was rarely in his office, however, with the full blessing of the also newly arrived consul general, Kita Nagao, and his vice consul, Okuda Otojiro, who both knew of and fully supported his mission, which was to reconnoiter all U.S. Army and Navy bases and airfields on Oahu, with special emphasis on Pearl Harbor, where he was to observe and report regularly on ship movements.

Yoshikawa was not the first to undertake this work. The consular treasurer, Seki Kohichi, who had briefly attended Japan's naval academy at Eta Jima, made regular observations at Pearl Harbor, seven miles distant from the consulate, in 1940 and in the first months of 1941. But Yoshikawa, a graduate of Eta Jima, was the first agent in Honolulu with a professional espionage background. On paper he had a thorough knowledge of the U.S. fleet, and, soon, with the help of a Navy-wise taxi driver named John Yoshige Mikami and a young dual citizenship–holding Nisei with a 1937 Ford named Richard Masayuki Kotoshirodo, Yoshikawa was making regular observations of ship movements in and out of Pearl. The ships were easily observable from various highway and street sites, from Aiea Heights, from Kamehameha Highway, between Aiea and Makalapa, from a pier at Pearl City, northwest of the harbor, and from a telescope-equipped teahouse on Alewa Heights that overlooked both the harbor and Hickam Field. Driving with Mikami along the Kokokahi Road on the east coast of Oahu, he also studied the Kaneohe Naval Air Station, home of the patrol bomber (PBY) wing. Twice he and Mikami drove by the Army's Schofield Barracks, and once, in autumn, he took a geisha friend on a tourist airplane flight over southern Oahu that provided excellent views of Pearl and Hickam as well as of the airfields at Wheeler and Ewa. Everything he saw—ships, airstrips, aircraft, hangars—he reported regularly and in detail to Tokyo, utilizing the consulate code room and radio facilities.[49] It was his information, for example, that produced the ship movements signal that reached *Akagi* on 2 December.

On 24 September, Foreign Minister Togo, acting on the request of the Naval Staff's Third Bureau (Intelligence), directed the Honolulu consulate to generate a second series of reports, these to focus not on ship movements but on berths and anchorages of major warships *in port*. The "strictly secret" Message No. 83 read:

1. The waters [of Pearl Harbor] are to be divided roughly into five sub areas. (We have no objection to your abbreviating as much as you like.)

    Area A. Waters between Ford Island and the arsenal [navy yard].

    Area B. Waters adjacent to the island south and west of Ford Island. (This area is on the opposite side of the island from Area A.)

    Area C. East Loch.

    Area D. Middle Loch.

    Area E. West Loch and the communicating water routes.

2. With regard to the warships and aircraft carriers, we would like to have you report on those at anchor (these are not so important), tied up at wharves, buoys, and docks. (Designate types and classes briefly. If possible we should like to have you make mention of the fact when there are two or more vessels alongside at the same wharf.)[50]

After consulting with Yoshikawa, Consul General Kita responded to No. 83 on the twenty-ninth. His message proposed an even more precise reporting system utilizing code designators:

1. Repair dock in the Navy Yard (the repair base referred to in my message to Washington #48): KS.
2. Navy dock in the Navy Yard (Ten Ten Pier): KT.
3. Moorings in the vicinity of Ford Island: FV.
4. Alongside at Ford Island: FG (east and west sides will be designated A and B respectively).

On 18 November another area, N, was added to the grid.[51]

The effect of these five designators was to place what has been called an "invisible grid" over Pearl Harbor. Togo's and Kita's messages, which were sent in a low-grade consular cipher known as J-19 (but also under the umbrella of Magic), were intercepted by U.S. Navy operators in Station Hypo at Pearl Harbor, named after the "H" of Heeia on the east side of Oahu where the Pacific Fleet's radio intercept towers were located. But Commander Rochefort, chief of the Combat Intelligence Unit of the Fourteenth Naval District, was under orders from Main Navy to send all consular intercepts, unread, by Clipper pouch to Washington, for decryption and evaluation there. This meant, said Kimmel's intelligence officer Layton, that "the Pacific Fleet, the principal instrument of our military power in the Pacific, was not equipped to monitor the enemy beyond its harbor wall."[52] In Washington, where consular traffic was given a low priority, Togo's message of 24 September was not decrypted (by the Army) until 9 October; and Kita's scheme was not read (by the Navy) until the following day. Colonel Rufus C. Bratton, chief of the Far Eastern Section in Army G-2, routed Togo's message to Stimson, Marshall, and Gerow, chief of War Plans, but none found it of special interest, much less alarming. On the Navy side, Lt. Comdr. Alwin D. Kramer, of ONI's Translation Section, Communications Division (OP-20-GZ), routed Togo's and Kita's messages through his own hierarchy of Knox, Stark, and Turner, eliciting the same indifference.

There were several reasons why the messages received scant attention. Some midlevel Navy officers thought that the grid system represented an attempt to reduce either the volume or the expense of radio traffic; or that it was a plan for sabotage or for a submarine attack. Others were more impressed by the fact that "ships in harbor" messages had been requested of Japanese embassies and consulates elsewhere: during 1941 there would be six such messages from Seattle, Washington, eighteen from Panama, fifty-five from Manila, and sixty-eight from Honolulu. That the greatest number originated from Honolulu was explained for some by the presence there of the greatest concentration anywhere of U.S. naval strength. No one seems to have thought on the basis of those messages that Pearl Harbor stood out as especially pinpointed for hostile action—except that Honolulu *alone* was asked to divide harbor waters into precise sectors and to provide such detail as ships moored alongside each other—though one or more unnamed Navy officers did propose to Kramer that the grid "might be a plan for an air attack."[53] In any event, said Kramer, he was under the "impression" that the grid messages were sent to Hart and the Asiatic Fleet with either "an action addressee or information addressee to Admiral Kimmel."[54] The Navy file copy stamp shows it went to Hart but *not* to Kimmel. Nor was Kimmel sent any of Yoshikawa's grid reports that followed.

Since Hart was equipped with the Purple decryption machine and regularly read the Magic messages that his cryptanalysts (at Cast Station, located at Cavite Navy Yard, outside Manila) generated, it is ironic in retrospect that Main Navy found it necessary to send him duplicates of what he already had, while withholding the same messages from Kimmel, whose fleet was the grid's objective. And, grid in hand, Manila relayed no secondary warning to Pearl. Of course, there is no certainty that a Purple-equipped Pearl Harbor would have performed any better than Main Navy or Manila in separating out the relevant warning signals from the background "noise" of competing, irrelevant signals, except that what came to be known as the Pearl Harbor "bomb plot" messages presumably would have made more of an impression on Kimmel's staff than they apparently made on Main Navy or Manila; and it might be noted that the intelligence track record of Rochefort and Layton in predicting Midway as Nagumo's target on the 4 June following proved to be far more discerning and accurate than the record of their counterparts in Washington who insisted otherwise, both as regards target and date.

When, several years later, Layton was shown the bomb plot messages, he pronounced himself "astonished and outraged." The failure of OpNav to send them to Pearl he attributed to "blind stupidity at the least and gross neglect at best."[55] When Short saw them in 1944, he called the messages "a bombing plan for Pearl Harbor."[56] And Kimmel, who was the most directly affected, and who fought hard and successfully to have all Magic decrypts from 1941 made available to the NCI in 1944, forcefully characterized the Navy Department's dereliction in failing to send him the messages as "affirmative misrepresentation," in that he had been promised all intelligence relating to the fleet, and his estimates and actions had been based on what he had received. Now the Magic decrypts disclosed that he had been misled:

> These Japanese instructions and reports [withheld from me] pointed to an attack by Japan upon the ships in Pearl Harbor. The information sought and obtained, with such painstaking detail had no other conceivable usefulness from a military standpoint. . . . Its effective value was lost completely when the ships left their reported berthings in Pearl Harbor. . . . No one had a greater right than I to know that Japan had carved up Pearl Harbor. . . . Knowledge of these intercepted Japanese dispatches would have radically changed the estimate of the situation made by me and my staff [and] afforded an opportunity to ambush the striking force as it ventured to Hawaii.[57]

The senior command personnel in the War and Navy Departments were asked about the bomb plot messages in the JCC hearings. Marshall answered that he had no recollection of seeing them.[58] Gerow stated that he had seen the messages but was unable to explain why their contents had not been communicated to Kimmel and Short. The reason was that Marshall had ordered that not even the "gist" of Magic decrypts should be distributed outside of Washington to the theaters. But when asked, "Were you aware that information and enemy intelligence was [sic] being withheld from G-2 in Hawaii?" Marshall answered, "I was not aware of that, sir."[59] Miles also saw the message of 24 September but averred that it was not his responsibility to evaluate it because it pertained to naval matters, best left to ONI.[60] On the Navy side, Turner testified that he never saw the messages, but if they should have been sent to Kimmel it was Wilkinson's job to do so.[61]

Wilkinson remembered seeing the messages, and spoke at length about them. "The Japanese for many years had the reputation," he testified, "and the facts bore out that reputation, of being meticulous seekers for every scrap of information. . . . I thought that [the grid] was an evidence of their nicety of intelligence." He thought at the time that the information sought was for the purpose of projecting how long a time it would take individual ships to sortie from harbor. The inside vessels at double-banked berths, for example, "might take some time to go out." He said that he discussed the 24 September message with McCollum and "possibly" with Turner or Ingersoll. In a later appearance before the JCC he allowed that a day-by-day mapping of ship locations according to five sectors would mean more to CINCPAC than to anyone in Washington who was "less immediately concerned." But, as ONI director, he was forbidden to send Kimmel any decrypt information of an operational nature.[62]

From the department's top echelon, Ingersoll could not recall seeing the bomb plot messages, but upon learning about them he thought that Kimmel should have been informed.[63] His chief, Stark, thought the same, in marked contrast to Marshall's strict Army proscription against sending even the gist of Magic information to the theaters. Though he had not seen the 24 September message at the time it was decrypted and translated, and, while he thought that those who did see it might have considered it "as just another example of [the Japanese's] great attention to detail,"

> in the light of hindsight it stands out very clearly, with what we can read into it now [January 1946], as indicating the possibility or at least

the groundwork for a Japanese air raid on Pearl Harbor. . . . This particular dispatch would have been of particular interest, if they [ONI] had so considered it, to Admiral Kimmel. They could have simply sent it out as it was. If they had thought it vital, they could have also brought it to what we call the front office; that is, to Ingersoll or myself, or come through Turner, but I have no recollection of this dispatch having been discussed, certainly not with regard to what in the light of hindsight we would now read into it.[64]

An Army Chief of Staff orders that no operational intelligence drawn from Magic be sent to his menaced commander in Hawaii, then later states that he was unaware that enemy intelligence was denied him. . . . An Army intelligence chief, representing the service specifically charged with defending the fleet at Pearl, punts on the grounds that fleet ships, after all, belong to the Navy. . . . A Navy war plans chief states that any transmission of operational intelligence of this kind should have been sent out by ONI, something he himself never permitted to happen. . . . A director of naval intelligence discerns in bomb plot messages no more than Japanese curiosity and "nicety" of detail about the time required for ships to sortie from harbor. . . . And a CNO, as uninformed at the time on this espionage as was the Army Chief of Staff, states four years later that ONI should have sent the information to Kimmel—in direct violation of restraints that his own OpNav office had placed on ONI. . . . Surely, if ever there was a "fog of pre-war," it hung low over Washington in the fall of '41.

The Tokyo-Honolulu traffic reached a suggestive crescendo with three messages outside the usual ship movements and bomb plot categories. The first from Tokyo, dated 2 December, and sent in the J-19 code, read in part:

> Wire me in each case whether or not there are any observation balloons above Pearl Harbor or if there are any indications that they will be sent up. Also advise whether or not the warships are provided with anti-torpedo nets.[65]

The balloons the message had in mind were what were called in the West "barrage" balloons. Tethered to ground moorings, they trailed beneath them steel cables that could cripple low-flying aircraft. Such balloons had been used by the British in defending cities and harbors against the German Luftwaffe. Mention of antitorpedo nets particularly evokes images of a Taranto-type air attack on a fleet at anchor. It stretches credulity to think that Washington would not pick up on these straightforward clues, but we shall never know what the reaction there was, since the message, intercepted by the Army's communication centers at Fort Shafter, was sent unread by surface mail to Washington, where it arrived on the twenty-third.

The Honolulu consulate duly investigated the subjects cited and replied in two separate messages sent on the same day, 6 December (Hawaiian time). In the first, No. 253, the consulate reported that, though the Army had begun training barrage balloon troops in North Carolina, and had ordered 400 or 500 balloons, at Pearl Harbor they had not as yet set up mooring equipment:

> At the present time there are no signs of barrage balloon equipment. In addition, it is difficult to imagine that they have actually any. However . . . because they must control the air over the water and land runways of the airports in the vicinity of Pearl Harbor, Hickam, Ford and Ewa, there are limits to the balloon defense of Pearl Harbor. I imagine that in all probability *there is considerable opportunity left to take advantage for a surprise attack against these places* [emphasis added].

The message concluded with: "In my opinion the battleships do not have torpedo nets."[66]

This extraordinary document might well indeed have altered history if its contents had been read in a timely way by the sometimes obtuse Washington evaluators, for whom the Pearl Harbor grid portended nothing, but who, we may assume, could hardly have missed the overt meaning of "surprise attack." (How Yoshikawa and consul general Kita learned or surmised that this was their country's intent has not been explained.) And one may state the same for the second message of 6 December, No. 254, which reported: "It appears that no air reconnaissance is being conducted by the fleet air arm."[67] Unfortunately for Admiral Kimmel and General Short, who may not have been advised of the contents of these dispatches *even if* decrypted and evaluated in a timely manner, both messages, sent in a very low-grade PA-K2 cipher—the consulate's J-19 having been burned—fell victim to Washington's strong preference for Purple messages. Though captured by the Army intercept station at San Francisco at 12:58 P.M. and 6:01 P.M., respectively, and forwarded to the War Department by fast teletype, the two messages were not decrypted until Monday the *eighth*. Commander Safford said afterward that message No. 253 could have been decrypted in about an hour and a half, and No. 254 in less than an hour.[68] But both were delayed in surfacing to view by Washington's denigration of ciphers employed by mere consulates.[69]

★

There were other provocative messages picked up by intercept stations operated by the two services.[70] Particularly ominous where imminence of war in the Pacific (though not necessarily at Pearl Harbor) was concerned was a series of orders sent by Tokyo beginning on 30 November (Washington time) directing embassies to destroy certain codes and ciphers, and, in some cases—the first were London, Singapore, Hong Kong, and Manila— their cipher machines. On 2 December the embassy in Washington was ordered to burn various ciphers, codes, message files, and secret documents. In the same order Washington was also told to "destroy completely" one of its two Purple machines.[71] Similar orders were sent to embassies or consulates in Ottawa, Havana, Panama, Los Angeles, Portland, Seattle, Vancouver, and Honolulu. On 5 December the Washington embassy acknowledged the destruction order, but requested from Tokyo "your approval of our desire to delay for a while yet the destruction of one [cipher] machine" for use in the "continuing" negotiations. Tokyo confirmed this understanding of its order on the following day.[72]

The burn and destroy signals were decrypted by Army and Navy cryptanalysts, and on 3 December OpNav sent two radio messages to Kimmel paraphrasing their contents. This was one of the first information items based on Magic transmitted to CINCPAC since the previous July, and, in a curious lapse of security, the second of the two messages, initiated by Safford, included not only the phrase "Purple machine" but also the Tokyo message serial number (2444). Kimmel and Layton puzzled over the expression "Purple," but were later advised by fleet security officer Lt. Comdr. Herbert M. Coleman, a recent arrival from Washington who was in the know, that it was "an electric diplomatic coding machine" used by Japan. In Kimmel's mind, the messages bore little relation to Pearl Harbor.

Cipher and code destruction worldwide would be part of the Japanese war preparation for invading Southeast Asia, as the 27 November "war warning" had predicted Japan would do. And Kimmel noted that the messages did not order diplomatic and consular posts to destroy *all* their codes and ciphers. Nor was Kimmel surprised when, on 6 December, he learned from Layton that the consulate at Honolulu had been burning papers for the past two days. He himself was sent an instruction from OpNav on the same day authorizing him, "in view of the international situation," to authorize the destruction of secret and confidential documents on Midway, Wake, and the outlying islands.[73]

EIGHT

IMPERILED

Even on the morning of December 7, four or five hours before the attack, had the Navy Department for the first time seen fit to send me all this significant information, and the additional fact that 1:00 P.M., Washington time, had been fixed for the delivery of the Japanese ultimatum to the United States, my light forces could have moved out of Pearl Harbor, all ships in the harbor would have been at general quarters, and all the resources of the fleet in instant readiness to repel an attack.

The Pacific Fleet deserved a fighting chance.

Rear Admiral Husband E. Kimmel, USN (Ret.), 1954

What later became the most controversial, though inconsequential, of the Japanese messages intercepted during the weeks immediately prior to 7 December were two so-called Winds Code transmissions from Tokyo to Washington on 19 November, which, because they were sent in the low-priority J-19 cipher, were not decrypted and translated until the twenty-sixth and twenty-eighth of that month. The messages established a code that would be followed in advising the Washington embassy essentially which course or courses of war Japan had decided to take. The embassy was to monitor all Japanese short-wave voice radio news broadcasts around the clock and listen for mention of one or more weather conditions that identified the nation or nations with which Japan was "in danger" of severing diplomatic relations: The phrase *higashi no kazeame* (east wind rain) would point to the United States; *kitanokaze kumori* (north wind cloudy) would point to the Soviet Union; and *nishi no kaze hare* (west wind clear) would point to Great Britain.[1] The code was devised as a means of communicating this information when and if commercial international transmission facilities such as those operated by the Mackay System and Radio Corporation of America (RCA) were shut down.

The War and Navy Departments took the winds code more seriously than they did the more foretokening bomb plot messages, if one may judge from the amount of time and the number of personnel that were devoted to monitoring its "execute." Several intercept stations of both services were put on twenty-four-hour alert for the key phrases. Teletype traffic from those stations increased from three to four feet per week to 200 feet per day.[2] Six three-by-five prompt cards containing the phrases and their meanings were distributed by Admiral Noyes to the Navy's Magic recipients. The Army's General Miles and Colonels Bratton and Carlisle C. Dusenbury were equipped with similar cards. The watch officers manning teletypes from the intercept stations were authorized to signal reception of an execute directly to one of the card-carrying senior officers, bypassing ordinary channels.

In another unusual step, Bratton and Dusenbury, who knew that Short had no access to Magic, either raw, gist, or paraphrase, but who thought that Rochefort's Station Hypo at Pearl was decrypting the Purple, J-19, and other traffic, drafted a signal, approved by Miles, to Rochefort's opposite number at Fort Shafter, Col. Kendall J. Fielder (G-2), which read: "Contact Commander Rochefort immediately thru Commandant Fourteen Naval District regarding broadcasts from Tokyo reference weather. Miles."[3] By this means the officers apparently sought to circumvent Marshall's directive not to give Magic to theater commanders. Rochefort would give it. They were wrong on two counts. Rochefort was not Magic-equipped, though he had been sent the winds code information on the twenty-eighth—"our first piece of Magic diplomatic intelligence in four months," Layton later wrote[4]—and had been asked by Noyes to listen for a winds-execute from his post, which in fact he never heard. On the second count, Rochefort, like Layton, was forbidden by Navy Department regulations to pass on to Army personnel any intelligence received from Washington, unless specifically directed to do so.[5] For example, Kimmel did not tell Short about the code-destruction messages.

According to Safford's testimony before the JCC, an execute message came into the Navy's Cheltenham Station M in Maryland beginning at 0830 Washington time on Thursday 4 December (elsewhere he says the third). The source was an overseas news broadcast from station J-A-P in Tokyo on 11980 kilocycles. From Cheltenham the execute was teletyped to the Navy Department (OP-20-GY) where the "weather conditions" were translated by Kramer. According to Safford, Kramer rendered the code phrases in pencil or crayon directly onto the incoming teletype sheet: "War with England (including NEI, etc.); war with the U.S.; peace with Russia." Kramer testified that the message arrived on the morning of the *fifth*, that he did not recall writing on the teletype sheet, and that he definitely would not have used the word "war." Safford stated the entire message was two hundred or so words in length; Kramer said that it was not more than a line or two. These conflicts of memory were but the beginning of a long and bizarre series of contradictions, inconsistencies, changes in testimony, missing documents, and charges of conspiracy to follow from 1944 through 1946.

Among the more notable events in that bleak procession were: Kramer insists in 1944 that the teletype sheet contained the phrase meaning a break in relations with the United States, then in 1945 testifies that he is "under the impression" that the phrase he saw was the one that meant instead a break of relations with "England and possibly the Dutch";[6] allegations swirl that the Navy Department bureaucracy, acting in self-protection, brought pressure to bear on Kramer to amend his testimony; the one alleged copy of the execute and all the prompt cards carried by senior officers disappear from the Navy's sequentially numbered message file sometime before 1945; Japanese communications officers deny after the war that any winds-execute was sent; British and Dutch witnesses come forward to say that they did receive it; five U.S. Navy radiomen from intercept stations separately give sworn affidavits that they knew nothing about the winds code or its execute, each adding in identical (formulaic?) language, "until I read about it in the newspapers"; and one radioman named Ralph T. Briggs, who was on duty at Cheltenham M in December 1941, is not asked by the JCC to sign an affidavit or to testify but comes forward in January 1977 to say that he intercepted the execute and was prevented from saying so by his commanding officer, Captain John H. Harper, who allegedly told him, "Someday you will understand the reason for this."

Furthermore, finding in 1960 that all his signal sheets for the first week in December are missing from the station's records, Briggs writes another entry specifying his receipt of the "winds message warning code" onto the original duty personnel log sheet, not for 4 but for 2 December.[7]

For writers unsatisfied with the knowledge that history is often untidy, like an Agatha Christie mystery without an orderly ending, and who search instead for the logic and clarity that conspiracy provides, here are plot lines aplenty. Using this material it would not be difficult to construct a conspiracy theory according to which the Navy Department's top brass tried to prevent a warning message that should have been sent to Kimmel and Short, but was not, from coming to public notice; or, if it did come to light, to extinguish it. Certain popular authors and so-called revisionist historians have taken that route. Others, historians like Gordon W. Prange and Roberta Wohlstetter, have tended toward the position articulated by Vice Admiral H. Kent Hewitt, who in 1945 made an independent investigation of this and other matters relating to the Pearl Harbor attack at the behest of then Secretary of the Navy James V. Forrestal. After exhaustive examination of the winds affair, Hewitt concluded that if an execute had been received on the day (days) specified—and he concluded that none did, the preponderate weight of evidence being that Safford was "honestly mistaken"—"such fact would have added nothing to what was already known concerning the critical character of our relations with the Empire of Japan," and, furthermore, "would not have conveyed any information of significance which the Chief of Naval Operations and the commander in chief, Pacific Fleet, did not already have."[8] This writer tends in the same direction.

The "winds" was not the only new code at play in this period. After 27 November the Japanese employed *ingo denpo*, or the "hidden word" code. A plain language message in that code was translated by the Navy on the morning of 7 December, and it was placed in a Magic pouch that Kramer delivered to Stark that same morning; it may also have reached Marshall's office in the Army's first Sunday delivery. As translated it read: "Relations between Japan and England are not in accordance with expectations"[9]— which was no more revelatory than the putative winds execute. However, a few days after the Pearl Harbor attack, Army cryptanalyst Col. William F. Friedman discovered that the translator had made two errors, and that the message should have read: "Relations between Japan and England and the United States are on the brink of catastrophe"[10]—which should have triggered the tocsins in War and Navy, particularly since the departments had an even more incendiary alarum on their desks that Sunday morning, as will be shown.

While fleet and Army intelligence officers in Hawaii were not informed of the Honolulu-Tokyo espionage traffic that was being read in Washington, they did come into possession of one curious piece of transoceanic communication that put them on their guard temporarily. It was a lengthy, two-hundred-dollar radiotelephone call on 3 December from a Tokyo newspaperman to Dr. Motokazu Mori, a Japanese dentist in Honolulu. (Some accounts state that the recipient of the call was Mrs. Mori, but that appears unlikely since in the caller's last remark he says, "Best regards to your wife.") The caller was responding, he said, to a telegram sent him by one or both Moris. Tapped by the Federal Bureau of Investigation, the conversation was translated on the afternoon of the sixth and given to Special Agent in Charge Robert L. Shivers, who had long had Dr. Mori on a suspect list. To Shivers's eyes questions addressed to Mori from the Tokyo caller about daily flights of aircraft, ship movements, the presence of searchlights, and the number of sailors in Oahu appeared to be more than ordinary civilian talk, and Mori's mention of "flowers in bloom," the hibiscus, poinsettia, and Japanese chrysanthemum in particular, seemed suspiciously like a code.[11] Later that afternoon, Shivers showed the transcript to Army Lt. Col. George W. Bicknell, assistant G-2, who thought it worrisome enough to pass upstairs to his chief, Lt. Col. Kendall J. Fielder, at the latter's residence. Fielder suggested that they show the transcript to Short, who lived next door. For about three-quarters of an hour the three officers discussed the transcript and decided that they could not "attach any military significance to it."[12] What most struck the three in the end was the very ordinariness of the military information given; and the fact that the hibiscus, poinsettia, and chrysanthemum *were* in bloom.

✷

In the Station Hypo basement offices, known to its occupants as the "dungeon," beneath the Administration Building of the Fourteenth Naval District, Rochefort and his cryptanalysis team brooded over the blank pages that once were filled with data on the physical locations of ships and air units that constituted the Japanese Combined Fleet. Prior to 26 November it had been possible to track at least some elements of the fleet by their call signs, which were not enciphered, by radio direction-finding (HF-DF), and by the signature "fists" of individual Morse senders. On that date, however, a general silence fell over the fleet and Rochefort's data source on the operational forces blacked out, particularly where the carriers were concerned. Perhaps, Rochefort reasoned, some carriers were moored in harbor and were communicating with headquarters by landline. In any event, his Communication Intelligence Summary issued on the twenty-seventh stated: "Carriers are still located in home waters."[13] That was two days after six of the carriers, including the flagship *Akagi,* sortied from the Kuriles to begin their 3,150-mile voyage through the Vacant Sea.

On the twenty-eighth Rochefort reported "no indication of movements of any Combined Fleet units." On the thirtieth he thought he heard a tactical radio circuit in operation between *Akagi* and several supply ships (which would have been a violation of radio silence). On 1 December he stated, "As to the First [Air] Fleet [the core of the Hawaii Striking Force], nothing indicated that it was operating as a fleet outside of Empire waters." It did appear, though, that the submarine force had taken up positions eastward of Yokosuka-Chichijima, Japan, in the Marianas, north-northeast of Guam. On the second: "The First Fleet appeared relatively quiet. . . . Almost a complete blank on the Carriers today. . . . Not one Carrier call has been recovered. . . . Carrier traffic is at a low ebb." On the third there was "no information on Submarines or Carriers." Nor was there any over the three days following, other than that the Commander Submarine Force "is definitely in the Marshalls." In the next month's Roberts Commission hearings, Rochefort told chairman Justice Owen J. Roberts and commissioner Rear Admiral Joseph M. Reeves that he had speculated that the carriers *Akagi* and *Kaga* (Carrier Division 1) were in the Marshalls, and that there might be another division in Thai waters.

ROBERTS: But if there were two in each of those places it would have left them a maximum of six [unaccounted for]?
ROCHEFORT: Yes, sir, including the converted carriers it left them that.
REEVES: There were either four or six whose whereabouts you didn't know?

ROCHEFORT: Yes, sir, but these we did—
REEVES: Well, when did you hear of these carriers again?
ROCHEFORT: The 7th of December, sir.[14]

Equally deaf to the presence of the six-carrier Striking Force in the mid–North Pacific was Station Negat, or Code and Signal Section, the naval code-breaking unit of OP-20-G, the Operational Intelligence Center in the sixth wing of Main Navy. There a memorandum on Japanese fleet locations, produced on 1 December, placed all ten carriers in home waters at Kure and South Kyushu.[15] So Washington was no help. Like Rochefort, Layton was concerned that some of the carriers had left their nests, but with no radio traffic from them excepting the unexplained *Akagi*–supply train blip, and with an unexpected change of call signs made by Japan on 1 December, there was nothing definite that Layton could report in his daily intelligence presentation to Admiral Kimmel. During the morning briefing of 2 December, as Layton remembered it, Kimmel responded:

> "You mean to say that you are the intelligence officer of the Pacific Fleet and you don't know where the carriers are?"
>
> "No, sir, I don't."
>
> He then said, "For all you know, they could be coming around Diamond Head [on Oahu], and you wouldn't know it?"
>
> I answered, "Yes, sir, but I hope they'd have been sighted by now."[16]

Had Rochefort and his talented team of cryptanalysts at Hypo not been limited by Washington to breaking, if they could, the Japanese so-called Flag Officers Cipher—which proved month after month to be a fruitless assignment—and had they instead been tasked to penetrate the Japanese Navy's operational cipher, known as the Fleet General Purpose System, a "five-numeral" cipher that became known eventually as JN-25-B, Hawaii's knowledge of Japanese operational intentions in October, November, and December likely would have advanced into a galaxy of irresistible clues. But the authority to attack JN-25 was held tightly in Washington.

Navy cryptanalysts in Negat had acquired a commendable success rate in breaking into the Japanese diplomatic ciphers, starting with high-grade Purple and descending through J-19, J-17K6, J-18K8, J-22, then PA-K2 and LA, and they had made a start at JN-25B recoveries. "On 4 January

1941," as one of Rochefort's traffic analysts, (later) Captain Jack S. Holtwick, Jr., remembered, "it was reported that about 2,000 values had been recovered out of 33,000 possible" in JN-25B—which was slightly more than 6 percent.[17] Captain Safford in OP-20-G stated from memory in August 1970, "By December 1st 1941, we had the code solved to a readable extent."[18] The Philippines' Station Cast (which had moved in November to the island fortress of Corregidor), British cryptanalysts at Singapore, and the Dutch crypto unit in Java were given equal credit for the accomplishment. When, after 7 December, Hypo was at last relieved of the Flag Officers Code (which never was cracked sufficiently to provide intelligence) and given shared responsibility for JN-25B, the list of code group recoveries sent it from Washington numbered about 10 to 15 percent of the total—meaning that about 10 to 15 percent of each message broken surrendered some information, though not necessarily text.[19] The percentage did not mean that 15 percent of the intercepts could be read, or even that 15 percent of the words in a given message could be read.

It is important to recognize that *no naval operational message text in JN-25B was read by the United States prior to 7 December,* several revisionist writings to the contrary.[20] Ten to 15 percent of code groups was not sufficient to read message texts and very little usable intelligence derived from that level of penetration. Our living authority for that asseveration is Rear Admiral Donald M. "Mac" Showers, USN (Ret.), who joined the Hypo team as an ensign in February 1942 and stayed until January 1945. He crowned his career as chief of staff of the Defense Intelligence Agency. At a colloquium on Admiral Kimmel held in Washington on 7 December 1999, Showers told the audience, "If you would write a letter only using ten percent of the words in the dictionary, I challenge you to complete your task. We were not reading ten percent or fifteen percent of the text of JN-twenty-five messages in those days [prior to Pearl Harbor]."[21]

Lack of skilled manpower was one reason why work on JN-25B advanced as slowly as it did during 1941 in OP-20-G, where effort was also being expended on attempts to gain entry to the German naval Enigma cipher used by the Atlantic U-boats. Another was the Code and Signal Section's decision to concentrate resources on mining Japan's diplomatic (DIP) rather than naval ciphers. It is not recorded whether that decision to go the diplomatic route was taken under pressure from outside the Navy, e.g., from Roosevelt and/or Hull, but in retrospect one may wonder if JN-25B was not the better way to go, in view of its specific operational content. DIP gave advance disclosure only to Japan's diplomatic schemes and deadlines, not to her military intentions, although it was the source of three highly charged last-minutes messages, to be shown below, that did augur military action. A case can be made for either cipher, though certainly none can be made for the impervious Flag Officers cipher on which the talent pool at Hypo was squandered. Absent that bureaucratic miscalculation, which has less charitably been characterized as "a major blunder,"[22] the Navy likely would have had in hand *both* JN-25 and DIP prior to Pearl Harbor.

Rochefort was delayed in getting started on JN-25B by Op-20-G's decision to send him its list of code recoveries by surface mail aboard a transport that experienced foul-ups at both ends of its West Coast–Honolulu passage,[23] but by the end of December Hypo was going after the naval cipher at four bells.[24] Less than *five months* later, Rochefort's team was solving JN-25B message text in sufficient measure to be able to predict the Japanese attack on Midway in June.

Had Rochefort been tasked to work JN-25B five months before Pearl Harbor, and had he forced it to shed its veils at the same pace as that achieved after the attack, what operational clues to Japan's Hawaii Operation might he have captured? We have a very good idea because during the period from September 1945 through May 1946, OP-20-G's as yet not demobilized crypanalysts, with no more war traffic to monitor, were assigned to have a look at the JN-25B intercepts acquired, but never decrypted, from the three months preceding Pearl Harbor. Altogether, 26,581 naval messages were harvested, of which 2,413 were considered "of sufficient interest for translation." And of that number 188 were discovered to contain clues to the Pearl Harbor attack plan. These were messages exchanged during the Striking Force's training period as well as signals transmitted from shore to the force while it steamed toward Hawaii. Many of the clues uncovered would be obscure to a layman's eyes, e.g., the first mentions in October of "Striking Force" and "Advance Expeditionary Force," but a trained intelligence evaluator's eyes might well have widened at mention later that same month of "Type 91 torpedoes equipped with stabilizers" and of sixty additional torpedo technicians requested by the 1st

Air Fleet for Carrier Divisions 1, 2, and 5, where the "lack of personnel is causing grave delays."[25]

Even a layman would be unlikely to miss the import of three signals dating from 1, 3, and 4 November, which read in part, "Ambush and completely destroy the U.S. enemy," "In 3rd Special Drill in ambushing, 54 shipboard bombers will carry out bombing and strafing attack in sight of the Saeki Base," and "Pick up and take to Kagoshima the torpedoes (total of 4) which Cardivs 1 and 2 are to fire against anchored capital ships on the morning in question."[26] (In the imagination one can see Rochefort racing from the Dungeon to Kimmel's office.) Other intercepts from November ordered: heavy containers for storing fuel on the decks of the carriers *Akagi, Soryu,* and *Hiryu;* additional fueling hoses; an additional tanker to be assigned to the 1st Air Fleet; and, after 26 November, radio silence aboard all ships of that Combined Fleet. In yet other decrypts historians and cryptanalysts have found clues to the *direction* to be taken by the attacking force—a 30 November advisory to Admiral Nagumo that he might encounter Russian westbound freighters "in the northern Pacific"—and to the *date* for the attack: the 1208 appended twice to the "Climb Mount Niitakayama" order of 2 December.[27]

Though the 188 intercept translations were completed by May 1946, when they were placed in the hands of the then CNO, Admiral Nimitz, their contents were not shared with the members of the JCC, who remained in session until July of that year. That the Navy's cryptanalysts had attempted to acquire message text from the naval operational cipher was barely mentioned in the hearings. The "five-numbered system" or "JN-25" appears fleetingly on just five pages of the hearing's record of its own proceedings and of all previous commissions, board, courts, and investigations. In the most extensive mention, Lt. (later Comdr.) Rudolph J. Fabian, a veteran of Cast at Corregidor, stated during the Hewitt investigation that his unit "was working on the naval system known as JN-25. . . . We were exchanging values [with the British unit at Singapore], both code and cipher recoveries; but we had not developed either to the point where we could read enemy intercepts." Fabian concluded this provocative moment by acknowledging that information on the location, and movements of Japanese warships was obtained from traffic analysis and not from decryption.[28] It is a curiosity that no member of the JCC, either solon or counsel, having read the Hewitt record, ever raised this question in the hearings: Were those enemy intercepts ever decrypted at a later date?

At the Navy Department the 1945–46 translations were deep-sixed on arrival. Comdr. Baecher, whose Liaison Office was responsible for supplying the still-sitting committee with all pertinent Pearl Harbor evidence in the hands of the department, either was not apprised of the existence of the translations, or he participated in their burial. It is hard to think ill of Admiral Nimitz in this or in any other connection, but someone in his department made the decision to keep the translations away from the eyes of the committee. The cover-up prevented the JCC and the general public from knowing that, prior to Pearl Harbor, the Navy was in possession of intercepts that, if decrypted, would likely have warned the country of Japan's impending attack. Since from 1946 until at least 1995, when the department conceded for the first time that the responsibility for Pearl Harbor "should not fall solely on the shoulders of Admiral Kimmel and General Short; it should be broadly shared [see epilogue note 50]," the department consistently deflected blame onto the shoulders of its designated scapegoats, it may well be that the forty-five-year concealment of the JN-25B translations was part of that general policy. On 20 July 1946 the department accepted without objection the JCC's finding that Kimmel had committed "errors of judgment." Princely self-esteem and institutional sclerosis prevented it from acknowledging misjudgments of its own.

*

On 3 December, *Kido Butai* rendezvoused as planned at 42 degrees north, 170 degrees west and undertook refueling of all warships, despite their rolling and pitching in heavy seas. Replenishment completed, the 2nd Supply Train, consisting of tankers *Toho Maru, Toei Maru,* and *Nihon Maru,* together with an escort destroyer, *Arare,* broke away from the fleet to await its return leg a short distance to the south. *Toho Maru* hoisted flags wishing the attackers success. Admiral Nagumo let his force know that the attack was still set for the eighth (seventh Hawaii time), that war might break out in the Far East before that date, and that so far there were no indications that their approach had been detected by the Americans.[29] On that same date, to what must have been his great relief, Nagumo also had in hand intelligence that had originated at the Honolulu consulate: "So far no indications of sea patrol flights being conducted."[30] From the rendezvous position, Point C on *Akagi's* chart, which was about 1,000 miles north-northwest of Oahu, the fleet hauled around onto a course that would take them southeast to the next rendezvous point, D, which was 575 nautical miles directly north of Oahu.

On 5 December, the Striking Force sighted a passing westbound freighter "of a third nation." That encounter, denied to have taken place by Fuchida during his postwar interrogation in October 1945, also went unmentioned in the official Japanese history of the attack, *Hawai sakusen,* published in 1967, although that history does recount that an alert was sent to *Kido Butai* that it might encounter a Soviet merchant vessel along the reciprocal of its route. The Japanese government later acknowledged the sighting, without identifying the vessel. It is believed to have seen either the *Uzbekistan* or the *Azerbaidjan,* which departed San Francisco for Vladivostok on 12 and 14 November, respectively.[31] Yamamoto's biographer wrote in 1979 that the task force observed the vessel "with an extraordinary degree of tension," and stated that, had it made a radio transmission, "it would probably have found itself at the bottom of the sea within a few minutes."[32] In his account of the Pearl Harbor attack, Layton suggests that there was some prior collusion between Tokyo and Moscow on this midocean meeting, leading to the absence of any customary sighting signal in Morse from the freighter. It would have been in Moscow's interest, he argues, for the Japanese to be consumed by a war with the United States; the force requirements of such a conflict would compel Japan to withdraw divisions from the Siberian border.[33] The existence of such collusion has never been proved, however.

★

After bucketing through riled-up seas and thick weather, the Striking Force found calmer conditions as, in the early-morning hours of the sixth, it reached its next rendezvous position D, at 31 degrees north, 157 degrees west. It was a noteworthy feat of seamanship that the fleet navigator, prevented by the leaden overcast from taking sun and star sights, hit his mark by dead reckoning. There at 1130, the attack force began a final refueling before action. When completed, the 1st Supply Train, consisting of oilers *Kyokuto Maru, Kenyo Maru, Kokuyo Maru,* and *Shinkoku Maru,* together with the escort destroyer *Kasumi,* was dispatched from the main body to sail for home waters.[34] Admiral Nagumo ordered up twenty-four knots, course due south on 180 degrees, for *Kido Butai's* daring daylight dash (until twilight at 0508) over the remaining distance to Point E, 230 nautical miles north of Oahu, where the first wave of aircraft would be launched into flight. The *Akagi* broke out a "DG" signal flag on the masthead to signify the same message to ships that Admiral Togo Heihachiro had signaled from the flagship *Mikasa* thirty-six years earlier at the Battle of Tsushima Strait: THE FATE OF OUR NATION DEPENDS ON THIS BATTLE—ALL HANDS WILL EXERT THEMSELVES TO THEIR UTMOST.[35] Cheering resounded on every deck. Then the crews prepared themselves for battle by prayer and by bathing for the first time since departing Tankan Bay; that is, all but the crews aboard *Soryu* and *Hiryu*, where on each carrier 550 tons of fuel oil were deck-loaded in 200-liter drums and bucket brigades were kept busy emptying their contents into the main fuel bunkers.

Chief ordnance officer Chigusa aboard the destroyer *Akigumo* observed in his diary that the dash south was favored by fair winds: "The wind fortunately changed from the northwest to the north. It was now just a fair breeze of about 10 m [twenty knots]. I should feel that even God was now with us. But strong swells still remain on the surface."[36] Three submarines scouted 100 nautical miles ahead. And *Akagi's* communications officer reported that normal programming on Honolulu commercial radio stations KGMB and KGU indicated that there was no sign of alarm or tension on Oahu. American patrol planes were flying, but radio bearings taken on their chatter showed that they were south of Oahu.[37] From Combined Fleet intelligence came a mix of good and bad news:

> Vessels now at anchor in Pearl Harbor consist of eight battleships and two heavy cruisers.[38]
>
> . . . No balloons, no torpedo-defense nets deployed around battleships. No indications observed from enemy radio activity that ocean patrol flights are being made in Hawaiian area. *Lexington* left harbor yesterday and recovered planes. *Enterprise* is also thought to be operating at sea with her planes on board.[39]

The Honolulu consulate agent missed picking up on the PBY dawn patrol flown each day out of Kaneohe over the operating areas to the south, as well as the 400-miles-out PBY flights to the north and northwestward of Oahu on the first, second, third, and fourth. But it was true that no patrols were being flown this Saturday over *Kido Butai*'s line of advance. The bad news was that neither of the Pacific Fleet's carriers was in harbor. "It is most regrettable," commented air operations officer Genda, "that no carriers are in."[40] Other bad news came from submarine *I-72*: "American Fleet is not in Lahaina Anchorage."[41] In the planning for this attack it had always been a distant hope that the Pacific Fleet would not be in Pearl Harbor, after all, but in the deep, open anchorage off Maui, where twenty-nine fathoms of water ensured that vessels sunk there would never be refloated. The near hope was realized, however: the battleships were in Pearl. As Nagumo's chief of staff Kusaka concluded, "We may take it for granted that all eight battleships will be in the harbor tomorrow. We can't do anything about carriers that are not there. I think we should attack Pearl Harbor tomorrow."[42] That became Nagumo's decision.

✯

Saturday the sixth was a hectic day for cryptanalists and translators at the War and Navy Departments. Traffic volume was heavy and all circuits were overloaded. At 0720 the Navy station on Bainbridge Island in Puget Sound intercepted a message from the Japanese Foreign Ministry to its Washington negotiators Nomura and Kurusu. Translated by the Army, it announced the coming, at last, of Japan's formal answer to Secretary Hull's uncompromising Ten-Point note of 26 November. The text, later to become known in Pearl Harbor lore as the "pilot message," called attention to the forthcoming transmission of another "very long" memorandum, in fourteen parts:

> The situation is extremely delicate, and when you receive it I want you to please keep it secret for the time being.
> Concerning the time of presenting this memorandum to the United States, I will wire you in a separate message. However, I want you in the meantime to put it in nicely drafted form and make every preparation to present it to the Americans just as soon as you receive instructions.[43]

During that day the first thirteen parts of message No. 902 came tapping over the teletype from Puget Sound in nonsequential order: parts 4, 1, 2, and 3 by 1149, parts 9 and 10, 5, 6, 7, 8, 11, 12, 13 by 1451. After decryption they required no translation since the text was in English. The content of all thirteen parts was familiar to Commander Kramer, who assembled the decrypts, since it was no more than a rehearsal of previously stated Japanese positions. Much of the language was an attempt at justifying "the China Affair."[44] What was different about it was a harsh tone in which the United States was both blamed for the failure of negotiations and imputed to have base motives. Part fourteen had not yet arrived when Kramer, with Wilkinson's permission, personally undertook the Magic distribution. Stopping first at the White House at about 2130, he left the locked pouch with assistant naval aide Lt. Lester R. Schulz, who, accompanied by an usher, immediately carried it to President Roosevelt, who was in his second floor study with adviser and confidant Harry Hopkins.

Just before dinner that evening, the President had dictated a radiogram to his secretary, Grace Tully. Addressed to Emperor Hirohito, one head of state to another, the message read in part: "I am confidant that both of us, for the sake of the peoples not only of our own great countries but for the sake of humanity in neighboring territories, have a sacred duty to restore traditional amity and prevent further death and destruction in the world." As a practical matter Roosevelt offered to discuss the neutralization of Indo-China. He sent it by way of his ambassador, who had the right of audience. "Shoot this to Grew. I think can go in gray code—saves time—I don't mind if it gets picked up." It reached the hands of the Emperor about twenty minutes before the first bombs dropped on Pearl Harbor.[45]

While Schulz stood by, Roosevelt read slowly through the somewhat turgid prose of the thirteen parts, and, after reflecting on the next-to-last paragraph with its reference to Hull's Ten Points—"Therefore, viewed in its entirety, the Japanese government regrets that it cannot accept the proposal as a basis of negotiation"—he handed the message to Hopkins. When Hopkins finished reading the text, Roosevelt turned toward him and said, famously: "This means war."[46]

On 15 February 1946, then Commander Schulz testified about this incident before the JCC. He recalled that Hopkins, concerned that the Japanese would attack when it was convenient for them, expressed the view that "it was too bad that we could not strike the first blow and prevent any sort of surprise." Roosevelt nodded, but said, "No, we can't do that. We are a democracy and a peaceful people." Then he raised his voice and added, "But we have a good record." Schulz went on to testify about other things that were said or not said by the two men:

> During this discussion there was no mention of Pearl Harbor.... The time at which war might begin was not discussed, but from the manner of the discussion there was no indication that tomorrow was necessarily the day. I carried that impression away because it contributed to my personal surprise when the news did come. . . .
>
> There was no mention made of sending any further warning or alert. However, having concluded this discussion about the war going to begin at the Japanese convenience, then the President said that he believed he would talk to Admiral Stark. He started to get Admiral Stark on the telephone . . . but I believe the White House operator told the President that Admiral Stark could be reached at the National Theater. . . . The President went on to state, in substance, that he would reach the admiral later, that he did not want to cause public alarm . . . if he [Stark] had left [the theater] suddenly.

When questioned if anything was said about telephoning anybody else besides Stark, Schulz answered, "No, sir; there was not."[47] Stark's biographer says that, later that night, Stark and Roosevelt discussed the Japanese message "on the private telephone line from Stark's quarters to the White House."[48]

Kramer's next stop on his courier run was Secretary Knox's apartment in the Wardman Park Hotel. While Kramer waited, Knox studied the document, intermittently talking to Kramer and making telephone calls, at least one to Secretary Hull.[49] Kramer's final stop was at Wilkinson's home in Arlington, Virginia, where the DNI was entertaining his Army opposite number, General Miles, and the President's naval aide, Capt. John R. Beardall. All three read the message and commented on its significance as a sign that negotiations were shut off, but they apparently saw in it nothing of a military nature. About the other Magic-reading principals on the Navy side there is some confusion in the record. Kramer had not been able to locate Stark, but the CNO would have learned the basics of the Japanese message from Roosevelt, if indeed they spoke by telephone that night. He may also have been called by Wilkinson. Ingersoll and Turner both stated later that they had read the thirteen-part message on the evening of the sixth; but Kramer testified that he did not reach them that night and, instead, returned to the Navy Department about 0030 where he placed the Magic pouch in a safe.[50]

On the Army side there is much conflicting (in one case altered) testimony about who saw what and when they saw it.[51] It will suffice to say simply that Colonel Bratton, who was in charge of Army distribution of the Magic pouch, apparently made only one delivery that evening, to the duty staff officer at the State Department, before heading home at about 2230. It is believed that Hull, and Stimson, too, did not see their copies until the following morning. Generals Marshall and Gerow both stated in testimony that they had not received the thirteen parts on the evening or night of the sixth. Only Miles acknowledged that he saw them, at Wilkerson's home, but did not inform Marshall by telephone or other means. Marshall stated before the JCC that he could not account for his movements that Saturday evening; he did not recall where he was, though he thought that he was in his quarters at Fort Myer.[52] If he had read the back files of the *Washington Times Herald* for 7 December 1941, he would have learned that he spent the evening of the sixth at a reunion of World War I veterans at the capital's University Club on 16th Street. (Stark, too, would have trouble later remembering that he, his wife, and his aide were in the audience for *The Student Prince* that evening.)

✴

Meanwhile, at Hamilton Field in California, General "Hap" Arnold was readying another ferry flight of B-17s to a staging stop at Hickam Field, Hawaii. The Air Corps chief told his bomber pilots that they might fly into a war on this journey, which was no comfort to crews who knew that their guns, still covered in Cosmoline, had no ammunition. Furthermore, there were no gunners aboard to use the weapons even if they could have been fired. The fourteen Fortresses were going to go with five-man skeleton crews in order to save weight, hence fuel, for the long hops before them. Arnold was right about their meeting up with a war. He just did not guess how soon. This flight would arrive over Hickam in the middle of the Japanese attack.[53]

In Hawaii, on that last evening of tropical peace, General Short and Lieutenant Colonel Fielder, with their wives, dined in the Officers' Club at Schofield Barracks, their conversation still fixed on the Mori call. Admiral Kimmel, too, dined out, at the Halekulani Hotel on Waikiki Beach, among about a dozen other guests of Rear Admiral H. Fairfax Leary, Commander Cruisers, Battle Force. Under the circumstances, their conviviality could not have evaded entirely the adumbrations of war, despite the attending strains of "Sweet Leilani" and "Lovely Hula Hands." Following dinner, and his usual single drink, Kimmel retired to his quarters in Makalapa Heights at about 2200, and immediately turned in. Below his bedroom window lay the long, gray Battleship Row, with gun crews aboard each of the seven moored dreadnoughts (and *Pennsylvania,* which was in drydock) standing by antiaircraft weapons through the night. To the south, two minesweepers, USS *Condor* and *Crossbill,* swept the waters in and the approaches to the entrance channel, while a destroyer, USS *Ward,* trolled for submarines in the navigable waters between bearings 100 degrees to 250 degrees (true) from entrance buoy No. 1 to a distance of two miles. As he drifted off into his last unburdened sleep, Kimmel could take comfort from the fact that, as he thought, General Short's Army defense force was on full alert. He was not aware that, at the same time, Short was under the impression that, since 27 November, Patrol Wings 1 and 2 had been flying 360-degree distant reconnaissance; as similarly he was unaware that, back home, Main Navy assumed that his entire Battle Force was out to sea.[54]

During the same midnight hours, the Japanese carrier task force, having made its high-speed daylight approach from the north undetected, slowed from twenty-four knots and undertook final deck and hangar procedures to ready aircraft for takeoff. Arming and fueling were done both on deck and in the hangars below. Ample gasoline outlets existed and all points could be reached by hoses. Three elevators served the flight deck, where aircraft were spotted abaft the beam centerline. Warm-up was never done in the hangar. On deck the aircraft were secured by chocks fore and aft of the main wheels and by wing and tail lashings to ring bolts that folded flush into the deck. The forward 230 feet of the deck was used as the takeoff length. For night launch operations the flight deck was marked by rows of flush white lights that ran down the center and sides of the deck. The command islands of *Akagi* and *Hiryu* stood on the port side; the other four carriers had starboard-side islands.[55]

While the deck crews went about their work, the pilots and bombadiers, breakfast of red rice with sea bream and chestnuts under their belts, were given their final briefings in ready rooms just below the flight decks in the vicinity of the islands. They were all "Division I" veterans of combat operations in China. For the last fifteen days they had rehearsed the various segments of the attack plan. Everyone assigned to strike Pearl Harbor possessed a packet including, among other things, an air chart of Oahu, a diagram of ship positions in the harbor, and a code table for making reports by voice or Morse key. ("Each pilot," Admiral Kimmel would write to Stark on 12 December, "judging from my material from unburned or partially burned planes, carried a book of silhouettes of our ships. The charts of Pearl Harbor in planes were as good as anything we have.")[56] Those pilots and bombadiers assigned to hit airfields carried diagrams showing the runways, warming-up aprons, and hangars of those installations. When group and squadron commanders finished their sum-ups and exhortations, the first wave airmen, already in their flying togs, with pistols, mounted their aircraft. The six carriers had reached their final rendezvous, Point E, 230 nautical miles from Kahuku Point on the north shore of Oahu. Admiral Naguno now ordered a fleet course change toward the northeast, into the strong trade winds, for launching.

✦

Part fourteen of the No. 902 Japanese response to Secretary Hull's Ten-Point note was intercepted by the Puget Sound station at 0300 Washington time and was decrypted by the Navy for distribution at some time between 0730 and 0800. Crafted in the same strident, accusatory language of the first thirteen parts, the final part contained nothing substantially new or different. It concluded:

> The Japanese Government regrets to have to notify hereby the American Government that in view of the attitude of the American Government it cannot but consider that it is impossible to reach an agreement through further negotiations.[57]

Shortly after the fourteenth part arrived, an instruction message was intercepted:

No. 904
Re my No. 902
There is really no need to tell you this, but in the preparation of the aide memoire [memorandum] be absolutely sure not to use a typist or any other person.

Be most extremely cautious in preserving secrecy.[58]

When Roosevelt was handed his copy of the fourteenth part by Captain Beardall, he commented only that it looked "as though the Japanese are going to sever negotiations." Beardall testified later that there was nothing in the President's manner to suggest that he was expecting an attack within hours; that there "was no alarm" and "no mention of war."[59] When Kramer arrived at his desk on the second deck of Main Navy at 0730 he seems to have been unaware that two far more critical messages had been intercepted after 0437 and sent over to the Army, since there were no Navy cryptanalysts on duty at that hour. The first of these was a time of delivery message, later to become known as the "one o'clock message":

No. 907 (Urgent–Very important)
Re my No. 902.
Will the Ambassador please submit to the United States Government (if possible to the Secretary of State) our reply to the United States at 1:00 p.m. on the 7th, your time.[60]

The second message read:

No. 910 (Extremely Urgent)
After deciphering part 14 of my No. 902 and also Nos. 907, 908 and 909, please destroy at once the remaining cipher machine and all machine codes. Dispose in like manner also secret documents.[61]

Kramer would not have these two messages in hand until "about 1100." In the meantime, at 0900, when Stark came in, he made delivery of the full fourteen parts to the CNO's office, where he found "quite a number [of officers], possibly 15 or more, standing around, not yet seated. . . . I hardly glanced at them, more than to note that Adm. Turner, Noyes, and Wilkinson, the principal other usual recipients, were also there, and consequently it would not be necessary to run them down in the building for separate individual delivery. . . . I don't believe I spent as much as a minute in his [Stark's] office." In January 1944, admittedly "hazy" about his brief conversation with Stark, he allowed as though it went "most likely along the lines of":

STARK: My God! This means war!

KRAMER: Admiral, it has meant war for the past three months.

STARK(picking up a message blank): I must get word to Admiral Kimmel. Does General Marshall know of this?

KRAMER: Most of it was sent over to his office last night. This last part [part 14] was sent over ten minutes ago and should be on the General's desk by now.[62]

Stark's alleged concern, expressed here, to warn Kimmel seems unlikely in view of his reaction to the one o'clock message, as shown below.

At 1000 Kramer delivered the full fourteen parts to Secretary Knox (who had read the first thirteen the night before), who was meeting with Stimson and the secretary of State in Hull's office. He would make another Magic run "about 1100" when he had the decrypts of the one o'clock and code destruction messages. Obviously struck by the specificity of the Sunday time of delivery—an hour when, as the Japanese must have known, secretaries of State did not normally make themselves available to foreign diplomats—Kramer made a point of calling it to the attention of each recipient, as well as the fact "that 1300 [Eastern Standard Time] was 0730 [an hour after sunrise] at Pearl, and 0300 approximately or shortly before morning twilight at [the beaches of] Kota Bharu [in northern Malaya]." In a comment to Captain Safford made in January 1944, Kramer wrote that he especially drew Knox's attention to the correlation of times—Washington, Pearl, Kota Bharu:

I distinctly remember that the tieup of those times would be apparent to experienced naval officers, but that a civilian (Mr. Knox) might overlook it. Hence the pains I took to point it out at the State Dept. I repeated this point at least half a dozen times that morning to others.[63]

At the War Department, Colonel Bratton was even more alarmed than Kramer by the time-of-delivery message, which was placed in his hands about 0900. "This immediately stunned me into frenzied activity," he would say later, ". . . trying to locate various officers of the General Staff," starting with the chief, whose quarters at Fort Myer he called shortly after 0900. One of Marshall's orderlies answered the phone and informed Bratton that the general was out horseback riding.

> I said, "Well you know generally where he has gone. You know where you can get hold of him?"
>
> He said, "Yes, I think I can find him."
>
> I said, "Please go out at once, get assistance if necessary, and find General Marshall, ask him to—tell him who I am and tell him to go to the nearest telephone, that it is vitally important that I communicate with him at the earliest practicable moment."
>
> The orderly said that he would do so.[64]

The orderly did not do so, though he may have tried. That Sunday morning, for a man who had much of the world on his shoulders, Marshall was moving in an unaccustomed leisurely manner, as though he deserved a respite before that world exploded. He had slept late and had breakfast an hour or so beyond his normal time on Sundays. Afterward, he sent for his horse and rode for about fifty minutes along the Virginia shore of the Potomac, first at a trot, then at a canter, and finally at a full gallop across the grounds of a government experimental farm, where the Pentagon stands today.[65] After his return to quarters, where he learned of Bratton's call, Marshall telephoned. The time, Bratton remembered, was, "between 10 and 10:30; sometime closer to the half-hour."[66] Bratton explained that he had "a most important message" and that he would be glad to drive it over. Marshall said, no, don't bother. "I am coming down to my office. You can give it to me then."[67] His office was seven minutes away.

After his first failure to reach Marshall, Bratton called Miles, at his home. The G-2 chief arrived on the scene "around 10 o'clock," and immediately conferred with Bratton. Miles, too, was struck by the singularity of the 1300 hour, and agreed with Bratton that it signified that some target in the Pacific or Far East was going to be hit at that time. Neither officer expressed particular concern about the ships in Pearl Harbor, because, as Bratton said, "We all thought they had gone to sea."[68]

✷

At 0530 (Hawaii time) the Japanese cruisers *Chikuma* and *Tone* each catapulted an Aichi E13A1 Jake floatplane into the morning twilight, which began at 0510. *Chikuma*'s twin-float plane would reconnoiter Pearl Harbor at high altitude and break radio silence to report ships present. *Tone*'s would double-check *I-72*'s signal that no elements of the Pacific Fleet were in Lahaina Roads. Without waiting for their reports, Admiral Nagumo ordered the engines of all his aircraft on six flight decks started and warmed up. The flattops pitched and rolled in the still heavy seas, and there was not yet a visible horizon. Still, Genda and Fuchida were confident that their first wave aircraft would lift off all right. Before entering their cockpits, each airman tied a cloth *hachimaki,* or headband, around his leather helmet; on it was the word *Hissho,* meaning "Certain Victory."

At 0600 a launch officer on the foredeck of each carrier swung a green lamp as a signal to take off. The light-gray-painted Type 21 Reisen Zero fighters, under the command of Lt. Comdr. Itaya Shigeru, were the first to push their carburetors to full power. More nimble because they carried no bombs or torpedoes, they needed the least space to take off. In Japanese carrier practice, aircraft were not individually signaled by a dispatcher. Instead, deck crews removed the forward wheel chocks in planned order, and planes taxiing out of their spots began their takeoff runs as soon as they could. Deck hands cheered every launch, waving their caps overhead. *Banzai!* After the fighters came the green-painted Type 97 Kate high-level bombers, with Fuchida as observer in the lead plane off *Akagi*'s deck, all carrying a single 1,760-pound converted 16-inch armor-piercing gun shell. Next came Type 99 Val dive-bombers, and last, the Kates fitted with the modified, shallow-water torpedoes, on which so much of Japan's hopes rested.

As the roaring sound gathered and circled in the gray haze overhead, Genda counted only three dive-bombers that failed to get airborne because of mechanical malfunctions. With Fuchida in overall command, 183 aircraft formed up under light signals in well-rehearsed, disciplined attack groups—43 fighters, 49 level bombers, 51 dive bombers, and 40 torpedo bombers. By prearrangement, the signal for the first wave to shape course for Oahu was to be Fuchida leading the level bombers across *Akagi*'s bow. This he did at about 0620. The entire air fleet swung south and homed in on the Hawaiian music playing over Honolulu's radio station KGMB.[69]

★

Finally, at 1125, General Marshall entered his office, where Bratton had laid out the fourteen-part message on his desk. Bratton and Miles stood by impatiently while Marshall read through the No. 902 pages. When he finished, Bratton handed him the No. 907 time-of-delivery.

On 15 December, responding to a request from Marshall that he put into writing what he recalled of that moment, Miles wrote the chief:

> You then asked what Col. Bratton and I thought should be done about it, or what it signified. We said that we believed there was important significance in the time of the delivery of the reply—1:00 p.m.—an indication that some military action would be undertaken by the Japanese at that time. We thought it probable that the Japanese line of action would be into Thailand, but it might be any one or more of a number of other areas.
>
> I urged that the Philippines, Hawaii, Panama and the West Coast be informed immediately that the Japanese reply would be delivered at one o'clock that afternoon, and to be on the alert. You then picked up the telephone and got Admiral Stark. You told him you thought we should send out warning as indicated above.[70]

Bratton's recollection in 1945 was that he and Miles both told Marshall "that we were convinced it meant some *American* installation in the Pacific at or shortly after 1 o'clock that afternoon [emphasis added]." He also mentioned that, during the discussion, they were joined by Gerow and Bundy, who also, according to Bratton, concurred in the estimate that the Japanese intended to attack "us" at about that hour.[71] In a *Rashomon*-type disparity, Miles's aide-mémoire similarly notes the arrival of Gerow and Bundy but states that they concurred only in that the Japanese reply and timing "probably meant Thailand"; no American installation was mentioned. Bratton, when asked during the JCC hearings, "Was there any discussion that 1 p.m. meant 7:30 Hawaiian time?" answered, "No, sir."[72]

At the Navy end of Marshall's telephone line, Stark was in his office, where he had arrived sometime before 10:30, conferring on his copy of the one o'clock message with OpNav's liaison officer with the State Department, Capt. Roscoe E. Schuirmann, "when General Marshall called me on the phone to ask if I knew of it":

> I told him I did, and he asked me what I thought about sending the information concerning the time of presentation on to the various commanders in the Pacific. My first answer to him was that we had sent them so much already that I hesitated to send more. I hung up the phone, and not more than a minute later I called him back, stating that there might be some peculiar significance in the Japanese Ambassador calling on Mr. Hull at 1 p.m. and that I would go along with him in sending the information to the Pacific. I asked him if his communications were such that he could get it out quickly because our communications were quite rapid when the occasion demanded it. He replied that he felt they could get it through very quickly. I then asked him to include [in] the dispatch instructions to his people to inform their naval opposites.[73]

Stark's account corresponds to that of Miles's in these respects. Marshall thereupon drew a piece of scrap paper toward him, picked up a pencil, and wrote out in longhand a message to the commanders in the Philippines, Hawaii, and Panama:

> The Japanese are presenting at 1 P.M. Eastern Standard Time, today, what amounts to an ultimatum. Also they are under orders to destroy their code machine immediately. Just what significance the hour set may have we do not know, but be on alert accordingly. Inform naval authorities of this communication. Marshall.[74]

Miles states that when Marshall completed this message, which, it bears mention, contains the first use of the word *alert* in a Pacific warning since the Marshall-authored alert to General Herron on 17 June 1940, he handed it to Bratton and ordered it taken at once to the WD Signal Center. As Bratton hurried out, Gerow called after him, "Tell them to give first priority to the Philippines if there is a question of priority." At 11:50 A.M. Bratton had the message in the hands of Col. Edward F. French, the Signal Center director. Because neither French nor his clerk could read Marshall's handwriting, Bratton read it out while the clerk typed. French said later that he had "never seen [Bratton] more excited." When Bratton returned to Marshall's office, he was ordered back to inquire from French how much time it would take to encipher and transmit the dispatches. Returning a second time, Bratton reported, as Miles remembered, that "they would have them encoded in three minutes, on the air in eight, and in the hands of the recipients in (I think) twenty."[75]

From that point Murphy's Law took hold. French learned that, owing to atmospheric interference, his radio equipment had been out of contact with Honolulu since approximately 11:20 that morning. Not aware that the Navy had offered to send the messages on its more powerful transmitters, and without advising Colonel Bratton of what he was about to do—Miles quotes Bratton as saying that French gave him "no intimation" that all the messages would not go out direct to their addressees[76]—French decided on his own to send the dispatch intended for General Short by commercial means. In the past he had used the Navy's transmitters when experiencing problems with his own, but he thought that the message for Short would be delayed in reaching him if it had to be carried from Pearl Harbor to Fort Shafter. Commercial circuits seemed to him the more expeditious route to take. Accordingly, he filed the Hawaii dispatch by teletype with Western Union in Washington at 12:17 P.M. (6:47 A.M. Hawaii time) for overland transmission to RCA (across the street from Western Union and connected by pneumatic tube) in San Francisco. From there RCA, with forty kilowatts of power compared with his own ten kilowatts, transmitted the message by radio to its offices in Honolulu, where it was received at 1:03 P.M. (Washington time, which was three minutes past the one o'clock deadline), 7:33 A.M. in Hawaii, where the attack on Pearl Harbor would begin in twenty-two minutes. From Honolulu the message would have been transmitted by teletype to the Signal Center at Fort Shafter—*except* that that circuit was not operating at that hour. RCA assigned the message, which carried no priority designation, to a messenger boy named Tadao Fuchikami, who placed the message envelope, along with others, in his pouch and took off by motorcycle on his rounds. The traffic jams and roadblocks that quickly followed the start of the Japanese bombardment at 0755 made it impossible for the messenger to reach Shafter until after the last attacking aircraft had withdrawn. The alert was delivered to the office of the signal officer at 1145. After decryption it reached Short's office at 1458.[77] Short hit the ceiling. Kimmel rolled his copy into a ball.

★

Earlier, at 0358, the World War I–vintage flush-deck destroyer *Ward* (DD-139) received a flashing-light signal from the nearby minesweeper *Condor* off the channel entrance to Pearl. *Condor*'s crew had sighted an object that looked like a submarine proceeding to westward. *Ward*'s skipper, thirty-five-year-old Lt. William W. Outerbridge, set general quarters, slowed to ten knots, and began a sonar search. After an hour of fruitless "pinging," Outerbridge signaled *Condor,* asking for verification of the target's distance and course. *Condor* replied that the object when sighted was about 1,000 yards from the entrance on a course of 020 magnetic. That was not to westward. Outerbridge asked to be informed of any further sightings, secured from general quarters, and retired to his bunk in the emergency cabin. He sent no report of the sighting to headquarters, Fourteenth Naval District (hereafter 14ND).[78]

At 0600, three PBY-5 Catalinas, each fitted with four live Mark-17 325-pound depth bombs with hydrostatic fuses that hung in racks from hard points near both ends of the 104-foot wings, and each bristling with .50-caliber machine guns in the waist blisters and .30-caliber guns in the bows and tunnels, formed up for takeoff on Kaneohe Bay. That morning's dawn patrol—sunrise was due at 0626—their mission was to scout for Japanese submarines to a distance of 300 nautical miles over the operating area south of Pearl. Group leader that morning was a young ensign named William P. Tanner, from Rossmoor, California. Not only was this his first flight as group leader, it was also his first as a patrol plane commander. But he had gained many hours of seasoning and proficiency flying right seat to Commander Thurston Clark, commanding officer of Patrol Squadron 14. Tanner's Catalina was marked 14P1. His after-station crew reported that the ladder was in, sea anchors were in, and waist hatches were secure.

When the three aircraft received clearance for takeoff, Tanner reached overhead and slowly pushed the throttles to the wall. The two fourteen-cylinder, 1,200 horsepower Pratt & Whitney R-1830-82 engines on the wing above his head put out a thunderous din. With so much apparent thrust, it seemed to many novice pilots that the Catalina should fairly leap off the water. But pilots of Tanner's experience knew that the PBY was, in fact, underpowered, and that the boat's hull had difficulty breaking the suction and drag of the water's surface, particularly when it was calm. As power was applied, the nose came up, and Tanner held the elevator control back in his stomach in order to prevent water from spraying into the engines and reducing power. At sixty-five knots the boat was "on the step," riding on a notch at the base of the V-bottomed float. Then, abruptly, 14P1 broke away and became airborne. Tanner recorded the time as "just after 0600."[79]

Following a signal to the plane captain in the cabane strut to raise the wingtip floats, Tanner began his climb out at 2,450 rpm, thirty-six inches manifold pressure, or 800 feet per minute. At 1,000 feet, he stood on the right rudder pedal and turned the aileron control slightly to starboard. The lumbering Catalina responded and took a compass heading of 220 degrees, which would take Tanner and his crew of seven over the channel entrance to Pearl. There they were to establish the first leg seaward of their assigned search sector. Ensigns Fred Meyer and Tommy Hillis, piloting the other two PBYs, would work on grids to port and starboard. At 2,000 feet, Tanner nosed over into level cruise and reduced power to 2,000 rpm, pulling thirty inches, 110 knots indicated. The nonspecular blue-gray paint scheme of 14P1 blended in with the surrounding sky as morning twilight gave way to dawn. Looming ahead was the cloverleaf-shaped harbor with its stately array of battlewagons moored snugly to concrete quays.

When the Catalina had roared past Ford Island, Tanner made a slight turn to southward, took up his assigned heading, and cranked in the autopilot. As the Pacific came up, all crew members went to glasses, Bausch & Lomb 7×50s. "We were a little south of Pearl when we spotted the submarine," Tanner said years later. It was tailing a target repair ship, USS *Antares* (AG-10), just arrived off Pearl from Canton and Palmyra with a 500-ton steel barge in tow, standing in to Honolulu harbor, ten miles east. Crewmen aboard *Antares* sighted a suspicious object 1,500 yards on the starboard quarter. Tanner and his crew made the same sighting from the air, at about the same time, 0630. So did *Ward*, nearby. "Riding the wake some 200 yards aft," as Tanner estimated the distance, "with its conning tower barely awash, was this submarine—clearly outside the established sanctuaries [where USN submarines operated]."

Going off autopilot, Tanner called for mixture at auto rich, forty-three inches, and 2,400 rpm. With that, he pushed over into glide attack mode and descended at 140 knots to 100 feet off the deck. When he neared the optimum point of release, he slowed to near-stalling speed and ordered a crewman in the tunnel to drop two smoke pots to mark the sub's position. These released, Tanner kicked left rudder, pulled into a climbing turn, and looked aft. "The USS *Ward* was nearby but we didn't have immediate radio contact with her. . . . I guess the *Ward* spotted it [the submarine] about the same time we did because she started bearing down hard."

On board *Ward,* Lt. (jg) Oscar W. Goepner, who had the deck, roused Outerbridge: "Captain, come on the bridge!" When Outerbridge scanned the moving object that Goepner and the helmsman had sighted, he pronounced it probably to be the conning tower of a submarine, but, as he put it in May 1945, "we didn't have anything that looked like it in our Navy, and they [Goepner and the helmsman] had never seen anything like it." The tower belonged to one of the Japanese midgets. Outerbridge set general quarters, ordered speed increased from five to twenty-five knots, and directed guns 1 and 3 manned and readied. At a range of 100 yards a shot from No. 1 gun passed directly over the midget's strange-looking conning tower. After closing to 500 yards, the No. 3 gun scored a direct hit at the waterline junction of the tower and hull. The submarine was observed to heel over to starboard and start to sink. Passing over the position, Outerbridge dropped four depth charges.

Tanner and his crew above observed this action, and, sometime between the gun action and the depth charges, employed weapons of their own. "We made as tight a turn as we could," Tanner said, "and bracketed the sub with our own depth charges. But now, with the *Ward* closing and firing, we pulled up and watched her launch four depth charges from the fantail."[80] A patch of oil came up to cover the surface where the midget was found. Tanner sent an action report to the PatWing 2 command center on Ford Island.

Tanner and Outerbridge had fired the first shots in the Battle of Pearl Harbor. Acting under orders from Admiral Kimmel (who was acting in violation of his orders from Admiral Stark), Tanner and Outerbridge had not waited for the enemy to "commit the first overt act" but had skillfully taken the initiatives expected of them.

At 0653 Outerbridge sent a voice message *in the clear* to 14ND: "We have attacked, fired upon, and dropped depth charges upon submarine operating in defensive sea area."[81] The message was received by Lt. Oliver H.

228 // PEARL HARBOR BETRAYED

Underkofler, who was on loudspeaker watch at 14ND communications. At 0712, after a delay of nineteen minutes, Underkofler handed the message to Lt. Comdr. Harold Kaminski, district watch officer. Realizing the importance of the dispatch, Kaminski dialed the number of the CINCPAC duty officer, Comdr. Vincent Murphy, assistant in war plans to Soc McMorris. The call was taken by Murphy's assistant, Lt. Comdr. R. B. Black, who passed the message on to Murphy, who was in his quarters dressing. Murphy directed Black to call Kaminski back to find out what he was doing about the report, and whether he had reported the action to 14ND commandant Admiral Bloch. But Kaminski's line was busy and remained so. It was tied up because the watch officer was attempting to reach Bloch's aide, and, failing there, Bloch's chief of staff, Capt. John B. Earle, whom he reached after "quite a while." "Around 0720" he also reached 14ND war plans officer Commander Charles B. Momsen.

Earle directed Kaminski to signal the ready-duty destroyer USS *Monaghan* (DD-354) and "send her out at once" to investigate. (In his testimony before the Roberts Commission the following month, Kaminski stated that he sent out the *Monaghan* on his "own responsibility"—"I had instructions, yes, to use my own judgment"—*before* he talked with Earle. Murphy testified that it was Bloch who had ordered out the ready-duty destroyer and had ordered the standby destroyer to get up steam.) Earle telephoned Bloch at his quarters and notified him of the situation. Earle's impression was "that it was just another one of these false reports which had been coming in off and on . . . for a period of a year . . . but this seemed to be a little bit more serious. Apparently there had been an actual attack made." Bloch reacted in much the same way: "My thought was, Is it a correct report or is it another false report? Because we had got them before. I said, 'Find out about it.'" That order was given to Momsen, who lived next door to Bloch. Neither Bloch nor Momsen notified the Army, the latter saying, "It was a naval matter." Momsen went to 14ND headquarters to seek verification, but no further word was heard from him, and no messages to *Ward* are recorded on the radio log. Bloch later stated, "I did not hear anything until I heard the explosion in close proximity to my house, and that was around 7:55."[82]

In the meantime, Commander Murphy received a call at his office from Lt. Comdr. Logan Ramsey, operations officer of PatWing 2, who reported receipt of a signal from patrol aircraft 14P1, "to the effect that a submarine had been sunk in the Defensive Sea Area" one mile off the entrance. Murphy now called Admiral Kimmel. The time was "about 7:30." Eighteen minutes had passed since *Ward's* message was placed in the hands of Kaminski. Kimmel, who had not yet shaved, dressed, or breakfasted, said, "I will be right down." He testified in the following month that "I was telephoned at my quarters that an attack had been made on a submarine near Pearl Harbor. We have had many reports of submarines in this area. I was not at all certain that this was a real attack."[83]

But it was, and the sunken submarine had tipped off Pearl Harbor that an attack was afoot—just as Fuchida had feared. In the twenty minutes remaining, however, no one went to full alert. And the Army was never notified.[84]

NINE

THIS IS NO DRILL

Our air force . . . achieved a great success unprecedented in history by the Pearl Harbor attack. . . . This success is owing to the Imperial Navy's hard training for more than twenty years. . . . Nothing could hold back our Imperial Navy, which kept silent for a long time. But once it arose it never hesitated to dare to do the most difficult thing on this earth. Oh, how powerful is the Imperial Navy!

Commander Sanagi Sadamu
Operations Section, Japanese Naval Staff
Diary entry for 8 December 1941

Kimmel was unaware of it, as was Short, as was every other commander or senior staffer in the two services who was capable of doing anything about it, but one of the Army's mobile radar (AWS) stations picked up the incoming Japanese air fleet and reported it to the Army's Information Center at Fort Shafter. On 7 December, the six radar stations positioned around Oahu shut down operations at 0700, which was just over a half hour after sunrise, the predicted danger period.[1] There is no document found by this writer to indicate that the Japanese knew that General Short's radar stations stood down at that hour on Sundays, or that they even knew that Oahu was equipped with this detection technology. Even Kimmel did not know that Short's radar screens went dark on schedule at 0700 that morning.[2] It was only luck, it appears, that led the Japanese aircraft to approach the island just "over" the radar—with one notable exception.

That exception was the long-range mobile station at Opana, near Kahuku Point, 230 feet above sea level, at the northern tip of Oahu. Until 25 November there had not been a radar set at the site, but on that date an SCR-270B training set at Schofield Barracks was relocated there.[3] On the morning of 7 December, the two Army privates operating the radar equipment at Opana decided to keep the five-inch diameter oscilloscope on power after the normal 0700 shutdown hour. "We figured that we might as well play around," said Joseph Lockard, of Harrisburg, Pennsylvania, the more experienced of the two, "because the truck had not come in yet to take us back for chow." He was about to hand the controls over to the "new man," George Elliott, from Chicago, so that he could get some training in, when an anomaly—"it looked like two main pulses"—appeared on the scope. He looked at the clock. The time was 0702.

At first, he thought there might be something wrong with the equipment, but "finally decided that it must be a flight of some sort." He asked Elliott to start plotting the jagged vertical lines both on the Record of Readings and on an overlay chart with a mileage radius rule and grid lines running true north imprinted on transparent paper. Position: five degrees northeast of azimuth. Range: 136 miles. By the time the range reached 132 miles, Lockard decided that this was "the largest group [of aircraft] I had ever seen on the oscilloscope," and he directed Elliott to use the direct-line telephone for a sighting call to the Information Center at Fort Shafter.[4]

The telephone operator at the center, Private Joseph McDonald, wrote down the message, including the information that the scope image seemed to have been generated by "an unusually large number of planes." McDonald told Elliott that he was the only person in the center: taking advantage of their first day off in a month, the seven or eight plotters had packed up and left promptly at 0700. Elliott asked him to look around for *anyone* who could handle this information. He was speaking "in a very nervous tone of voice." Against regulations, McDonald left his switchboard and did find someone, an Air Corps fighter pilot named Lt. Kermit Tyler, who was sitting at the plotting table with "nothing to do," waiting to be relieved at 0800.[5] A four-year veteran, Tyler had been sent to the center to be trained as a "pursuit officer." His responsibilities, once oriented, were to assist the center controller in directing Army planes to intercept enemy planes. This was his second day: his first tour was on the preceding Wednesday, and he still did not know what all his duties were.[6] At Opana Lockard grabbed the phone and asked McDonald to put Tyler on. "I gave him all the information that we had—the direction, the mileage, the apparent size of whatever it was." Tyler's reply was, "I told him not to worry about it."

The time was approximately 0725. Fuchida's air fleet was now sixty miles distant from Opana.[7]

Tyler's reasoning was that the flight was one of two possibilities. The first was that it was a flight of B-17s, a bit off course, coming into Hickam from the West Coast. A bomber friend-pilot had told him that when the B-17s staging through Hawaii approached the islands, the local radio stations played Hawaiian music through the night to serve as identifiable signals for the pilots to home in on. That morning, before 0400, as he drove to the center, Tyler had listened on his car radio to the wistful music of the islands and surmised that bombers were coming in—and they were, *just three degrees off Fuchida's course and five minutes behind*. The other possibility that occurred to Tyler was that those aircraft were a Navy launch from an aircraft carrier north of Oahu. Frequently, when the carriers came into port from exercises on Saturdays or Sundays, their aircraft would participate in air raid drills on Sunday mornings.[8] On this particular Sunday, though Tyler did not know it—"The movement of the Navy was usually secret, more so than we are"—two of the three carriers were at sea to the west and west-northwest, and the third was in overhaul on the West Coast.[9]

Suppose the planes were the enemy's? During the 1944 Army Pearl Harbor Board, Maj. Gen. Henry D. Russell bore home on that *third* possibility:

GENERAL RUSSELL: You knew that the pursuit officer in that information center was there to get planes in the air, to intercept incoming hostile planes if they appeared, did you?

COLONEL TYLER: Yes, sir.

GEN. RUSSELL: And you knew the only thing you had to do was to get in touch with the people who could put those up, isn't that true?

COL. TYLER: That is not exactly true, sir, because we had nothing on the alert. We had no planes.[10]

The Army aircraft were at parade attention in closed ranks to prevent sabotage. General Short conceded that, if Tyler had sounded the alarm at 0720, there would not have been enough time to arm, refuel, and warm up the engines of fighter aircraft before the dive-bombers were overhead. But there would have been sufficient time, he said, to disperse many of the planes, which probably would have reduced losses.[11] The Army would also have been able to man and arm some of its AA guns.

On the Navy side, the thirty-minute window that Tyler's alert would have provided (if the Army shared the alert with its sister service) an opportunity for all ships in harbor to sound general quarters, which would have meant among other actions taken, that all AA guns would be manned with ammunition boxes at the ready, and all ships would go to material readiness Condition Zed, which required that all double bottoms, compartments, passageways, and access openings be closed, except for those necessary to fight the ship. As a result, the battleship *California* might have been saved from sinking, with the loss of ninety-eight lives, by the closing of manhole covers that had been left open for maintenance.[12]

★

It has often been pointed out that, if General Marshall or Admiral Stark had used the scrambler telephones on their respective desks in Washington to call Short and Kimmel, the window of emergency preparedness in Hawaii would have been a more gainful one hour and thirty-five minutes. Why did they not do so? Marshall, who was the more concerned of the two about alerting Hawaii to the one o'clock trigger, stated in 1944 and 1945 that he never considered using the scrambler because it was not secure. If the Japanese had succeeded in tapping and descrambling the transpacific lines, as he was sure the Germans had done with the transatlantic cable, his mention of one o'clock would have given away the fact that the United States was reading the Purple cipher. "I had a test made of induction from the telephone conversations on the Atlantic cable from Gardiners Island [off the eastern tip of Long Island]," he testified. "I found that that could be picked up by induction. I talked to the President not once but several times. I also later, after we were in the war, talked with the Prime Minister [Churchill] in an endeavor to have them be more careful in the use of the scrambler." This line of reasoning is persuasive. But another reason Marshall offered for not having used the scrambler strains credulity. It was that the heightened defensive posture adopted by the Army in Oahu as a result of his alert call would have been taken by Japan as an overt provocation justifying a Japanese declaration of war. In the JCC hearings the general was asked by Senator Homer Ferguson (R. Mich.), "Now, how could the use of that telephone to Hawaii have been an overt act of war by America against Japan in alerting Hawaii?" Marshall answered: "I think, Senator, that the Japanese would have grasped at most any straw to bring to such portions of our public that doubted our integrity of action that we were committing an act that forced action on their part."[13] Surprisingly, Senator Ferguson did not follow up his question. If he had, these additional questions would have been appropriate: Why then did you send the cabled alert, which, though slower in reaching Hawaii, would have had exactly the same effect? Why did you send General Short your warning of November 27, which you have testified was meant to put the Army on full alert? Why was that warning not provocative and this one was? Do you mean to tell me that every time the Army held field maneuvers there, or practiced air raid defense, Japan would feel justified in declaring war?

Marshall stated further that, if he had used the telephone, he would not have called Hawaii first. The Philippines would have come first, and the Panama Canal second. "We were open in a more vulnerable way in the Panama Canal than we were in Hawaii."[14]

Stark, who was reluctant at first to send an alert to Kimmel, similarly mistrusted the security of the scrambler phone. But he had a better reason than Marshall for not using his scrambler to call Hawaii. *The Navy had no descrambler at the other end.*[15] Stark may have been averse to using telephones of any kind for transoceanic communications. Kimmel had a regular commercial line in his office, but Stark, despite their long association and friendship, had never called him on the telephone during the whole of 1941.[16] When asked in 1960 why he did not urge Stark to pick up a telephone and call Kimmel, Kelly Turner answered, obliquely:

> Why weren't I and a lot of others smarter than we were? I didn't put all the Two's and Two's together before Savo [the Battle of Savo Island, 8–9 August 1942, a U.S. Navy defeat] to get four. Maybe I didn't before Pearl, but damned if I know just where. If Noyes had only known that Kimmel couldn't read the diplomatic Magic, If Kimmel had only sent out a few search planes. If the words "Pearl Harbor" had only survived the redrafting of the warning messages. . . . You find out the answers and let me know.[17]

Admiral Richardson, whom Kimmel had relieved at the start of the year, was unforgiving on this point. He delayed publication of his somewhat intemperate book, *On the Treadmill to Pearl Harbor*, until 1973, after Stark's death:

> I consider that "Betty" Stark, in failing to pick up the telephone and give Kimmel a last-minute alert on the morning of Pearl Harbor, committed a major professional lapse, indicating a basic absence of those personal military characteristics required in a successful war leader. I believe his failure in these respects were far more important derelictions than those of any of his subordinates.[18]

In the interest of preserving the secrecy of Magic, which was one of Marshall's arguments, much was sacrificed at Pearl: many of the 2,403 lives and the reputations of two commanders. The losses could have been much less. One is reminded of the false story—still circulating—of Churchill sacrificing Coventry to the Luftwaffe rather than warn its population and thus betray Britain's penetration of the German Enigma cipher.[19] In the present true case there was no credible intent on the part of Marshall and Stark to make such a sacrifice: after all, they did send a message. Their failure was in their decision not to use the most expeditious means: the telephone.

Stark, like Marshall, was probably chary of spoken use of the one o'clock information. He need not have mentioned it. Taking a cue from the British, who were adept at masking their use of Enigma-derived information by making certain that the same information could have come from another, more conventional, source, Stark might have camouflaged his real purpose with a spoken message such as the following: "In view of the deteriorating state of U.S.-Japanese relations, I remind you of OpNav's message to you last April first advising that 'Axis Powers often begin activities in a particular field on Saturdays and Sundays or on national holidays of the country concerned.' I hereby advise you, if it has not already been done, that you go on maximum alert immediately—repeat immediately—and that you maintain such highest state of alert on all subsequent Saturdays and Sundays, as well as on Christmas and New Year's. More to follow."

It would have been good advice, regardless.

Of course, a different personality might have taken this tack: "To hell with the diplomatic cipher! There's not going to *be* any more diplomacy. I'd rather risk Purple than my people. Get Admiral Kimmel on that telephone!"

Of course, too, Stark could have sent an enciphered explicit message by means of what he called the Navy's "quite rapid" radio system.

But he did none of these things. And, by 1944, it was clear that he regretted it. "There is only one thought," he told the NCI "—that doesn't mean that I am right—in my mind there is only one thought that I regretted. What the effect would have been I don't know—and that was the dispatch which was sent by the Army on the morning of December 7, that I had not paralleled it with my own [radio] system, or that I had not telephoned it. . . . That is the one regret, that I have had."

Pacific Fleet intelligence officer Layton wrote, "Admiral Kimmel [after he learned of it in 1944] considered the delayed warning of Tokyo's one o'clock deadline as the most shocking example of Washington's mishandling of the whole matter of intelligence."[20] And Kimmel would hold his old friend Stark primarily to blame.

✯

Commander Fuchida's air armada droned south both through and beneath the unbroken cloud cover that he measured at 2,000 meters. Then, as Kahuku Point came up, the clouds suddenly broke, and the first faint rays of the rising sun enabled the flight leader to look around at his fleet: forty-nine level bombers in triangular formations astern; forty torpedo planes to starboard and slightly below; fifty-one dive-bombers at about 200 meters overhead; and forty-three fighters, unable to keep to the low 125-knot base speed, snarling back and forth like warrior bees over the entire argosy.

Ahead he could see partly cloudy skies, except that the mountains were thickly wreathed with clouds at 1,000 meters. He had had no midair collisions to that point, and did not want to risk any in the mountains. So he banked to starboard as a signal that all aircraft, except those fighters detailed to strafe the Army's Wheeler Field, north-northwest of Pearl, would divert to the west, circle that shore of the island, and attack Pearl from the west and south. About fifteen miles to the west of Pearl, the torpedo bombers would divide into two groups, one of twenty-four Kates that would swing south and around the channel entrance and attack Battleship

Row from the southeast over Merry Point and the submarine base; and another of sixteen Kates that would strike from the northwest across the West Channel against ships moored to the northwest of Ford Island.

Fuchida's second signal did not work as planned. When he thought he had achieved surprise—which he now did think since there were no American fighters airborne to contest him—he was to fire *one* flare from his Very pistol. On that visual signal the torpedo planes were to sweep in low and make the first strikes at Pearl. The level bombers would follow next, and then the dive-bombers. The planner had not wanted the dive-bombers to attack first in the event of surprise because the smoke generated by their bombs would obscure targets assigned to the torpedo and level bombers. If, however, surprise was not achieved, Fuchida was to fire *two* flares, in which case the dive-bombers would attack first to sow panic and confusion. In either case, the fighters were to peel off for their assigned duties of strafing airfields and interception of any American fighters that might be climbing to oppose them. As it happened, however, the air fleet demonstrated that Murphy's Law applied in the Orient as well as in the West.

Convinced of surprise, at 0740 Fuchida raised his signal pistol above the canopy and fired a single "black dragon" flare. At that his level bombers assumed the 3,000-meter altitude they would maintain through their bombing runs, the dive-bombers climbed to 4,000, and the torpedo bombers began a slow descent to near sea level. The fighters, however, flew on as before instead of banking left toward their targets. Apparently, at their high altitude they had missed seeing the signal because of clouds beneath them. Fuchida thereupon fired a second flare in their direction, which got their attention. But it also got the attention of the commander of dive-bombers, Lt. Comdr. Takahashi Kakuichi, who saw the flare as the second of two indicating "dive-bombers first." He promptly ceased his climb to altitude and pushed his fifty-one-plane flight into fast forward. Seeing this, and apparently thinking that his own flight of torpedo bombers was slow off the mark, Murata hurried his descent. Fuchida now realized that Genda's carefully crafted plan had gone awry. The dive-bombers would strike five minutes before Admiral Yamamoto's firmly established start time of 0800. At this moment the *Chikuma's* scout seaplane broke radio silence to report—not very accurately—that ten battleships, one heavy cruiser, and ten light cruisers were anchored in the harbor. The pilot also reported on meteorological conditions at Pearl: "Wind at 14 meters from bearing 080, 7-density clouds at 1,700 meters."[21]

There was nothing to do but go ahead with the final attack order. Fuchida turned to the radio operator aft and called out: "*To-renso.*" The operator began tapping with his Morse key, repeating the single first syllable of *Totsugeki* (Charge!): "*To, to, to, to, to, to . . .*" The time was 0749, and the attack was irrevocably on. Because of the total surprise achieved, the slight hitch in attack sequence and timing was not likely to make any real difference in the result. As he looked forward through his windshield with binoculars at the immobile array of unexpectant warships, Fuchida would be forgiven if he imagined himself Napoleon in 1800, after taking his army across the St. Bernard Pass before the snow had melted, catching entirely by surprise the rear of the Austrian army besieging Genoa. He called out a second order to the radio operator: transmit the prearranged code signal to Admiral Nagumo indicating that complete surprise had been achieved: "*Tora, Tora, Tora.*" The time was 0753.

Thanks to an unusually reflective ionosphere, the code signal was received 3,400 miles away in the radio shack of Yamamoto's flagship *Nagato,* anchored in Hiroshima Bay. The message was rushed to the admiral in the ship's operations room, where the creator of *Hawai sakusen* was seated on a folding chair, his eyes shut, his mouth set. When the news was read to him, he opened his eyes and nodded.[22]

At 0755 the first dive-bomber struck, placing a delayed-fuse bomb on the PBY ramp at the south end of Ford Island. Its explosion was followed by others in rapid succession as the torpedo Kates, pouncing from the southeast and northwest, launched their first missiles starting at 0757. Lieutenant Goto Jinichi later described himself as "shocked to see the row of battleships in front of my eyes." He squared off at *Oklahoma:*

> Three things were the key elements to the attack: speed must be 160 knots, the nose angle zero [horizontal to the sea], an altitude of 20 meters. We were told if one of these were off, it would change the angle and the torpedo would go deep under the water and miss the target. I didn't have time to say "ready" so I just said "fire." The navigator in the back pulled the release lever. The plane lightened with the sound of the torpedo being released. I kept on flying low and flew right through, just above the ship. . . . I asked my observer, "Is the

torpedo going all right?" . . . I saw two water columns go up and go down. . . . But then I realized we're being attacked from behind. . . . I was avoiding bullets by swinging my plane from right to left. I felt frightened for the first time and thought my duty was finished.[23]

Meanwhile, bombers and fighters simultaneously bombed and strafed Army and Navy aircraft parked at the Hickam, Wheeler, Ford Island, Kaneohe, and Ewa bases. It was a predicate of operational success that American air strength be neutralized so that the first and second Japanese waves could work over the battleships and cruisers unimpeded. Fighters and dive-bombers also struck the U.S. Army's Schofield Barracks and Fort Kamehameha, adjacent to Hickam. At Pearl, the level bombers struck last, but only moments later than the other attackers. Fuchida had formed them into a single column with intervals of 200 meters, his best pilot and bombadier in the lead:

> As my group made its bomb run, enemy anti-aircraft suddenly came to life. Dark gray bursts blossomed here and there until the sky was clouded with shattering near misses which made our plane tremble. Shipboard guns seemed to open fire before the shore batteries. I was startled by the rapidity of the counterattack which came less than five minutes after the first bomb had fallen. Were it the Japanese fleet, the reaction would not have been so quick, because although the Japanese character is suitable for offenses, it does not readily adjust to the defensive.
>
> Suddenly, the plane bounced as if struck by a huge club. "The fuselage is holed to port," reported the radio man behind me, "and a steering-control wire is damaged." I asked hurriedly if the plane was under control, and the pilot assured me that it was.[24]

Because of clouds that obscured their target, Fuchida's group missed their release point, and had to circle around for another try. As they did so, Fuchida could see between the fleecy clouds tall columns of black smoke and waterspouts rising from the harbor below—then, startlingly, one enormous explosion of "dark red smoke" erupted in Battleship Row. It was *Arizona* in fiery death. He called the pilot's attention to the scene. "Yes, Commander," the pilot answered, "the powder magazine must have exploded. Terrible indeed!" Smoke from the fractured ship covered *Nevada*, directly astern, which was the group's target, and Fuchida saw that *Tennessee,* ahead of *Arizona* at quay F-6, was already burning, so he ordered the Kates, still in single line ahead, to release their bombs over *Maryland,* inboard of the capsizing *Oklahoma,* at F-5. As they did so, Fuchida lay flat on the deck and watched through a peephole as the armor-piercing bombs fell toward their target. Most of what he saw was misses—"wave rings in the water"—but two small flashes led him to shout: "Two hits!"[25] *Maryland* did suffer two hits: one bomb exploded prematurely on an awning rope, another struck frame 14, penetrated, and detonated, holing the shell, decks, and bulkheads forward of frame 24. Like *Tennessee* astern, she escaped more threatening damage that would have come from torpedoes by virtue of her inboard berthing position.[26] Fuchida ordered all other bombers in his group that had made their bomb drops to return to their carriers, while he and his crew remained over Pearl to direct operations, take photographs, and estimate damage.

> During the attack many of our pilots noted the brave efforts of the American flyers able to take off who, though greatly outnumbered, flew straight in to engage our planes. Their effort was negligible, but their courage commanded the admiration and respect of our pilots.[27]

★

By 0825, their fury spent, the remaining aircraft of the first wave were on northerly headings back to the carriers. (Given the confusion that existed later in American commands over the location of those carriers, it is curious that no service personnel from Pearl north to Kahuku seemed to have noticed and reported that the retiring air armada overhead was flying *north.* Nor was the Lockard-Elliott plot at Opana consulted by the Army's Information Center. The first wave was remarkably intact, having lost only five torpedo planes (all from *Kaga*), three fighters, and one dive-bomber. Fuchida remained over Pearl awaiting the arrival of the second wave. Launched 200 nautical miles north of Oahu, by 0840 that flight was east of Kahuku Point and descending on a course just off the island's east shore. It consisted of eighty-one Val dive-bombers to make additional attacks on the fleet; fifty-four Kate level bombers to make secondary attacks on Kaneohe Naval Air Station and Hickam Field; and thirty-six Zero fighters to make strafing attacks on airfields and targets of opportunity.[28] No torpedo Kates were in this wave, their vulnerability now too heightened by the absence of surprise.

As Fuchida watched from overhead, the new arrivals at Pearl had difficulty sighting ship targets through the dense pall of black smoke that rose from the crippled battleships and from oil fires on the water. Particularly high columns of smoke drifted over the harbor from *Tennessee,* afire from two bomb hits and flaming debris from *Arizona,* seventy-five feet astern, herself a ghastly funeral pyre; from *West Virginia,* which absorbed no fewer than nine torpedoes; and from *California,* which burned fiercely from two torpedo hits and a bomb explosion amidship. But Fuchida would not be aware of those details. He concentrated on trying to ascertain which of the battleships had sunk.

Eventually, the second wave pilots found more than enough work to do. Level-bombing Kates and Val dive-bombers got a bomb into the starboard side of the fleet flagship, *Pennsylvania,* which was immobilized in Drydock One alongside Ten-Ten Dock in the navy yard; and more heavily damaged two other occupants of the drydock, destroyers *Cassin* (DD-372) and *Downes* (DD-375). Three hundred yards distant, eight bombs fell on Floating Drydock Two, which held the destroyer *Shaw* (DD-373) and a tug, heavily damaging the former and sinking the latter. One of the three hits scored on *Shaw* ignited the forward ammunition magazine, which shot skyward in a blinding ball of fire that Fuchida had to have seen.

Nor did the bombers ignore the cruisers. Already one light cruiser, *Helena* (CL-50), had been heavily damaged by a first wave torpedo, the blast from which sank a minelayer, *Oglala* (CM-4), moored alongside her at Ten-Ten Dock. At 0910, the bombers went after another light cruiser, *Raleigh* (CL-7), moored on the northwest side of Ford Island. *Raleigh* was already hurting, having taken one of the first three torpedo hits during the first wave attack. Now, a diving Val dropped a dud that penetrated three decks and the ship's side aft below the waterline. The jettisoning overside of all portable heavy weapons and equipment topside by the crew helped keep the ship afloat. The light cruiser *Honolulu* (CL-48) attempted to get under way from her berth east of Ten-Ten, but just barely had steam up at 0925 when a near miss from Vals blew open a twenty-by-six-foot hole underwater at frame 40 on the port side. With flooding and other damage, she aborted her sortie.

✷

If Fuchida had been able to observe the activities of the midget submarines at Pearl, he would have been sorely disappointed. These seventy-four-by-six-foot submersibles of the Sixth Fleet's "Special Naval Attack Unit," each armed with two torpedoes and operated by a two-man crew, were assigned to penetrate the harbor and conduct attacks on Battleship Row in concert with the air fleet. According to the most recent research, of the five Type A *Ko-hyoteki*-class midget submarines cast off from mother boats for this purpose, only one managed to make it inside the harbor. Possibly it was *I-16 tou,* which we know from the record was the first released from the heavy clamps that held it to its mother, *I-16.* The time was 0042 on the seventh, the position was seven nautical miles bearing 212 degrees from the channel entrance buoy. A recent analysis concludes that a single midget cleared both the antitorpedo net, which also served as an antisubmarine net to defend against standard-sized submarines—the U.S. Navy having no knowledge of the existence of Japanese midgets—and an electric light barrier at the channel entrance during the period 0230–0240, and proceeded into the inner harbor. Unaccountably, the antitorpedo net, opened at 0458 to permit passage of the two minesweepers, was left open until 0840, but no midgets took advantage of the laxness; from the beginning the midgets understood that they would have to pass beneath the net.

The same analysis suggests, on the basis of a photograph of the water's surface off Battleship Row during the attack, that the lone intruder launched her two torpedoes at *West Virginia* and *Oklahoma.*[29] That intruder was later engaged by two seaplane tenders, *Curtiss* (AV-4) and *Tangier* (AV-8), as well as by *Monaghan,* the ready-duty destroyer under way to assist *Ward.* Sighting the midget's tower "bobbing and weaving," the two tenders opened fire. *Monaghan,* alerted by a flag hoist on *Curtiss,* also fired but decided to ram the vessel as the best means of disposing of it. Her crew observed a torpedo from the midget that passed alongside and grounded harmlessly against Ford Island. (If that observation was correct, the intruder could not have launched two torpedoes at Battleship Row.)

Following a successful collision, *Monaghan* dropped two depth charges—at peril to herself in shoal water where the reflected blast effect could hole her. She survived the shock waves, but, unable to slow her advance, got fouled briefly in the anchor cables of a derrick barge off Beckoning Point. Once free, she reported the submarine sunk, as indeed it was.[30] The damage to her bows from both collisions was minimal, and she proceeded out to sea. The scrappy *Curtiss* took a brace of more serious hits when, at 0905, AA fire from her own guns and from those of nearby ships struck a Val bomber that was pulling out of a dive, and the aircraft slammed into her starboard side, starting a furious fire on the boat deck. Then, at 0912, a group of Vals dropped four bombs against the stricken ship. One of them detonated in the tender's hangar, spreading death and destruction across a radius of thirty feet. Twenty-one men died, fifty-eight were wounded. By 0936 *Curtiss* had her fires out, but damage to the engine room had forced her to signal CINCPAC at 0930 that she could not stand out to sea.[31]

Twelve ships did sortie during the second wave battle before the Japanese aircraft began to break off at 0945, after suffering high losses of fourteen Val dive-bombers and six Zero fighters to the ferocity of U.S. fire. These were nine destroyers, USS *Helm* (DD-388), *Dale* (DD-353), *Monaghan*, *Blue* (DD-387), *Henley* (DD-391), *Alwyn* (DD-355), *Phelps* (DD-360), *Bagley* (DD-386), *Patterson* (DD-392); two destroyer minesweepers, *Trever* (DD-339) and *Wasmuth* (DD-338); and one light minelayer (converted flush-deck destroyer), *Breese* (DM-18). A light cruiser, *St. Louis* (CL-49), one of the newest ships (1939) in the harbor, would follow, heading out the channel at 1005. Outside the channel, *Helm* was slightly damaged by two near bomb misses off the port bow at 0915. Other ships, too, capable of getting under way, cleared the channel by 1216; these were the light cruisers USS *Detroit* (CL-8) and *Phoenix* (CL-46); destroyers *Cummings* (DD-365) and *Worden* (DD-352); and light minelayers (converted DDs) *Ramsay* (DM-16) and *Montgomery* (DM-17).[32]

In the channel approaches, *Blue*, *Wasmuth*, *Henley*, *Ramsay*, and *Breese* made sonar contacts with what they identified as submarines and dropped depth charges over the contacts. *Blue*'s attack at 0950 brought up "a large slick and air bubbles." *Wasmuth*'s attack at 1036 brought up "large quantities of oil, but no wreckage." *Breese* attacked at 1135 and an "oil slick with debris appeared."[33] The other attacks had no visible results, but these three may account for the two midgets thought to have been lost off the entrance. A recent analysis concluded that the midget *I-20 tou* malfunctioned and sank on her own.[34] From other, clearly evident sources we know that midget *I-24 tou*, beset by gyroscope and battery-gas problems, twice rammed into a reef, then, following the current, carried its two unfortunate crewmen, unconscious from the foul battery fumes, around Diamond Head to the east shore of Oahu, where she beached them in heavy surf about six hundred yards off the end of the runway at Bellows Field. Both the midget and one crewman survived.[35]

The crewmen of these fragile undersea craft must have known from the beginning that their mission was suicidal. Though their orders were to rendezvous after the attack at a point seven nautical miles west of Lanai Island, where they would be taken aboard their mother boats, there was doubtless little real expectation on anyone's part, including their own, that they would ever show up. When asked by U.S. Navy interrogators after the war why these crewmen might have volunteered for such a death-defying endeavor, Captain Watanabe Yasuji, Yamamoto's staff gunnery officer, replied, "It was a morale factor. Young naval officers very much admire the bravery of Italian officers in torpedo boats and small submarines. . . . They also want to show bravery in submarines."[36]

It should not go unmentioned that owing to aggressive patrolling by U.S. Navy destroyers and PBYs, and probably also to the incompetence of their commanders, not a single one of the twenty large I-class submarines deployed around Oahu sank or damaged a Pacific Fleet warship.

★

While Fuchida would not have been able to follow the fate of the midgets from his perch overhead (except that he may have observed the plumes of depth charge explosions in the entrance channel approaches), and while he may not have taken much notice of the sorties made by light cruisers and destroyers, we know that he was totally and excitedly aware of the attempt made by a surviving but heavily damaged 29,000-ton occupant of Battleship Row, USS *Nevada* (BB-36), to transit the channel and stand out to sea. During the first ten to twelve minutes of the first wave attack, *Nevada*, the northernmost battlewagon in line, was struck by a torpedo twenty feet below the waterline. The resulting explosion tore a hole in the port bow, around frame 41, that measured some forty-eight feet long and thirty-three feet high. Further but less serious damage resulted from two or three bombs dropped on her armored deck. As the ship began to list slightly to port, crewmen counterflooded and endeavored to restore watertight integrity to the lower compartments forward, while AA batteries topside put up withering fire against their attackers. When *Arizona*'s magazine blew up at 0810, showering *Nevada* with debris and burning oil, the senior officer present—the skipper being absent—ordered the vessel to get under way. By chance she had two hot boilers. That and the fact that she was moored singly enabled her to pull slowly away from quay F-8 at 0840.

As *Nevada* then limped down the East Channel toward the entrance, she caught the attention of Fuchida, overhead. He recognized at once the opportunity to sink a ship that size in the narrow entrance channel and thus bottle up the harbor for weeks or months. Accordingly, he ordered the Val dive-bombers to that task. As Fuchida remembered his thoughts twenty-two years later: "Ah, good! Now just sink that ship right there!"[37] At 0907 those Vals with bombs still on their racks screamed down upon *Nevada* in an effort, apparently, to cripple her progressively, so that when she was ready to sink she would do so where the cork best fit the bottle.

The old 1916-vintage ship took a merciless pounding as three or four bombs—it was impossible to say accurately—struck home against the foredeck and superstructure. Despite heavy casualties on the AA guns, the crew never wavered. Only the navy yard signal tower, which tumbled to what was afoot, called off *Nevada*'s lunge for the sea and directed her to go aground on Hospital Point, which she did to the disappointment of Fuchida, at around 0910.[38] When that action was observed from the air, the Vals lifted their siege. For about an hour and a half tugboats hosed down *Nevada*'s fires, after which they floated and moved her mangled hulk to the beach at Waipio Point on the channel shore opposite. There her officers made a thorough count of casualties: 3 officers and 47 men killed, 5 officers and 104 men wounded. Among the many decorations for gallantry awarded later to enlisted men of this ship were two Congressional Medals of Honor.

★

After the second wave of aircraft broke off their attack beginning at 0945, Fuchida directed his pilot to circle over the harbor one last time so that he could make a final tally. "I counted four battleships definitely sunk and three severely damaged. Still another battleship appeared to be slightly damaged and extensive damage had also been inflicted upon other types of ships."[39] It was a fairly accurate estimate. *Arizona, Oklahoma, West Virginia,* and *California* had been sunk, *Nevada* heavily damaged, and *Tennessee, Pennsylvania,* and *Maryland* damaged to lesser degree. Heavy damage had been inflicted on the light cruisers *Raleigh* and *Helena,* lesser damage on *Honolulu.* The only heavy cruisers in the harbor that day, *San Francisco* and *New Orleans,* escaped harm. Fuchida's interest probably did not descend to the level of destroyers, minecraft, or auxiliaries sunk or damaged. Or to that of target ships. USS *Utah* (AG-16) was a target ship. It was *supposed* to be bombed. Constructed as a 19,800-ton battleship in 1909 and converted later to a target vessel, she was hardly worth wasting torpedoes on, but probably because of her size, and the fact that *Chikuma's* scout plane had reported the presence of ten battleships, two Kate torpedo bombers placed their missiles in her port side during one of the first two such attacks of the morning.[40] Within a matter of minutes, *Utah* capsized, and later sank.

As Fuchida's plane made its final pass over the smoke-ridden dismantlement below, he observed that, except for a few Army fighters that had gotten airborne,

> it was readily apparent that no planes on the fields [Ford Island and Hickam] were operational. In the three hours that my plane was in the area we did not encounter a single enemy plane. It seemed that at least half of the island's air strength must have been destroyed. Several hangars remained untouched, however, and it was possible that some of them held planes which were still operational.[41]

This time Fuchida's estimate was off the mark. Army Air losses in terms of aircraft destroyed were 28 percent of total air strength.[42] Lost at Hickam, Wheeler, and Bellows Fields were 4 B-17s and 14 other bombers; 32 P-40 pursuit planes; and 27 other aircraft. Thirty-four bombers, 88 pursuit planes, and 6 reconnaissance aircraft were damaged (though 80 percent eventually would be salvaged).[43] Human casualties were heavy, particularly at Hickam Field. The totals were 163 killed, 43 missing, and 336 wounded. Damage to ground installations was extensive, again particularly at Hickam. Nineteen pilots managed to fuel, arm, and get airborne in P-40 and P-36 pursuit planes at Wheeler, Bellows, and Haleiwa, an aux-iliary field north of Wheeler. They accounted for six Japanese aircraft shot down, while losing five of their own.

The most notable Air Corps achievement that day was experienced by the twelve B-17s arriving in two separate flights from California, on the very tail of the Japanese first wave. (Fourteen had started out from Hamilton Field, but two had turned back shortly after wheels up.) With no armament and marginal fuel in their wing tanks, two bombers of the first flight, under the command of Major Richard H. Carmichael, suc-cessfully put down on the 1,200-foot runway at Haleiwa; three others passed through the thicket of Japanese air attack and American ground AA fire to safe landings at Hickam; and one landed on a golf course. The second flight, led by Major Truman H. Landon, was harried by Zero fighters as it made its own approach and landings, two bombers at Haleiwa, one at Wheeler, one at Bellows, and seven at Hickam. Remark-ably, the sturdily built Flying Fortresses suffered minimal casualties: one was destroyed, three were heavily damaged; only two crewmen were seri-ously injured.[44]

Proportionately, naval aviation assets on Oahu were more severely impacted than were those of the Army. The total number of aircraft of all types at Ford Island, Kanoehe Naval Air Station, and Ewa Marine Air Sta-tion was 301. Of 69 patrol planes, most of them PBY-3 and PBY-5 Catali-nas, 24 were destroyed and 34 damaged. The Patrol Wing 1 base at Kaneohe Bay, the first site on Oahu to be struck that morning, at 0750, was particularly devastated by bombing and strafing attacks during both Japa-nese waves; 18 men were killed. Of 24 fighters, 9 were destroyed, 15 dam-aged. Of 60 SBD scout bombers, 31 were destroyed, 15 damaged. Of 92 battleship and cruiser reconnaissance aircraft, 10 were destroyed, 71 damaged. And of 54 noncombatant utility and transport aircraft, 6 were destroyed, 32 damaged.[45]

The Navy also had planes flying into Oahu airspace while the raid was under way. While 215 miles west of Oahu on her return voyage from Wake, *Enterprise* flew off (at 0615 and 0637) eighteen SBD Dauntless dive-bombers toward the air stations at Ford Island and Ewa. Like the B-17 crews who stumbled into the Pacific war, the Navy pilots were stunned as they closed the shore to find Oahu under enemy fire. Four of the planes were shot out of the air by Zeros, killing two pilots. American

AA fire mistakenly accounted for another. At 0908 14ND radioed to all ships: "Do not fire on our planes coming in"; and, again, at 0921: "To all hands. Reported that enemy ships [sic] has [sic] red dot on bottom of fuselage."[46] (The red rising sun roundel, later called the "meatball" by U.S. servicemen, was actually on the underside of the wings.) One SBD crashlanded at a field on Kauai Island. The remainder found dangerous havens at Ford or Ewa.[47] Damage to ground installations at Ford, Ewa, and Kaneohe was heavy.

✳

Fuchida's Kate departed Oahu with the rear guard of fighters and, about noon, finding the carriers recovering the last of their aircraft on a northeast heading, successfully caught one of the arresting cables on *Akagi*. Not every plane before his had been so fortunate. Newly aroused seas had the carriers rolling and pitching. Numerous returning aircraft crashed onto the decks. When Fuchida tallied the casualties from AA fire and landing accidents, he reported 14 dive-bombers and 6 fighters lost from the second wave of 171 aircraft, for a total of 29 lost in both waves, and 74 damaged. "How many did you expect to lose?" he was asked in a postwar interrogation. "About half," he answered, "and we thought we would lose half our ships."[48] When Fuchida and Genda energetically clasped hands on *Akagi*'s flight deck it was with relief as well as with elation and triumph.

Fifty-five officers and men had been lost.

✳

How did the American principals seen earlier on this day first learn of the Japanese air attack? A few minutes before 0800, Ensign Tanner's 14P1 began to crackle with "frenzied" voice and coded Morse messages, one of which, eventually, was directed to him. Base headquarters at Kaneohe turned his flight of three patrol bombers northwest and north to search between 270 and 360 degrees for Japanese carriers responsible for an attack under way against Oahu. Tanner and his crew found nothing in that sector, but one of the other PBYs in his flight, searching due north, encountered Zero fighters and took a number of hits in the aft fuselage. That bomber, commanded by Ensign Fred Meyer, continued scouting but also came up empty. Tanner later wrote, "I have often thought of the hour-plus warning we had, based on the action with the Jap submarine. I've wondered why we didn't better use that time to mount a defense of the island."[49] The hour-plus of which Tanner wrote would be correct if one counted from *Ward's* message at 0653; but not from the time of his own message, which was sent coded at 0715 and was not decoded until 0735. Still, any warning would have helped.

✷

Ward's skipper, Lt. Outerbridge, continued to be busy following his famous attack and message. He brought in a sampan that had been found in restricted waters and he made more depth charge attacks on submarine contacts. *Ward* was still at general quarters when the ship's executive officer, standing next to Outerbridge on the bridge, pointed toward the harbor and said, "They are making a lot of noise over there this morning, Captain." Outerbridge replied, "Yes, I guess they are blasting the new road from Pearl to Honolulu." The Exec said, "Look at those planes. They are coming straight down." Outerbridge looked, as the Exec added, "Gosh, they are having an attack over there." Outerbridge said, "They certainly are."[50]

✷

Lt. Comdr. Kaminski was still at his watch officer station in 14ND head-quarters when, at approximately 0755, "I heard a plane approaching from the south. I saw it from [the] southerly lanai [porch] of [the] administration building. I could discern the Rising Sun of Japan under the wings. The plane was joined shortly by others with the same insignia on [them]. This plane was flying very low and hedge-hopping, just going over the roof."[51]

✷

At Opana, Privates Lockard and Elliott closed down the radar operation when the return signal from "an unusually large number of planes" reached a distance of about twenty-two miles and became distorted by a back wave off the mountains. Anyway, the truck had arrived to take them down for breakfast at the eighteen-man tent camp nine miles away at Hawailoa. As Elliott remembered it:

About a quarter way away from the camp, we noticed from our truck all of the men from the camp driving very fast in the opposite direction in which we were going. They were going to the [radar] unit. They had their field packs, and helmets, and what not. We still had no indication as to what had happened until we arrived at the camp, when we were told that we had been attacked by the Japanese.[52]

There the two privates turned over their record of readings to platoon commander 2nd Lt. John Upson. "We were very proud of the reading that we had gotten," said Elliott. "We brought it back to show it off, so to speak."[53] There is no information in the surviving documents that this writer has found to explain what Upson did with the readings—whether, for instance, he communicated the report to his superior, Capt. W. H. Tetley, or to overall AWS commander Lt. Col. C. A. Powell, both at Schofield Barracks. Lockard said later that, in camp, the men remaining were "looking at the sky," where, to the south, they could see "black oil smoke," and that they were aware that Pearl Harbor was being attacked by Japanese aircraft. He turned to Elliott and said, "I bet that is what we saw"—or "something like that."[54]

When in 1945 Elliott was asked in the JCC hearings, "Did anybody come to you during that day and ask you to tell them what you saw in the radar at seven o'clock that morning?" he answered, "No sir; only the men at our individual camp that were interested to know just what had gone on." So all the men there had the information? "Yes, sir; very definitely, sir." And if anyone had called your camp on the telephone they could have gotten that information from practically anybody there? "Yes, sir."[55] When, later, Lockard was asked, about the information, "When was it first taken notice of officially?" he answered, "It must have been about a week." Actually, a copy of the radar plot reached CINCPAC on Tuesday the ninth.[56]

At the Information Center at Fort Shafter, operator Private McDonald was relieved from his switchboard at 0730:

I took this message [from Opana] with me. By the way, it was the first time I ever did that, but I wanted to show the fellows, up at the tent; so they all saw it; and when the planes were coming over there, I began to get a little shaky. . . . When they started coming down and diving all around I just started running for the nearest pile.[57]

★

Lt. Tyler, who had told Lockard and Elliott "not to worry about it," stated on 20 December that:

> At about 0750 I heard some airplanes outside and looking toward Pearl Harbor saw what I thought to be a navy [sic] practicing dive bombing runs. At a little after 0800, Sergeant Eugene Starry, A[ir]. C[orps]., Wheeler Field called me to tell me that Wheeler Field had been attacked. I immediately had the telephone operator call all men back to duty. . . . I remained on duty . . . until about 1615, 8 December 1941, with the exception of rest periods.[58]

★

Lt. Comdr. Ramsay was in his operations office at PatWing 2 on Ford Island when he received a call from the staff duty officer reporting Ensign Tanner's message from patrol bomber 14P1. He immediately reported in turn to the CINCPAC duty officer, Commander Murphy, and went to the PatWing 2 Command Center, where, together with the staff duty officer, he observed what both thought was a U.S. Navy aircraft diving ("flathatting") over the southern seaplane ramp on the island. They did not see that the plane had dropped a bomb near the VP-22 hangar until the delayed fuse detonated at 0757. "Never mind: it's a Jap," he said, and at 0758 broadcast a voice alert, in the clear on all frequencies, that Samuel Eliot Morison later called "a message that shook the United States as nothing had since the firing on Fort Sumter":[59]

AIR RAID PEARL HARBOR. THIS IS NO DRILL.[60]

The alert was repeated by the signal tower in the navy yard to all ships and stations at 0800.[61]

★

Admiral Bloch, as noted earlier, first became aware of the air attack when "he heard the explosion in close proximity to my house, and that was around 7:55."[62] He went "as fast as I could" to 14ND headquarters, where he sent notice that Oahu had been attacked to Washington, Manila, Guam, and all ships at sea. He then issued the following orders:

> Close all Navy Yard gates to traffic. Have Captain of the Yard detail fire parties. Notify Marines to make all men available to assist in fighting fires. Notify Marines to bring in from Salt Lake Camp all available Marines. Notify Yard to flood drydock. Make arrangements for civilian workmen to be rounded up and brought to the Yard to assist in damage control. Notify hospital to establish emergency measures for caring for killed and wounded.[63]

★

Bloch's opposite number, General Short, heard the first bombs "about 7:55" at his quarters in Fort Shafter. He thought at first that the Navy was conducting exercises about which either he had not been made aware or had forgotten. When some more explosions sounded, he went out on the back porch to have a look—Pearl Harbor was only four statute miles distant—"and about that time the chief of staff [Colonel Phillips, who lived nearby] came running over to my quarters about three minutes after eight, and said he had just received a message from Wheeler or Hickam, or both—I have forgotten which—that it was the real thing."[64]

Short told Phillips to put into effect Alert No. 3. By 0810, with telephone calls to the Army's four major units, that was done. Because of the manner in which the full alert plans had been written and practiced, every unit down to the company level sprang into action. "We didn't have to issue a long winded order," Short said in the following month. "Everybody knew exactly what his job was, because there was no confusion." The Army's 24th and 25th Divisions took up battle positions against the possibility of a land invasion. And the AA batteries scrambled for their ammunition.[65]

★

Admiral Kimmel was buttoning on his white uniform at his quarters when Captain Murphy called for a second time, to report that *Ward* was towing a sampan into Honolulu Harbor. Before Murphy could finish that message, a yeoman interrupted him to say, "There's a message from the signal tower saying the Japanese are attacking Pearl Harbor and this is no drill."[66]

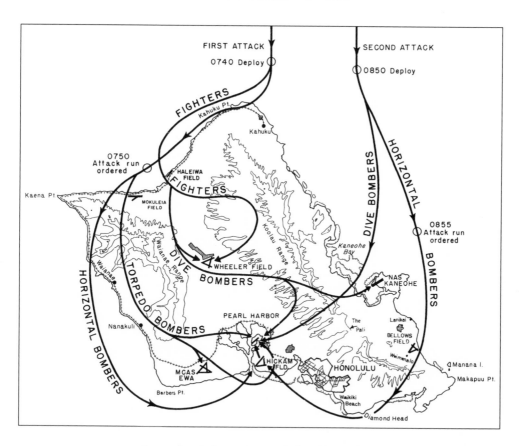

drawn by Robert M. Berish for The Rising Sun in the Pacific,
courtesy National Historical Center

Murphy relayed that message to Kimmel, who bounded out the front door toward the automobile door held open for him by his driver. There would be no golf game as scheduled with General Short this morning. Seeing Captain Earle's wife standing on her front lawn looking down on Battleship Row, he paused to follow her eyes, first, toward the black oil smoke beginning to rise over the Battle Force, then overhead to the Japanese aircraft with their red roundels flying figure-eight bombing runs across the harbor. Mrs. Earle later told historian Gordon W. Prange that, for that brief wordless moment, Kimmel seemed to be in a state of "utter disbelief and completely stunned." His face, she said, was "as white as the uniform he wore."[67]

Within ten minutes Kimmel was in his corner office on the second deck of the submarine base, absorbing information and issuing messages and orders, including these:

At 0816:
FROM THE COMMANDER IN CHIEF TO ALL SHIPS AND STATIONS X
HOSTILITIES WITH JAPAN COMMENCED WITH AIR RAID ON PEARL X

At 0817:
FROM CINC TO COMPATWING-2 X LOCATE ENEMY FORCE

At 0832:
FROM CINC TO ALL SHIPS PRESENT PEARL X JAPANESE SUBMARINE
IN HARBOR

At 0902:
FROM CINC TO COMTASKFORCE 38 AND 12 AND ALL SHIPS PACIFIC
FLT X EXECUTE WPL46 AGAINST JAPAN[68]

★

At Washington, Admiral Stark was talking with Navy Secretary Knox in the latter's office when a dispatch arrived from Pearl Harbor. It was Lt. Comdr. Ramsey's terse composition: "Air Raid Pearl Harbor: This Is No Drill." Knox was disbelieving. "My God!" he barked. "This can't be true, this must mean the Philippines." But Stark checked the point of origin on the signal, and said, "No, sir, this is Pearl."[69] Knox then called the President, who was with Harry Hopkins. As Hopkins wrote later that day,

> I lunched with the President today at his desk in the Oval Room. We were talking about things far removed from war when at about 1:40 Secretary Knox called and said that they had picked up a radio from Honolulu from the Commander-in-Chief of our forces there advising all our stations that an air raid attack was on and that it was "no drill."[70]

For twenty minutes, while awaiting confirmation of the message and additional details, Roosevelt discussed the likelihood of the report being true, as against Hopkins's belief that "there must be some mistake and that surely Japan would not attack in Honolulu."[71]

*

Army Secretary Stimson, after an hour and a half meeting with Secretaries Hull and Knox in the secretary of State's office that broke up at noon, returned home for lunch. His diary entry for that Sunday records:

> And just about 2:00 o'clock, while I was sitting at lunch, the President called me up on the telephone and in a rather excited voice asked me, "Have you heard the news?" I said, "Well, I have heard the telegrams which have been coming in about the Japanese advances in the Gulf of Siam." He said, "Oh, no. I don't mean that. They have attacked Hawaii. They are now bombing Hawaii." Well, that was an excitement indeed.[72]

General Marshall left the office of the Chief of Staff at noon, directly after filing an alert to General Short (copy to Admiral Kimmel), and had his driver take him to his quarters at Fort Myer for lunch. Before leaving, he had asked Col. John R. Deane, secretary of the general staff, to keep the office open and to have some of the commissioned and civilian personnel report for duty. As Deane remembered events six months later:

> At about 1:30 P.M. an enlisted man from the Navy rushed into my office out of breath with a pencil note, which was supposed to have been a message from the Navy radio operator at Honolulu and which said, as I recall: "Pearl Harbor attacked. This is no drill." I immediately telephoned General Marshall at his quarters at Fort Myer. . . . He directed me to contact Hawaii if possible and verify the message. Before I could do this another and more official message came, indicating the correctness of the first message that had been received. General Marshall was in his office within ten minutes.[73]

*

This Sunday as on every Sunday since he first entered the State Department in 1933, Cordell Hull was in his office: first, as planned, to meet with Knox and Stimson; second, as expected since about ten o'clock when he was handed the "one o'clock" Magic decrypt, to receive the Japanese emissaries Nomura and Kurusu. The formal request made by them to have that audience at 1:00 P.M. came by telephone shortly before noon. Hull agreed to remain in his office for that purpose. But shortly after the agreed-upon hour, Nomura called to ask for a postponement until 1:45. The two men entered State's diplomatic waiting room, in fact, at 2:05, the exact time when Hull received a call from Roosevelt advising him in a "steady but clipped" tone that "there's a report that the Japanese have attacked Pearl Harbor." Hull asked if the report had been confirmed, and the President answered that it had not. (Stark would telephone in the confirmation to Roosevelt at 2:28, adding that there was damage to the fleet and loss of life.) Hull told Roosevelt that Nomura and Kurusu were waiting outside his office. The President advised him to go ahead and receive them, not to mention that he possessed news about an attack, but to receive their fourteen-part message "formally and coolly and bow them out."[74]

Part of the mythology of Pearl Harbor is the explanation commonly given for Nomura's and Kurusu's failure to make the deadline imposed on them by Tokyo. The assumption of many is that Japan intended to break off negotiations with the United States as a substitute for a formal declaration of war, and to do so a half hour prior to the opening of hostilities. Article I of the Second Hague Peace Convention (1907), which Japan had signed, required that hostilities undertaken by one nation against another should not commence "without an explicit warning, in the form of either a reasoned declaration of war or of an ultimatum with conditional declaration of war."[75] Apparently, Japanese Foreign Minister Togo interpreted the fourteen-part response to Hull's Ten-Point note as meeting the stipulations of the last phrase cited. Roosevelt, too, after reading the first thirteen parts, said, "This means war"; as described above. Thus, according to a widely held belief, Japan's surprise attack would be considered in that country at least to be "honorable." The delay in meeting that "half-hour prior" deadline has traditionally been attributed to the tardiness of the Japanese embassy in preparing the fourteen-part message for presentation. Ordered by a dispatch that had followed the pilot message that they "be absolutely sure not to use a typist," Nomura and Kurusu relied upon an embassy official named Okumura Katsuzo, whose typing skills were at best "hunt and peck." His slowness at the typewriter, so the story goes, forced the postponement of the presentation until after the attack.

Conservative historians in Japan have promoted this account to support their views, first, that the United States forced their country into war, and, second, that the only factor preventing the onset of hostilities from being entirely honorable was a bumbling embassy staff in Washington. In 1999 those views were challenged by Professor Takeo Iguchi, of the faculty of law and international relations at the International Christian University in Tokyo. Iguchi has turned up papers in the Foreign Ministry archives, as well as the war diary of the Imperial General Staff, which suggest that Japan's diplomatic and military leaders deliberately retarded the delivery of the fourteen-part message as a means of assuring the success of a surprise attack. A 7 December entry in the war diary notes with satisfaction that "our deceptive diplomacy is steadily proceeding toward success." The diplomatic documents include an earlier draft of the fourteen-part message, dated 3 December, that more closely tracked the Hague requirement of a warning, in that it stated that Washington "would be held responsible for any and all the consequences that may arise in the future." But the war diary shows that the Army and Navy staffs objected to that warning and forced the adoption of the weaker, non-threatening language contained in the final message. Professor Iguchi maintains that the delay in presenting the message was also deliberately planned by the military with the cooperation of a pliant Minister Togo. His evidence is the unusual number of "garbles" in the original enciphered text—significantly more than one finds in other diplomatic traffic. (These garbles, it may be noted, seem not to have slowed down the U.S. Navy cryptographers.) Iguchi observed that many leading historians in his country have described the embassy's fumbling performance as an "ugly blemish" on Japan's modern history. "But," in his own view, "the blemish belongs to those who engaged in deliberate deception, or who have failed to ever go into the documentary evidence."[76]

✮

At 2:20 Secretary Hull directed that Nomura and Kurusu be brought into his office. He stood to meet them with one of his aides, Joseph W. Ballantine, alongside. Believing that there was but "one chance out of a hundred that [the Pearl Harbor attack] was not true," he received the two Japanese with a stern face, and did not invite them to be seated. Nomura said that he had been instructed by his Foreign Ministry to deliver a message to the secretary at one o'clock, but had been delayed in putting it into proper form. Hull took the document and asked what the significance of one o'clock was. Nomura said he did not know. Hull skimmed through the fourteen parts—he had read them before—and then fixed a cold eye on Nomura:

I must say that in all my conversations with you during the last nine months I have never uttered one word of untruth. This is borne out absolutely by the record. In all my fifty years of public service I have never seen a document that was more crowded with infamous false-hoods and distortions—infamous falsehoods and distortions on a scale so huge that I never imagined until today that any Government on this planet was capable of uttering them.[77]

With that, he nodded toward the door. The two emissaries silently with-drew, their heads bowed. They would learn about the attack when they reached the embassy.

✲

At 3:00 P.M. President Roosevelt met with Hull, Stimson, Knox, Marshall, Stark, and Hopkins. We are indebted to Hopkins for a short contempora-neous account of the discussion: "The conference met in not too tense an atmosphere because I think that all of us believed that in the last analysis the enemy was Hitler and that he could never be defeated without force of arms; that sooner or later we were bound to be in the war and that Japan had given us an opportunity. Everybody, however, agreed on the serious-ness of the war and that it would be a long, hard struggle. During the con-ference the news kept coming in indicating more and more damage to the fleet."[78] No doubt Stark was one of those present who was eager to duke it out with Hitler. But war with Japan by no means meant that Germany would necessarily declare war against the United States as a consequence of the Japanese attack. There was no known pact requiring it. Nor was it certain that the Congress would vote for a U.S. declaration against Ger-many, absent a German attack or declaration. (Four days later, in one of history's more baffling decisions—improvised and unnecessary, it doomed his war—Hitler declared war on the United States. On the same day, the U.S. Congress reciprocated.)

At 4:00 that afternoon, Washington time, Japanese Imperial Headquar-ters formally declared that a state of war existed between that country and both the United States and Great Britain. Prime Minister Churchill called the White House from England. He had heard the news. He would learn later that Singapore had been attacked, and that landings had been made at Khota Baru in Malaya. Roosevelt told him, "We are all in the same boat now."[79] In the evening, beginning at 8:30, Roosevelt met with his entire cabinet in the Oval Room. "The President nodded as we came in," wrote Secretary of Labor Frances Perkins, "but there was none of the usual cordial, personal greeting. This was one of the few occasions he couldn't muster a smile." She mentioned "the terrible shock of Pearl Harbor, the destruction of his precious ships. . . ."[80] The President sat at his desk with the cabinet in a semicircle in front of him. "He opened by telling us that this was the most serious meeting of the Cabinet that had taken place since 1861," Stimson recorded in his diary, "and then he proceeded to enumerate the blows which had fallen upon us in Hawaii."[81] After which, he read slowly from the very brief draft statement that he intended to present to Congress the next day. Most of the members supported Hull's suggestion that the President deliver a more lengthy address covering the entire range of Japan's lawless conduct. But Roosevelt demurred; he thought a short statement centered on the attack at Hawaii would be both more widely read and more effective. Forgoing the proffered help of Hull and his staffers, he would write the finished statement himself. No one present supported Stimson's advocacy of a request to Congress that war also be declared against Germany. At about 9:30 P.M., as FDR's aides had arranged, the cabinet meeting was enlarged to include Vice President Henry Wallace and ten leading senators and representatives of both the Democratic and Republican parties. "The President began by a very frank story of what had happened, including our losses," Stimson recorded. "The effect on the Congressmen was tremendous. They sat in dead silence and even after the recital was over they had very few words."[82] Among those few words, we learn from another source, were these from Senator Thomas T. "Tom" Connally (D. Tex.), chairman of the Foreign Relations Committee: "Well, they were supposed to be on alert. . . . I am amazed at the attack by Japan, but I am still more astounded at what happened to our Navy. They were all asleep. Where were our patrols? They knew these negotiations were going on."[83]

The stigmatization of Kimmel had begun.

★

Churchill had spent the evening of the seventh at his country home in Chequers entertaining, appropriately, U.S. ambassador to Britain John G. Winant and Roosevelt's special representative W. Averell Harriman. While in their company Churchill heard the news of Pearl Harbor from his butler, who had caught it on the radio. Within minutes Churchill placed his call to Roosevelt, who confirmed the report. That night, as he prepared for bed, the prime minister's mind filled with positive, even exultant, thoughts: "To have the United States at our side was to me the greatest joy." Britain's long, lonely nightmare was over. "So we had won after all!" Saturated with such emotion, "I went to bed and slept the sleep of the saved and thankful."[84]

★

Shortly after noon on Monday the eighth, Roosevelt appeared before a joint session of the Congress and delivered substantially the same talk that he had tested before the cabinet. In it he did not ask Congress to declare a war before the commencement of hostilities. Rather, he asked Congress to declare that "since the unprovoked and dastardly attack by Japan," a state of war "has existed" between the two nations. The speech lasted only six minutes and thirty seconds. It contained two sentences that have been securely graven into the monument of American oratory:

> Yesterday, December seventh, 1941—a date which will live in infamy—the United States of America was suddenly and deliberately attacked by naval and air forces of the Empire of Japan. . . .

> With confidence in our armed forces—with the unbounded determination of our people—we will gain the inevitable triumph—so help us God.[85]

Thirty-three minutes later, Congress passed a joint resolution affirming the state of war. The vote in the Senate was 82 to 0, in the House 385 to 1 (Representative Jeannette Rankin [R. Wy.]). At 4:10 P.M. the declaration was signed by the President.

A largely isolationist nation had become overnight a virtually united internationalist nation.

A fighting patriotism swept the land. Popular-music tastes changed, as though in an instant, from "Rockabye My Baby, There Ain't Gonna Be No War" to "Let's Remember Pearl Harbor!"

No doubt, on the other side of the world, it was borne home on Admiral Yamamoto Isoruoku, who had certainly anticipated it, that an awful avenging force had been unleashed.

EPILOGUE

I have always felt that Kimmel and Short were held responsible for Pearl Harbor in order that the American people might have no reason to lose confidence in their Government in Washington. This was probably justifiable under the circumstances at that time, but it does not justify forever damning these two fine officers.

Admiral Raymond A. Spruance
1961

At 1330 Admiral Nagumo ordered his Striking Force to shape course for home. The decision not to pursue further the defeated American fleet was taken at the urging of First Air Fleet chief of staff Kusaka, and against the strenuous objections of Genda and Fuchida. The two airmen argued that, since the air force was still virtually intact, and, although the aerial torpedoes had been expended, there were still plenty of bombs for the Kates and Vals, hence another air assault should be mounted. The pilots and crews on *Akagi,* as Fuchida could personally attest, were unanimously in favor of pressing the attack further, against the elusive carriers, if they could be located, or if not, against remaining targets on Oahu.

Fuchida thought that *Enterprise* and *Lexington,* with their accompanying heavy cruisers, were exercising in calmer waters to the south of Oahu. He recommended to Nagumo that, instead of retiring basically by the same route it had taken on the voyage out, the fleet should travel to the south of Oahu, thence in the direction of the Marshalls, all the while carrying out air searches for the American carriers. Two carriers could not stand up to Nagumo's six. But Nagumo and Kusaka raised what Fuchida later called "one insuperable obstacle." That part of the tanker train that had detached at rendezvous Point C on the voyage out was standing by on the northwestern withdrawal route to refuel the fleet. If redirected southward it would not be able to catch up with the fast carriers. (Though no one on *Akagi's* bridge knew it, the American carriers were not south of Oahu but to the west and northwest.) Dashed, Fuchida recommended another pounding of Oahu, but he did not identify exactly which targets.[1] But Nagumo firmly said no. Later, the once reluctant commander of *Kido Butai*, now its surprised victorious commander, committed his reasons to writing:

1. The first attack had inflicted practically all the damage that we had anticipated, and a further attack could not have been expected to augment this damage to any great extent.
2. Even in the first attack, the enemy's antiaircraft fire had been so prompt as virtually to nullify the advantage of surprise. In a further attack, it had to be expected that our losses would increase out of all proportion to the results achievable.
3. Radio intercepts indicated that the enemy still had at least fifty large-type aircraft in operational condition, and at the same time the whereabouts and activities of its carriers, heavy cruisers, and submarines were unknown.
4. To remain within attack range of enemy land-based planes was distinctly to our disadvantage, especially in view of the limited range of our own air searches and the undependability of our submarine patrol then operating in the Hawaiian area.[2]

There may have been other reasons besides, which Nagumo would be reluctant to acknowledge. For one thing, as Combined Fleet Chief of Staff Ugaki entered in his diary on the day following the attack, "We haven't yet had a plan like that."[3] His Navy had not thought sufficiently ahead or broadly to consider the possibility that *Kido Butai* might carry off a surprisingly easy victory, which it did. An overly cautious operations staff had prepared no contingency plan for that eventuality. And Nagumo probably was not willing to improvise. Capt. Tomioka Sadatoshi, chief of the Operations Section of the Naval General Staff, told the historian Gordon

Prange after the war that Nagumo acted in character with a pervasive defect in the officers list: inflexible compliance with orders combined with the inability to adapt to new situations and to go beyond instructions.[4] A second possible reason was that Nagumo, who had initially opposed the Hawaii Operation, and now was sensible of the fact that he had met the bare requirements of his mission, was not willing to exploit the unanticipated opportunity before him. Protecting his fleet assumed more importance than inflicting additional damage on the enemy. In Prange's deft expression, "The admiral felt like a gambler who has staked his life's savings on the turn of a card and won. His only idea was to cash in and go home as quickly as possible."[5]

When Nagumo broke radio silence to inform Admiral Yamamoto both of the unexpectedly successful results of the raid and that he was retiring, staff officers on board the flagship *Nagato* objected that Nagumo should return to wipe up. Yamamoto is reported to have told them, "It would be fine, of course, if it were successful. But even a burglar hesitates to go back for more. I'd rather leave it to the commander of the task force. . . . He isn't going to do it just because he's prodded from a distance. I imagine Nagumo doesn't want to."[6] But late in 1942, at Truk, Yamamoto said to Vice Admiral Ozawa Jisaboro, commander, Third Battleship Division: "Events have shown that it was a great mistake not to have launched a second attack against Pearl Harbor."[7] The reason: the first attack had hit the *wrong targets*.

✻

To Admiral Kimmel the immediate problem was locating the Japanese carriers. At 0817 he had ordered the PBYs to "locate enemy carriers." With that, Ensign Tanner's dawn patrol flight of three PBY-5s was diverted from the operating area to southward to the sea approaches to Oahu between 310 and 360 degrees, northwest to north. Logan Ramsey, who had made that canny decision, was one of the few persons in command that morning who got it right: the carriers were either to the northwest or north. Tanner's flight did not find the carriers but one of his PBYs on a due north heading tangled with Zero fighters. Kimmel seems not to have known at the time of his order that PatWing 2's flight line lay in fiery ruin—only one PBY got into the air from Ford Island that day; it flew a pie sector search to the northwest without seeing anything but *Enterprise* with her three cruisers and nine destroyers.[8] And little help could be expected from PatWing 1 at Kaneohe where damage to the PBYs was proportionately even more severe. But four other PBY-5s were in the air that morning over the operating area conducting intertype exercises for communication and recognition with USN submarines. Ramsay redirected these four to the sector 245 degrees to 285 degrees west of Oahu. But these, of course, would not be in positions to sight the Japanese carriers.[9]

Kimmel had briefly entertained what he called "a hunch" that the attack had come from the northward, so that the planes could fly downwind with their bomb loads. But he failed to follow up on it. During the second wave bombing, cryptanalyst "Ham" Wright called Layton from Station Hypo to say that a direction-finding bearing had been acquired on a Japanese radio transmission. Unfortunately, it was a "bilateral" bearing: either 003 degrees or its reciprocal, 183 degrees. There was no way to correct it by reference to the Navy's large-array direction finder on a peak north of Pearl, since, for some reason, the Army had unplugged the telephone lines to that installation. When Kimmel asked Layton what information he had on the carriers' position, Kimmel became "uncharacteristically testy" when all Layton could report was: either north or south. "Goddammit!" he quoted Kimmel as saying, "We're under attack here . . . and you don't even know whether they're north or south. For Christ's sake!"[10]

Later, at 1046, bearings on another radio transmission indicated the "probability" of an enemy carrier to the southward at 178 degrees from Barbers Point on the southwest corner of Oahu. Kimmel had that position transmitted to Halsey on *Enterprise,* whose Task Force 8 was then about two hundred miles south by west of Pearl, standing to eastward. Halsey launched fifteen Douglas "Dauntless" dive-bombers with 1,000-pound bombs and altered course to a more southerly heading. At the time, Task Force 12 (Vice Admiral Newton), composed of the carrier *Lexington,* three cruisers, and five destroyers, was positioned at 23°45' N, 171°15' W, or 425 miles southeast of Midway and 300 miles west of French Frigate Shoals on a westerly course to land eighteen Marine F4F fighters on Midway. Newton cancelled the fly-off when he learned of the attack on Pearl, and, subsequently, Kimmel ordered him to proceed at fastest speed to join up with Halsey south of Oahu. The search by both carriers would be fruitless, of course, but, in one of that Sunday's kinder blunders, the erroneous heading saved both U.S. carriers from extinction. If, by contrast, the *Enterprise* and *Lexington* had steamed to the northward and had encountered the retiring *Kido Butai,* the odds against them would have been three to one, and, absent a "five-minute miracle" such as would happen at Midway, the carriers probably would have gone down with all hands.[11]

At Pearl, Kimmel scratched together thirty-four surviving aircraft of varying types and sent them on search missions 200 to 300 miles out. Short, too, got five B-17 and three B-18 bombers into the air, along with one A-20A medium bomber. At the same time, warships that had cleared the harbor, as well as those that now could, were organized as Task Force 1 and directed by Kimmel to join up with Halsey's Task Force 8 "to assist in locating and destroying the enemy."[12] All such efforts proved futile, and only after the recovery of flight charts from downed Japanese aircraft did the Hawaiian commanders learn that the attack made against them had been flown from the north. Admiral Newton said later that he had wondered from the start why anyone thought that the Japanese would be to the south, since that was the fleet's training area and all commercial shipping had been routed to southward, hence the Japanese carriers would likely have been observed before they launched their aircraft.[13]

In any event, both surface and air searches of the approaches to Oahu continued with what assets were available during the days and weeks that followed, since both Kimmel and Admiral Nimitz, who relieved him on the seventeenth and formally took command on the thirty-first, believed that the Japanese, after reflecting on the ease with which they had broken through Oahu's door, would return. The Navy Department helped by sending the newly refitted carrier *Saratoga* (CV-3) from the West Coast, and, from the Atlantic, the carrier *Yorktown* and three battleships that had been detached in the preceding April and May. Every available PBY was also rushed to Oahu. Nimitz would write on 7 January to the Navy's new CINCUS (that office now having been severed from CINCPAC) Admiral Ernest J. King:

> The attack of 7 December will be followed by others. The enemy has exploited the element of surprise. He can, however, use it again, although to a lesser extent because of local alertness measures, if adequate search is not maintained. In any case, his strength in carriers and heavy ships is such that he need not depend on surprise. . . .

Japanese aircraft carrier aviation, with all due allowance for the advantage of surprise, proved itself to be in a very high state of development. This applies with full force not only to material and to the training, skill and determination of personnel, but also to the unquestionably brilliant manner in which the entire expedition was conceived, planned and handled. This arm of the Japanese fleet has been greatly underestimated. Its potential must be recognized from now on.[14]

The Japanese carriers would not return to Pearl. But, in the June following, they would attempt to ambush the U.S. carriers off Midway, and, for all their "brilliance" and "potential," suffer there a crushing defeat. On that occasion it was the Japanese force that was surprised.

★

Before leaving the subject of surprise hostile attack, it bears mentioning that a carrier-borne air strike proved during the Pacific War to be the most difficult of all forms of naval attack to defend against, as the Japanese learned again and again, to their sorrow. First, because the attacking carriers made but a tiny mark on a very large ocean, thus were hard to detect. Second, because the weapons delivery systems that they launched reached their appointed targets with unprecedented speed. From 1 February 1942 to 13 August 1945 there were 72 major raids by U.S. carrier-based planes in which the element of surprise was a factor. Of those, 21 (29.2 percent) achieved complete surprise; 32 (44.4 percent) achieved partial surprise; 15 (20.8 percent) achieved no surprise; and 4 (5.5 percent) achieved an unknown element of surprise.[15] Overall, it was demonstrated that it was practically impossible to prevent or deflect an air attack once it was launched, remarkably even in those cases where the recipient of the attack was aware of the presence of enemy forces in the vicinity—the Halsey-Doolittle raid on Tokyo and other Japanese cities on 18 April 1942 was undeterred even though the carrier *Hornet* had been reported by picket boats—and even in some cases where the recipient was fully alerted.

Examples of the latter are the raids on Rabaul Harbor in New Britain conducted by Task Force 11 under Vice Admiral Wilson E. Brown in February 1942, and by Task Force TF 38 under Rear Admiral Frederick C. Sherman and Task Force 50.3 under Rear Admiral Alfred E. Montgomery in November 1943. One may cite, too, the attack in February 1944 by Vice Admiral Marc A. Mitscher's Task Force 58 on Truk, in the Carolines, where the carrier force was sighted twenty-four hours out by a Japanese scout plane.[16] In Admiral Kimmel's case at Pearl, where the advance warnings from Opana and *Ward* were not recognized for what they were because of a systems breakdown, Kimmel was under no illusion, either before or after the attack, that with the available forces and weapons he and Short could *repel* a determined air assault. The most he thought they could do was to make the aggressor pay a heavy price—which, as we know from Japanese staff planning, the *Kido Butai* expected to pay. The very nature of a surprise leaves defenders paralyzed in its opening minutes by the question, Are those enemy planes or *ours*? Short stated in the month following the attack that "I will say, this: that if we had been absolutely on the alert for this kind of an attack, I believe that those low flying planes that came in at two hundred feet would probably have gotten in regardless." Unlike Kimmel's AA, his own Army AA batteries had been far from being on the alert, and their tardy performance had been spotty at best.[17]

There were many instances in World War II, and there have been numerous since, where surprise occurred and no advance warning was immediately recognized. One thinks of the Ardennes in both 1940 and 1944, of the Yalu in 1950, Tet in 1968, Yom Kippur in 1973, the Beirut Marine barracks in 1983, Kuwait in 1990, Khobar Towers in 1996, the East African embassies in 1998, and the USS *Cole* (DDG-67) in 2000. Place Pearl Harbor at the head of that list. At Oahu Island the Japanese executed a cunning and audacious operational plan, under the strictest secrecy, and achieved complete tactical surprise, even though, as learned later, the possibilities of American foreknowledge were present. And it was not only at Oahu that Japan achieved surprise that day. At many of the other targets she struck on 7 December (Washington times) complete or partial surprise was effected: Singapore at 1500; Khota Baru at 1540; Davao Gulf, the Philippines, at 1810; Guam at 1810; Hong Kong at 1900; and Wake at 2000.[18] The only sites where there was full foreknowledge and warning that day were Clark and Iba U.S. Army Air bases, north of Manila, Luzon Island, in the Philippines. There a flight of level bombers and Zero fighters from Formosa (now Taiwan), 500 miles to the north, arrived overhead and unmolested at lunchtime on the eighth, local time (on the other side of the International Dateline). Depending on the source consulted, the advance warning time between receipt of the signal about Pearl Harbor at Army and Navy headquarters and the Japanese air strike on Clark and Iba was a startling *seven to ten hours*.[19] And yet General MacArthur's bomber and fighter squadrons on Luzon were caught flatfooted on the ground, where in a single stroke he lost almost half of his Far East Air Force, including half his fleet of B-17s, to bombs and strafing fire.

★

Admiral Yamamoto knew, even before he demonstrated it in a single morning, that the primacy of the battleship in ocean warfare had ended. Hence, it was ironic that he expended so much energy, and took such great risks, to prove the point. The U.S. Navy was not essentially diminished by the sinking, capsizing, disabling, or damaging of eight battleships. Those slow, obsolescent vessels would have had no roles to play in the major carrier battles that developed soon afterward at Coral Sea (7–8 May) and Midway (4–6 June). Nor would they have been capable of cruising to the western Pacific to interdict or harass Japan's Southern Operation anytime in the next six months, for lack of a supply train. And when, finally, they were needed to soften up invasion beaches and to engage Japan's own big-gun ships in blue-water exchanges of fire, six of those battleships would be ready. And that was owing to the fact that the navy yard was able quickly to repair the damaged vessels—*Maryland* by February 1942, *Nevada* by December 1942, *Pennsylvania* by January 1943, *Tennessee* by May 1943—and to refloat, repair, and modernize *California* by May 1944 and *West Virginia* by July 1944. (Only *Arizona* and *Oklahoma* were total losses.) *California* and *West Virginia* could be raised readily because the harbor water was shallow and their hulls had settled on even keels in the muck.

If any of the stricken battleships had been caught at sea, off soundings, in the vicinity of Oahu where Nagumo's aircraft flew, instead of where they were, it is not likely that any would have survived. And the number of deaths would have been greater by many thousands. That accounts for the paradox uttered by Admiral Nimitz in 1965: "It was God's mercy that our [battleship] fleet was in Pearl Harbor on December 7, 1941."[20] Two of the sunken and two of the damaged battleships—*California, West Virginia, Tennessee,* and *Maryland*—would participate in the largest naval battle in history, Leyte Gulf, in 23–25 October 1944, when the once-wounded veterans of Battleship Row "capped the T" on the battleships *Yamashiro* and *Fuso* in Surigao Strait.

What, then, *should* the Japanese have targeted at Pearl? The navy yard.

First, the two above-ground tank farms east and west, with their several million barrels of oil. That reserve had been barely sufficient to fuel the fleet on a training basis; oil was depleted faster than the supply line could haul it from the West Coast. Even the reduced fleet after 7 December expended 750,000 barrels of fuel oil in the first nine days after the attack, when the most that all the available Navy and commercial tankers could transport to Pearl at a time was 760,000 barrels.[21] Incineration of the tank farms would have totally immobilized the fleet. Second, the maintenance and repair shops, together with the drydocks, that kept the fleet ready for sea and, after 7 December, returned to the fleet two sunken and four damaged battleships, three damaged cruisers, three damaged destroyers, and the damaged *Curtiss, Oglala,* and *Vestal.*

Destruction of the tank farms and the shops, combined with demolition of the power plant and five submarines (*Gudgeon, Tautog, Cachalot, Narwhal,* and *Dolphin*) moored at the yard piers would have taken the Fleet out of the Pacific War for a conservatively estimated three months. On assuming command at Pearl, and expecting a second air strike, Admiral Nimitz observed, "There remain untouched the very important and tempting objectives of fuel supply, navy yard industrial establishment and drydocks, commercial docks and the city of Honolulu."[22] But by the date of those remarks, 7 January 1942, Nagumo's carriers were moored back in home waters, having shot their bolts in the wrong direction. Though they may not have realized it yet, their great tactical victory had become a strategic defeat. Attacking Pearl Harbor, as shown earlier, was not even necessary to protect their warlords' seizure of rubber, tin, tungsten, and oil. And for their pains they had riled up an American public as no other act in our history had. Said historian Morison in an oft-quoted judgment, "One can search military history in vain for an operation more fatal to the aggressor."[23]

★

Admiral Kimmel was given, and then denied, one last opportunity to fight the Japanese enemy, at Wake Island. Actually a volcanic atoll with three small islands above the ocean's surface, Wake was first attacked on 8 December (local time) by thirty-six twin-engined bombers from Japanese bases at Kwajalein Atoll, 620 nautical miles to southward in the Mandates. Defending Wake were a detachment of Marines, of the 1st Defense Battalion,

Fleet Marine Force, and Marine fighter squadron VMF-211, consisting of twelve F4F-38 Grumman Wildcats that had been flown off *Enterprise* on the fourth. After just ten minutes of bombing, nearly all the ground facilities on Wake were destroyed, nine Wildcats were destroyed or damaged, and twenty-three Marine officers and men and ten civilian workers were left dead or dying. Second and third bombing attacks hit the wounded garrison on the ninth and tenth, after which a small invasion force, with 450 naval landing troops, appeared off the beaches on the eleventh. The besieged garrison made surprisingly good use of its coastal artillery and surviving Wildcats, sinking two destroyers, damaging two light cruisers and setting fire to a transport, killing an estimated five hundred Japanese, and preventing an amphibious landing—all for the loss of a single American life.

At Pearl, Kimmel and his war plans staff were drawing up plans for sending a reinforcement expedition to the exposed base, when, on the same day that Wake held, CINCPAC headquarters was distracted by the arrival in Hawaii of Secretary of the Navy Knox, who had come to make a personal inspection of fleet losses. (A parallel mission from the War Department was frustrated when the aircraft carrying Col. Charles W. Bundy, of the War Plans staff, crashed into the High Sierras while on course to California.) After Knox's four-engine PB2Y Coronado flying boat set down in Kaneohe Bay, amid the burned wreckage of PBYs and hangars, he was driven to the Royal Hawaiian Hotel at Waikiki Beach. Kimmel greeted him there and, shortly afterward, escorted him and his aide Captain Beatty to CINCPAC headquarters, from which the secretary could plainly see the broken remains of Battleship Row, the *Arizona* still smoking. There, too, he heard a detailed briefing on what had happened from Kimmel and his staff, during which one unidentified staff officer made a "fervent plea" for the dispatch of a reinforcement expedition to Wake. Knox would state later that those in responsible position showed a willingness "to assume their share of the blame."[24]

Following the briefing, the secretary allowed that no one in the Department of the Navy, including Kelly Turner, had expected an attack on Pearl. (But Knox would be among those who would make sure that the two men, Kimmel and Short, who had the *least* information to go on would be the ones held responsible for knowing what was going to happen.) If that was true, it put another of his remarks in a very curious light: "Did you get Saturday night the dispatch the navy department sent out?"[25]

Kimmel answered that no warning had been received after 27 November, except for the Army's grossly delayed alert of 7 December. "Well, we sent you one," Knox insisted.[26] Poco Smith particularly recalled that Knox used the phrase "on the Saturday preceding Pearl Harbor."[27] Beatty later asked each staffer, in turn, "Did you receive our message of the sixth?" (Later investigation turned up no such warning or warning draft directed to Pearl Harbor in Navy Department files.) Knox studied closely every photograph of the attack and its effects that intelligence officer Layton had collected; met twice with General Short; visited the burn ward at Hospital Point—"The sight of those men made me as angry as I have ever been in my life"[28]—and, after thirty-two hours of investigation, reboarded his aircraft for the flight home. Shortly after takeoff he commented to Beatty, "Frank, you will be glad to hear that a decision was finally reached and relief forces for Wake will soon be on its way."[29]

★

Kimmel had long regarded Wake as both a defensible position and a bait: "If Wake be defended," he had written to OpNav the previous 18 April, "then for the Japanese to reduce it would require extended operations of their naval force in an area where we might be able to get at them, thus offering us an opportunity to get at naval forces with naval forces."[30] Now he and his staff settled on an improvised task force built around the carrier *Saratoga,* then racing back to Pearl from repair at San Diego. "Sara" was the choice over "Big E" and "Lady Lex" because she embarked eighteen new Marine Corps Wildcats with full personnel and equipment. The other two carriers would provide diversion and support. In company with three cruisers and a destroyer squadron, *Saratoga* sortied from Pearl to Wake at 1115 on 16 December, under the overall command of Rear Admiral Frank Jack Fletcher.

Unfortunately for Kimmel, on that same Tuesday a dispatch arrived from Stark ordering him to relinquish his command effective 1500 on the following day. The blow was not unexpected. On the day after the attack, while talking in his office with Soc McMorris and operations officer Captain DeLany, Kimmel said, "If I were in charge in Washington I would relieve Kimmel at once. It doesn't make any difference why a man fails in the Navy, he has failed."[31] Both men protested that nothing like that would happen. In public Kimmel had kept up his spirits, and had tried to do the same for others. On the eleventh he had issued a joint statement with Bloch:

> We Americans can receive hard blows but can deliver harder ones. In these days when we face the task that lies ahead with calm determination and unflinching resolve, it is truly great to be an American.
>
> Victory for us is assured.
>
> Never have we been so proud as when we saw Sunday's magnificent response to the call of duty by civilian employees of the government and contractor firms—whom we call un-uniformed fighters—and officers and men of the Navy, Marine Corps, and Army.[32]

In private, however, it was clear to his closest associates that Kimmel's spirits had flagged. Rear Admiral Walter S. Anderson, who as commander, Battleships, Battle Force, had his own reasons to be downcast, became particularly distressed about the emotional state of his friend:

> I used to go over to see ol' Kimmel and try to cheer him up because I was worried about him, you know, because he was awfully depressed. I talked to "Poco," and he showed me some of the files and there was that well-known telegram [of 27 November] which, paraphrased, ordered "You must allow the Japanese to attack first." "Poco" had written on it "They did!"[33]

Kimmel's removal from command was owed to the self-serving report of findings that Knox presented to Roosevelt immediately upon his arrival in Washington, at 2000 on the fourteenth. While granting that "neither Short nor Kimmel, at the time of the attack, had any knowledge of the plain intimations of some surprise move, made clear in Washington, through the interception of Japanese instructions to Nomura, in which a surprise move of some kind was clearly indicated by the insistence upon the precise time of Nomura's reply to Hull, at one o'clock on Sunday," three times Knox stated that Short and Kimmel were not in "a state of readiness" for an air attack. He praised the fighting spirit of the crews aboard ships, which he called "superb," and pointed out that the ships' AA batteries were firing within four minutes after the first torpedo was dropped, "and this fire grew rapidly in intensity." At the same time, he wrote critically of the Army's AA performance: "All Army personnel were in their quarters and the guns were not manned or in position for firing, save only those in fixed positions." In a summing-up a sentence he wrote, "Army preparations were primarily based on fear of sabotage while the Navy's were based on fear of submarine attack."[34]

On the fifteenth Roosevelt decided that a "formal investigation" should be conducted to determine if there had been "any dereliction of duty prior to the attack." He also directed that Knox and Stimson should give press conferences and release those parts of Knox's report that would not give helpful information to the enemy. The services were to accept equal responsibility and blame. Accordingly, Knox told the press that six warships had been sunk: *Arizona* (hit by a bomb "said to have literally passed down through the smokestack"), *Utah*, three destroyers (*Cassin, Downes,* and *Shaw,* all heavily damaged but not in fact sunk), and minelayer *Oglala; Oklahoma* had capsized, he also reported. He omitted mention of Magic intelligence that had been withheld. The Army and Navy, he said, "were not on the alert against the surprise air attack on Hawaii." He claimed that, nonetheless, forty-one Japanese planes (as against twenty-nine actual) were destroyed. Knox stated that any action taken against the Hawaiian commanders would be "dependent on the facts and recommendations made by [an] investigating board."[35] But that restraint lasted just one day.

At the order of Roosevelt, who wanted to restore the public's confidence in the two services as quickly as possible, the Navy and War Departments issued simultaneous orders on the sixteenth relieving Admiral Kimmel of his command and displacing General Short as well as his Hawaiian Air Force commander General Martin. Yielding both CINCPAC and CINCUS, Kimmel was assigned to "temporary duty in the Fourteenth Naval District." Rear Admiral Chester W. Nimitz was assigned to CINCPAC and (temporarily) to CINCUS with the rank of admiral. Pending Nimitz's arrival at Pearl, temporary command of the Pacific Fleet would be held by Vice Admiral Pye, commander, Battle Force. The Army replaced its ground and air commanders in Hawaii with two Air Corps officers, Lt. Gen. Delos C. Emmons and Brig. Gen. Clarence L. Tinker, respectively. Martin apparently paid the price for Short's decision to bunch up his aircraft on the ground, where many were easily destroyed. Altogether, *The*

New York Times declared, the changes in command constituted "one of the most drastic shake-ups in American military and naval history."[36]

Knox's published report of Navy losses at Pearl combined with the relief of Kimmel had the effect of fixing Kimmel in the public mind as the principal miscreant in the debacle, however weak the evidence against him. The Army, which had primary responsibility for protecting Pearl and the fleet, was barely mentioned in the recriminations that now swept the country. Nor were the War and Navy Departments cited as having any particular responsibility for the defeat. The lion's share of the blame belonged to Kimmel, the country was led to believe, because he was the one who lost the ships and most of the lives. Kimmel's discharge from command before the "formal investigation" even began had the further effect of branding him publicly as derelict in his duty.

★

In CINCPAC headquarters, at 1500 on the seventeenth, Rear Admiral Kimmel and Vice Admiral Pye read their orders to each other and shook hands. Kimmel said good-bye to his downhearted staff and retired to his quarters. Pye now inherited direction of the Wake relief expedition being led at sea by Fletcher in *Saratoga*. At 1000 on the twenty-first (Wake time) Wake radioed that it was under heavy air attack by carrier-borne dive-bombers; at noon it reported severe damage inflicted by seventeen heavy bombers. Certain to follow in a day or two was a second and larger landing force. By 2000 on the twenty-first Fletcher was just 500 miles distant from the beleaguered atoll. But instead of pressing forward at twenty knots to be in position to attack such a landing force at or before dawn on the twenty-third he took a time-out—ten hours—on the twenty-second to refuel four of his eight destroyers from the fleet oiler USS *Neches*, which Kimmel had dispatched ahead. As a result, by 0800 on the twenty-third *Saratoga* was only ninety miles closer to Wake than she had been twenty-four hours earlier. Meanwhile, the bombing of Wake continued, and, as expected, a formidable invasion force, attended by carriers *Soryu* and *Hiryu* as well as by heavy cruisers *Tone* and *Chikuma,* all detached from Nagumo's *Kido Butai* on its homeward voyage, assembled offshore. Landings began at 0235 on the twenty-third and by 0500 an overwhelming number of Japanese troops controlled a solid beachhead.[37]

At Pearl, Pye, his chief of staff, Rear Admiral Milo F. Draemel, and Soc

McMorris deliberated on what further could be done. All three concluded that Wake could no longer be relieved. But should *Saratoga* proceed to engage the enemy, regardless? The country needed a victory. Pye decided no. He ordered Fletcher to retire. To Stark he reported, "The conservation of our naval forces became the first consideration." On *Saratoga* the order to withdraw angered officers from the bridge to the flight deck; Marine pilots bent on saving their service-mates on Wake raged at the pusillanimity. But it was too late for Wake, which surrendered directly after Pye's order. *Saratoga*'s aircraft may not have reached the Japanese carriers and cruisers even if they tried, since that supporting force began retiring to the westward shortly after the landings. Even so, the withdrawal of *Saratoga* left a bitter taste in the mouths of many Navy and Marine personnel—more bitter for some than what had happened on the seventh. Samuel Eliot Morison, the official historian of U.S. naval operations in World War II, concluded in his account of the fiasco, "If Admiral Kimmel had been allowed to retain the Pacific Fleet command a few days longer, Wake might have been relieved, and there would certainly have been a battle."[38]

★

On 16 December Roosevelt appointed a five-man commission consisting of two Army officers, two Navy officers, and a civilian "to investigate the losses and to make recommendations."[39] White House press secretary Stephen Early stated that "if it [commission] finds that negligence contributed to the losses it will fix responsibility for them."[40] Upon the recommendation of Stimson, Roosevelt chose for the chairman Owen J. Roberts, Associate Justice of the Supreme Court. Roberts had gained national attention as a prosecutor in the Teapot Dome oil scandal. As the only member of the Court who had not been appointed by Roosevelt—Herbert Hoover named him in 1930—Roberts was thought to be a neutral, objective choice, and press reaction was favorable. For the Navy members Knox chose Admiral William H. Standley, Retired, chief of Naval Operations from 1933 to 1937, and a member of the United States delegation to the London Disarmament Conference in 1934; and white-whiskered Rear Admiral Joseph M. Reeves, Retired, holder of the Navy Cross and first naval aviator to serve as Commander in Chief, United States Fleet, from 1934 to 1936. Stimson chose Maj. Gen. Frank R. McCoy, Retired, holder of the Silver Star, veteran of campaigns in Cuba and the Philippines, and member of the general staff in France (1918); and General Marshall selected an airman and the only actively serving officer on the commission, Brig. Gen. Joseph T. McNarney, a World War I Army Air Service veteran.

The commission got off to a questionable start on 17 December by accepting Stimson's invitation to meet privately with him and Knox in the former's office. Their conversation was unsworn and unrecorded. Conversations of the same character took place the next day between the commission members and such key witnesses as Marshall, Stark, Turner, Gerow, Wilkinson, Miles, and Bratton.[41] It is unlikely that the leadership of the War and Navy Departments did not exploit this unusual opportunity to prepare the ground for the commission's deliberations, if not its findings. Certainly, in unsworn and unrecorded testimony, the temptation to deflect blame from the departments in Washington to Hawaii would have been strong.

In the course of those meetings, somewhat surprisingly, the commissioners were briefed on Magic, though the import of the decryptions seems not to have impressed Roberts: "The magic was not shown to us," he told the JCC in 1945. "I would not have bothered to read it if it had been shown to us. All I wanted to know was whether the commanders had been advised of the criticalness of the situation."[42] As Robert Neuleib has pointed out, Roberts's 1945 testimony implied "that he viewed the purpose of the commission much like that of a grand jury investigation. He was to see if there were enough facts to indict, and it would be up to someone else to gather the proper evidence for an actual trial." Roberts thus had set a low threshold for damaging statements to be made and accepted against the Hawaiian commanders without any care for their probative value. The fact that the decrypted intercepts *existed* and that, on their basis, Kimmel and Short had been sent a warning, "was sufficient for an indictment."[43]

✱

The Roberts Commission, as it came to be called, commenced sworn, recorded hearings in Hawaii on 22 December. Short was the first major witness, on the twenty-third. Kimmel's first appearance was on the twenty-seventh. Both former commanders made strong, confident defenses of their performances. At the same time, both acknowledged that they had made mistakes. Short said, "I think that we [the Army] made a very serious mistake when we didn't go to an alert against an all out attack."[44] Kimmel conceded that he underestimated the importance of the code burning message, and that his judgment on torpedoes running in Pearl's shallow water had been "entirely wrong."[45] The commanders' testimony, and that of other principals, has been considered in the Pearl Harbor literature many times and need not be repeated here. But one constant refrain in the commission's questioning does bear mention: it was the charge advanced time and again that Kimmel and Short failed to confer with each other about the meaning of the warning messages sent them on 27 November by the War and Navy Departments and about the specific actions that each intended to take in the light of those messages. No single matter is dealt with at greater length in the commission record than that one.[46] Although it recognized that the two men did confer at length on 27 November, 1, 2, and 3 December, the commission observed that the subjects of their conversations seemed not to include the defensive deployment each had made, with the result that each was unaware of the other's exact alert status; as specific examples, Kimmel did not know that Short's radar was operating only for a limited number of hours each day, and Short did not know that Kimmel was not conducting distant aerial reconnaissance.

When the commission members wrote the report of their findings, which was presented to Roosevelt on 24 January, it was the "no conference on warnings or orders" issue that they chose as the frame within which to deliver their predictable indictment: dereliction of duty.[47]

Roosevelt released the entire report to the press and radio on the following day. The charge of dereliction that it contained was red meat to the reporters, as it was also to an angry public clamoring for someone to blame. Kimmel and, far less so, Short were roundly condemned in every public arena for "permitting" the catastrophe of Pearl Harbor to take place. Since the commission had found no major fault with their subordinate commanders or with their superiors in Washington, Kimmel and Short were singled out for a nation's vilification. Kimmel received scores of abusive letters, some suggesting that he be made to retire without a pension, others that he make the only honorable expiation for his treachery, which was suicide. Even U.S. Representative Andrew J. May, chairman of the House Military Affairs Committee, proposed in a speech at Pikeville, in Kimmel's home state of Kentucky, that the admiral should be shot.[48] Others in the

House demanded a court-martial. Kimmel kept copies of those letters and threats, but it should be pointed out that the collection of his papers at the University of Wyoming contains an equal or greater number of letters showing understanding and support.

What stung him most was the charge of dereliction of duty. Although there was no such specific charge in the Articles of War, the contrived censure offended his honor as one who had always and faithfully performed his duty. After years of sterling service, it was a tarnish that he found impossible to accept, particularly at the hands of a body of men who had looked at his difficult but faithful duty at Pearl for no more than thirty-four days. He knew, as Neuleib has noted, that it would be difficult for the American people to dislodge this judgment from their minds. The Roberts Commission had provided the nation a "correct" perception: "Kimmel had violated the public image of what an admiral should be and do."[49]

The dereliction charge would not be repeated in any of the findings of the subsequent eight formal investigations, boards, inquiries, and hearings about the Pearl Harbor attack that took place from 1944 to 1995.[50] Indeed, some thirteen years after the Roberts report was disseminated, one of the commission members, Admiral Standley, looking back on what he called the "irregularity," "inaccurate reporting," and "unfairness" of the commission's proceedings, expressed his regret that Kimmel and Short had not instead been given general courts-martial, in which they would have been afforded rights denied them by the commission: to have counsel, to introduce evidence, to be present during the testimony of witnesses, and to cross-examine witnesses. (Kimmel was not permitted to read the full testimony of others until 1944.) Said Standley: "Thus, these two officers were martyred, as it were, for in my opinion, if they had been brought to trial, both would have been cleared of the charge of neglect of duty."[51]

Kimmel, like Short, retired from his service soon afterward. But, unlike Short, he fought back vigorously throughout the next two years. Specifically, he sought a court-martial. The Navy finally, in July 1944, granted him an equivalent court of inquiry, in which he would have all the same rights as a defendant in a court-martial. While preparing for those proceedings, he was approached by cryptanalyst Capt. Laurance Safford, who, angered to discover that Kimmel had been denied Magic, gave the former CINCPAC a verbal account of the most critical decrypts affecting Hawaii. "This information made me almost sick," Kimmel told Prange in 1963.[52] With the help of attorneys Charles Rugg, Capt. Robert A. Lavender, USN, and Lt. Edward F. Hanify, USNR, Kimmel forced the Navy to provide him access to the pre–Pearl Harbor Magic. *And he broke off all personal relations with Stark.*

Presiding over the Navy court of inquiry were Admiral Orin G. Murfin, USN (Ret.), Admiral Edward C. Kalbfus, USN (Ret.), and Vice Admiral Adolphus Andrews, USN, with Comdr. Harold Biesemeier, USN, judge advocate. After three months of taking testimony and reading documents, the court found, among eighteen specific findings:

> That relations between Kimmel and Short were cordial, and that there was "no failure to cooperate on the part of either, and that each was cognizant of the measures being undertaken by the other for the defense of the Pearl Harbor Naval Base to the degree required by the common interest."

> That Kimmel's action "in ordering that no routine, long-range reconnaissance be undertaken was sound and that the use of fleet patrol planes for daily, long-range, all-around reconnaissance was not possible with the inadequate number of fleet planes available. . . ."

> That Kimmel's decision "to continue preparations of the Pacific Fleet for war was sound in the light of the information then available to him."

> That the "war warning" message of 27 November "directed attention away from Pearl Harbor rather than toward it."

> That Admiral Stark "failed to display the sound judgment expected of him" in that, on the morning of 7 December, "he did not transmit immediately the fact that a message had been received which appeared to indicate that a break in diplomatic relations was imminent, and that an attack in the Hawaiian area might be expected soon."

> That, even with a last-minute telephoned warning, "there was no action open to Admiral Kimmel which could have stopped the attack or which could have had other than negligible bearing upon its outcome."[53]

The findings constituted the first time that anyone in high position in the Navy Department was brought to account as wholly or partially responsible for what happened at Pearl Harbor. Stark's performance was held to two standards, or principles, that were policy in 1941, as they are today:

> He who denies intelligence to commanders shares in the blame for any disaster that results.
>   When a commander denies information to subordinates who command the forces he provided them to accomplish the missions he assigned he controls what they do and do not do.[54]

An Army Pearl Harbor Board was in session during the same three months. In October it submitted to the War Department a set of findings that came down hard on General Gerow, less severely on General Marshall, and least harshly on General Short. Gerow was declared to have "failed in his duties" in that (1) he failed to keep Short "adequately informed" on the impending war situation; (2) he approved a warning message to Short on 27 November that "contained confusing statements"; (3) he failed to correct Short's actions pursuant to the 27 November message; and (4) he did not take steps to implement the existing joint defense plans of the Army and Navy in Hawaii. Marshall was criticized for (1) not having kept Short informed of the "growing tenseness" of the Japanese situation; (2) for, like Gerow, not correcting Short's reply to the 27 November warning; (3) for not sending additional warnings to Short on the evening of 6 December and in the early morning of the seventh; and (4) for not investigating and determining the "state of readiness of the Hawaiian Command between 27 November and 7 December." Short was concluded to have "failed in his duties" by (1) adopting an alert against sabotage only instead of guarding "against surprise to the extent possible"; (2) failing to implement the joint Army-Navy defense plans; and (3) by not informing himself "of the effectiveness of the long-distance reconnaissance being conducted by the Navy."[55]

Before Kimmel learned of his exculpation it was snatched away from him by CNO-CINCUS Admiral King. In a second endorsement (opinion) to the court of inquiry dated 3 November 1944, King overturned its findings where Kimmel was concerned. His reason: CINCPAC should have conducted long-range air searches at least "in the more dangerous sectors."[56] Which these were he did not say, but on that basis he charged Kimmel anew with "dereliction," and urged the newly appointed Secretary of the Navy James V. Forrestal to concur, which the secretary did in his own endorsement.[57] On the dismal anniversary day of 7 December 1944 King invited Kimmel to his office to convey the bad news in person. When he heard it, Kimmel wondered if the testimony and the findings of the court were not to the contrary (they were), and in an aide-mémoire written afterward he expressed his stupefaction in capital letters: "KING SAID THAT HE HAD NOT READ THE TESTIMONY GIVEN BEFORE THE COURT."[58] (Nor, it turned out, had Admiral King written his own endorsement; it was authored by Vice Admiral Richard S. Edward, his deputy chief of staff.[59] Nor had King even *read* his endorsement before signing it.[60]) Perhaps King read the court testimony in the postwar years, since in 1948 he wrote to the secretary of the Navy softening the language of his endorsement—Kimmel's were "errors of judgment," he wrote, "as distinguished from culpable ineffi-ciency"—though without retracting the word "dereliction."[61]

✯

Although the Navy court recommended "that no further proceedings be had in the matter," the United States Congress decided to intervene in September 1945, when it authorized a Joint Congressional Committee on the Investigation of the Pearl Harbor Attack (JCC), its membership to be five senators and five representatives, six Democrats and four Republicans. Its proceedings, which consisted mostly of the taking of testimony, lasted from 15 November 1945 to 15 July 1946. Though the hearings amassed a huge amount of data, not much of what was new information was essential to understanding the Pearl Harbor event. At their weary conclusion, the committee announced findings that divided fairly closely along party lines. The majority (Democratic) report cited twelve "errors of judgment and not dereliction of duty" on the part of the Hawaiian commanders. It also con-cluded that Stark and Marshall should share in the blame. Roosevelt was completely exonerated. Two Republicans on the committee took a middle-of-the-road approach, finding fault with both the Hawaiian commanders and official Washington. A minority report was submitted by the two other Republicans. While not entirely exculpating Kimmel and Short, that report focused on failures it attributed to Roosevelt, Stimson, Knox, Marshall, Stark, and Gerow. It fell short, however, of charging Roosevelt with having foreknowledge of the Japanese attack that he did not share with his Hawai-ian commanders—a favorite conspiracy theory that would soon become a cottage industry, one alive and well to this day.[62]

General Short, who had not publicly struggled with the charges made against him beginning with the Roberts Commission, joined Kimmel in a friendly relationship during the hearings, and gave a scrappy performance at the witness chair, after which he retired again into desired obscurity. He died on 3 September 1949 in Dallas, Texas, and was buried with full military honors in Arlington National Cemetery. (He was preceded in death by Japanese admirals Yamamoto and Nagumo. On 18 April 1943, acting on a decrypted Japanese itinerary for an inspection tour of the northern Solomon Islands by Yamamoto, U.S. fighters intercepted the admiral's aircraft and shot it down. During the last stages of the U.S. Marine and Army conquest of Saipan Island [June–July 1944], Nagumo and all but one of his staff shot themselves rather than be taken alive.) Kimmel kept fighting to overcome the stain of "dereliction" dripped on him by King. In letters, articles, and a book he defended his performance and his honor, not ceasing in that labor until a heart attack claimed him in his eighty-sixth year, on 14 May 1968, in Groton, Connecticut. Sometime during the last year of his life he drafted, but never sent, a response to a letter received from his onetime friend Admiral "Betty" Stark. The language expressed his deep pain at recalling a professional association and a long friendship gone terribly wrong. As he vented his feelings, probably with no real intention of placing them in a mailbox, there was overt bitterness in every use of the word "betrayed":

> You betrayed the officers and men of the Fleet by not giving them a fighting chance for their lives and you betrayed the Navy in not taking responsibility for your actions; you betrayed me by not giving me information you knew I was entitled to and by your acquiscence [sic] in the action taken on the request for my retirement; and you betrayed yourself by misleading the Roberts Commission as to what information had been sent to me and by your statements made under oath before the Court of Inquiry that you knew were false.
>
> I hope that you never communicate with me again and that I never see you or your name again that my memory may not be refreshed of one so despicable as you.[63]

Looking back over the preceding chapters, I have resisted the temptation to summarize or to draw last conclusions. I leave that to the reader.

"Truth is the daughter of time."

$\star$ $\star$ $\star$

NOTES

Pearl Harbor has become one of the most exhaustively examined and debated single events in United States history—more so than the assassination of President John F. Kennedy or the Watergate political scandal. The documents from eight official commissions, courts, boards, inquiries, or investigations conducted from December 1941 through May 1946 fill 23 volumes, 40 parts, and 25,000 closely printed pages. The personal archive of Admiral Husband E. Kimmel amounts to another 35,000 pages in typescript, some of it duplicative. More than 140 books and innumerable articles have been written on the subject.

"Defeat cries out for explanation; whereas success, like charity, covers a multitude of sins."

Alfred Thayer Mahan

Chapter One: Disaster

1. *Pearl Harbor Attack* [hereafter PHA], *U.S. Congress, Joint Congressional Committee* [hereafter JCC] *on the Investigation of the Pearl Harbor Attack*, 79th Congress, 40 parts (Washington, D.C.: U.S. Government Printing Office, 1946), Pt. 32, p. 444.

2. For precise details on these torpedo actions the writer has relied on the best recent study, by John F. De Virgilio, "Japanese Thunderfish," *Naval History* (winter 1991), pp. 61–68.

3. Ibid., p. 64 and n. 9, pp. 67–68 and n. 18.

4. Ibid., p. 65.

5. PHA, Pt. 23, p. 724.

6. De Virgilio, "Thunderfish," pp. 66–67.

7. Interview with Mr. Howard Huseman, Gainesville, FL, 6 March 2001. PHA, Pt. 12, p. 354, "Damage to United States Naval Forces and Installations Resulting from the Japanese Attack on the Island of Oahu on 7 December 1941 [hereafter "Damage to United States Naval Forces]."

8. National Archives and Records Administration, Archives II, College Park, Maryland, Modern Military Branch [hereafter NARA], Record Group [hereafter RG] 80, Pearl Harbor

Liaison Office [hereafter PHLO], Box 14, Commanding Officer USS *Arizona* to Chief of Naval Operations, January 28, 1942, "Information on Damage Control." Admiral Husband E. Kimmel Collection [hereafter KC], University of Wyoming, on microfilm, Roll 4, Memorandum Prepared for Vice Admiral [William S.] Pye, Commander, Battle Force, Pacific Fleet, Air Raid, December 7, 1941 [hereafter Memorandum for Pye], p. 19.

9. Michael Slackman, *Target: Pearl Harbor* (Honolulu: University of Hawaii Press and Arizona Memorial Museum Association, 1990) contains an excellent account of the attack on *Arizona* with special focus on human interest details. The author times a bomb at "between 8:12 and 8:13" based on a Marine private's stopped watch; p. 113. However, the Navy's "Analysis of Loss of *Arizona*," dated 31 October 1944, states: "All the references agree that the bombs which struck *Arizona* fell between 0815 and 0820"; NARA, RG 80, PHLO, Box 14, p. 3.

10. Ibid., "Analysis of Loss of *Arizona*," pp. 3–7.

11. Captain Joseph K. Taussig, Jr., U.S. Navy (Ret.), "A Tactical View of Pearl Harbor," Paul Stillwell, ed., *Air Raid: Pearl Harbor!* (Annapolis, Maryland: Naval Institute Press, 1981), p. 138.

12. De Virgilio, "Thunderfish," p. 65; Morison, *Rising Sun*, p. 112.

13. NARA, RG 80, PHLO, Box 14, "Condition of Water-Tight Integrity of Major Vessels"; 11 December 1945.

14. De Virgilio, "Thunderfish," p. 68; PHA, Pt. 12, p. 355, "Damage to United States Naval Forces," p. 355.

15. KC, Roll 4, Memorandum for Pye, pp. 19–20.

16. Rear Admiral Edwin T. Layton, USN (Ret.), with Captain Roger Pineau, USNR (Ret.), and John Costello, *"And I Was There": Pearl Harbor and Midway—Breaking the Secrets* (New York: William Morrow and Company, Inc., 1985), p. 315.

Chapter Two: Too Thin a Shield

1. Stimson to Secretary of the Navy Knox, quoted in "Statement of Admiral Harold R. Stark, U.S. Navy, Before the Joint Committee on the Investigation of the Pearl Harbor Attack, 31 December 1945 [hereafter "Statement of Stark"]," p. 65; KC, Roll 1.

2. *Collier's, The National Weekly*, vol. 107, no. 24 (14 June 1941), pp. 11–12, 75–78. *Time* magazine, too, stated, "Except for the Japanese spies that teemed in Honolulu, the Navy felt safe in its base"; 15 December 1941.

3. PHA, Pt. 33, Exhibit No. 6, Joint Action of the Army and the Navy, Chapters I–V, pp. 1018–1047.

4. PHA, Pt. 15, Exhibits, p. 1601. A short Army-originated history in typescript of the "Hawaiian Department and Successor Commands," composed in 1945 or shortly afterward, enumerates the Army's responsibilities on Oahu but makes no mention of its primary mission to protect the fleet. The document is found in the "Pearl Harbor Retainer File," Modern Military Branch NARA.

5. KC, Roll 3, Commander in Chief, U.S. Fleet to Chief of Naval Operations, Pearl Harbor, T.H., 25 January 1941.

6. Ibid., Roll 4, Extracts from Secret Letters Exchanged Between the Commander in Chief and the Chief of Naval Operations [hereafter Extracts from Secret Letters], p. 1; Kimmel to Stark, 27 January 1941.

7. Ibid., Roll 4, The Pacific Fleet in the Command Organization of the Navy as of December 7, 1941, p. 3.

8. Ibid., Roll 1, Statement of Stark, p. 60.

9. PHA, Pt. 15, Exhibits, p. 1601. In a conference held in his office the day before, Marshall acknowledged that "the planes in Honolulu were, in general, obsolescent, and that we should have a reasonable number of top flight planes which would out-perform any the Japa-

nese could bring on their carriers." KC, Roll 3, Conference in the Office of the Chief of Staff, Thursday Morning, February 6, 1941; Subject: Defense of Pearl Harbor.

10. Ibid., Roll 1, Statement of Stark; letter, Secretary Stimson to Secretary Knox, 7 February 1941, pp. 65–67. At that date there were only thirty-six pursuit (fighter) planes of which nineteen were outmoded Curtiss P-36A Hawks and seventeen were even more obsolescent. Under the title Hawaiian Project, Stimson promised to have thirty-one more P-36As assembled at San Diego for shipment to Hawaii within the next ten days. He also pledged to have assembled and shipped by carrier "about March 15" fifty of the new Curtiss P-40B Warhawk pursuit planes, with liquid-cooled Allison engines, self-sealing tanks, and pilot-protecting armor. (Though no match for the Japanese Zero in maneuverability, the P-40B could fight the Zero on otherwise almost equal terms. The P-36A would be at a distinct disadvantage.)

Where antiaircraft guns were concerned, there were 82 3-inch AA guns then present on Oahu, 109 50-caliber AA machine guns, and 20 37-mm AA guns "en route." Stimson pledged to provide a total force of 98 3-inch, 120 37-mm, and 308 .50-caliber machine guns.

It was expected, he said, that land-based radar sets, called at that date the Aircraft Warning Service (AWS), might be available for delivery in June. Barrage balloons might be available sometime in the summer. The value of smoke for screening the fleet had, he said, been judged "impractical." (Neither balloons nor smoke was in place by 7 December. And twelve days before the seventh, both the War and Navy Departments authorized the transfer of 50 percent of Oahu's P-40Bs to Wake and Midway Islands; PHA, Pt. 6, p. 2519.)

11. NARA, Record Group [hereafter RG] 38, Strategic Plans Division Records, Box 147J: Plans, Strategic Studies, and Related Correspondence (Series IX), Part III: OP 123 War Plans and Related Correspondence, WPL-46—WPL-46-PC. Folder: WPL-46 Letters.

12. KC, Roll 4, Extracts from Secret Letters, Kimmel to Stark, 18 February 1941, p. 2; Roll 1, Statement of Stark, p. 65.

13. KC, Roll 4, Kimmel, Outline of Testimony Before the Navy Court, August 1944, p. 1.

14. PHA, Pt. 22, p. 32. KC, Roll 1, Statement by Major General Walter C. Short, U.S. Army, Retired, Before the Joint Congressional Committee, January 1946, p. 1.

15. Ibid., Pt. 32, p. 283.

16. NARA, RG 80, General Records of the Secretary of the Navy, Pearl Harbor Liaison Office [hereafter PHLO], Boxes 68–69; Original Transcript [hereafter OT], Proceedings of the Naval Court of Inquiry [hereafter NCI]. The quotation from Senator Truman comes from *Colliers,* also from the United Press, *The New York Times,* and the *New York Herald Tribune,* all 21 August 1944. Kimmel's letter to Truman, written from Bronxville, NY, on 20 August 1944, is found in KC, Roll 26. Kimmel struck back hard at this canard one month later, on 25 September, when responding to a question raised during the NCI Was he aware of rumors that he and Short were not cordial, did not cooperate, and held few conferences? Kimmel answered: "I believe every man, woman, and child in the United States who can read has read such statements. I wish to state that all such statements are malicious lies. . . . There was absolutely no basis for the rumors, and I am forced to the conclusion that this was part of a deliberate campaign to smear me and General Short." NARA, RG 80, PHLO, NCI, OT, Boxes 68–69, Thirty-second day, 25 September 1944.

Kimmel's brother Manning M., a colonel commanding the 6th Replacement Regiment (A.A.) at Fort George Meade, MD, wrote Kimmel on 2 May 1944 reporting on a conversation he had there with Colonel Walter C. Phillips, who had been General Short's chief of staff from 1 March 1941 forward. Phillips had identified Short's other principal staff officers: Lieutenant Colonel (Lt. Col.) Russell C. Throckmorton, G-1 (Personnel); Lt. Col. Kendall J. Fielder, G-2 (Intelligence); Major William E. Donegan, G-3 (Operations and Training); Lt. Col. Morrill W. Marston, G-4 (Supply); and assistants: Lt. Col. George W. Bicknell, G-2, Major Robert J. Fleming, Jr., G-4, and Lt. Col. William S. Lawton, G-3.

Manning reported to his brother Colonel Phillips's statement that "Each of these officers could, and no doubt would, give favorable statements, particularly on the close cooperation and frequent consultation of the staff officers in your headquarters and General Short's headquarters. He said that they will no doubt testify and be able to produce documents to prove that all information received in one headquarters was immediately transmitted to the other, also that all plans formulated in one headquarters was done so [sic] with the full cooperation and assistance from the other. Also that copies of all orders issued relating to operations were interchanged between the two headquarters," KC, Roll 26. Kimmel's chief of staff, Captain William W. Smith, testified in 1944 that "They [Kimmel and Short] were together, I should say, at least twice a week, very frequently with their staffs, and sometimes more frequently than that"; PHA, Pt. 26, p. 44.

17. KC, Roll 3, Joint Coastal Frontier Defense Plan, Hawaiian Department and Fourteenth Naval District, 28 March 1941, signed 2 April 1941.

18. NARA, RG 38, Joint Coastal Frontier Defense Plan, Hawaiian Coastal Frontier, 11 April 1941, Basic Joint, Combined, and Navy War Plans and Related Documents, 1905–1941, Box 1.

19. NARA, RG 80, PHLO, Box 1, PHA, Pt.4, p-1896. The Martin-Bellinger estimate is reproduced in PHA, Pt. 1, pp. 349–54; Pt. 33, pp. 1182–86.

20. Ibid.

21. Ibid.

22. Admiral Nimitz to Commander in Chief, United States Fleet [Admiral Ernest J. King], 7 January 1942, quoted in PHA, Pt. 6, p. 2533; the entire Nimitz report, "Airplane Situation, Hawaiian Area," is found in NARA, RG 80, PHLO, Box 25.

23. Conference in the Office of the Chief of Staff, 25 February 1941; NARA, RG 80, PHLO, Box 2. In a General Council meeting on 19 February, Marshall stated: "Out in Hawaii the Fleet is anchored but they have to be prepared against any surprise attack. I don't say any probable attack but they have to be prepared against a surprise attack from a trick ship or torpedo planes. Our whole Navy power in general is concentrated there; they can't cruise for [the] next six months." Ibid., Box 3.

24. Marshall to Short, 5 March 1941; ibid., Box 2. This box includes additional correspondence between the two men during 1941.

25. Short to Marshall, 19 February and 15 March 1941; ibid., Box 2. Short said that so many planes were based at Hickam that they could not be sufficiently dispersed on the field itself to prevent losses by that means alone in an air raid.

26. Marshall to Short, 28 March 1941; ibid., Box 2.

27. Harry J. Malony, "Dispersion and Protection of Aircraft, Hawaiian Department," ibid., Box 3.

28. KC, Roll 1, Statement of Major General Walter C. Short, U.S. Army, Retired, January 1946 [hereafter Short Statement], pp. 3–4.

29. KC, Roll 1, Short Statement, p. 6; see also the more detailed Statement of Major General Walter C. Short of Events and Conditions Leading Up to the Japanese Attack, December 7, 1941 [hereafter Events and Conditions], in PHA, Pt. 24, pp. 1769–1933, particularly pp. 1785–89.

30. NARA, RG 80, PHLO, Box 2: Short to Marshall, 6 March 1941; William Bryden to Short, 15 March 1941.

31. KC, Roll 1, Short Statement, pp. 4–8; Events and Conditions, PHA, Pt. 24, pp. 1769–1933, 1842–44.

32. PHA, Pt. 24, pp. 1842–44, Short to Adjutant General, War Department, 28 October 1941.

33. PHA, Pt. 6, p. 2519; NARA, RG 80, PHLO, Box 29, Stark to Kimmel, 19 August 1941.

34. NARA, RG 80, PHLO, Box 2, Short to Marshall, 14 April 1941.

35. See, for example, NARA, RG 80, PHLO, Box 2, Short to Marshall, 29 May 1941.

36. General Short was outspoken on this point in his answers to the Roberts Commission:

"I think that the Navy has been perfectly conscious in the last two or three years that this was too restricted an area for the fleet; that a bay like Manila Bay, extending from Cavite to Manila Bay probably 60 miles long would be an immensely safer place to put a fleet in view of an air attack, because you could disperse them and you wouldn't have such an enormous target. All you had to do was to drive by down here when the fleet was all in; you can see that they just couldn't be missed if they had a serious air attack. There were too many—there was too little water for the number of ships. . . . I am implying that it would be practically impossible to protect the ships in such a restricted area against a serious attack, no matter how much you tried. . . ." PHA, Pt. 22, p. 104. (For every thirty-one operating days at sea a navy task force required fifty-five days of upkeep in port.)

37. KC, Roll 3, OT of Admiral Husband E. Kimmel's Statement Before the NCI [hereafter Kimmel Statement], pp. 1–3.

38. NARA, RG 80, PHLO, Box 29, Stark to Kimmel, 13 January and 29 January 1941.

39. Ibid., Boxes 2 and 18, Pacific Fleet Confidential Letter No. 2 CL-41, 15 February, revised 14 October 1941. Captain Willard A. Kitts, fleet gunnery officer, testified that "The letter [2CL-41] was issued again by Admiral Nimitz, with Admiral Kimmel's name on it, in middle of summer 1942. He used this letter as an enclosure to be sent to Fleet and merely stated in the letter that the former letter was to remain in effect. . . . Plans that Kimmel made prior to Pearl Harbor were to be used after Pearl Harbor. Instructions as to watches and states of conditions of readiness did not change." KC, Roll 4; PHA, Pt. 32, p. 400.

40. KC, Roll 3, Kimmel, Memorandum with Respect to Security of Fleet in Port, 5 July 1944, pp. 1–13. Fleet gunnery officer Kitts testified that on 29 April 1941 Vice Admiral William S. Pye, Commander, Battleships, Battle Force, made modifications on the manning of guns that made AA preparedness on battleships "equal to or better than the condition of readiness 3" laid down in Port Security 2CL-41; PHA, Pt. 32, p. 397. The Battle Force consisted of all battleships; Cruiser Divisions 3 and 9; Carrier Divisions 1 and 2; Mine Squadron One (Divs. 1, 2, and 3); and Destroyer Flotillas 1 and 2. Kimmel's appeal for Bofors and Oerlikon AA armament is in NARA, RG 80, PHLO, Box 25, Kimmel to Stark, "Survey of Conditions in the Pacific Fleet," 26 May 1941, p. 9. The normal antiaircraft armament of battleships was eight 5-inch $\neq$.25-caliber guns, six to eight 3-inch $\neq$ .50-caliber guns, and about twelve .50-caliber machine guns; that of cruisers, eight 5-inch $\neq$ .25-caliber guns, except for two which had 5-inch $\neq$.38-caliber guns, and eight to twelve .50-caliber machine guns. Percentages of officers and crews aboard are given in PHA, Pt. 22, p. 537; and in KC, Roll 4, Memorandum Prepared for Vice Admiral Pye, Commander Battle Force, Pacific Fleet, Air Raid, December 7, 1941; n.d. but probably late in the same month. Testimony about sobriety is found in ibid., Pt. 32, pp. 315, 339; Pt. 23, p. 747.

41. NARA, RG 80, PHLO, Box 25, Kimmel to Nimitz, 16 February 1941. On 3 March Nimitz replied, pointing out that so many ordnance plants were opening up to provide weapons and ammunition for the British Royal Navy that it was necessary to detach trained officers from the fleet.

42. Quoted by Kimmel in his Statement Before the Joint Congressional Committee [hereafter JCC] on the Investigation of the Pearl Harbor Attack; OT in KC, Roll 1, p. 16.

43. NARA, RG 80, PHLO, Box 37, the Chief of Naval Operations to the Secretary of the Navy, 10 June 1941.

44. Kimmel, Statement Before the JCC, OT in KC, Roll 1, pp. 14–15.

45. NARA, RG 80, PHLO, Box 48, 19 May 1941, Commander Arthur C. Davis, Fleet Aviation Officer, to Chief of Staff William Ward Smith, "Subjects for Possible Discussion with the Secretary of the Navy." There was also a continuing shortage into December of .50-caliber ammunition for the fleet's AA machine guns, necessitating such economy in training as limiting the number of rounds an individual gunner could fire in drills. PHA, Pt. 32, p. 392.

46. Ibid., Box 29, the Chief of the Bureau of Aeronautics to the Chief of Naval Operations, 5 March 1941.

47. Gordon W. Prange interview with Bloch, 28 November 1962; cited in Gordon W. Prange, *At Dawn We Slept: The Untold Story at Pearl Harbor* (New York: Penguin Books, 1981), p. 68

48. NARA, RG 80, PHLO, Box 29, Stark to Kimmel, 13 January 1941.

49. Ibid., Stark to Kimmel, 29 January 1941.

50. KC, Roll 4, Exercises for the Combined Training of Aircraft, Sky Lookouts, and Antiaircraft Batteries in the Hawaiian Area—Promulgation of; 3 July 1941.

51. NARA, RG 80, PHLO, Box 14, Memorandum of the Under Secretary of the Navy reporting information given by Rear Admiral Roscoe F. Good, who (as a commander) had been an assistant operations officer on Kimmel's staff.

52. Rear Admiral Edwin T. Layton, USN (Ret.), "Admiral Kimmel Deserved a Better Fate," in Stillwell, ed., *Air Raid, Pearl Harbor!,* p. 277.

53. PHA, Pt. 32, p. 398.

54. William F. Halsey, *Admiral Halsey's Story* (New York: McGraw-Hill Book Co., 1947), pp. 70, 82.

Chapter Three: Opposite Numbers

1. Hiroyuki Agawa, *The Reluctant Admiral: Yamamoto and the Imperial Navy,* translated by John Bester (Tokyo, New York: Kodansha International Ltd., 1979), p. 220. Oikawa may have burned Yamamoto's letter, as requested. But a copy, in a sealed envelope, was left by Yamamoto with an academy classmate, Vice Admiral Hori Teikichi, who made the document public on 9 November 1949. See Professor Jun Tsunoda, Kokushikan University, Tokyo, and Admiral Kazutomi Uchida, JMSDF (Ret.), "The Pearl Harbor Attack: Admiral Yamamoto's Fundamental Concept," *Naval War College Review,* vol. XXXI, no. 2 (fall 1978), pp. 83–88.

2. This scenario is best presented in Stephen E. Pelz, *Race to Pearl Harbor: The Failure of the Second London Naval Conference and the Onset of World War II* (Cambridge, MA: Harvard University Press, 1974), pp. 34–39. Pelz interviewed a number of Japanese naval strategists from the pre–Pearl Harbor period. Though the scenario cited represented traditional Japanese naval thinking, it should not be thought that it excluded any thought of a surprise attack on Pearl Harbor. Lt. Comdr. Kusaka Ryunosuke, an instructor at the Kasumigaura Aviation Corps, committed such a Pearl Harbor plan to writing in 1927 or 1928. See Agawa, *Reluctant Admiral,* p. 193.

3. Quoted in Gordon W. Prange, *At Dawn We Slept: The Untold Story of Pearl Harbor* (New York: Penguin Books, 1982), p. 16. Cf. Tsunoda and Uchida, "Yamamoto's Fundamental Concept," pp. 84–85.

4. Tsunoda and Uchida, "Concept," p. 85. See also p. 88: "To do so they [the Japanese Navy] must, first of all, clear both sides of the route to the south, which meant the occupation of the Philippines as well as of Singapore." "Hawaii Operation" would be the Japanese Imperial Headquarters' official, not so secret, code name for the Pearl Harbor attack.

5. Quoted in Agawa, *Reluctant Admiral,* p. 220. The writer has taken the liberty of altering the third person, as given by Agawa, to the first person.

6. Ibid., p. 65.

7. Ibid., p. 28.

8. Asada Sadao, "The Japanese Navy and the United States," in Dorothy Borg and Shumpei Okamoto, eds., *Pearl Harbor as History: Japanese-American Relations, 1931–1941* (New York: Columbia University Press, 1973), p. 232; Pelz, *Race to Pearl Harbor,* pp. 14–16.

9. Agawa, *Reluctant Admiral,* p. 33.

10. Pelz, *Race to Pearl Harbor,* p. 40. On the clear superiority in this period of Japanese cruisers and destroyers, torpedoes, star shells and parachute flares, optics for night work, regular issue binoculars, and possibly also gunnery, navigation, ship-handling tactics, and fighting spirit, see Samuel Eliot Morison, *History of United States Naval Operations in World War II,*

Vol. III, *The Rising Sun in the Pacific, 1931–April 1942* (Boston: Little, Brown and Company, 1948), pp. 22–24.

11. Agawa, *Reluctant Admiral*, p. 51; Sadao, "Japanese Navy," p. 243.

12. Pelz, *Race to Pearl Harbor*, pp. 159–64.

13. Agawa, *Reluctant Admiral*, p. 8.

14. Construction of these two superbattleships began in secret, in 1937. The *Yamato* was launched in December 1941, the *Musashi* in August 1942. Their main gun turrets bristled with 18.1-inch guns that fired 3,200-pound projectiles over a greater range than that achieved by 16-inch guns. Armor plate 25.5 inches thick protected the hulls of these "unsinkable" monsters. *Musashi* would be sunk on 24 October 1944 during the Battle of Leyte Gulf; *Yamato* would go down on 7 April 1944 during the Battle of Okinawa.

15. Sadao, "Japanese Navy," pp. 237–38.

16. Ibid., p. 237. Vice Foreign Minister Shigemitzu Mamoru had earlier expressed concern that the Navy wanted to "fight with the United States around 1936"; ibid., p. 240.

17. By 7 December 1941, the U.S. Pacific Fleet consisted of nine battleships, three aircraft carriers, twelve heavy cruisers, nine light cruisers, sixty-seven destroyers, and twenty-seven submarines. An advance force, named the Asiatic Fleet and commanded by Admiral Thomas C. Hart, USN, was based at Manila, in the Philippines. It consisted of three cruisers, thirteen destroyers, and twenty-nine submarines. British, Dutch, and Free French naval forces in the South Pacific consisted of two battleships, one heavy cruiser, eleven light cruisers, twenty destroyers, and thirteen submarines. The Japanese Combined Fleet consisted of ten battleships, ten carriers, eighteen heavy cruisers, twenty light cruisers, one hundred and twelve destroyers, and sixty-five submarines.

18. John Deane Potter, *Yamamoto: The Man Who Menaced America* (New York: The Viking Press, 1965), pp. 34–36.

19. Agawa, *Reluctant Admiral*, p. 6.

20. Ibid., p. 189.

21. Ibid. A more familiar rendering of the original Japanese of Prince Konoye's *Memoirs* (a "Japanese-schoolboy translation," Samuel Eliot Morison called it) goes: "If I am told to fight regardless of consequence, I shall run wild considerably for the first six months or a year, but I have utterly no confidence for the second and third years"; Morison, *Rising Sun*, p. 46.

22. Agawa, *Reluctant Admiral*, p. 192.

23. Vice Admiral Shigeru Fukudome, "Hawaii Operation," *U.S. Naval Institute Proceedings*, Vol. 81 (December 1955), p. 1317.

24. Ibid., p. 1318.

25. Ibid.

26. Kimmel Family Papers [hereafter KFP]. A miscellaneous collection of Admiral Kimmel–related papers, including a three-page biography of the admiral, is in the possession of the admiral's only surviving son (of three), Edward R. Kimmel, of Wilmington, Delaware. During an interview with Mr. Kimmel on 22–23 May 2000, the writer received a copy of the biographical statement, examined genealogical entries in the family bible, and recorded Mr. Kimmel's personal recollections of his father. Another short biographical statement, titled "Brief Biography of Rear Admiral H. E. Kimmel, U.S. Navy, Commander, Cruisers, Battle Force," appears in Roll 23 of the KC. The same collection contains items of Kimmel's early personal correspondence, most of it to and from family members, from 1907 to 1909, but, unaccountably, none from 1909 to 1924. In the latter year there begins a comprehensive collection of both official and personal correspondence that continues until his death in 1968. Additional important biographical material was collected by Donald Grey Brownlow, who conducted numerous interviews with Admiral Kimmel in the 1960s, and published his gleanings in a book, *The Accused: The Ordeal of Rear Admiral Husband Edward Kimmel, U.S.N.* (New York: Vantage Press, 1968).

27. Peter Karsten, *The Naval Aristocracy: The Golden Age of Annapolis and the Emergence of Modern American Navalism* (New York: The Free Press, 1972), p. 41. The author cites two sources for this finding. Historian Ronald H. Spector has summarized the academic situation: "1!.e naval academy [at the turn of the century] was parochial, spartan, intellectually sterile, and pedagogically backwards"; Spector, *Eagle Against the Sun: The American War with Japan* (New York: Vintage Books, 1985), p. 18.

28. Karsten, *Naval Aristocracy*, pp. 40, 42.

29. Dorothy and Thomas Cassin Kinkaid were children of Admiral Thomas Wright Kinkaid (class of 1880).

30. Brownlow, *The Accused*, p. 35.

31. Quoted in ibid., p. 74. Husband E. Kimmel, *Admiral Kimmel's Story* (Chicago: Henry Regnery Company, 1955), p. 6. Concurrently with Kimmel's appointment, the Navy Department created three separate fleets: Pacific, Asiatic, and Atlantic.

32. Ibid., p. 6. A mischievous rumor circulated in Washington to the effect that Kimmel owed his appointment to a relationship that his wife, Dorothy, had with Senator Alben W. Barkley of Kentucky. But Dorothy was not related to the majority leader, nor had she ever met him; KC, Roll 1, "Statement of Rear-Admiral Husband E. Kimmel, U.S. Navy Retired, May 1942," p. 37.

33. Nimitz, personal letter to Brownlow, 25 February 1962; *The Accused*, p. 69.

34. Stark, interview with Brownlow, Washington, D.C., 23 April 1966; *The Accused*, p. 69.

35. Ibid., pp. 69–70. Kimmel asserted in 1962 that he considered turning the job down, but decided that that would be "foolish." Besides, with close friends like Stark and Royal E. Ingersoll as CNO and assistant CNO, respectively, he would be kept "completely informed of all developments;" ibid., p. 75.

36. PHA, Pt. 15, Exhibits, p. 1601.

37. Interview with Edward R. Kimmel, Wilmington, DE, 23 May 2000.

38. Thomas K. Kimmel, personal letter to Brownlow, 18 June 1966; *The Accused*, pp. 169–70.

39. Edward S. Miller, *War Plan Orange: The U.S. Strategy to Defeat Japan* (Annapolis, MD: Naval Institute Press, 1991), p. 273. On the same date the small squadron at Manila in the Philippines was retitlted the Asiatic Fleet. See E. B. Potter, *Nimitiz* (Annapolis, MD: Naval Institute Press, 1976), p. 5.

40. Quoted in Eric Larrabee, *Commander-in-Chief: Franklin Delano Roosevelt, His Lieutenants, and Their War* (New York: Harper & Row, 1987), p. 155.

41. Rear Admiral Kimmel's temporary designation as a four-star admiral was made under existing law, Act of May 22, 1917, 65th Cong., 1st Sess., Ch. 20, sec. 18, 40 Stat. 59, permitting the President to designate six officers as commanders of fleets or subdivisions thereof with the rank of admiral or vice admiral. When an officer of those designated ranks was detached from the command of a fleet or subdivision thereof, "he shall return to his regular rank in the list of officers of the Navy." The office of CINCUS (hardly an appropriate-sounding acronym) meant that command of other fleets as well as his own would be exercised only when two or more fleets operated together, or when it became necessary to proscribe "uniform procedures or training standards for all forces afloat." Theoretically, the title was to be rotated among the three fleet commanders, Pacific, Asiatic, Atlantic, but that chance never came.

The "custom of the service" had been for officers to serve as CINCUS for a tour of eighteen to twenty-four months. Thus, Admiral Claude C. Bloch held the command from January 1938 to January 1940 (24 months), Admiral Arthur J. Hepburn from June 1936 to January 1938 (18 months), and Admiral Joseph M. Reeves from June 1934 to June 1936 (24 months). Richardson assumed command on 6 January 1940. His career is described in James O. Richardson, as told to Vice Admiral George C. Dyer, USN (Ret.), *On the Treadmill to Pearl Harbor: The Memoirs of Admiral James O. Richardson, USN (Retired)* (Washington, D.C.: Department of the Navy, Naval History Division, 1973). Cf. B. Mitchell Simpson III, *Admiral Harold R. Stark: Architect of Victory, 1939–1945* (Columbia: University of South Carolina Press, 1989), p. 54.

42. PHA, Pt. 14, p. 1044.

43. Ibid., Pt. 36, p. 368.

Chapter Four: The Brewing Storm

1. The nine powers were the United States, Japan, the British Empire, France, the Netherlands, China, Portugal, Italy, and Belgium.

2. Quoted in Akira Iriye, "The Role of the United States Embassy in Tokyo," in Dorothy Borg and Shumpei Okamoto, eds., *Pearl Harbor as History: Japanese-American Relations, 1931–1941* (New York: Columbia University Press, 1973), p. 116.

3. Iris Chang, *The Rape of Nanking: The Forgotten Holocaust of World War II* (New York: Basic Books, 1997).

4. Patricia Neils, ed., *United States Attitudes and Policies Toward China: The Impact of American Missionaries* (Armonk, NY: M. E. Sharpe, Inc., 1990), *passim*. The same Gallup poll is cited in Morison, *Rising Sun*, p. 39, n. 8.

5. Quoted in James C. Thompson, Jr., "The Role of the Department of State," in Borg and Okamoto, eds., *Pearl Harbor as History*, p. 99.

6. Dispatch, Grew to State Department, 1 December 1939, cited in Herbert Feis, *The Road to Pearl Harbor: The Coming of the War Between the United States and Japan* (Princeton, NJ: Princeton University Press, 1950), p. 43.

7. Quoted in Iriye, "Embassy in Tokyo," in *Pearl Harbor as History*, p. 125.

8. Thompson, "Department of State," ibid., pp. 99–101; cf. Feis, *Road to Pearl Harbor*, pp. 90–93. The President was given authority to control or end the exports of war material to Japan by the passage in Congress in June of "An Act to Expedite the Strengthening of the National Defense" (H.R.9850). The first sentence of Section IV reads: "Whenever the President determines that it is necessary in the interest of national defense to prohibit or curtail the exportation of any military equipment or munitions, or component parts thereof, or machinery, tools, or material or supplies necessary for the manufacture, servicing or operation thereof, he may by proclamation prohibit or curtail such exportation, except under such rules or regulation as he shall prescribe." Ibid., p. 73. Hull had written on 22 May to the Chairman of the Senate Committee on Military Affairs urging enactment of this legislation, which gave Roosevelt sweeping powers to embargo, which he would employ again in the months ahead.

9. Ibid., pp. 92–93. Here, and for much of the account of the U.S. diplomatic measures taken against Japan that follows, the writer has relied on the work of Professor Feis.

10. Quoted in Morison, *Rising Sun*, p. 42.

11. Appendix 2, "The System of Government in Tokyo During the Years Preceding the Outbreak of War," in Major General S. Woodburn Kirby, et al., *The War Against Japan*, Vol. 1, *The Loss of Singapore* (London: Her Majesty's Stationery Office, 1957), pp. 479–80.

12. Attributed to Leon Samson, in Christopher Morley, ed., *Familiar Quotations, John Bartlett* (Boston, MA: Little, Brown and Company, 1951), p. 999.

13. Agawa, *Reluctant Admiral*, p. 189.

14. Grew to Department of State, 12 September 1940, quoted in Feis, *Road to Pearl Harbor*, p. 102.

15. Address at Teamsters Union Convention, Washington, D.C., 11 September 1940. Cited in ibid., p. 102. Roosevelt famously made an even stronger pledge in Boston, on 30 October, when he told an audience: "I have said this before, but I shall say it again and again and again: Your boys are not going to be sent into any foreign wars." Ibid., p. 133.

16. William L. O'Neill, *A Democracy at War: America's Fight at Home and Abroad in World War II* (New York: The Free Press, 1993), p. 27; and see pp. 10–26, *passim*.

17. *The Gallup Poll: Public Opinion, 1935–1971*, Vol. 1., *1935–1948* (New York: Random House, 1972). Poll of 22 January 1941, showing 68 percent of respondents in support of Lend-Lease, 26 percent disapproving, p. 261.

18. Ibid., pp. 259, 274.

19. Ibid., pp. 263, 268.

20. Ibid., p. 276.

21. Ibid.

22. Ibid., pp. 208, 246.

23. Ibid., pp. 266, 268.

24. Ibid., p. 296. The same question was asked on 14 November, when the responses were 64 percent yes, 25 percent no, with 11 percent having no opinion.

25. Ibid., p. 311.

26. NARA, RG 80, PHLO, Box 29, Stark, Memorandum for the President, 11 February 1941, p. 2. In this memorandum Stark summed up in writing for the President's benefit the arguments he had made in person earlier.

27. Ibid., Box 5, Stark to Kimmel, 10 February 1941, Narrative Statement of Evidence at Navy Pearl Harbor Investigations [hereafter Statement of Evidence], p. 260.

28. Ibid.

29. Ibid., Kimmel to Stark, 18 February 1941, p. 261.

30. Ibid., Stark to Kimmel, 25 February 1941, p. 263.

31. PHA, Pt. 16, p. 2163.

32. Ibid., pp. 2163–64. The northwestern cruise would have been made by one aircraft carrier, a division of heavy cruisers, and one squadron of destroyers, with tankers as necessary, to Attu, Aleutian Islands, then to Petropavlovsk in Siberia for a three-day visit. The phrase "to say 'Boo!' " is borrowed from Morison, *Rising Sun,* p. 57.

33. PHA, Pt. 16, pp. 2175–77.

34. Winston S. Churchill, *The Second World War,* Vol. 3, *Their Finest Hour* (Boston: Houghton Mifflin Company, 1949), p. 404.

35. For a more detailed presentation of these Atlantic events, see Michael Gannon, *Operation Drumbeat: The Dramatic True Story of Germany's First U-Boat Attacks Along the American Coast in World War II* (New York: Harper & Row Publishers, 1990), pp. 83–89.

36. As examples of recent works that date the "shoot on sight" order to the post-*Greer* period one may list: Clay Blair, *Hitler's U-Boat War,* Vol. 1, *The Hunters, 1939–1942* (New York: Random House, 1996), p. 360; Peter Padfield, *War Beneath the Sea: Submarine Conflict, 1939–1945* (London: BCA, 1995), p. 164; O'Neill, *Democracy at War,* p. 31; William K. Klingaman, *1941: Our Lives in a World on Edge* (New York: Harper & Row, 1988), pp. 370–71; and Waldo Heinrich, *Threshold of War: Franklin D. Roosevelt and American Entry into World War II* (New York: Oxford University Press, 1988), p. 167.

37. Naval Historical Center Library, Rare Books, Operation Plans Nos. 4-41 and 5-41 (1 and 18 July 1941, respectively), in MS, dated 1946, CINCLANT, Administrative History No. 139, "Commander Task Force Twenty-Four," pp. 61–62. Confirming copies of the same orders are found in Operational Archives [hereafter OA/NHC], Box CINCLANT (June–Sept. 1941), Operation Plan 5-41, Serial 00120, 15 July 1941; NARA, RG 80, Records of the CNO Headquarters COMINCH 1942, Box 11, cited in Task Force Fifteen, USS *Idaho,* Flagship, Secret Serial A4-3 (005), 29 August 1941; and Washington National Records Center, Suitland, Maryland, RG 313, Box 108, CINCLANT, cited in Task Force Three, USS *Memphis,* Flagship, n.d., but presumed July 1941. Operation Orders Nos. 6-41 and 7-41 were found in OA/NHC, Box "CINCLANT, Jun.–Sept. 1941." All the above-cited archival collections, though not the NHC Library, have been moved to NARA, Archives II, Modern Military Branch, in College Park, MD.

38. Ibid.

39. Interview with Jürgen Rohwer, Stuttgart, Germany, 16 December 1986. Dr. Rohwer described the *Admiral Scheer* incident in his "Die USA und die Schlacht im Atlantik 1941," Jürgen Rohwer and Eberhard Jäckel, eds., *Kriegswende Dezember 1941* (Koblenz: Bernard & Graefe Verlag, 1984), pp. 81–103.

40. The conversations and text of the agreement are given in PHA, Pt. 15, pp. 1485–1550. An ABC-22 staff agreement for joint United States-Canadian defense was incorporated into ABC-1.

41. Rear Admiral Turner, who was one of two flag officers representing the Navy in the staff conversations, stated in 1944: "It would be a grave error for anyone to get the idea that the war in the Central Pacific was to be purely defensive. Far from it." PHA, Pt. 26, p. 265.

42. Morison, *Rising Sun*, pp. 53–54.

43. WPPac-46, with four annexes, is given in PHA, Pt. 37, pp. 837–71.

44. Here again the writer relies on Feis, *Road to Pearl Harbor*, pp. 150–59.

45. Cordell Hull, *The Memoirs of Cordell Hull*, Vol. II, (New York: The MacMillan Company, 1948), p. 987.

46. Ibid., p. 995.

47. From postwar interrogation of Admiral Nagano Osami, chief of the Naval General Staff, cited in Feis, *Road to Pearl Harbor*, p. 217 and n. 20.

48. PHA, Pt. 32, p. 560. On the same date that the President issued his freeze order he federalized the Philippine Army and appointed Douglas MacArthur its commanding general. By this same date the American Volunteer Group, composed of American pilots who called themselves the "Flying Tigers," were flying Curtiss P-40B fighters in missions against the Japanese in China.

49. NARA, RG 80, PHLO, Box 29, Stark to Cooke, 31 July 1941.

50. Morison, *Rising Sun*, p. 63, n. 37. In placing controls on oil exports Roosevelt intended to permit low-grade gasoline for civilian and commercial purposes to continue flowing at 1936 levels, and so informed Ambassador Nomura. However, Secretary Ickes and Assistant Secretary of State Dean Acheson enveloped the flow in so much red tape that the embargo became total. See John Costello, *Days of Infamy: MacArthur, Roosevelt, Churchill—The Shocking Truth Revealed* (New York: Pocket Books, 1994), p. 57.

51. As naval historian Samuel Eliot Morison assayed the moment: "The oil embargo and assets-freezing order of 26 July 1941 made war with Japan inevitable unless one of two things happened, and neither was humanly possible. The United States might reverse its foreign policy, restore trade relations and acquiesce in further Japanese conquests; or the Japanese government might persuade its army at least to prepare to evacuate China and renounce the southward advance [which would surely] have been disregarded by an Army which, as the facts show, would accept no compromise that did not place America in the ignominious role of collaborating with conquest." Morison, *Rising Sun*, p. 63.

Chapter Five: An Air of Inevitability

1. Morison, *Rising Sun*, p. 68.

2. Hull wrote later: "We could not forget that Konoye had been Premier when Japan had invaded China in 1937; he had signed the Axis Alliance in 1940 and had concluded the treaty with the puppet government in Nanking designated to give Japan the mastery of China." Hull, *Memoirs*, II, p. 1024.

3. Ibid., pp. 1019–34; Feis, *Road to Pearl Harbor*, pp. 253–76; Morison, *Rising Sun*, pp. 68–70.

4. PHA, Pt. 14, p. 1402, CNO to CINCPAC, CINCAF, CINCLANT, 16 October 1941.

5. NARA, RG 80, PHLO, Box 25, Kimmel to Stark, 22 October 1941; Kimmel, *Kimmel's Story*, pp. 40–41. Two days before the warning of 16 October, Kimmel reissued security order No. 2 CL-41, which contained the advisory that a Japanese declaration of war may be preceded by "a surprise attack on ships in Pearl Harbor."

6. PHA, Pt. 5, pp. 2382–84.

7. NARA, RG 80, PHLO, Box 29, Stark to Cooke, 31 July 1941.

8. PHA, Pt. 5, pp. 2175–76.

9. Ibid., Pt. 5, pp. 2176–77.

10. Ibid., Pt. 5, p. 2019; 1975. Turner identified the three times he claimed he received the denials by Noyes that Kimmel had Magic decryption equipment in January, July or August, and early November, all in 1941. Ibid., p. 2040.

11. For Noyes see ibid., Pt. 33, p. 897. Noyes later testified that Turner, if he asked such a question as that suggested, may have had "traffic analysis" and "decrypted traffic" confused in his mind; ibid., pp. 1975–77, 2029; Pt. 10, pp. 4714–15. Or, as Roberta Wohlstetter has theorized, Turner may have had "intercepts" (which Kimmel had) confused with decrypts and translations (which he did not have); Wohlstetter, *Warning and Decision,* pp. 182–83. For Beatty, see *U.S. News & World Report* (28 May 1954), pp. 49–50. In his posthumously published book, *"And I Was There,"* pp. 19–20, then Rear Admiral (Ret.) Layton recounted how, when a personal guest of Admiral Nimitz on board his flagship *South Dakota* during the Japanese formal surrender ceremonies on 2 September 1945, then full Admiral Turner, another personal guest, strode into the wardroom. "The war had made 'Terrible' Turner a naval legend," Layton wrote. "As commander of Nimitz's amphibious forces, he had executed all our landing operations from Guadalcanal to Iwo Jima with brilliant distinction." His booming voice stopped all conversation. " 'That goddamned Kimmel had all the information and didn't do anything about it. They should hang him higher than a kite!'

"Turner continued to hold forth. Time and again he said, 'Kimmel was given all that information and didn't do anything about it.'

"I sat there stunned. I knew that what he was saying was not only untrue, but a monstrous slur on my former commander in chief." Rear Admiral Edwin T. Layton, USN (Ret.), with Captain Roger Pineau, USNR (Ret.), and John Costello, *"And I Was There": Pearl Harbor and Midway—Breaking the Secrets* (New York: William Morrow and Company, Inc., 1985.)

Before the JCC on 21 December 1945, Turner was forced by evidence that had been presented earlier to the NCI, to admit that he "was entirely in error as regards the diplomatic codes"; PHA, Pt. 4, p. 1976.

Others who believed that Kimmel was Magic-equipped were Rear Admiral Theodore S. Wilkinson, Director of the Office of Naval Intelligence (ONI) who testified to that effect before the Roberts Commission in January 1942 (ibid., Pt. 24, p. 1361), and three Army G-2 officers at the War Department: Brig. Gen. Sherman Miles, chief of military intelligence (G-2); Lt. Col. Moses Pettigrew, executive officer of G-2; and Col. Carlisle Dusenbury, assistant to Col. Rufus S. Bratton, chief, Far Eastern Section, G-2. "I understood," Dusenbury testified, "the Navy had about four or five hundred Naval personnel in Hawaii doing monitoring, breaking, and translating of the Japanese diplomatic codes." Ibid., Pt. 35, p. 25.

The accuracy of Turner's predictions of Japanese intent and action may be measured right up to the morning of 6 December, when this exchange took place between the War Plans chief and Secretary Knox: " 'Are they going to hit us?' Knox asked. To which Admiral Turner replied, 'No, Mr. Secretary, they are going to attack the British. They are not ready for us yet.' " Vice Admiral Frank E. Beatty, "The Background of the Secret Report," *National Review* (13 December 1966), p. 1261.

12. The Knox-Turner exchange was recorded by Knox's aide Captain Frank E. Beatty. See Vice Admiral Frank E. Beatty (Ret.), "Another Version of What Started War with Japan," *U.S. News & World Report* (28 May 1954), p. 49. The Morison letter is found in KC, Roll 18, Morison to Shafroth, Northeast Harbor, ME, 1961, no date, but shortly before Morison's article "The Lessons of Pearl Harbor" appeared in the *Saturday Evening Post* (28 October 1961), pp. 19–27.

13. PHA, Pt. 32, pp. 560–62.

14. E.g., ibid., Pt. 14, p. 1062.

15. Ibid., Pt. 32, p. 560.

16. Memorandum, "Reinforcement of the Philippines," Gerow to Marshall, 14 August 1941, cited in Costello, *Days of Infamy,* p. 84.

17. Forrest C. Pogue, *George C. Marshall: Ordeal and Hope, 1939–1942* (New York: The Viking Press, Inc., 1966), pp. 185–87.

18. PHA, Pt. 16, pp. 2211–12; NARA, RG 80, PHLO, Box 29, Memorandum, Marshall to Stark, 12 September 1941. Cf. Wesley Frank Craven and James Lea Cate, *The Army Air Forces in World War II*, vol. 1, *Plans and Early Operations, January 1939 to August 1942* (Chicago: University of Chicago Press, 1948), pp. 178–79.

19. PHA, Pt. 16, pp. 2211–12.

20. PHA, Pt. 3, pp. 1119–20.

21. NARA, RG 80, PHLO, Box 29, Stark to Cooke, 31 July 1941.

22. Ibid., Box 25, Kimmel to Stark, 26 May 1941.

23. See PHA, Pt. 16, p. 2229, Kimmel to Stark, 18 February 1941; ibid., p. 2160, Stark to Kimmel, 22 March 1941, ibid., p. 2160; ibid., pp. 2233–38, Kimmel to Stark, 26 May 1941, also found in NARA, RG 80, PHLO, Box 25; ibid., Box 29, Stark to Kimmel, 19 August 1941. For Kimmel's letter to Stark of 12 September, see ibid., Box 29; and for Stark's interrogation see ibid., Box 23, NCI, OT, vol. 1, p. 129 ff.

24. Ibid., Box 29, Stark to Kimmel, 17 October 1941.

25. Cecil Woodham-Smith, *The Reason Why* (New York: McGraw-Hill Book Company, Inc., 1953), pp. 228–34.

26. Gannon, *Operation Drumbeat*, pp. 90–92.

27. NARA, RG 80, PHLO, Box 29, "Betty" to "Mustapha," 25 November 1941.

28. Ibid., Kimmel to Betty, 12 August 1941.

29. Ibid., Box 25, Kimmel to Betty, 22 August, and Betty to Mustapha, 12 September 1941.

30. Ibid., Box 29, Kimmel to Stark, 15 November 1941; cf. Box 25, Kimmel to Stark, 26 May 1941.

31. Ibid., Box 25, Kimmel to Stark, 22 October 1941.

32. Ibid., Kimmel to Stark, "Survey of Conditions in the Pacific Fleet," 26 May 1941. He could have mentioned the role of battleship gunfire in softening up invasion beaches, but as late as Betio Island, Tarawa, in the Gilberts on 20 November 1943, it was not understood how important it was to saturate a landing beach with heavy, sustained bombardment. Kimmel's prediction that carriers and light forces would dominate sea warfare in its opening stages was confirmed by the Japanese Navy not only at Pearl Harbor but in their advances, built around air power, through the Philippines and the NEI. See Fleet Admiral Ernest J. King, U.S. Navy, *U.S. Navy at War, 1941–1945: Official Reports to the Secretary of the Navy* (Washington, D.C.: United States Navy Department, 1946), p. 42. Of course, the main confirmations of the primacy of the carriers and air power came in the battles of the Coral Sea (7–8 May 1942) and Midway (3–6 June 1942).

33. Ibid., Box 25, Kimmel to Stark, 26 May 1941. See Chapter 4 *infra* for the tanker numbers, and see Kimmel to Stark, 2 December 1941.

34. Ibid., Box 25, Kimmel to Stark, 2 December 1941.

35. Ibid., Box 29, Betty to Mustapha, 25 November 1941.

36. Fukudome, "Hawaii Operation," p. 1316.

37. This point was made during the Hart Inquiry in 1944 by then Captain Vincent R. Murphy, who had been Kimmel's assistant war plans officer: "I did not think they [the Japanese] would attack at Pearl Harbor because I did not think it was necessary for them to do so, from my point of view. We could not have materially affected their control of the waters that they wanted to control, whether or not the battleships were sunk at Pearl Harbor. In other words, I did not believe that we could move the United States Fleet to the Western Pacific until such time as auxiliaries were available." PHA, Pt. 26, p. 207. Cf. Morison, *Rising Sun*, p. 132.

Admiral Stark wrote to Roosevelt a month before the attack: "At the present time the United States Fleet in the Pacific is inferior to the Japanese Fleet and cannot undertake an unlimited strategic offensive in the Western Pacific . . . [which] would require tremendous merchant tonnage, which could only be withdrawn from services now considered essential." KC, Roll 7, Memorandum for the President, 5 November 1941, p. 2.

38. See Miller, *War Plan Orange,* pp. 294–308. The Navy Plan Option Dash One that *was* approved by the Navy Department, on 9 September 1941, is summarized in NARA, RG 80, PHLO, Box 5, Statement of Evidence, pp. 103–16. Cf. ibid., Box 25, Kimmel to Stark, 2 December 1941.

39. Miller, *War Plan Orange,* pp. 306–07. Another version of his statement, and the one used here, appears in Miller, "Kimmel's Hidden Agenda," *MHQ, The Quarterly Journal of Military History* (autumn 1991), p. 42.

40. Frederic L. Borch III, "Guilty As Charged?" *MHQ: The Quarterly Journal of Military History* vol. 13, no. 2 (winter 2001), p. 61.

41. NARA, RG 80, PHLO, Box 5, Statement of Evidence, Japanese Diplomatic Dispatches, pp. 332–33. Neither of these two messages was sent to Kimmel or Short.

42. Kirby et al., *Loss of Singapore,* pp. 90–93.

43. For Proposal A, see Feis, *Road to Pearl Harbor,* p. 295; for Proposal B, see William A. Langer and S. Everett Gleason, *The Undeclared War, 1940–1941* (New York: Harper & Brothers Publishers, 1953), pp. 233–34. Neither of these two proposals, decrypted as Magic, was sent to Kimmel or Short.

44. NARA, RG 80, PHLO, Box 5, Statement of Evidence, Japanese Diplomatic Dispatches, p. 334. This message was not sent to Kimmel or Short.

45. Ibid., Box 29, Stark to Kimmel, 17 October 1941.

46. PHA, Pt. 3, p. 1167.

47. NARA, RG 80, PHLO, Box 5, Statement of Evidence, Estimate Prepared by Admiral Stark and General Marshall for the President, 5 November 1941, pp. 355A–58; PHA, Pt. 14, pp. 1061–62. This estimate was sent to Kimmel. The estimate did recommend that military action should be taken against Japan in the following contingencies: "(1) A direct attack of war by Japanese armed forces against the territory or mandated territory of the United States, the British Commonwealth, or the Netherlands East Indies. (2) The movement of Japanese forces into Thailand to the west of 100° east or south of 10° north; or into Portuguese Timor, New Caledonia, or the Loyalty Islands."

48. KC, Roll 3, Stimson, Statement of Facts as Shown by My Current Notes and My Recollection as Refreshed Thereby, typescript, pp. 12–42.

49. KC, Roll 8, Sumner Welles, Memorandum of Conversation, Monday, August 11, 1941, at Sea, p. 10. Welles noted further that "Mr. Churchill dissented very strongly from" the President's insistence that "no future commitments had been entered into." See Costello, *Days of Infamy,* p. 77 and n. 38.

50. KC, Roll 3, Address of Winston S. Churchill, 27 January 1942. The address was not published in the United States at the time.

51. Quoted in Costello, *Days of Infamy,* p. 145. See his Chapter 6, "If the British Fought, We Would Have to Fight," pp. 131–49.

52. NARA, RG 80 PHLO, Box 23, ALUSNA SINGAPORE TO CINCAF Ø61526. As the reader will notice, "A firm" [sic], "Baker," and "Cast" are code for A, B, and C; double Xs represent periods. In 1946 then Captain John X. Creighton, USN, testified that he was the officer who sent the cable to Hart but that his memory was blank about its particulars. He doubted that he had received the information from Brooke-Popham because he was not close to the air marshal. For Creighton see PHA, Pt. 10, pp. 4803, 4809, 4818–19, 5075, 5080–89; Pt. 11, 5207, 5484, 5514–15; Pt. 18, p. 3344; Pt. 33, p. 838; Pt. 40, n. 170, n. 414.

53. CINCAF to OPNAV, 6 December 1941, reproduced in Kemp Tolley, *The Cruise of the Lanikai* (Annapolis: U.S. Naval Institute Press, 1973), p. 265.

54. NARA, RG 80, PHLO, Box 23, Stark's Testimony Before the NCI, OT, vol. 1, p. 129.

55. Ibid., Kimmel's Testimony Before the NCI, excerpt.

56. Hull, *Memoirs,* II, p. 1062.

57. NARA, RG 80, PHLO, Box 9, "Pencilled Memorandum Given By the President to the Secretary of State (Not Dated but Probably Written Shortly After November 20, 1941)."

According to Langer and Gleason, "Logic as well as internal evidence" work against the post–20 November dating; *Undeclared War*, p. 872.

58. White's memorandum was entitled "Suggested Approach for Elimination of United States-Japanese Tension; see ibid., p. 875 ff. The full text is given in PHA, Pt. 19, p. 3667ff.

59. PHA, Pt. 12, p. 155.

60. PHA, Hull, Statement to JCC; *Memoirs*, p. 1070.

61. See, e.g., Langer and Gleason, *Undeclared War,* p. 880; Feis, *Road to Pearl Harbor,* pp. 310–11; Roberta Wohlstetter, *Pearl Harbor: Warning and Decision* (Stanford, CA: Stanford University Press, 1961), p. 234.

62. PHA, Pt. 12, pp. 156–57.

63. Wohlstetter, *Pearl Harbor,* p. 234. It may be added here that the centrality of the China issue was recognized by both sides when Nomura and Kurusu met with Hull on 1 December. According to Nomura's account, "We then said that behind the problems at hand, there has always been the China problem. . . . It is of the utmost importance for us to avoid standing by and watching our own respective countries die just because of the China problem. Hull indicates his agreement with this." NARA, RG 80, PHLO, Statement of Evidence, p. 571.

64. NA, RG 80, PHLO, Box 5, Statement of Evidence, Japanese Diplomatic Dispatches, pp. 337–38. This message was not sent to Kimmel or Short.

65. PHA, Pt. 14, pp. 1103–07.

66. Ibid., p. 1300. This message did not arrive at the White House until 12:55 A.M. on the twenty-sixth.

67. Ibid., Pt. 4, p. 1167 ff; Pt. 2, p. 774.

68. PHA, Pt. 11, p. 5433, Stimson diary entry, 25 November 1941.

69. Ibid., pp. 5433–34, diary entries 25, 26 November 1941.

70. Hull's memorandum is reproduced in the Exhibits of the JCC, Pt. 14, pp. 1176–77. In his *Days of Infamy,* pp. 126–31, 384 n. 79, 386 n. 30, John Costello has used second- and third-hand evidence to support his contention that "it was the president who took the decision to abandon the modus vivendi that Wednesday morning, over the secretary of state's strongly voiced objections." In the first instance, he cites a letter from Max Bishop, a career State Department official who "kept the files of all American-Japanese conversations during the summer and fall of 1941." In a letter to former ambassador to Japan Joseph C. Grew, dated 14 October 1955, Bishop related what he had been told by another State official, Landreth Harrison, who had been in Hull's office "just a day or so before November 26." As Bishop related Harrison's experience: "Hull was summoned by private telephone to the White House. He asked Mr. Harrison to wait in the office for he, Secretary Hull, expected to return immediately. The Secretary was gone only 15 minutes or so and came back in a very agitated frame of mind. He said something like this: 'Those madmen over there [White House—he may have used the term "madmen" but Harrison doesn't want to go that far] do not believe me when I tell them the Japanese will attack us. You cannot give an ultimatum to a powerful and proud people and not expect them to react violently.' "

In the second instance, Costello cites the same letter from Bishop as his source for a supposed exchange of letters between Hull and Hornbeck on 27 November. Bishop prefaced his relation of the text with the story that, sometime after 7 December, Hornbeck asked Bishop for the return of all his "personal memoranda." Bishop complied, but not without first arranging to have them copied "because of their historical significance." According to Bishop, the 27 November exchange went as follows: "In days to come," Hornbeck is supposed to have written to Hull, "you will look upon the decision which was made and the action you took yesterday [holding back the modus vivendi] with great satisfaction." He went on to reassure Hull that the modus vivendi note had little chance of success, since the Japanese would have viewed it as a "not . . . completely honest document" expressly crafted "to give us more time to prepare our weapons of defense." Hull, according to the account, was angered by this oleaginous compliment and wrote back at once to say, "We differ so entirely . . . that I must in writing offer my dissent." "It is no answer to the question of whether this proposal is sound and desirable at this most critical period," he told Hornbeck, "to say that it probably would not have been accepted by Japan in any event. If that sort of demagoguery stuff would be rung into this sort of understanding, then there could never be any settlement between countries except at the point of a sword." This sounds like a Hull proud of what he had attempted to produce as a truce or compromise.

The Harrison recollection is secondhand hearsay. Where the Hornbeck-Hull exchange is concerned, one must say that in history nothing substitutes for examination of the original documents. And here the original (alleged) Hornbeck-Hull correspondence of 27 November is missing. In the matter of Pearl Harbor much mischief has been created through appeal to secondary "sources" that, time and again, have proved to be worthless or wrong. The dialogue and correspondence reproduced in the Bishop letter may have in fact occurred in that or similar fashion (and "similar" means that the hearer or the reader might well have skewed what he heard or read). But in the effort of establishing that Roosevelt abandoned the modus vivendi over Hull's passionate objections, as Costello contends, the Bishop letter, one must conclude, has questionable probative value.

71. PHA, Pt. 14, p. 1083. The memorandum was signed on the twenty-sixth and delivered on the twenty-seventh. Rear Admiral Turner is said to have fashioned the first draft. It should be remarked here that neither the modus vivendi note nor the Ten-Point note was sent to Kimmel and Short in Hawaii.

72. NARA, RG 80, PHLO, Box 14, Hornbeck to Hull, 31 October 1941. On 3 November Hornbeck read a Statement to the Joint Board Meeting (Stimson, Knox, Marshall, Stark, and their respective War Plans staffs), in which he said of a U.S.-Japan war: "With Japan as comparatively weak as she is . . . we need not fear unduly the military outcome—or even the immediate consequence—of such a conflict"; NARA, RG 80, PHLO, Box 14, p. 2. Later in the meeting, Rear Admiral Royal E. Ingersoll, Stark's assistant CNO, objected to such brashness and declared that he for one did not accept State's view "that Japan could be defeated in military action in a few weeks"; PHA, Pt. 14, p. 1064. For a short profile of Hornbeck, see Thompson, "Department of State," in Borg and Okamoto, eds., *Pearl Harbor as History*, pp. 81–106, *passim*.

73. Ibid., Pt. 5, p. 2089.

74. See, e.g., the diary of Adolf A. Berle, Jr., Assistant Secretary of State, entry of 1 December 1941. Franklin D. Roosevelt Library, Hyde Park, NY., microfilm of typescript in the University of Florida Libraries.

75. Ibid.

76. Julius W. Pratt, *Cordell Hull, 1933–44* (New York: Cooper Square Publishers, 1964), vol. II, p. 515.

77. Robert Dallek, *Franklin D. Roosevelt and American Foreign Policy, 1932–1945* (New York: Oxford University Press, 1979), p. 308 and n. 48; cf. Wohlstetter, *Pearl Harbor*, p. 244; Feis, *Road to Pearl Harbor*, p. 320. For Roosevelt's and the American public's absorption with Europe and the Atlantic see Wohlstetter, *Pearl Harbor*, p. 230: "President Roosevelt was so deeply interested in the European situation that he left Far Eastern matters almost entirely to Secretary Hull."

78. See Appendix B. Hull recalled, in May 1946, that after the emissaries read the document, "Mr. Kurusu said that he felt that our response to their proposal [B] could be interpreted as tantamount to meaning the end"; PHA, Pt. 11, p. 5369.

79. Reproduced in Feis, *Road to Pearl Harbor*, p. 321, n. 4. Stimson took a different view of the Ten Points document in his testimony before the JCC in March 1946: "The statement contained a reaffirmation of our constant and regular position without the suggestion of a threat of any kind. I personally was relieved that we had not backed down on any of the fundamental principles on which we had stood for so long and which I felt we could not give up without the sacrifice of our national honor and prestige in the world. I submit, however, that no impartial

reading of this document can characterize it as being couched in the terms of an ultimatum, although the Japanese were of course only too quick to seize upon it and give it that designation for their own purposes." Stimson, Statement before the JCC, PHA, Pt. 11, p. 5423. Among the diplomatic historians, Herbert Feis disputes the characterization of the Ten-Point program as an "ultimatum," *Road to Pearl Harbor,* p. 321. According to Stimson, Roosevelt called it a "magnificent statement"; ibid., p. 5435. On 27 October 1945, anxious to exculpate Hull from a charge made by the Army Pearl Harbor Board in 1944 that Hull's Ten-Point program was "the document that touched the button that started the war," Secretary of the Navy James Forrestal announced that Japanese documents taken from the heavy cruiser *Nachi,* sunk in Manila Bay, disclosed that the order implementing the Pearl Harbor attack (Combined Fleet Top Secret Operation Order No. 2) was dated 7 November, twenty days before Hull delivered the Ten-Point document. NARA, RG 80, PHLO, Box 23, Speech by Secretary of the Navy James Forrestal at the Navy League Dinner, Waldorf-Astoria Hotel, New York City, 27 October 1945. A similar exculpation, based on the same evidence, was issued to the press on 31 October 1945 by Secretary of State James F. Byrnes; *New York Times,* sec. 1, p. 2, 1 November 1945. The Army Board's charge originated from a misinterpretation of testimony given before it by former Ambassador Grew; PHA, Pt. 29, pp. 2148, 2151–53; Pt. 3, p. 137.

80. Ibid., Pt. 11, p. 5422, Stimson diary entry, 27 November 1941. Asked to explain this statement during the JCC investigation, Hull answered: "From November 22 on it was my individual view that Japan was through with any serious conversations looking to a peaceful settlement. From that day I and my associates had reached a stage of clutching at straws in our effort to save the situation." PHA, Pt. 2, pp. 404, 554. In his *Memoirs,* published in 1948, Hull denied making the Pilate-like "washed my hands" statement: "I did not make, and could not have made in the light of what occurred, the statement later attributed to me that I had 'washed my hands' of the matter. As long as there was the most microscopic possibility of peace, I intended to continue working toward that end as the record shows" (II, p. 1080).

Chapter Six: War Warnings

1. PHA, Pt. 11, p. 5435.
2. Ibid., pp. 5423, 5425.
3. Ibid., p. 5424.
4. PHA, Pt. 11, p. 5424.
5. Ibid., Pt. 14, p. 1330. The dates and times given are from KC, Roll 2, "Summary of Evidence Concerning Time of 27 and 28 Nov 41 War Department Warning Messages to Hawaii and Replies Thereto," pp. 1–2.
6. NARA, RG 80, PHLO, Box 5, Messages from the War and Navy Departments, 1941, p. 10; also PHA, Pt. 7, p. 2935.
7. Ibid. Pt. 14, p. 1330.
8. Ibid.
9. Short replied on 29 November and 4 December, respectively, to the warnings from Adams and Arnold; ibid., pp. 1331, 1333.
10. The Army levels of alert and what each required are given in Standing Operating Procedure, Hawaiian Department [5 November 1941] in Pt. 15, pp. 1440–44.
11. Ibid. Wohlstetter explains how Short arrived at his three levels of alert in *Pearl Harbor,* Appendix, pp. 403–04; see also her p. 47.
12. PHA, Pt. 10, p. 4860.
13. For Short see ibid., Pt. 7, p. 2984. For Kimmel see KC, Roll 20, "My Knowledge of Condition of Army Alert November 27 to December 7, 1941." Kimmel's chief of staff, Captain "Poco" Smith, told him that the Army had gone on all-out alert, and Bloch did not know the alert was for sabotage only until Short told him after the attack; see Prange, *At Dawn We Slept,* p. 730.

14. PHA., Pt. 35, pp. 217–18.

15. Ibid., Pt. 23, p. 1106.

16. Ibid., Pt. 7, p. 3016. As shown in the present text, directly below Short's quotation, Short did institute radar reconnaissance, and in so doing accurately reflected Stimson's thinking. In his Statement before the JCC, Stimson praised "what I regarded as a most effective means of reconnaissance against air attack and one to which I had personally devoted a great deal of attention during the preceding months. I refer to the radar equipment with which the Hawaiian Department was then provided. This equipment permitted approaching planes to be seen at distances of approximately 100 miles; and to do so in darkness and storm as well as in clear daylight." Ibid., Pt. 11, p. 5425.

17. Ibid., p. 2930.

18. Ibid. Marshall gave his reasons for declaring the alert in a letter addressed to Herron on 26 June, but never sent; ibid., Pt. 15, p. 1597.

19. Ibid., p. 1594.

20. Ibid., p. 1600.

21. Ibid., Pt. 7, p. 2930.

22. Ibid.

23. Ibid., p. 2935.

24. Ibid., p. 2941.

25. Ibid., p. 2985.

26. Ibid., p. 2942.

27. Ibid., pp. 2942–43.

28. Ibid., p. 2936.

29. Ibid., p. 2922. In a "Memorandum for the Record," dated 31 January 1942, Brigadier General Sherman Miles, who was stepping down as assistant chief of staff, Military Intelligence Division (G-2), wanted the world to know that, while he considered Short's acknowledgment message No. 959 "wholly inadequate," he regarded his 29 November detailed report of what he was doing under Alert No. 1 "a satisfactory answer." Neither message was approved or corrected. NARA, RG 80, PHLO, Box 26. Short's 29 November report was received in the War Department code room at 12:57 A.M., 30 November, Washington time.

30. PHA, Pt. 7, p. 2948.

31. Ibid., p. 2949.

32. Ibid., p. 2948.

33. Ibid.

34. Pogue, *Marshall: Ordeal and Hope*, p. 212.

35. The history of the routing of Short's No. 959 through the Munitions Building was developed by Lt. Comdr. John Ford Baecher, USNR, one of two Navy liaison officers assigned to supply evidence to the JCC. He was a graduate of Harvard Law School with three years naval service. His four-page routing document was entitled "Memorandum for Mr. Hidalgo," and was dated 14 March 1946. It is found in NARA, RG 80, PHLO, Box 26.

36. PHA, Pt. 32, p. 185; Pt. 22, p. 85; Pt. 27, p. 412; Pt. 28, p. 1497. On 20 December 1941, at Hickam Field, Lt. Col. Mollison gave an affidavit that included this language: "As this [sending Army pursuit planes to Midway and Wake] would unquestionably weaken the defenses of Oahu, Admiral Kimmel asked a question of Captain McMorris, his War Plans Officer, which was substantially as follows: Admiral Kimmel: McMorris what is your idea of the chances of a surprise raid on Oahu. Captain McMorris: I should say *none* Admiral [emphasis in the original]." In 1981, Rear Admiral Edwin T. Layton (Ret.), (a lieutenant commander in 1941), gave a more extended version of McMorris's reply: "Kimmel then sent for Captain Charles H. McMorris, his head of war plans, and I can still almost quote what he said: 'Soc . . . , Layton here and I have been discussing the chances of the Japanese making an attack on us here.' And McMorris replied, 'What's that?' 'We were discussing something that was written in Japanese

about a Japanese carrier task force making a strike on Pearl Harbor. Do you think there would be a chance of that?' McMorris answered him, 'Well, maybe they would; maybe they would, but I don't think so. Nope. Based on my studies, it is my considered opinion that there are too many risks involved for the Japanese to involve themselves in this kind of an operation.' " Layton, "Admiral Kimmel Deserved a Better Fate," Paul Stillwell, ed., *Air Raid: Pearl Harbor!* (Annapolis, MD: Naval Institute Press, 1981), p. 279.

37. PHA, Pt. 6, pp. 2519 and 2520. In the end, a squadron of Marine F4F fighters was sent to Wake and Midway in place of the P-40s.

38. Ibid., Pt. 7, p. 2922.

39. Ibid., Pt. 14, p. 1406. The writer has used the copy of the original message found in NARA, RG 38, Strategic Plans Division Records, Box 147J: Plans, Strategic Studies, and Related Correspondence (Series IX), Part III: OP-12B War Plans and Related Correspondence, WPL-46-WPL-46-PC. Cf. PHA, Pt. 14, p. 1406.

40. Ibid., Pt. 4, p. 2026.

41. Ibid., Pt. 14, p. 1405.

42. Vice Admiral George Carroll Dyer, *The Amphibians Came to Conquer: The Story of Admiral Richmond Kelly Turner* (Washington: Department of the Navy, 1969), p.191; Dyer interviews with Turner, March 1960.

43. The texts of the first four of these messages are given in PHA, Pt. 6, pp. 2512–13; the 16 October text is given in ibid., Pt. 14, p. 1402.

44. KC, Roll 4, Extracts from Secret Letters Exchanged Between the Commander in Chief and the Chief of Naval Operations, p. 11. Stark's reference to Russia recalls Turner's warning in August that the Japanese would likely invade the Maritime Provinces. But, by 27 November, his biographer tells us, Turner had backed off from that prediction. Dyer, *Amphibians*, p. 182.

45. "There is a certain sameness of tenor of such information as Admiral Stark sent to Admiral Kimmel"; King's second endorsement to the Record of Proceedings of the Naval Court of Inquiry, 6 November 1944, Pt. 39, p. 344.

46. This is according to Stark's biographer; Simpson, *Stark,* p. 269. Confirmed by the writer in a telephone conversation with Simpson, 13 November 2000.

47. PHA, Pt. 6, p. 2524.

48. Ibid., Pt. 3, p. 1434.

49. Ibid., Pt. 32, p. 52. See WPPac-46, Annex II, Phase IA, Task Force Nine; ibid., Pt. 37, pp. 863–66.

50. Ibid., Pt. 39, p. 321.

51. Ibid., Pt. 33, p. 877.

52. Ibid., Pt. 5, p. 2125.

53. Edward P. Morgan, "Confidential Report. An Approach to the Question of Responsibility for the Pearl Harbor Disaster. Respectfully Submitted at the Suggestion of the General Counsel for the Consideration, Assistance, and Sole Personal Use of the Joint Congressional Committee on the Pearl Harbor Attack. (Not to be released to the press, quoted from, published, or paraphrased in any way.)" (Washington: United States Government Printing Office, June 1, 1946), p. 125. Copy with the writer.

54. Ibid., Pt. 14, p. 1407.

55. KC, Roll 3, Kimmel, "Memorandum as to Cooperation and Coordination Between General Short and Admiral Kimmel," 17 July 1944, p. 9: "My own primary concern was the paralysing [sic] orders I had from the Navy Department to await an overt act by Japan."

56. The story of how Turner arrogated to himself the functions of naval intelligence is told in Jeffrey M. Dorwart, *Conflict of Duty: The U.S. Navy's Intelligence Dilemma, 1919–1945* (Annapolis, MD: Naval Institute Press, 1983), pp. 157–161; Dyer, *Amphibians*, pp. 182–87; and Layton, *"And I Was There,"* pp. 97–99, 100–01, 142–43, 256. In Layton's phrase, Turner tried to turn ONI into "nothing more than an intelligence drop-box." He recounts, from a

McCollum oral history, that when, in May 1941, the then director of ONI, Captain Alan C. Kirk, stated in handwriting on an intelligence summary, "In my view the Japs will jump pretty soon." Turner scribbled back his own prediction, "I don't think the Japs are going to jump now or ever!" p. 100.

57. PHA, Pt. 4, pp. 1975, 2029; Pt. 8, pp. 3388–90, 3412.

58. Ibid., Pt. 4, p. 1970.

59. Ibid., p. 2007.

60. Dyer, *Amphibians*, p. 189; and Dyer, interviews with Turner, March 1960, p. 193.

61. NARA, RG 38, Station US papers, Box 6, folder 5750–15. The memorandum is reproduced by Robert B. Stinnett, who discovered it, in his book *Day of Deceit: The Truth About FDR and Pearl Harbor* (New York: The Free Press, 2000), Appendix A, pp. 262–67.

62. Ibid., p. 9.

63. Ibid.

64. McCollum's memorandum, so far as is known, elicited only a "Do-Don't" response from Captain Dudley W. Knox, chief of the ONI library. He commented, "Be ready" and "We should not precipitate anything." Ibid., p. 6.

65. PHA., Pt. 8, pp. 3447–48.

66. Ibid., Pt. 26, p. 463.

67. Ibid., Pt. 4, pp. 1950–51.

68. Ibid., Pt. 26, p. 280.

69. Ibid., Pt. 5, pp. 2149–50, 2152; Pt. 32, p. 236.

70. Ibid., Pt. 32, p. 52.

71. See ibid., Pt. 37, Hewitt Inquiry, pp. 837–71, which includes WPPac-46 with four annexes and the following exhibit No. 36:

OP-12B-2–djm
(SC) A16/EF12
Serial 098912
D-33966
Secret
From: The Chief of Naval Operations
To: The Commander in Chief, U.S. Pacific Fleet
Subject: The U.S. Pacific Fleet Operating Plan, Rainbow
            No. 5 (Navy Plan O-1, Rainbow No. 5)
            WPPac-46, review and acceptance of
Reference: (a)CinCPac Secret let
            Serial 064W of 25 July, 1941.
            (1) The Chief of Naval Operations has reviewed
            subject Plan and accepts it
            (2) [Describes the means of delivery of this letter
            to be taken.]

                                                    H. R. Stark

72. Ibid. WPPac-46 was executed against Japan on 7 December 1941, J-Day.

73. Ibid. WPPac-46 provided a Phase I: "Initial Tasks—Japan not in the war," which did not include distant reconnaissance.

74. Ibid., Annex II; and Pt. 6, p. 2530. Task forces built around the carriers *Enterprise* and *Yorktown* would raid the Marshalls in late January 1942.

75. Ibid., Pt. 36, pp. 298–99.

76. Ibid., Pt. 33, pp. 1183–84. Cf. Pt. 8, pp. 3454–55. The Martin-Bellinger estimate was prepared "practically in toto" by Bellinger and his staff of Patrol Wing 2; Pt. 26, p. 140.

77. Ibid., Pt. 6, p. 2534.

78. Ibid., Pt. 17, pp. 2721–22, Memorandum, Bellinger to Kimmel, 19 December 1941.

Kimmel told the JCC that 250 aircraft would be required for distant reconnaissance (ibid., Pt. 6, p. 2533); Bellinger said "approximately 200" (Pt. 26, p. 124). On the number of flyable patrol bombers available to him at Oahu on 6–7 December, Bloch testified, "There were 72 patrol bombers available and two squadrons of 24 were at Midway, leaving 48, and 12 under overhaul, leaving 50. I meant 36" (Pt. 22, p. 487). Kimmel testified that 49 Navy patrol planes were in fly-able condition (Pt. 6, pp. 2532, 2722; Bellinger also said 49 [Pt. 22, p. 558]). Bloch had been promised an additional 108 patrol planes "at the earliest possible date," but none had arrived (Pt. 36, p. 550). The United Kingdom had first priority claim on the PBYs. On the operational B-17s see Pt. 27, p. 419; Pt. 12, p. 323; Pt. 7, p. 3203. Six long-range Army B-17D bombers, the only ones in operating condition on the island, were being used to train crews for the Philippine Air Force, but they were available in an emergency. The Army was also prepared to make avail-able twenty short-legged B-18 medium bombers, but they were useful only for inshore patrol; even there, General Martin's chief of staff, Lieutenant Colonel James A. Mollison, "complained bitterly" that the B-18 was "a very bad airplane for that purpose." Pt. 27, p. 423.

Responding to an inquiry from Navy Secretary James Forrestal, JCC liaison officer Lt. Comdr. Baecher, USNR, wrote to him on 28 March 1946, communicating a draft report from Mr. Seth W. Richardson, the second chief counsel of the committee. Richardson wrote:

> It was well known and recognized in Washington for at least a year prior to 7 December 1941 that adequate protection of the fleet in Hawaii, where Washing-ton ordered it to base rather than on the west coast, depended on having an ade-quate number of patrol and bomber planes with which to maintain reconnaissance and to defeat any approaching attacking force; that during the year 1941 there were manufactured in the United States a very large number of patrol and bomber planes, of which only a few were sent to Hawaii while a large and dispro-portionate number were diverted by Washington to Great Britain, in many instances under lend-lease; that if Washington had not so diverted these planes . . . the probability of the success of the Japanese attack on Pearl Harbor would have been greatly reduced; therefore, for such reasons, Washington must bear a large share of the burden of the blame for what occurred on 7 December 1941. (NARA, RG 80, PHLO, Box 23.)

In a handwritten aide-mémoire written in 1944 or 1945, Kimmel considered the fact that he had pleaded for additional patrol aircraft (PBYs): "In a conversation in the Navy Department with Admiral [John H.] Towers, then Chief of Bureau of Aeronautics, and Admiral Nimitz, then Chief of the Bureau of Navigation, in June 1941, I urged that additional patrol planes be sup-plied to the fleet." He referred to testimony he had given earlier:

> Both Admiral Bloch and I had been continually making such requests. I referred to the various requests of the Commandant of the 14th Naval District for patrol planes which I strongly and favorably endorsed. Had the Commandant been able to secure patrol planes for the 14th Naval District, it would have materially strengthened the base defense. The Chief of Naval Operations on November 25, 1941, wrote to the Commandant that the Department had no additional airplanes available for assignment to the 14th Naval District. 36 of the patrol plans which I had in Oahu arrived on November 23 and November 28, 18 arrived on October 28. They were all new planes experiencing shakedown difficulties and requiring substantial installations to get them into war condition. The Navy Department knew just how many patrol planes I had and knew that the number was not ade-quate for distant searches from Oahu. (KC, Roll 3.)

79. PH, Pt. 32, pp. 570–71. In March 1944 then Captain Vincent R. Murphy testified dur-ing the Hart Inquiry: "The question of patrol plane, all-around search, had come up many, many times. Much thought had been given to it. It was a question of wearing out our planes

over a considerable period of time, weakening out our pilots, and not knowing when to expect a declaration of war, to find ourselves completely worn out by practicing for war, including the psychological aspects thereof, and unable to fight it when it came." PHA, Pt. 26, p. 207.

80. Ibid., p. 307.

81. NARA, RG 80, PHLO, Box 5, Statement of Evidence, p. 405.

82. Ibid., Pt. 39, pp. 308–09.

83. Fleet Admiral William F. Halsey and Lt. Comdr. J. Byran III, *Admiral Halsey's Story* (New York: McGraw-Hill Book Co., 1974), p. 71.

84. PHA, Pt. 6, p. 2756. Elsewhere in the same hearings, Kimmel said: "I knew what Admiral Bellinger was doing. I didn't consider it necessary . . . to discuss it with a great many other admirals that I had in Pearl Harbor with me. The ones that I discussed it with were by no means all the admirals that we had out there." Ibid., p. 2652.

85. Ibid., pp. 2723, 2727.

86. Ibid., Pt. 39, p. 376.

87. Quoted in Paolo E. Coletta, *Patrick N. L. Bellinger and U.S. Naval Aviation* (Lanham, MD: University Press of America, Inc., 1987), p. 212. NARA (Washington, D.C.), RG 38, 80, 313, Records Relating to U.S. Navy Fleet Problems, I–XXII, 1923–1941, M964; Fleet Problem XIX in March–April 1938, Roll 24. Ernest J. King and Walter Muir Whitehill; *Fleet Admiral King: A Naval Record* (New York: W. W. Norton & Company, Inc., 1952), p. 281. Pearl Harbor had been "attacked" successfully three times before by U.S. Navy carrier-borne aircraft, in 1928, 1932, and 1933. In 1937 Lt. Comdr. Logan Ramsey published his *Proceedings* article, "Aerial Attacks on Fleets at Anchor," cited above. In it, among other points made, Logan emphasized that an attacking force had the advantage of choosing the time of attack; that the near approach could be made under cover of darkness; and that the immobilized fleet could not maneuver to avoid bombs.

C. Addison Pound, Jr., then an aviation cadet (at this date a resident of Gainesville, FL), piloted SBU-1 No. 42-S-6 on the Fleet Problem XIX attack of 30 March 1938. SB stood for bomber: the aircraft could carry two 200-pound bombs on its lower wing. The U stood for Chance-Vought, the manufacturer. Pound's VS-42 squadron, lacking oxygen, flew below 13,000 feet. "In the air at 5:00 [A.M.], . . ." he wrote in his diary. "Ahead were the piled cumulus masses marking Oahu, and we ran between two layers, one broken below and a solid above. . . . The group split, each squadron to its objective, and, as yet unseen—ours, Ford Island and the Patrol Base. We wheeled down into the rain and squared away on the hangers and beached PBY's—perfect—and steamed out to sea on the harbor channel at max[imum] manifold pressure, screaming by a group of A-11s [Curtiss two-seat attack bombers] that the Army [Air Corps] had picketed at low altitude. . . . These birds were funny as hell today with their coded calls, all names of whiskies: . . . 'Johnny Walker' . . . 'Hague & Hague' . . . 'Crab Orchard.' " Copy of diary page courtesy of Mr. Pound.

88. Kimmel told the NCI: "I would say that while all sectors are important, if I were restricted, I would probably search the western 180-degree sector first"; PHA, Pt. 32, p. 236. He told the JCC that, right after the attack on 7 December, he had a "hunch" that the Japanese aircraft had flown in from the north. "I did not know why, but I felt the carriers were to the northward, and I put that in a dispatch to Halsey. I did not want to make it much more than a hunch. Subsequently we got information which seemed to indicate the carriers were to the southward, and I had nothing more than this feeling, you might say." PHA, Pt. 6, p. 2603.

89. Ibid., p. 2535; cf. p. 2534.

90. Ibid., pp. 2723–24.

91. The writer is grateful for this meteorological information to Mark Jackson, of the National Weather Service, Pacific Region Headquarters, Honolulu; and to Henry Luu, meteorologist-forecaster at the National Weather Service Forecast Office, University of Hawaii, who showed the writer surface plots of the Pacific region north of Oahu during the month of December 2000.

92. Letter dated 13 January 2000, postmarked Julian, California, forwarded by Admiral Richardson to the writer.

93. NARA, RG 80, PHLO, Box 25, Commander-in-Chief, United States Pacific Fleet [Nimitz] to Commander-in-Chief, United States Fleet [King], Pearl Harbor, T.H., 7 January 1942.

94. Ibid., and Bellinger to King, via Nimitz, 30 December 1941, same Box 25.

95. See "Japanese Attack Plan" folder in NARA, RG 80, PHLO, Box 4; and reproductions of the Japanese tracking chart on the endpapers of Dull, *Imperial Japanese Navy,* and in Prange, *At Dawn We Slept,* p. 418.

96. NARA, RG 80, PHLO, Box 26, Colonel H. W. Allen, Assistant Adjutant General, General Headquarters, Supreme Commander for the Allied Powers, to Chief of Staff [Marshall], Tokyo, 1 November 1945.

97. Captain Mitsuo Fuchida, "I Led the Air Attack on Pearl Harbor," United States Naval Institute *Proceedings,* vol. 78, no. 9 (September 1952), pp. 942, 946.

98. NARA, RG 80, PHLO, Box 3, Naval Technical Mission, General Headquarters, Supreme Commander for the Allied Powers, "Pearl Harbor Attack," Interrogation of Captain Minoru Genda, Summary, 28 November 1945.

99. Unnamed and undated interrogation report in NARA, RG 80, PHLO, Box 40.

100. KC, Roll 3, Japanese Plan for the Attack on Pearl Harbor, p. 13.

101. Rear Admiral Sadao Chigusa (Ret.), "Conquer the Pacific Ocean Aboard the Destroyer *Akigumo*: War Diary of the Hawaiian Battle," in Donald M. Goldstein and Katherine V. Dillon, eds., *The Pearl Harbor Papers: Inside the Japanese Plans* (Washington, D.C.: Brassey's [US], 1993), p. 190.

102. PHA, Pt. 33, pp. 1183–84. Lt. Comdr. Logan Ramsey, chief of staff for Patwing 2, stated in 1944 that, "On the 360-degree circle from the Island, we took weather reports [from PBYs] covering a period of several months and found that approximately 20% in the area for a distance of 700 miles could be expected to have weather conditions where the visibility might go as low as zero." He was optimistic, however: "We stood an excellent chance of detecting any sizable group of surface vessels on any given day. . . . We might go out in rain squalls and miss them for a hour and get them on the return leg. If there was a widespread front, we might miss them entirely." PHA, Pt. 32, p. 447.

103. The Latin language maxim may be translated as: "In extreme circumstances extreme measures must be taken."

104. NARA, RG 38, Strategic Plans Division Records, Box 147J: Plans, Strategic Studies, and Related Correspondence (Series IX), Part III: OP-12B War Plans and Related Correspondence, WPL-46-WPL-46-PC, Chief of Naval Operations to the Commander-in-Chief, U.S. Pacific Fleet, 10 February 1941. On 23 June Stark mentioned sampans again to Kimmel: "It is also anticipated that at least five (5) sampans, recently condemned, will be available in the District"; KC, Roll 3.

105. Mitsuo Fuchida and Masatake Okumiya, *The Battle That Doomed Japan* (New York: Ballantine Books, Inc., 1955), pp. 68–71; Spector, *Eagle Against the Sun,* pp. 154–55.

106. PHA, Pt. 4, p. 2045.

107. Ibid., Pt. 36, p. 550.

108. NARA, RG 80, PHLO, Box 5, Statement of Evidence, p. 204, Ingersoll to Kimmel, 13 August 1941.

109. Morison, *Battle of the Atlantic,* pp. 275–76. A picket-ship line would have to be sustained on station by one or more tankers. The old destroyers, for example, required refueling every three days at sea. Kimmel had four tankers capable of refueling at sea. One could have operated to the north of Oahu, a second to the south. A third could be held in reserve. Even a fourth would be available up to 5 December, when it would be needed by Task Force 12, built around *Lexington*. Halsey on *Enterprise* did not take a tanker with TF-8. Carriers were fully

capable of refueling their accompanying ships. The writer is indebted to Vice Admiral David C. Richardson, USN (Ret.), former deputy commander in chief, Pacific Fleet, for these additional details.

110. PHA, Pt. 4, p. 2045.

111. KC, Roll 3, "Outline of Testimony Given Before Army Board Wash D.C., August 1944," p. 3.

112. PHA, Pt. 39, p. 308.

113. KC, Roll 20, "Additional Security Measures Taken November 27, 1941 and Thereafter," p. 1.

114. Ibid.

115. PHA, Pt. 6, p. 2537.

116. Ibid., p. 2538. The order was issued on the twenty-eighth with a copy sent to OpNav on that date. On 2 December Kimmel personally wrote Stark: "You will note that I have issued orders to the Pacific Fleet to depth bomb all submarine contacts in the Oahu operating area;" NARA, RG 80, PHLO, Box 29, Kimmel to Betty, 2 December 1941. Cf., Pt. 6, p. 2662.

117. KC, Roll 20, "Additional Security Measures," p. 2.

118. Ibid., p. 2.

119. PHA, Pt. 6, p. 2532.

120. Ibid.

121. KC, Roll 20, "Additional Security Measures," p. 1.

122. See exchange of letters, Kimmel to Ramsey, 6 December 1945, and then Captain Ramsey to Kimmel, 25 December 1945, in KC, Roll 28.

123. PHA, Pt. 6, p. 2534. Also see Lt. Comdr. Baecher to Mr. Seth W. Richardson, 4 April 1946, communicating Operation Plan No. 9-1, Section (a), Search Squadron, dated 15 November 1941, signed by Bellinger. NARA, RG 80, PHLO, Box 18.

124. An oral report presented to the JCC on 15 November 1945 by Rear Admiral T. B. Inglis, who had never been stationed at Pearl Harbor, contained the statement that these three patrol planes were scheduled to take off at 0527 but did not take off until 0640. PHA, Pt. 1, pp. 37 and 41. But the group leader of that flight, Ensign William P. Tanner, stated that "It was just after 0600 when we got up on the step and lifted off the water in Kaneohe Bay." Quoted in Mel Crocker, *Black Cats and Dumbos: WWII's Fighting PBYs* (Blue Ridge Summit, PA: Tab Books, Inc., 1987), p. 2.

125. PHA, Pt. 36, p. 550; Pt. 6, p. 2530. NARA, RG 80, PHLO, Statement of Evidence, pp. 578–80. From the immediately foregoing paragraphs in this chapter 6, it would be difficult to sustain a charge that Kimmel did nothing by way of stiffening his defenses after 27 November. Such a charge was made at a Colloquium on Pearl Harbor and the Kimmel Controversy, held in Washington, D.C., on 7 December 1999, by professor of history Robert W. Love, of the U.S. Naval Academy. "Why was Kimmel unready?" Love asked, when other commanders in the Asiatic Fleet, the Philippines, the Western Defense Command, Alaska, and the Caribbean Defense Command put their forces on alert or took other defensive measures. "Kimmel's counterparts moved," Love asserted. "They acted, whereas in Gordon Prange's memorable phrase, Kimmel failed to cease polishing the sword and pick up the shield." (Audio tape with the writer.) The evidence is to the contrary.

126. *Chicago Tribune*, Monday, 27 October 1941.

Chapter Seven: Climb Niitakayama

1. The foregoing information is given in Agawa, *Reluctant Admiral*, pp. 214–26. Agawa states that he relied on Volume 10, *Hawai sakusen* [Hawaii Operation], in the Japanese Defense Agency's series, *History of the War*. This would be the 102-volume *Senshi sosho* [War History] edited by Boeicho Boei Kenshujo, Senshishitsu (Asagumo Shinbunsha, 1966–1980).

2. NARA, RG 80, PHLO, "Reconstruction of Jap Attack Plan for the Attack on Pearl Harbor,"

Box 18; "The Japanese Plan for the Attack on Pearl Harbor," Box 4. Also see Agawa, *Reluctant Admiral,* p. 228.

3. Ibid., p. 229.

4. Fukudome, "Hawaii Operation," *Proceedings,* p. 1322.

5. See the newly published Herbert P. Bix, *Hirohito and the Making of Modern Japan* (New York: HarperCollins Publishers, 2000), *passim.*

6. Quoted in Bix, *Hirohito,* p. 422.

7. Ibid., pp. 425–26.

8. Fukudome, "Hawaii Operation," *Proceedings,* pp. 1322–23.

9. Quoted in Prange, *At Dawn We Slept,* p. 330

10. The Operational Order No. 1 is given in PHA, Pt. 13, p. 431 ff; also in NARA, RG 80, PHLO, Box 36. A copy of the order was recovered at war's end from the Japanese cruiser *Nachi,* sunk in Manila Bay.

11. Quoted in Prange, *At Dawn We Slept,* p. 332.

12. Agawa, *Reluctant Admiral,* p. 236.

13. Rear Admiral Walter C. Ansel, USN (Ret.), "The Taranto Lesson," in Stillwell, ed., *Air Raid, Pearl Harbor!,* p. 74. After the war, some curious remarks about the attacks at Taranto and Pearl were made by Admiral William V. Pratt, USN (Ret.), a former CNO as well as a former CINCUS: "Didn't the Taranto sinkings, which happened in November 1940, mean anything? There three Italian battleships and two cruisers, lying in an enclosed harbor, with a water depth of 42 feet and less, were sunk in a British air torpedo attack. The water depth at Pearl Harbor was 45 feet. And now [it is said] it was not thought a successful torpedo attack could be made in that depth of water. What is a Commander-in-Chief for?" *Newsweek,* 10 September 1945. (In 1933, the reader will remember, Pratt called Kimmel "a humdinger.") One should have thought that a former CNO would have access to nautical charts. The writer consulted a chart of the Port of Taranto and Mare Grande, with soundings in meters, in the Map Library, University of Florida Libraries (D5.356.54061/1997).

14. The best recent analysis of the Type 91 modification 2 torpedo is De Virgilio, "Japanese Thunderfish," pp. 61–68. The writer is grateful to Daniel A. Martinez, National Park Service historian at the USS *Arizona* Memorial, at Pearl Harbor, who explained to him the aft section of a Japanese torpedo that was recovered from the harbor bottom. See also Prange, *At Dawn We Slept,* pp. 160, 324, 332–33. The 17.7-inch Type 91 had a 2,200-yard range, 42-knot speed, and a 452-pound warhead (explosive charge).

15. PHA, Pt. 33, p. 1283.

16. Ibid., Pt. 23, p. 1138. In the attack at Taranto torpedoes were dropped at distances of 400, 600, 700, 800, 1,000, and 1,300 yards from targets. The water allowances for aerial torpedo runs against the battleships and cruisers at Pearl Harbor were 1935 yards from the navy yard to berths off northeast Ford Island, measured from Merry Point Landing, and 800 yards from Pearl City Peninsula southeast to berths off northwest Ford Island.

17. Ibid., Pt. 33, p. 1284.

18. NARA, RG 80, PHLO, Box 5, "Statement of Evidence," p. 226.

19. Ibid., p. 227. NARA, RG 80, PHLO, Box 8, "Information Derived from Alusna London Confidential Dispatch to OPNAV, 22 November 1940."

20. Ibid., p. 228; and PHA, Pt. 23, p. 1138.

21. NARA, RG 80, PHLO, Box 5, "Statement of Evidence," pp. 229–30.

22. PHA, Pt. 39, p. 362.

23. NARA, RG 80, PHLO, Box 5, "Statement of Evidence," pp. 230–31.

24. Ibid., Box 8, untitled and undated list, probably drawn up by Lt. Comdr. Baecher.

25. Ibid., Box 8, Intelligence Report, from Naval Attaché, London, No. 855 (Secret), issued by the Intelligence Division, Office of Chief of Naval Operations, 15 May 1941, no. 8 of 9 copies.

26. See above, n. 24.

27. Ibid., Box 8, Intelligence Report, from Naval Attaché, London, No. 1347 (Secret), 26 June 1941, no. 3 of 20 copies. This weapon was dropped regularly at 2,000 feet by Beaufort bombers equipped with specially adapted bombsights. It was found that the point of entry in the water could be controlled within a maximum error of 200 yards. Successful drops, it was reported, had been made from as high as 10,000 feet.

28. Ibid., Box 8, Intelligence Report, from Naval Attaché, Ottawa, No. 570–41 (Confidential), 5 September 1941. See A. J. Smithers, *Taranto 1940: "Prelude to Pearl Harbor"* (Annapolis, MD: Naval Institute Press, 1995), p. 84. From a 15 July 1941 report of Capt. C. A. Lockwood, USN, Naval Attaché in London, the Royal Navy Fleet Air Arm 18-inch Mark XII aerial torpedo then in use *"may be dropped in water as shallow as 4 fathoms [24 feet]"* [emphasis added]." NARA, RG 38, Box 75, Intelligence Report, Summary of Rear Admiral Mediterranean Carrier's report dated 5 February 1941 (0575/577/16), "Air Attacks on Italian Harbors by Naval Aircraft." The routing slips and distribution lists accompanying intelligence reports from London do not clearly specify that the 15 July report was shared with CINCPAC.

29. See above, n. 24. The actual language reads: London Report No. 1347, 26 June 1941: "The report was sent to C. in C. U.S.," Ottawa Report No. 570-41, 5 September 1941: "The report was sent to C. in C. U.S."

30. PHA, Pt. 32, p. 391.

31. NARA, RG 80, PHLO, Box 15, Kimmel to Chief of Naval Operations, 18 October 1945 (signed by R. A. Lavender, by direction).

32. Ibid., Box 34, Information Furnished to Rear Admiral H. E. Kimmel, USN (Ret.).

33. KC, Roll 3.

34. NARA, RG 80, PHLO, Box 4, "Japanese Plan for the Attack on Pearl Harbor," p. 3. See also ibid., Box 36, "Combined Fleet Top Secret Operation Order 1, Flagship NAGATO, Saeki Bay 5 Nov 41" and "Combined Fleet Secret Operation Order 2, Flagship NAGATO, Saeki Bay, 7 Nov. 41."

35. Fukudome, "Hawaii Operation," *Proceedings*, pp. 1325–26; Prange, *At Dawn We Slept*, pp. 204, 338. The enumeration of the main body of the Striking Force differs slightly in the accounts given by Fukudome and Fuchida. Cf. PHA, Pt. 13, pp. 487–88.

36. NARA, RG 80, PHLO, Box 18, "Reconstruction of Jap Attack Plan," pp. 9–10.

37. PHA, Pt. 12, pp. 195, 206. Roberta Wohlstetter has presented the argument that the fraudulent character of these negotiating tactics could be deduced by Magic readers only after 7 December, since, in her view, "there is not enough evidence of fraud in the dispatches alone to arouse suspicion." Furthermore, she cites Ambassador Grew's belief that Foreign Minister Togo "had no prior knowledge that an act of war was to be committed by the Japanese forces [against the United States]"; Wohlstetter, *Warning and Decision*, pp. 202 and n. 100, 205. Her, and Grew's, position is debatable given the recent findings (1999) of Professor Takeo Iguchi in the Foreign Ministry archives. There Iguchi discovered documents revealing that a "pliant" Foreign Ministry connived in the military's deceit stratagem; and he quotes from a 7 December (Japan time) entry in the Imperial General Staff's war diary: "Our deceptive diplomacy is steadily proceeding toward success." *New York Times*, 9 December 1999, p. A3.

38. Agawa, *Reluctant Admiral*, p. 244. See, for example, Fukudome, "Hawaii Operation," *Proceedings*, p. 1326; Fuchida, "Attack on Pearl Harbor," ibid., p. 942. Robert B. Stinnett, in *Day of Deceit: The Truth About FDR and Pearl Harbor* (New York: The Free Press, 2000), identifies a radio intercept traffic chief for the Pacific Fleet named Homer Kisner, who claims now to have "detected the Japanese advance on Hawaii" from intercepts of messages transmitted by ships of the striking force; p. 54. If so, as he said he would have done if he had seen McCollum's eight-point memorandum, he did not go "direct to Admiral Kimmel" and alert him to this bombshell information. In a review of Stinnett's book, the noted cryptographer David Kahn wrote: "Central to the surprise was the radio silence of the strike force. The Japanese, commanders and radio operators alike, say unanimously that they never transmitted any messages whatever, not even on low-power ship-to-ship [radio]. Except for Kisner, an American

intercept operator, everyone else who was listening for Japanese messages says the same thing. And the naval communications intelligence summaries produced in Hawaii have only one statement to make about the Japanese aircraft carriers after November 26 [Japan time], when the strike force sailed: 'Carriers are still located in home waters.' On December 3, in the last mention before the attack, the summaries say, 'No information on submarines or Carriers.'" *New York Review of Books* (November 2, 2000), p. 59. The contention that radio transmissions from the Striking Force were intercepted was also made in John Toland, *Infamy: Pearl Harbor and Its Aftermath* (New York: Doubleday & Company, Inc., 1982), chapter 14, "The Tracking of Kido Butai," pp. 287–321. But Admiral Genda Minoru answered Toland in a letter to *The New York Times*: "We kept absolute radio silence"; 13 March 1982.

39. NARA, RG 80, PHLO, Box 4, "Japanese Plan for the Attack on Pearl Harbor," p. 4; ibid., Interrogation of Yoshio Shiga, pp. 4–5, The unnamed pilot in the alleged 5 October briefing was adopted as the official source in the U.S. Navy's presentation of evidence during the opening sessions of the JCC.

40. Ibid., p. 8.

41. PHA, Pt. 13, p. 421.

42. Ibid., p. 377.

43. Most of the foregoing is drawn from Prange's account of his interviews with Kusaka, Genda, and Fuchida; *At Dawn We Slept*, pp. 373–88. Fuchida's comments about what would be done if the American fleet was not in harbor are given in "Reply to a Questionnaire Concerning the Pearl Harbor Attack," Allied Translator and Interpreter Section, United States Army Forces, Pacific, 1 November 1945; NARA, RG 80, PHLO, Box 26.

44. Chigusa, "War Diary," Goldstein and Dillon, eds., *Pearl Harbor Papers,* pp. 183–84.

45. Ibid., pp. 177–78, 208.

46. The Torres Strait order is found in PHA, Pt. 14, p. 1403; cf. Pt. 4, p. 1943. It was repeated in short form on 25 November; Pt. 14, p. 1406, where CINCPAC and CINCAF were ordered to provide escorts. A discussion of the order before the JCC by Kelly Turner is given in ibid., Pt. 4, pp. 1942–44. In his conspiracy book, *Day of Deceit,* Stinnett quotes from a sentence in Turner's testimony. He presents the quotation as a full and accurate sentence complete with a period: "We sent the traffic down via Torres Strait, so that the track of the Japanese task force would be clear of any traffic." The full and accurate sentence in fact is as follows:

> We sent that down via Torres Straits so that the track that the Japanese task force actually took would cross the composite great circle course close to Japan and they would be clear of any traffic that would be there in a very short time and that traffic that went on that composite course went through the normal operating areas where the Japanese held their maneuvers.

Granted that is a difficult locution, but to excise and cite only a segment as standing for the full sentence and context is less than forthright, especially when in an end note, most kindly described as sly, Stinnett reveals his agenda: "The significance of his admission that the North Pacific was cleared for the Japanese carrier force did not register with Congress or with the news media covering the 1945–46 investigation" (p. 349, n. 10). Kelly Turner had his faults, but complicity with the enemy was not one of them.

47. Fuchida, "Air Attack," *Proceedings,* pp. 942–43. NARA–RG 457, SRH 406, "Pre–Pearl Harbor Japanese Naval Dispatches," p. 114.

48. "Pearl Harbor Attack," Interrogation of Captain Minoru Genda, Naval Technical Mission, General Headquarters, Supreme Commander for the Allied Powers, 28 November 1945; NARA, RG 80, PHLO, Box 3. Picked up by U.S. Navy radio antennas on Bainbridge Island in Puget Sound, WA, the "Climb Mount Niitakayama" order was not decrypted and translated until 1945.

49. This information comes from Prange's interviews with Yoshikawa, Okuda, and Kotoshirodo; *At Dawn We Slept,* pp. 70–77, 133, 148–49, 155–56.

50. PHA, Pt. 12, p. 261.

51. Ibid., p. 262–63. A subsequent message from Tokyo on 29 November refined the request: "We have been receiving reports from you on ship movements, but in future will you also report even when there are no movements"; ibid., Pt. 12, p. 263. This was translated by the Navy on 5 December.

52. Layton, "And I Was There," pp. 144, 163. Layton points out that reports to Tokyo from the consulate in Manila were read in Washington more quickly because the consulate there transmitted in the Purple cipher, regarded as more productive of first-rank intelligence.

53. PHA, Pt. 9, p. 4534. The same may be said for another Tokyo-Honolulu dispatch dated 20 November: "Strictly secret. Please investigate comprehensively the fleet [air?] bases in the neighborhood of the Hawaiian military reservation." Ibid., Pt. 12, p. 263.

54. Ibid., Pt. 9, pp. 4195–96. Kramer's "impression" was mistaken. Noyes testified to the JCC that the consular decrypts had not been sent to Kimmel as an information addressee. "It wouldn't be sent out for information to anybody," he stated. On the Army side Major General Miles described the grid messages as just part of a routine effort of the Japanese to track the movements of U.S. naval vessels worldwide, though he did allow that the Pearl Harbor reports were unusual "in the sense of dividing any particular waters." PHA, Pt. 2, p. 795.

55. Layton, "And I Was There," pp. 144, 167.

56. PHA, Pt. 7, pp. 2956–57.

57. Ibid., Pt. 6, pp. 2540, 2542–43. Layton wrote, much later, "Whether it would have enabled us to spring an 'ambush on the Japanese striking force as it approached Hawaii' is a matter of debate"; Layton, "And I Was There," p. 168. On 7 December 1999, at a Washington, D.C., colloquium on Admiral Kimmel, Vice Admiral David C. Richardson, USN (Ret.), who had been aboard the carrier USS Yorktown at the time of Pearl Harbor, and since became an expert authority on the attack, addressed the question of the Pacific Fleet's chances in a sea engagement with Nagumo's force. Among his remarks were the following: "Their [Japan's] carriers at top speeds exceeded thirty knots—their weapons range three hundred miles. Kimmel's battleships' speeds were seventeen knots—weapons range fifteen miles. Kimmel was literally incapable of harming the Japanese force. Even had his two carriers been suitably placed, given Japan's submarine presence, the odds against him still exceeded three-to-one." Pearl Harbor and the Kimmel Controversy: The Views Today, cited earlier.

58. PHA, Pt. 3, p. 1102.

59. Ibid., Pt. 2, pp. 791, 793, 810, 812; Pt. 3, pp. 1210, 1369.

60. Ibid., Pt. 2, pp. 890, 894–95, 904.

61. Ibid., Pt. 4, pp. 1922–23, 1927–28, 2018–19.

62. Ibid., pp. 1746–48, 1830, 1853.

63. Ibid., Pt. 9, pp. 4235–37.

64. Ibid., Pt. 5, p. 2174; Pt. 4, p. 1748.

65. Ibid., Pt. 12, p. 266.

66. Ibid., p. 269.

67. Ibid., p. 270.

68. NARA, RG 80, PHLO, Box 15, Re-intercepted Message of 6 December 1941, 3 pp.

69. Another message from consul general Kita to Tokyo during this period contained what came to be called the "lights code." Dated 3 December and encrypted in PA-K2, the code consisted of an elaborate system for signaling information to submarines, by night with shore light patterns including house lights and bonfires, by day with a star and Roman numerals on a boat sail, and by want ads broadcast over a Honolulu commercial radio station. The bizarre plan, which was never implemented, originated with a Nazi German resident of the city named Bernard Julius Otto Kuehn. A sometime agent for the consulate, he generally was kept at arm's length. The dispatch of his plan was translated by the Navy on 11 December. It is found in PHA, Pt. 12, pp. 267–68. See also Pre-War Espionage in the Hawaiian Islands, District Intelligence Office, Honolulu, 7 November 1945; NARA, RG 80, PHLO, Box 48.

70. The Army's intercept stations were located at Fort Hunt, VA, Fort Hancock, NY, San Antonio, TX, Panama, Honolulu, and Manila. The Navy's main stations were at Bainbridge Island, WA, Winter Harbor, ME, Cheltenham, MD, and Cavite in the Philippines. The Army's intercepts were handled by the Signal Intelligence Service (SIS), supervised by Colonel Otis K. Sadtler. Cryptanalysis was supervised by Col. William F. Friedman, inventor of the Purple machine. Col. Rufus S. Bratton, head of Far Eastern Intelligence, G-2, made the evaluations. In the Navy Department a Communications Security unit handled the intercepts. Commander Lawrence F. Safford supervised cryptanalysis and Lieutenant Commander Kramer oversaw the evaluation process. The services shared in the distribution of Magic, which went only to the President, the secretaries of state, war, and navy; the army Chief of Staff; the Chief of Naval Operations; and the heads of each service's war plans and intelligence offices. See Wohlstetter, *Warning and Decision*, pp. 170–86.

71. PHA, Pt. 12, pp. 215, 236.

72. Ibid., p. 237.

73. Ibid., Pt. 6, p. 2765, Pt. 14, p. 1408.

Chapter Eight: Imperiled

1. Ibid., Pt. 12, pp. 154–55. The phrases given are from the first messages. They are reduced to single words in the second message: HIGASI, KITA, NISHI.

2. Wohlstetter, *Warning and Decision*, pp. 217–18.

3. PHA, Pt. 9, p. 4347.

4. Layton, *"And I Was There,"* p. 219.

5. Wohlstetter, *Warning and Decision*, pp. 62, and n. 138, 181, n. 25, 186.

6. PHA, Pt. 36, p. 81.

7. See SRH 210, Collection of papers relating to the "Winds Execute Message, U.S. Navy 1945," 80 pp., NARA, RG 457, Records of the National Security Agency; Graydon Lewis, "Higashi No Kaze Ame," *Cryptolog*, vol. 8, no. 1 (fall 1986), pp. 1, 2, 21; Layton, *"And I Was There,"* pp. 219–20, 264–69, 517–23, 568 n. 46; Prange, *At Dawn We Slept*, pp. 360–61, 457–59, 665–66, 680–81, 713–19; Wohlstetter, *Warning and Decision*, pp. 51, 214–19, 307–08; NARA, RG 80 PHLO, Box 19, correspondence of Comdr. Baecher re: futile search for winds code prompt cards, 9, 17, 23 April 1946; Morgan, "Confidential Report," Appendix C, "The 'Winds Code,' " pp. 285–302.

8. PHA, Pt. 39, p. 514. Prange wrote: "Why the 'winds' message caused such a stir when the much more significant 'bomb plot' series did not is another of the Pearl Harbor mysteries. Certainly no one in Washington needed the Japanese Foreign Ministry to tell him that diplomatic relations with Japan were 'becoming dangerous'; " *At Dawn We Slept*, p. 361. Wohlstetter wrote: "An authentic execute would have told Washington nothing that it did not already know on December 4"; *Warning and Decision*, p. 219.

9. PHA, Pt. 12, p. 251.

10. Ibid., Pt. 36, p. 308. See Wohlstetter, *Warning and Decision*, pp. 224–25.

11. A transcript of the Mori conversation appears in PHA, Pt. 35, pp. 274–76. Layton and Prange maintain that the Honolulu conversant was Mrs. Mori; Wohlstetter states that it was Dr. Mori.

12. Ibid., Pt. 28, p. 1542; Pt. 22, p. 175. Layton did not learn of the Mori transcript until a year later; *"And I Was There,"* p. 276. See KC, Roll 3, The Dr. Mori Telephone Conversation, 5 pp.; also NARA, RG 80, PHLO, Statement of Evidence, pp. 581–86.

13. Communication Intelligence Summary—1 November 1941–6 December 1941; NARA, RG 80, PHLO, Box 49. Comintel quotations that follow are from the same Pearl Harbor source. "Home waters" or "Empire waters" were understood to be the Inland Sea, the approaches to Kyushu, the Isai Bay area, the coastal offshore area out to forty or sixty miles surrounding

Honshu, Shikoku, and Kyushu; but not Etorofu or sites in northern Japan such as Hokkaido and the Kuriles.

14. PHA, Pt. 23, p. 680. Kimmel's chief of staff, Captain (later Vice Admiral) Smith, testified before Admiral Hewitt that he had found "nothing very alarming" in the Combined Fleet's radio silence: "Our own forces while at sea exercising maintained radio silence. We had a very large force, almost half [*sic*] of the Pacific Fleet, in May, 1941, proceed to the Atlantic and no traffic was heard from them for a period of some six weeks. So the absence of radio traffic from the forces at sea doesn't indicate anything to me." PHA, Pt. 36, pp. 213–14.

15. NARA, RG 80, PHLO, Box 6, Japanese Fleet Locations, 1 December 1941, p. 2.

16. Rear Admiral Edwin T. Layton, USN (Ret.), "Admiral Kimmel Deserved a Better Fate," in Stillwell, ed., *Air Raid: Pearl Harbor!*, p. 281. Cf. Layton, *"And I Was There,"* p. 244.

17. NARA, RG 457, SRH 355, Naval Security Group History to World War II, prepared by Captain J. S. Holtwick, Jr., USN (Ret.), June 1971, p. 398.

18. Ibid.

19. Ibid., p. 399; Layton, *"And I Was There,"* pp. 231–32, 534 n. 5.

20. The most recent writer to make the claim that the United States was reading Japan's naval operational messages prior to Pearl Harbor is Stinnett, *Day of Deceit,* pp. 5, 21–23, 71–77, 83. Stinnett's claim is rejected by two noted authorities in cryptology, David Kahn, in a review of Stinnett's book in the *New York Review of Books*, 2 November 2000, pp. 59–60; and Stephen Budiansky, "Too Late for Pearl Harbor," Naval Institute *Proceedings,* vol. 125/12/1, 162 (December 1999), pp. 47–51. See also Budiansky, *Battle of Wits: The Complete Story of Codebreaking in World War II* (New York: The Free Press, 2000), pp. 8–9, 364. Both Kahn and Budiansky draw the reader's attention to an archived official history of the cryptanalytic section of OP-20-G that reported the number of Japanese naval messages read in 1941. The number was "none." Duane L. Whitlock, a veteran of Station Cast on Corregidor, attested in 1986: "The reason that not one single JN-25 decrypt made prior to Pearl Harbor has ever been found or declassified is that no such decrypt ever existed. It simply was not within the realm of our combined [U.S.-British-Dutch] cryptologic capability to produce a usable decrypt at that particular time." Cited in Costello, *Days of Infamy,* p. 323 and n. 81. Costello provides a discussion of British and Dutch attacks on JN-25B in pp. 316–30.

21. R. Adm. Mac Showers, USN (Ret.), "Comment and Questions," in David F. Winkler, Ph.D., and Jennifer M. Lloyd, eds., *Pearl Harbor and the Kimmel Controversy: The Views Today* (Washington, D.C.: Naval Historical Foundation, Washington Navy Yard, 2000), p. 42.

22. Layton, *"And I Was There,"* p. 94; cf. Costello, *Days of Infamy,* p. 282.

23. NARA, RG 457, SRH 355, p. 399.

24. Leading the attack, besides Rochefort, were cryptanalysts Lt. Comdrs. Thomas H. Dyer and Wesley A. "Ham" Wright.

25. "Pre–Pearl Harbor, Japanese Naval Dispatches," dated 1946, declassified 21 October 1991, found in NARA, RG 457, SRH 406, p. 10.

26. Ibid., pp. 9, 12.

27. Ibid., pp. 12, 13, 18, 114.

28. PHA, Pt. 36, pp. 48, 446–67; Pt. 18, pp. 3335–36.

29. PHA, Pt. 4, p. 1676.

30. Fuchida, "Air Attack," *Proceedings,* p. 943.

31. See Layton, *"And I Was There,"* pp. 260–61; Costello, *Days of Infamy,* p. 291 and n. 33.

32. Agawa, *Reluctant Admiral,* p. 251.

33. Layton, *"And I Was There,"* pp. 261–63. There is a fertile literature on alleged radio signals emanating from the mid-Pacific on either naval or marine frequencies during the first week of December. Those transmissions, never proven to have come from *Kido Butai* or from a Soviet merchant ship, are examined by Layton on pp. 261–62.

34. Chigusa, "War Diary," Goldstein and Dillon, eds., *Pearl Harbor Papers,* p. 190.

35. Cited in Layton, *"And I Was There,"* p. 273.

36. Chigusa, "War Diary," p. 191.

37. NARA, RG 80, PHLO, Box 3: General Headquarters, Supreme Commander for the Allied Powers, Additional Data with Reference to Japanese Attack on Pearl Harbor, 13 December 1945, pp. 2–3.

38. Agawa, *Reluctant Admiral,* p. 252.

39. Fuchida, "Air Attack," p. 944.

40. Quoted in ibid., p. 944.

41. Ibid.

42. Ibid., pp. 944–45.

43. Message No. 901, PHA, Pt. 12, pp. 238–39.

44. Ibid., pp. 239–45.

45. Ibid., Pt. 14, pp. 1238, 1240–45; Waldo H. Heinrichs, Jr., *American Ambassador: Joseph C. Grew and the Development of the United States Diplomatic Tradition* (Boston, MA: Little, Brown and Company, 1966), p. 357.

46. PHA, Pt. 10, p. 4662.

47. Ibid., pp. 4662–63.

48. Simpson, *Stark,* p. 112.

49. NARA, RG 80, PHLO, Box 4, Kramer questionnaire, filled out for Capt. Safford, 28 December 1943 and 22 January 1944, pp. 2 and 6.

50. PHA, Pt. 8, pp. 3903–04, Pt. 4, pp. 1762–63.

51. The reader who wishes to investigate the Army muddle, which includes charges of altered testimony, may consult Henry C. Clausen and Bruce Lee, *Pearl Harbor: Final Judgement* (New York: Crown Publishers, Inc., 1992), pp. 29–300 *passim;* and Costello, *Days of Infamy,* pp. 204–15, 400–01.

52. PHA, Pt. 3, pp. 1110, 1430; Pogue, *Ordeal and Hope,* pp. 223–24.

53. Ibid., Pt. 3, p. 1121; Pt. 18, p. 2965; Pt. 22, p. 45, Pt. 27, p. 96; Arnold, *Global Mission,* pp. 266–69.

54. Bratton testified that, "Nobody in ONI, nobody in G-2, knew that any major element of the fleet was in Pearl Harbor on Sunday morning the 7th of December . . . because that was part of the war plan, and they had been given a war warning." PHA, Pt. 9, p. 4534. Washington's ignorance of the fleet's actual dispositions did not speak well of the two intelligence services. Judging from their testimonies in the various Pearl Harbor investigations and hearings, operations staffers seem to have been under the same misapprehension. It is one of Pearl Harbor's enduring ironies that Tokyo knew more about U.S. Pacific Fleet daily location of ships and aircraft than did the Navy Department.

55. NARA, RG 80, PHLO, Box 49, Japanese Aircraft Carrier Operations, Interrogations of Captains Kawaguichi Susuma, Nagaishi Marataka, and Aoki Taijiro; 4–5 October 1945.

56. Ibid., Box 40, Weekly Intelligence, United States Pacific Fleet and Pacific Ocean Areas, Vol. I, No. 52 (9 July 1945), pp. 17–19. NARA, RG 80, PHLO, Box 25, Kimmel to Betty, 12 December 1941.

57. PHA, Pt. 12, p. 245.

58. Ibid.

59. Ibid., Pt. 11, p. 5274.

60. Ibid., Pt. 12, p. 248. This is probably the single most critical Magic decrypt. Where most Magic information would have had little warning value for Kimmel and his staff except in hindsight, certain individual messages did have an immediate value. One thinks of the Japanese deadlines of 25 and 29 November; the "bomb plot" messages; the code destruction messages; the 14-part response to Hull's Ten-Point note; and this present message, which would become known as the "one o'clock" message—a something-is-going-to-happen message—Magic at its most vital moment.

61. Ibid., p. 249. The nos. 908 and 909 were messages of thanks to Namoru and Kurusu for

"all the efforts you two Ambassadors have been making," and to the embassy's commercial attaché for the same.

62. NARA, RG 80, PHLO, Box 4, Kramer questionnaire, filled out for Capt. Safford, 28 December 1943 and 22 January 1944, pp. 5–7. It is important to acknowledge that Safford's role in eliciting answers to his questionnaire was not a disinterested one. For two years he had wondered why Kimmel had ignored the Magic information. In the fall of 1943, when he discovered that Magic-originated intelligence had, for the most part, not been sent to Kimmel, he set about to defend both the admiral and General Short. In a letter accompanying a second questionnaire on 22 January 1944, addressed to "My dear Kramer-san," the newly converted advocate wrote: "I am just beginning to get things lines [*sic*] up on this end. No one in Op Nav can be trusted. Premature action would only tip off the people who framed Adm. Kimmel and Gen. Short, and will also get Safford [me] and Kramer [you] in very serious trouble . . . I knew Adm. Kimmel was a scapegoat from the start, but I did not suspect that he was a victim of a frame-up until about 15 Nov. 1943, could not confirm it until 2 Dec. 1943, and did not have absolute truth until about 18 Jan. 1944. Capt. Safford [I] has overwhelming proof of the guilt of Op Nav and the Gen Staff, plus a list of about fifteen reliable witnesses." The Stark-Kramer conversation of 7 December quoted here may not have happened exactly as given. Safford composed it, apparently on the basis of an earlier conversation with Kramer. For his part, Kramer said at one point in the questionnaire that he could not "verify" the conversation, but later in the document stated: "There were undoubtedly a few words exchanged with the Admiral, most likely along the lines you quote as my last reply. . . . The quoted exclamation of Adm. Stark would have been typical in character, because he had used emphatic exclamation once or twice before during the fall when particularly 'hot' items were being shown him. . . . With my mind focussed on the technical and messenger boy aspects that morning I simply do not recall the complete conversation in question."

63. Ibid., pp. 6–7. About this meeting Stimson recorded in his diary, "Hull is very certain that the Japs are planning some deviltry and we are all wondering when the blow will strike. . . ." Stimson Diary, 7 December 1941.

64. PHA, Pt. 9, p. 4524.

65. Pogue, *Ordeal and Hope*, p. 227.

66. PHA, Pt. 9, p. 4525.

67. Ibid.

68. PHA, Pt. 9, p. 4534; Pt. 3, p. 1114.

69. NARA, RG 80, PHLO, Box 49, Japanese Aircraft Carrier Operations; Fuchida, "Air Attack," pp. 945–46; Prange, *At Dawn We Slept*, pp. 490–91; and exhibits in the USS *Arizona* Memorial at Pearl Harbor. By carrier and type the aircraft launched in the first wave were (T for torpedo, B for bomb):

Akagi	*Kaga*
9 Zeros	9 Zeros
12 Kates (T)	12 Kates (T)
15 Kates (B)	15 Kates (B)
Soryu	*Hiryu*
9 Zeros	6 Zeros
8 Kates (T)	8 Kates (T)
10 Kates (B)	10 Kates (B)
Shokaku	*Zuikaku*
6 Zeros	6 Zeros
26 Vals	25 Vals

70. NARA, RG 180, PHLO, Box 5, Miles, Memorandum for the Chief of Staff, Subject: Sunday Morning, December 7, 1941; 15 December 1941.

71. PHA, Pt. 9, p. 4518.

72. Ibid.

73. PHA, Pt. 5, pp. 2132–33.

74. Ibid., Pt. 14, p. 1334.

75. NARA, RG 80, PHLO, Box 5, Miles, Memorandum, 15 December 1941. French's remark is in PHA, Pt. 34, p. 32; Pt. 23, p. 1105.

76. Ibid.

77. Ibid., Box 5, Memorandum for Record: Log of the Message; signed by Col. W. B. Smith, Secretary, General Staff, Washington, D.C., 15 December 1941.

78. PHA, Pt. 36, pp. 55–56.

79. Crocker, *Black Cats and Dumbos*, "Bill Tanner: One Hour Before the War," pp. 1–2.

80. For 14P1 and Tanner see ibid., p. 2. The flight procedures and engine numbers given in this narrative were standard for the PBY-5's takeoff, climb, cruise, and PBY-5 glide attack, as learned by the writer from flight manuals and interviews with former PBY-5 pilots. For *Ward* and Outerbridge see PHA, Pt. 36, pp. 56–57. Outerbridge made no mention of 14P1 in his testimony before the Hewitt Inquiry.

81. A shorter message sent two minutes earlier mentioned depth charges only; ibid., p. 57. The sending times are verified in the radio log of Section Base, Bishop's Point, Oahu, where they are recorded in equivalent Greenwich Mean Time: 1721 and 1723. Ibid., Pt. 37, p. 704. That the 0653 message was sent in *uncoded voice* is clearly stipulated in ibid., Pt. 36, p. 278, during the interrogation of Lieutenant Underkofler by Admiral Hewitt. It should be noted that the 14ND Control Post Watch Officer's Log (War Diary, Fourteenth District Naval Base Defense Force) logs in *Ward's* message at 0654 and states next: "0712. Message decoded and delivered to Duty Officer, Lt. Comdr. Kaminski." Pt. 24, p. 1649. If this is the accurate record of events, it would account for the delay in its passage to Kaminski. Either scenario is possible. But Hewitt's report, dated 12 July 1945, concluded: "The evidence indicates that the reports by the WARD were in plain language but that a request for verification by the WARD was later sent in code by the ComFOURTEEN Communication Officer at the direction of the ComFOURTEEN Duty Officer." NARA, RG 80, PHLO, Box 5, OT, Report of Further Investigation into the Facts Surrounding the Japanese Attack on Pearl Harbor, 7 December 1941, by Admiral H. K. Hewitt, U.S. Navy, p. 46. Outerbridge's official report to Commandant 14ND, dated 13 December 1941, is in PHA, Pt. 24, p. 1290.

82. For Kaminski see ibid., Pt. 23, pp. 1035–38; for Murphy see Pt. 26, pp. 209–10; for Earle see Pt. 23, pp. 1051–52; for Bloch and Momsen see Pt. 22, p. 499 and Pt. 32, p. 308; for the radio log see Pt. 37, pp. 704–05; for Ramsey see Pt. 32, p. 444; for Kimmel see Pt. 26, pp. 209–10, Pt. 23, pp. 1192–93. On the last-cited page, Kimmel is recorded as saying that, at the time of the Japanese air attack, he "had no report that an airplane had attacked a submarine;" he learned of it only "sometime later." The action report from PBY 14P1 was sent coded at 0715 and was decoded by 0735; ibid., Pt. 26, p. 135.

83. For Kaminski see ibid., Pt. 23, pp. 1035–37; for Earle ibid., pp. 1051–52; for Bloch ibid., Pt. 22, pp. 498–99; for Murphy ibid., Pt. 26, pp. 209–10; for Ramsey ibid., Pt. 32, p. 444; and for Kimmel ibid., Pt. 23, pp. 1125, 1193.

84. Ibid., Pt. 28, p. 1554.

Chapter Nine: This Is No Drill

1. Since 27 November the AWS daily schedule required the mobile radar sets to operate from 0400 to 0700 and to conduct training from 0700 to 1100 every day *except* Sundays. KC, Roll 2, Memorandum, Lt. Col. C. A. Powell, Signal Corps, Department Signal Officer, to General Short, 19 December 1941; also Capt. W. H. Tetley, Signal Corps, to Lt. Col. Powell.

2. KC, Roll 20, Changes Made in Pearl Harbor Defenses During the Period 1 February to 7 December 1941.

3. The other mobile radar emplacements were at Kawailoa, Wai'anae, Ka'a'awa, Koko Head, and Fort Shafter.

4. PHA, Pt. 27, pp. 531–32. The center was also called Interception Control Center.

5. Ibid., pp. 569, 532; Pt. 10, p. 5041.

6. Ibid., Pt. 32, p. 342; Pt. 22, p. 223.

7. Ibid., Pt. 27, p. 568. The Opana handwritten "Record of Readings" is given in ibid., Pt. 10, opposite p. 5058. A simplified drawing of the graphic plot is given on p. 137 of Morison, *Rising Sun*. On p. 138 of the same work Morison asserts, on the strength of information given him by Rear Admiral Inglis, that within a half hour prior to their 0702 radar sighting of the air fleet Lockard and Elliott made a radar sighting of one of the two Japanese reconnaissance float-planes; that they "reported it properly"; and the "the watch officer heard but did nothing." Morison's copy of the plot depicts the track of an incoming flight, at 200 miles per hour, recorded from 0645 to 0700. A photograph of the actual plot is given as an exhibit in PHA, Pt. 25, item 123. As Morison put it, the matter was "glossed over" in the JCC; see ibid., Pt. 1, pp. 39–40. But this writer has found no corroborating evidence that such a report was sent in to the information center or that the watch officer, presumably Lieutenant Tyler, "did nothing" about it.

8. Ibid., Pt. 7, p. 3075.

9. Ibid., Pt. 22, p. 223.

10. Ibid., Pt. 27, p. 569.

11. Ibid.

12. NARA, RG 80, PHLO, Lt. Comdr. Baecher to William D. Mitchell, Condition of Water-Tight Integrity of Major Vessels, 11 December 1945: "Only one vessel did not have an equivalent of the condition 'all water-tight openings below the third deck closed' at the time of the attack. That vessel, the USS *California*, had ten inner and outboard voids open for maintenance work."

13. PHA, Pt. 3, p. 1213.

14. Ibid., Pt. 29, p. 2313.

15. Ibid., Pt. 32, p. 294.

16. Ibid.

17. Dyer, *Amphibians*, pp. 192–93.

18. Richardson, *Treadmill*, p. 450. According to an oral history recorded years later by then Rear Admiral McCollum (Ret.) for the U.S. Naval Institute, Wilkinson asked Stark, "Why don't you pick up the telephone and call Kimmel?" McCollum stated that he saw Stark pick up the telephone, then place it back in its cradle, saying, "No, I think I will call the President." But he could not get through because Roosevelt was occupied on another call. Cited in Costello, *Days of Infamy*, p. 219 and n. 19.

19. R. V. Jones, *The Wizard War: British Scientific Intelligence, 1939–1945* (New York: Coward, McCann & Geoghegan, Inc., 1978), p. 150.

20. PHA, Pt. 32, p. 99; Layton, *"And I Was There,"* p. 321.

21. In developing this attack sequence, the writer has relied on the essential source, Fuchida, "Air Attack," *Proceedings*, pp. 945–52; as well as on Agawa, *Reluctant Admiral*, pp. 255–58. Contrary to the scout plane's report, the major vessels in harbor were eight battle-ships, two heavy cruisers, and six light cruisers; NARA, RG 80, PHLO, Box 24, List of Ships Present at Pearl Harbor at the Time of the Japanese Attack December 7, 1941, 3 pp.

22. Agawa, *Reluctant Admiral*, p. 258.

23. Lieutenant Goto, quoted in "Air Raid, Pearl Harbor. This Is No Drill," a map published by O.S.B. Map Mania Publishing, Phoenix, AZ, 1999.

24. Fuchida, "Air Attack," pp. 948–49.

25. Ibid., pp. 949–50.

26. KC, Roll 4, Summary of Damage Sustained by Ships of Pacific Fleet from Enemy Attacks At Pearl Harbor, 7 December 1941; CINCPAC, 21, December 1941, p. 1.

27. Fuchida, "Air Attack," p. 951.

28. By carrier and type the aircraft launched in the second wave were:

Akagi	*Kaga*
9 Zeros	9 Zeros
18 Vals	24 Vals
Soryu	*Hiryu*
9 Zeros	9 Zeros
18 Vals	18 Vals
Shokaku	*Zuikaku*
27 Kates (B)	27 Kates (B)

29. See Commander John Rodgaard, USNR, Peter Hsu, Carroll Lucas, and Captain Andrew Biache, USNR (Ret.), "Attack from Below," U.S. Naval Institute *Proceedings*, vol. 126/12/1, 174 (December 2000), pp. 64–67. The authors mention "antisubmarine and torpedo nets" at the harbor channel entrance. But Admiral Bloch, among whose responsibilities was the entrance defense, testified during the month after the attack: "The net is not an anti-submarine net proper. It is an anti-torpedo net. . . . It is our opinion—I refer to my opinion and the Navy Department's opinion—that any . . . regular-sized submarine could not come into the harbor without showing her periscope. . . . So we felt that there was no reason to put in anti-submarine nets, that an anti-torpedo net was sufficient." PHA, Pt. 22, p. 472. That the antitorpedo net was left open from 0458 to 0840 is confirmed in the net tender's log, PHA, Pt. 38, Items 133, 134. Excellent reproductions and a discussion of the photograph in question appear in Burl (William G., Jr.) Burlingame, *Advance Force—Pearl Harbor* (Kailua, Hawaii: Pacific Monograph, 1992), pp. 198–99.

30. Michael Slackman, *Target: Pearl Harbor* (Honolulu: University of Hawaii Press, 1990), pp. 155–57; Morison, *Rising Sun*, pp. 115–16.

31. KC, Roll 4, Rear Admiral Kimmel to Secretary Knox, Narrative of Events Occurring During Japanese Air Raid on December 7, 1941; 21 December 1941, pp. 47, 50, 56–57.

32. Ibid., pp. 44–85. A number of the ships that cleared the entrance channel did so in response to an order from Vice Admiral Pye, Commander, Battle Force, at 0921: TO ALL SHIPS PRESENT: GET UNDERWAY IMMEDIATELY; p. 54. At 1002, however, CINCPAC ordered: TO ALL SHIPS PRESENT: BATTLESHIPS REMAIN IN PORT PROBABLE CHANNEL MINED; and at 1015 CINCPAC ordered the commander, Task Force 1: DO NOT SEND ANY MORE CRUISERS TO SEA; KC, Roll 4, Messages and Orders from Headquarters of the Commander in Chief, Pacific Fleet, December 7, 1941.

33. Ibid., pp. 62, 71, 78.

34. Rodgaard et al, "Attack from Below," *Proceedings*, p. 66.

35. The survivor was the commanding officer, twenty-four-year-old Sub-Lieutenant Kazuo Sakamaki, from Okayama Prefecture, who was promptly designated by his capturers "Prisoner Number One" of the Pacific War. During his interrogation he stated: "My greatest mistake was being captured. This is the first time I have failed. Please do not advise Japan about this. Please kill me." NARA, RG 80, PHLO, Box 16, Report of Interrogation, 8 December 1941.

36. Ibid., Box 48, Interrogation of Captain Watanabe Y., Meiji Building, Tokyo, 15 October 1945, p. 3.

37. Interview with Fuchida conducted on 10 December 1963 by Prange; *At Dawn We Slept*, p. 536. Prange is also the source for the epigraph at the beginning of this chapter; p. 540.

38. Slackman cites statements of signal tower personnel as source for the grounding order; *Target: Pearl Harbor*, p. 167 and n. 36.

39. Fuchida, "Air Attack," *Proceedings*, p. 951.

40. The other first attack was made against *Raleigh*. See De Virgilio, "Japanese Thunderfish," p. 64. This is the best source for the effects of the torpedo-plane attacks. De Virgilio dismisses the notion that the Japanese pilots thought that *Utah* was an aircraft carrier because she

occupied the berth (F-11) normally filled by *Enterprise*. *Utah* was equipped with AA armament, but all ammunition was secured in magazines and all guns were either covered with steel housings or were dismounted and stowed below decks. See KC, Roll 4, Kimmel to Knox, Narrative of Events, 21 December 1941, p. 23.

41. Fuchida, "Air Attack," p. 952.

42. Wesley Frank Craven and James Lea Cate, *The Army Air Forces in World War II*, vol. 1, *Plans and Early Operations, January 1939 to August 1942* (University of Chicago Press, 1948), p. 200.

43. Prange, *At Dawn We Slept*, p. 539.

44. Craven and Cate, *Early Operations*, pp. 198–200.

45. KC, Box 4, Memorandum from Admiral Pye, Interim CINCPAC, to Mr. Walter Bruce Howe, Recorder of the Roberts Commission, on "Naval Airplanes on the Island of Oahu on the Day of the Japanese Air Raid, 7 December 1941"; 27 December 1941. Cf. PHA, Pt. 12, Item 12. Only one PBY at Pearl managed to get airborne, from the northwest side of Ford Island, at about 0830; Captain James R. Ogden, USN (Ret.), "Airborne at Pearl," U.S. Naval Institute *Proceedings*, vol. 119/12/1 (December 1993), pp. 60–62. Kaneohe, home to PBY Patrol Wing 1, was the first air station of either service to be struck, at 0745; PHA, Pt. 23, p. 741.

46. KC, Roll 4, Kimmel to Knox, Narrative of Events, 21 December 1941, pp. 48, 54. The observation that "red circles" were on the undersides of Japanese fuselages was also made by Comdr. Harold Montgomery Martin, commanding officer, Kaneohe Naval Air Station; PHA, Pt. 23, p. 739.

47. KC, Roll 4, Pye to Howe, "Naval Airplanes," 27 December 1941, p. 1. There are minor discrepancies in the secondary sources as well as in the original action reports as regards both the number of SBDs that formed the flight and the fate of individual planes. See Morison, *Rising Sun*, pp. 120–21, and n. 52; Prange, *At Dawn We Slept*, p. 520; Slackman, *Target: Pearl Harbor*, pp. 143, 149–50.

48. KC, Roll 4, Interrogation of Captain Fuchida Mitsuo, Tokyo, 10 October 1945, p. 2.

49. Tanner, "One Hour Before the War," in Crocker, *Black Cats and Dumbos*, pp. 3–5.

50. PHA, Pt. 36, p. 59.

51. Ibid., Pt. 23, p. 1038.

52. Ibid., Pt. 10, p. 5035.

53. Ibid., p. 5033.

54. Ibid., p. 5079–80.

55. Ibid., p. 5035.

56. Ibid., p. 5080. For their actions on 7 December Lockard was awarded a Distinguished Service Medal and Elliott a Letter of Commendation. Lockard was later given a commission.

57. Ibid., Pt. 29, p. 2122.

58. Ibid., Pt. 18, p. 3015.

59. Morison, *Rising Sun*, p. 101.

60. PHA, Pt. 32, p. 444.

61. KC, Roll 4, Messages and Orders, 7 December 1941, p. 1.

62. PHA, Pt. 22, p. 499.

63. Ibid., Pt. 32, p. 308.

64. Ibid., Pt. 32, p. 57.

65. Ibid.

66. Ibid., Pt. 26, p. 210.

67. Ibid., Pt. 23, p. 898; Prange, *At Dawn We Slept*, p. 507; Kimmel, *Admiral Kimmel's Story*, p. 8.

68. KC, Roll 4, Messages and Orders from Headquarters of the Commander in Chief Pacific Fleet, December 7, 1941, p. 1.

69. PHA, Pt. 8, p. 3829.

70. Quoted in Robert E. Sherwood, *Roosevelt and Hopkins* (New York: Harper & Brothers, 1948), pp. 430–31.

71. Ibid., p. 431.

72. PHA, Pt. 11, pp. 5438–39, Stimson diary entry, 7 December 1941.

73. NARA, RG 80, PHLO, Box 5, Col. J. R. Deane, Memorandum for Brig. Gen. W. B. Smith, June 8, 1941.

74. Hull, *Memoirs*, pp. 1095–96; Sherwood, *Roosevelt and Hopkins*, p. 431.

75. See Convention Relative to the Opening of Hostilities, Signed at the Hague, October 18, 1907, Article 1; in *Hague and Geneva Conventions* (Washington, D.C.: U.S. Navy Department, 1911), p. 42.

76. Howard W. French, "Pearl Harbor Truly a Sneak Attack, Papers Show," *New York Times*, 9 December 1999.

77. Hull, *Memoirs*, p. 1096.

78. Sherwood, *Roosevelt and Hopkins*, p. 431.

79. Ibid., p. 432; NARA, RG 80, PHLO, Box 17, Lt. Comdr. Baecher to Mr. Seth W. Richardson, Time Table of Japanese Attacks, 4 April 1946.

80. Frances Perkins, *The Roosevelt I Knew* (New York: Harper & Row Publishers, 1946), pp. 379, 368–69.

81. PHA, Pt. 11, pp. 5438–93; Stimson diary entry, 7 December 1941.

82. Ibid., p. 5439.

83. Ibid., Pt. 19, p. 3506.

84. Winston S. Churchill, *The Second World War*, vol. 3, *The Grand Alliance* (Boston, MA: Houghton Mifflin Company, 1977), pp. 606, 608.

85. *Congressional Record* 87: 95045 (December 8, 1941).

Epilogue

1. Fuchida and Okumiya, *Midway*, p. 42.

2. Quoted in ibid., p. 43. See another translation in Fuchida, "Air Attack," *Proceedings*, p. 952.

3. Ugaki diary, 9 December 1941 (Japan time), cited in Prange, *At Dawn We Slept*, p. 584.

4. Ibid., p. 550.

5. Ibid., p. 543.

6. Quoted in Agawa, *Reluctant Admiral*, p. 265.

7. Statement by Ozawa, 22 December 1948, quoted in Prange, *At Dawn We Slept*, p. 550.

8. Ogden, "Airborne at Pearl," *Proceedings*, pp. 60–62.

9. KC, Roll 4, CINCPAC, "Disposition of Task Forces," 20 December 1941, pp. 7–8.

10. Layton, *"And I Was There,"* p. 317.

11. Vice Admiral Richardson, in Winkler and Lloyd, *Pearl Harbor and the Kimmel Controversy*, p. 24.

12. NARA, RG 80, PHLO, Box 5, "Statement of Evidence," p. 660.

13. Ibid., p. 665.

14. NARA, RG 80, PHLO, Box 25, Commander-in-Chief, United States Pacific Fleet to Commander-in-Chief, United States Fleet, Pearl Harbor, T.H., 7 January 1942, pp. 1–2.

15. Ibid., Box 48, CINCPAC, "Surprise in Attacks by U.S. Carrier-Based Planes," 3 pp., n.d. but after 13 August 1945. Examples of complete surprise were the raids on the Marshalls (29 January 1944); Jaluit (20 February 1944); Aitape-Hollandia (21 April 1944); the Marianas (11 June 1944); Iwo Jima (24 June, 3 July, and 4 August 1944); Palaus (25 July 1944); Volcanoes-Bonins (31 August 1944); Mindanao (9 September 1944); Nansei Shoto (10 October 1944); Luzon (11 October, 5 November, and 14 December 1944); Yap (22 November 1994); Formosa–Nansei Shoto (3 January 1945); Indo-China (12 January 1945); Nansei Shoto (22 January 1945);

Tokyo (16 February 1945); Kyushu (15 April 1945); Tokyo (10 July 1945); and northern Honshu–Hokkaido (14 July 1945). U.S. naval air raids before 1944 achieved only partial or no surprise.

16. Ibid., Box 22, Secretary of the Navy James Forrestal to Major Correa, Subject: Pearl Harbor, 26 August 1945, p. 2.

17. PHA, Pt. 22, p. 99. Given the Army's No. 1 Alert, where air attack was not expected, the Japanese first wave met Army return fire from .50- and .30-caliber machine guns as well as from small arms. But the men manning the larger, more effective 3-inch guns had to travel varying distances for their ammunition, as Short explained:

> For instance, down at De Russy the ammunition was in the casemate. They had to carry it probably 75 yards, but their men were right there, and the guns were all set up and in position, but the ammunition was not right alongside of the guns. There were four batteries that had to go farther for their ammunition. . . . The first one of those batteries started drawing its ammunition at the Aliamanu Crater, where we had our ammunition in caves, at 8:15, to show how promptly that they got into action. And by 10:15 they had all drawn what we call a day of fire which for that particular battery is 300 rounds per gun. So there was no lost motion. (Ibid., p. 57.)

No lost motion, perhaps, but there was much lost time. With "ammo at the guns"— Kimmel's orders in violation of Naval Regulations—the battleships' AA batteries were firing as early as four minutes into the attack, while the four Army batteries were just starting to draw ammo twenty minutes into the attack; and by the time they had "a day of fire" the *second* wave attack was a half hour old. Four first-wave strafing aircraft were shot down by Army gunners, but they were wielding handheld Browning Automatic Rifles (BAR) or short-range machine guns. The commander of the first wave, Fuchida, remarked on the delay of shore-based AA to engage his aircraft. The Army's fixed 3-inch AA batteries at Fort De Russy and Sand Island on the other side of Honolulu from Pearl Harbor eventually went into action, as did a fixed 3-inch battery at Fort Kamehameha, adjacent to Hickam Field. But the Army's main AA strength lay in its mobile 3-inch AA guns, none of which were manned and deployed during the battle. Not until afternoon was the first mobile unit removed from the gun park and set in battle position. Ibid., Pt. 32, pp. 395–96. Prior to 7 December an Army AA company held tactical exercises on Ford Island with 37-mm guns, for which there were permanent emplacements. Neither the company nor the guns were present on the seventh. Army times of fire are given in ibid., Pt. 24, pp. 1831–32.

Naval AA shore batteries at Pearl performed only slightly better. At the air station on Ford Island there was a trained seaman guard of 200 men and a Marine detachment of approximately 100 men and two officers. Their heaviest weapons were .50- and .30-caliber machine guns. They were unusable throughout the first-wave attack because their ammunition was locked in armories. Unlike Kimmel's orders to the battleships, no orders had been issued requiring ammunition to be kept at or near the guns. Such orders would have come from Admiral Bloch or from the air station commander, Capt. James M. Shoemaker. The reaction of ground personnel at Kaneohe and Ewa was much faster and more effective.

18. NARA, RG 80, PHLO, Box 17, Lt. Comdr. Baecher, "Time Table of Japanese Attacks—Source of Material," 4 April 1946.

19. See the various time intervals given in NARA, RG 80, PHLO, Box 17, "Time Table of Japanese Attacks—Source of Material," p. 2; Costello, *Days of Infamy*, pp. 17, 32; Larrabee, *Commander in Chief*, p. 316; Spector, *Eagle Against the Sun*, p. 107, Pogue, *Ordeal and Hope*, pp. 233–34.

20. *Remembering Pearl Harbor* [pamphlet], The Pearl Harbor History Associates, Inc., 1990. Cf. Nimitz's remarks in 1962 quoted in Costello, *Days of Infamy*, p. 241.

21. PHA, Pt. 32, p. 593; Morison, *Rising Sun*, p. 133 and n. 75.

22. NARA, RG 80, PHLO, Box 25, Nimitz to King, 7 January 1942, p. 1.

23. Morison, *Rising Sun,* p. 132.

24. Vice Admiral Frank E. Beatty, "The Background of the Secret Report," *The National Review,* 13 December 1966, p. 1263.

25. Layton, *"And I Was There,"* p. 331.

26. Ibid.

27. Ibid. On 22 January 1946, Capt. Joseph R. Redman, chief of Naval Communications, wrote to the judge advocate general: "All appropriate files of the Naval Communication Service have been searched for any dispatches of a war-warning nature from the Navy Department to naval commanders in the field between noon, Eastern Standard Time, on 6 December 1941 and 2:30 p.m., Eastern Standard Time on 7 December 1941, inclusive. This will certify that no such dispatches are contained in those files." NARA, RG 80, PHLO, Box 17.

28. Beatty, "Background," *National Review,* p. 1263.

29. Ibid., p. 1264.

30. KC, Roll 4, Extracts from Secret Letters, Kimmel to Stark, 18 April 1941.

31. Brownlow, *The Accused,* p. 139 and n. 32; interview with Kimmel, Groton, CT, 13 February 1966.

32. *The New York Times,* 11 December 1941, p. 11.

33. Brownlow, *The Accused,* p. 140 and n. 33; interview with Anderson, New York City, 29 April 1966.

34. PHA, Pt. 5, pp. 2338–45, Report by the Secretary of the Navy to the President.

35. *The New York Times,* 16 December 1941.

36. Ibid., 18 December 1941. At the aforementioned Colloquium on Pearl Harbor and the Kimmel Controversy, held in Washington, D.C., on 7 December 1999, one of the speakers was Professor Robert W. Love, of the Department of History, U.S. Naval Academy. Among his various critical remarks about Admiral Kimmel on that occasion were the following: "Kimmel himself was on short tether and was scheduled to go ashore anyway once war broke out. . . . Stark explained in June 1941 to Admiral King . . . that Kimmel was completing the unexpired portion of his predecessor's [Richardson's] two-year tour as commander in chief, U.S. Fleet. . . . If the war broke out either in the Atlantic or in the Pacific, Stark intended . . . to send Admiral Nimitz to relieve Admiral Hart in command of the Asiatic Fleet and to replace Kimmel with Admiral Royal Ingersoll. . . . In effect, losing the Battle of Pearl Harbor merely hastened Kimmel's departure from Hawaii, which was scheduled to take place anyway." Audiotape with the writer. The source of that asseveration appears to be an undocumented footnote in King and White-hill, *Fleet Admiral King,* p. 357, n. 4. The asseveration was repeated by Thomas B. Buell in his biography of King, *Master of Sea Power,* p. 155. Commander Buell told the writer in a telephone interview on 2 May 2000 that he could not immediately recall the source for his repetition of that story. Stark's biographer B. Mitchell Simpson III told the writer in a telephone interview on 13 November 2000 that in his research he encountered no document attesting to that story. Absent an original document, the most telling witness is Mr. David W. Richmond, who as an attorney and lieutenant USNR in 1945–46, served as Admiral Stark's counsel in the JCC In a telephone interview conducted by the writer on 11 June 2000, Mr. Richmond said that, in the many mentions of Kimmel during his days of conference with Stark, during the JCC hearings, and during the years of friendship with Stark afterward, he never heard Stark speak of any plan to relieve Kimmel from his command upon the outbreak of war. So what was described as "Stark's idea" in King-Whitehill seems, upon investigation, to have been a chimera.

37. Morison, *Rising Sun,* pp. 243–49.

38. Ibid., pp. 249–50, 253.

39. Stimson diary, 15 December 1941; *The New York Times,* 16 December 1941.

40. *The New York Times,* 17 December 1941.

41. Prange, *At Dawn We Slept,* pp. 592–95.

42. PHA, Pt. 7, p. 3280.

43. Robert Neuleib, "Kimmel, the Roberts Commission and Public Myths," a lecture presented to the Tenth Naval History Symposium, U.S. Naval Academy, September 1991. The writer is grateful to Mr. Neuleib for a copy of his remarks.

44. PHA, Pt. 23, p. 987.

45. Ibid., Pt. 22, pp. 379, 418.

46. Short's testimony is given in ibid., Pt. 22, pp. 31–106, Pt. 23, pp. 975–92; Kimmel's testimony is found in ibid., Pt. 22, pp. 317–459, Pt. 23, pp. 893–901, 931–47, 1049–51, 1123–1244.

47. Ibid., Pt. 39, p. 21. The entire Report of the Roberts Commission is given in pp. 1–21.

48. Brownlow, *The Accused,* p. 148. The speech was given on 6 April 1942.

49. From the writer's notes of Mr. Neuleib's lecture; see n. 43, above.

50. These were, in abbreviated form, the:

Hart Investigation 12 February–15 June 1944	Clausen Investigation 24 January–12 September 1945
Army Pearl Harbor Board 20 July–20 October 1944	Hewitt Inquiry 14 May–11 July 1945
Navy Court of Inquiry 24 July–19 October 1944	Joint Congressional Committee 15 November 1945–23 May 1946
Clarke Investigation 4 August–20 September 1944	Dorn Investigation 27 April–1 December 1995

The last named investigation, directed by Edwin Dorn, Under Secretary of Defense for Personnel and Readiness, was prompted by a rising tide of support for Kimmel and Short that gathered from 1986 to 1995, and continues to the present. The crest of that tide has been formed by the Pearl Harbor Survivors Association, the Naval Academy Alumni Association, the Veterans of Foreign Wars, and thirty-four retired four-star admirals, whose numbers include two former chairs of the joint chiefs of staff and five former chiefs of naval operations. The Dorn Investigation resulted in five findings, the first of which was: "Responsibility for the Pearl Harbor disaster should not fall solely on the shoulders of Admiral Kimmel and General Short; it should be broadly shared." This finding constituted the first admission by the military establishment in fifty-four years that the War and Navy Departments of 1941 were guilty of mistakes, be they of commission or omission, in the matter of Pearl Harbor. Subsequently, the United States Congress, in Section 547 of the Defense Authorization Act for 2001, recommended that the President of the United States advance Kimmel and Short posthumously to their highest temporary rank held during the war, admiral and lieutenant general, respectively, as provided by the Officer Personnel Act of 1947, from which they alone, among flag and general officers, had been punitively excluded by the two services. There, at the date of this writing, the matter stands.

51. Quoted in Kimmel, *Admiral Kimmel's Story,* p. 144. The language "dereliction of duty" originated, apparently, in the White House executive order establishing the Roberts Commission, dated 18 December 1941. It mandated that the commission determine whether "dereliction of duty" or "errors of judgment" on the part of Army or Navy personnel had contributed to the Japanese success.

52. Prange, *At Dawn We Slept,* p. 622; interview with Kimmel, 1 December 1963.

53. Report of Navy Court of Inquiry and Addendum to Court's Finding of Facts, PHA, Pt. 39, pp. 319–21, 330.

54. Letter of Vice Admiral David C. Richardson, USN (Ret.), to the writer, 7 February 2001.

55. PHA 39, Army Pearl Harbor Board Report, pp. 175–76.

56. Ibid., p. 344. Use of the language "most dangerous sectors" reminds one of historian Gordon W. Prange, on two counts. First, because, as Prange wrote, the Martin-Bellinger estimate of 31 March 1941 was an "historic work" "famous to all students of the Pacific war," *At Dawn We Slept*, p. 93. Second, because he (or his two collaborators) wrote that the Martin-Bellinger estimate of 31 March 1941 postulated that the "most dangerous sectors" from which an air attack on Pearl might be mounted were "the north and northwest." Gordon W. Prange, with Donald M. Goldstein and Katherine V. Dillon, *Pearl Harbor: The Verdict of History* (New York: McGraw-Hill Book Company, 1986), p. 441. But Martin-Bellinger states no such thing; the text can be found in three places in the JCC record: Pt. 1, pp. 379–82; Pt. 22, pp. 349–54; and Pt. 33, pp. 1182–86. It appears that the "famous" "historic work" is also an unread work. Two other historians, Paolo E. Coletta and Michael Slackman, have also alleged that Martin-Bellinger stated that a Japanese attack would most likely come from the south or from the north, respectively. But Martin-Bellinger names no likely or most dangerous sector—neither "north," "northwest," nor "south," nor any equivalent nautical or numerical terms. See Paolo E. Coletta, "Rear Admiral Patrick N.L. Bellinger, Commander Patrol Wing Two, and General Frederick L. Martin, Air Commander, Hawaii," in William P. Cogar, ed., *New Interpretations in Naval History: Selected Papers from the Eighth Naval History Symposium* (Annapolis, Maryland: Naval Institute Press, 1989), p. 269; Slackman, *Target: Pearl Harbor*, p. 56. Elsewhere in his book Slackman makes the pertinent statement: "A body of folklore has developed around the Pearl Harbor attack as stories and 'facts' are passed from source to source with little critical examination;" p. ix.

57. Ibid., Pt. 16, pp. 2393–2431.

58. KFP, "Memorandum of Interview with Admiral King in Washington on Thursday, 7 December 1944," signed Husband E. Kimmel, 6 pp., n.d.

59. Simpson, *Stark*, p. 265.

60. Prange, with Goldstein and Dillon, *Pearl Harbor*, p. 230.

61. KFP (copy), King to Secretary John L. Sullivan, 14 July 1948.

62. The most recent such expression of that conspiracy revision appears in *Golden Age* (New York: Doubleday, 2000), a novel by Gore Vidal. Apart from the fact, several times mentioned in this volume, that no one has yet produced an original document connecting Roosevelt to perfidy on that scale, it offends credulity to think that FDR, a former assistant secretary of the Navy, who had a passionate affection for the naval service, would coldly and deliberately have sacrificed the heart of his fleet and the lives of 2,403 servicemen and civilians. As to the charge that he set up the Pacific Fleet for destruction or crippling damage as a means of getting the nation into war with Germany, two things might be said: (1) Germany was not obligated to declare war against the United States if Japan attacked the United States; and (2) in his address to Congress on 8 December FDR did not ask for a declaration of war against Germany. One need not hold FDR to blame for what happened at Pearl Harbor if one's wish is to exonerate Kimmel and Short. One need only cite the faithlessness and ineptitude of the War and Navy Departments, about which much has been written in these pages.

63. KC, Roll 35. The draft letter is undated, but it appears among Kimmel's correspondence and papers from 1968. As noted earlier, he broke off his friendship with Stark in 1944, when he first learned of the Magic information that had not been sent him. His feelings toward Stark in 1945 are revealed in a letter he wrote to his older brother Singleton on 15 February, in which he wrote about Stark's behavior at the time of Kimmel's retirement. Claiming that Stark said one thing but did another, Kimmel wrote: "I tell you this to show what an awful liar this fellow has turned out to be." KC, Roll 28.

☆　☆　☆

ACKNOWLEDGMENTS

I am grateful to many persons who assisted me in the research for this book. I thank archivists John E. Taylor, Barry Zerby, and Sandy Smith at the National Archives and Records Administration, Archives II, at College Park, Maryland; Sally A. Cravens and her fellow librarians in the Documents Collection of the University of Florida Libraries; and Jim Craig, of Micrographics, Inc. Leonidas Roberts, Professor Emeritus of Physical Sciences and Mathematics at the University of Florida and a Martin PBM Mariner pilot in the Pacific War, devoted many hours to helping me solve the time-to-intercept problem described in chapter 6. Daniel A. Martinez, National Park Service historian at the USS *Arizona* Memorial at Pearl Harbor, kindly conducted me on a detailed tour of the harbor and base installations. Vice Admiral David C. Richardson, former deputy commander in chief, Pacific Fleet, who has spent many years studying the operational history of the Pearl Harbor attack, generously shared his information with me at the admiral's home in Julian, California.

For biographical research on Admiral Husband E. Kimmel, I express my thanks to the admiral's sons, Thomas K., now deceased, and Edward R., in Wilmington, Delaware. The admiral's grandson, Thomas K., Jr., in McLean, Virginia, who is an accomplished Pearl Harbor scholar, has helped me on more occasions than I can count. Others from whom I have learned are: Captain Edward L. Beach, USN (Ret.), a distinguished naval historian and good friend; the late John Costello; B. Mitchell Simpson III; Commander Thomas Buell, USN (Ret.); Paul Stillwell; David Hackett Fischer; Robert Neuleib; David W. Richmond; George Victor; and David Chalmers.

A special thanks is given to my agent, Michael Congdon, and to my editor at Henry Holt, the esteemed Jack Macrae. Barbara Smerage assisted with preparation of the manuscript. And, as usual, my best helper, critic, and friend during the writing was my spouse, Genevieve.

Three paragraphs in chapter 2 and two in chapter 6 derive from my article "Reopen the Kimmel Case," in Naval Institute *Proceedings*, vol 120/12/1, 102 (December 1994), pp. 51-56. I thank the Naval Institute for their permission to use that material.

INDEX

About the Author

Michael Gannon is Distinguished Service Professor Emeritus of History at the University of Florida. The author of two previous books on World War II naval warfare, *Operation Drumbeat*, and *Black May*, he lives in Gainesville, Florida.